Sex, Time and Place

Sex, Time
and Place

Sex, Time and Place

Queer Histories of London,
c. 1850 to the Present

**EDITED BY SIMON AVERY AND
KATHERINE M. GRAHAM**

Bloomsbury Academic
An imprint of Bloomsbury Publishing Plc

B L O O M S B U R Y
LONDON · OXFORD · NEW YORK · NEW DELHI · SYDNEY

Bloomsbury Academic

An imprint of Bloomsbury Publishing Plc

50 Bedford Square
London
WC1B 3DP
UK

1385 Broadway
New York
NY 10018
USA

www.bloomsbury.com

BLOOMSBURY and the Diana logo are trademarks of Bloomsbury Publishing Plc

First published 2016

British Library Cataloguing-in-Publication Data
A catalogue record for this book is available from the British Library.

ISBN: HB: 978-1-4742-3492-4
ePDF: 978-1-4742-3494-8
ePub: 978-1-4742-3495-5

Library of Congress Cataloging-in-Publication Data
A catalog record for this book is available from the Library of Congress.

Cover design: Sharon Mah
Cover image © akg-images/A.F.Kersting

Typeset by Integra Software Services Pvt. Ltd.
Printed and bound in Great Britain

CONTENTS

List of Figures vii
List of Contributors viii
Acknowledgements xii

SECTION ONE   Framing Queer London 1

1   Structuring and Interpreting Queer Spaces of London
Simon Avery 3

2   Queer Temporalities, Queer Londons
Katherine M. Graham 23

3   Mapping This Volume
Simon Avery and Katherine M. Graham 41

SECTION TWO   Exploring Queer London 47

4   London, AIDS and the 1980s
Matt Cook 49

5   Bigot Geography: Queering Geopolitics in Brixton
Emma Spruce 65

6   Representations of Queer London in the Fiction
of Sarah Waters
Paulina Palmer 81

7   Are Drag Kings Still Too Queer for London?
From the Nineteenth-Century Impersonator
to the Drag King of Today
Kayte Stokoe 97

8 Claude McKay: Queering Spaces of Black Radicalism
   in Interwar London
   Gemma Romain and Caroline Bressey 115

9 The British Society of the Study of Sex Psychology:
   'Advocating the Culture of Unnatural and Criminal
   Practices'?
   Lesley A. Hall 133

10 Cannibal London: Racial Discourses, Pornography
   and Male–Male Desire in Late-Victorian Britain
   Silvia Antosa 149

11 'Famous for the paint she put on her face': London's
   Painted Poofs and the Self-Fashioning of Francis Bacon
   Dominic Janes 167

12 Mingling with the Ungodly: Simeon Solomon in Queer
   Victorian London
   Carolyn Conroy 185

13 Alan Hollinghurst's Fictional Ways of Queering London
   Bart Eeckhout 203

14 Sink Street: The Sapphic World of Pre-Chinatown Soho
   Anne Witchard 221

15 Chasing Community: From Old Compton Street to the
   Online World of Grindr
   Marco Venturi 239

16 Being 'There': Contemporary London, Facebook and
   Queer Historical Feeling
   Sam McBean 255

Bibliography 270
Index 291

LIST OF FIGURES

1.1 View of pavilion in Vauxhall Gardens. (De Agostini Picture Library/Getty Images.) 6

1.2 Grand view of Park Entrance and Vauxhall Tavern at Dusk. (Photo by View Pictures/UIG via Getty Images.) 16

7.1 Actress Vesta Tilley and her bicycle pose for a publicity postcard circa 1910 in London, England. (Photo by Transcendental Graphics/Getty Images.) 99

8.1 Jamaican writer and poet Claude McKay (1889–1948), 1926. (Photo by Berenice Abbott/Getty Images.) 116

11.1 'Portrait of an unidentified transvestite, possibly the artist Francis Bacon in drag, England pre-1945. The cleavage raises questions, but may be the result of photo manipulation.' (Caption provided by Getty Images. Photo by The John Deakin Archive/Getty Images.) 168

11.2 Francis Bacon, *Figure Study II* (1945–46), oil on canvas, 145 × 128.5 cm, Huddersfield Art Gallery, reproduced courtesy of the estate of Francis Bacon, all rights reserved, DACS 201x, photographed by Prudence Cuming Associates Ltd. 170

11.3 Fitzroy Sq., group, evidence presented at the Central Criminal Court, *Rex v. Britt and Others*, 1927, CRIM 1/387, reproduced courtesy of the National Archives, London. 177

14.1 Sandy's Bar. 232

LIST OF CONTRIBUTORS

Silvia Antosa is Associate Professor of English Literature at the University of Enna "Kore" (Italy). She is the author of *Richard Francis Burton: Victorian Explorer and Translator* (Peter Lang, 2012) and *Crossing Boundaries: Bodily Paradigms in Jeanette Winterson's Fiction 1985–2000* (Aracne, 2008), and editor of several interdisciplinary volumes on queer studies: *Queer Crossings: Theories, Bodies, Texts* (Mimesis, 2012), *Gender and Sexuality: Rights, Language and Performativity* (Aracne, 2012) and *Omosapiens II: Spazi e identità queer* (Carocci, 2007). She has published on Victorian fiction, poetry and travel writing and contemporary British fiction. She is co-editing with Joseph Bristow a special issue of *Textus* on Narratives of Gender, Sexuality and Embodiment in Modern and Contemporary English Culture.

Simon Avery is Reader in Nineteenth-Century Literature and Culture and co-director of the Queer London Research Forum at the University of Westminster, London, UK. His research interests include the relations between literature, politics and gender; historiography and queer histories; the 1890s; and the contemporary historical novel. His publications include *Elizabeth Barrett Browning* (Northcote House, 2011), *Poems of Mary Coleridge* (Shearsman, 2010), *Thomas Hardy: A Reader's Guide* (Palgrave, 2009) and the Broadview edition of Hardy's *The Return of the Native* (2013).

Caroline Bressey is Reader in the Department of Geography, UCL. Her research focuses on recovering the historical geographies of the black presence in Victorian and Edwardian Britain, especially the lives of women living in London. Her research draws out biographies from prison, hospital and asylum records as well as remapping the working lives of black women and their families. Parallel to this are her interests in ideas of race, racism, early anti-racist theory and identity in Victorian society. These themes were the focus of her first book on the historical geographies of Victorian anti-racist periodical publishing, *Empire, Race and the Politics of Anti-Caste* (Bloomsbury Academic, 2013).

Carolyn Conroy is an independent scholar, writer and researcher. She is a former post-doctoral tutor and researcher in the History of Art Department at the University of York and has worked on art historical research for private collectors and organizations such as the Paul Mellon Center for British Art at Yale University. She is currently writing a biography of the Anglo-Jewish homosexual Victorian artist Simeon Solomon and edits the Simeon Solomon Research Archive at www.simeonsolomon.com.

Matt Cook is Professor of Modern History at Birkbeck, University of London, Birkbeck Director of the Raphael Samuel History Centre and an editor of *History Workshop Journal*. He is the author of *London and the Culture of Homosexuality* (2003) and *Queer Domesticities* (2014), and editor of *A Gay History of Britain* (2007), *Queer 1950s* (2012 with Heike Bauer) and *Queer Cities, Queer Cultures* (2012, with Jennifer Evans).

Bart Eeckhout is Professor of English and American Literature at the University of Antwerp, Belgium, where he teaches queer fiction and queer studies and supervises doctoral dissertations in the field. His other long-term specializations are the poetry of Wallace Stevens and interdisciplinary urban studies. He has authored and edited more than twenty books and journal issues. His publications on LGBT/queer topics have appeared in *Queer in Europe* and the *Journal of Homosexuality*, and have repeatedly figured the writings of Alan Hollinghurst. He is currently co-editing a collection of essays entitled *LGBTQs, Media and Culture in Europe*.

Katherine M. Graham is a Lecturer in English Literature (Theatre) at the University of Westminster and co-director of the Queer London Research Forum. Her major research area is revenge, especially revenge in the drama of the early modern period. Katherine has forthcoming articles that consider the queerness of time and the queerness of the female revenger in late-Elizabethan and Jacobean revenge tragedies, as well as an article on John Fletcher's play *The Tragedy of Valentinian*. She also has a forthcoming chapter on gender and objects in *The Revenger's Tragedy*. Katherine works as a theatre reviewer for *The Morning Star* newspaper.

Lesley A. Hall is a Wellcome Library Research Fellow and Honorary Lecturer in History of Medicine, University College London. She has published several books and numerous chapters and articles on sexuality and gender in the UK from the nineteenth century to the present, including *Sex, Gender and Social Change in Britain since 1880* (2nd, revised expanded, edition, 2012), *The Life and Times of Stella Browne, Feminist and Free Spirit* (2011) and (with the late Roy Porter) *The Facts of Life: The Creation of Sexual Knowledge in Britain* (1995). Her website is www.lesleyahall.net, her blog lesleyahall.blogspot.co.uk, Twitter handle @erinacean.

Dominic Janes is Professor of History in the School of Humanities at Keele University. He is a cultural historian who studies texts and visual images relating to Britain in its local and international contexts since the eighteenth century. Within this sphere he focuses on the histories of gender, sexuality and religion. His most recent books are *Picturing the Closet: Male Secrecy and Homosexual Visibility in Britain* (Oxford University Press, 2015) and *Visions of Queer Martyrdom from John Henry Newman to Derek Jarman* (University of Chicago Press, 2015).

Sam McBean is Lecturer in Modern and Contemporary American Literature at Queen Mary University of London. She has published on contemporary literature, new media, queer theory and feminist theory in journals including *Feminist Review*, *Camera Obscura* and the *Journal of Lesbian Studies*. She is the author of *Feminism's Queer Temporalities* (Routledge, 2016).

Paulina Palmer has retired from a senior lectureship in English at Warwick University, where she helped establish the MA in Women's Studies. She has also lectured for the MA in Gender and Sexuality at Birkbeck, London University. Her publications include *Contemporary Women's Fiction: Narrative Practice and Feminist Theory*, *Contemporary Lesbian Writing: Dreams, Desire, Difference*, *Lesbian Gothic: Transgressive Fictions* and *The Queer Uncanny: New Perspectives on the Gothic*. She is currently writing a book entitled *Queering Contemporary Gothic* for Palgrave Macmillan.

Gemma Romain is a historian based in the Equiano Centre, Department of Geography, University College London. She is also an Honorary Fellow of the Parkes Institute for the Study of Jewish/non-Jewish Relations, University of Southampton. Her research explores modern Caribbean and Black British history, specifically in relation to visual cultures and queer histories. She also has a particular interest in public history, museums and curating and has curated/co-curated exhibitions and displays at institutions including Tate Britain, the Women's Library and the Petrie Museum, UCL. Her forthcoming biography of Patrick Nelson, a queer black Jamaican man who first migrated to Britain in 1937, will be published by Bloomsbury Academic.

Emma Spruce is a graduate researcher at the Gender Institute, London School of Economics. She is undertaking an ESRC-funded PhD that explores the appeal and effects of gay progress narratives. The project seeks to identify and analyse new discursive and material inclusions and exclusions, arguing that these borders have been reconfigured through the changing position of homosexuality in stories of progress that are told about the world, the nation, the city and the neighbourhood. Previously, Emma worked on LGBTQ asylum and the constrained sexual stories told through asylum applications.

Kayte Stokoe is a PhD candidate in French Studies at Warwick University. Her thesis, which re-evaluates three decades of French and Anglo-American queer and feminist reflection on drag performance, is supervised by Oliver Davis and funded by an AHRC studentship attached to the Queer Theory in France research project. Kayte's wider research interests include gender identity, expression and embodiment; and critical disability studies. Kayte is currently developing her paper 'Textual Drag in Woolf's Orlando and Wittig's Le Corps Lesbien' for *Queering the Second Wave*, a forthcoming special issue of *Paragraph*, edited by Lisa Downing and Lara Cox.

Marco Venturi is a final year PhD researcher in Gender and Sexuality Studies (CMII) at University College London. He is originally from Bologna, where he graduated in Foreign Languages and Literatures. In 2009, he moved to London and completed an MA in American Studies at King's College London with a dissertation on the political activism and street performances of the gay community during the AIDS crisis in the United States. He is currently writing up his PhD thesis titled 'Out of Soho, Back into the Closet: Re-Thinking the London Gay Community', which reconsiders the role of Soho for gay men in London as well as ideas of gay communities and gay spaces more broadly.

Anne Witchard is a Senior Lecturer in the Department of English, Linguistics and Cultural Studies at the University of Westminster. She is the author of *Thomas Burke's Dark Chinoiserie: Limehouse Nights and the Queer Spell of Chinatown* (Ashgate, 2007), *Lao She in London* (Hong Kong University Press, 2012) and *England's Yellow Peril: Sinophobia and the Great War* (Penguin, 2014). She is co-editor, with Lawrence Phillips, of *London Gothic: Place, Space and the Gothic Imagination* (Continuum, 2010) and editor of *British Modernism and Chinoiserie* (Edinburgh University Press, 2015).

ACKNOWLEDGEMENTS

A volume such as this is a collaborative effort in the widest sense and there are many people who have helped us bring it into being and to whom we would like to express our thanks here. The point of origin for the volume was the 'Queer London' conference which we held at the University of Westminster, London, in March 2013. Bringing together academics, practitioners, people working in charities and political and cultural institutions, and other interested participants, the conference enabled the speakers and delegates to debate a wide range of issues concerning the construction and workings of queer London from a variety of disciplinary perspectives. We would like to thank everyone who attended the conference for their contributions and enthusiasm and for confirming what an exciting and complex area of investigation Queer London studies is.

It was in the light of this that we subsequently established the Queer London Research Forum, housed in the Department of English, Linguistics and Cultural Studies at the University of Westminster. The aim of the Forum has been to extend that energetic discussion between people from different groups and backgrounds which was begun at the conference, and to establish a space where issues to do with London and its queerness can be examined in exploratory and expansive ways. To date, we have held a number of seminars on areas such as queer archives, queer literatures of London, queer London film and queer ageing, and we would like to thank our amazing speakers from these events: Jake Graf, Lesley A. Hall, Kate Hancock, Christa Holka, Nicola Humberstone, Jonathan Kemp, Sam McBean, Neil McKenna, Ian Iqbal Rachid, Sonny van Eden and Matt. Without their thoughtful, challenging and inspiring talks and presentations, the Queer London Research Forum could not have developed in the ways that it has. We would also like to thank the Research Management Group in the Department of English, Linguistics and Cultural Studies for financially supporting the Forum, and colleagues across the wider Faculty of Social Sciences and Humanities for their encouragement, enthusiasm and help. In particular, our thanks go to Alex Warwick, Martin Willis, John Beck, Monica Germanà, Anne Witchard, Lucy Bond, Matt Morrison, Nigel Mapp, Georgina Colby, Helen Glew and Francis Ray White.

It is within this context that we have been able to produce this volume of essays, and working with the contributors has been an enormous pleasure and privilege. Each of them has approached the project with commitment, patience and good humour, and our deep gratitude goes to them for their dedication to the volume over the past two years. It has been a wonderful experience to be able to bring together the work of such a diverse group of academics in order to address what Queer London might mean both historically and in its contemporary forms. Our thanks, too, go to Frances Arnold and Emma Goode at Bloomsbury, who have been enthusiastic about the volume throughout and offered valuable guidance along the way, as well as to the readers of our initial proposal whose comments and suggestions enabled us to think about the project in different ways. Thanks also to Chris Waters, whose thoughtful comments on the final manuscript were extremely helpful.

Finally, we would like to thank Dave, Sam McBean and Thomas Moore for their support, encouragement and help in so many ways, and for making Queer London even more interesting.

Framing Queer London

CHAPTER ONE

Structuring and Interpreting Queer Spaces of London

Simon Avery

The subtitle to this collection – 'Queer Histories of London, c.1850 to the Present' – provokes a number of pressing and complex questions. What do we mean by 'queer'? How do we construct models of history (and whose history are we constructing)? What do we define as 'London' and how might it be constituted? As the following chapters in the collection make clear, the answers to these questions are many and varied, and they point to the diverse ways – politically, ideologically, methodologically – that 'London' and its 'queerness' can be read. As these categories shift, overlap and are modulated by one another in ways which are both exhilarating and possibly bewildering, the complexity of thinking about 'Queer London' – or, more rightly, 'Queer Londons' in the plural – is clearly evident.

In this chapter, I consider the concept of queer urban space as a way of reading through, and framing, the range of material we have drawn together here. I am interested in how queer space might be structured, interpreted and theorized, and how queer spatial relations might operate in the urban matrix. To this end, I draw attention to the importance of both material and imaginative constructions in the formation of London's queer spaces and reflect upon the critical work that has been undertaken to date, as well as areas which would benefit from more extensive examination and analysis. In her chapter, Katherine M. Graham traces a history of the term 'queer'; here, I use 'queer' to indicate a series of approaches and politics to do with sexuality, desire and intimacy which trouble and disrupt orthodoxies and categories, particularly those which are 'normalized' by hetero-patriarchy or, increasingly, 'homonormativity', and which are also associated, in Heike Bauer and Matt Cook's phrasing, with 'the seeking out of blind spots in existing narratives about the present and the past'.[1] As Nikki Sullivan emphasizes, the queer project seeks 'to frustrate, to counteract, to delegitimise…heteronormative knowledges and institutions, and the subjectivities and socialities that are (in)formed by them and that (in)form them'.[2] Yet I am also drawn by the interactions between these definitions and the more colloquial meaning of queer as odd, strange and eccentric in the process of shaping space. Here, I am following Sara Ahmed's insistence in *Queer Phenomenology* that we keep both meanings in mind, in a way that 'allows us to move between sexual and social registers, without flattening them or reducing them to a single line'.[3] To this end, then, I would like to begin with a specific case study – that of the Vauxhall Pleasure Gardens. Although the Gardens were established earlier than the historical parameters of this collection, they nevertheless help to open up some of the key questions about queer space – regarding non-normative and perceived transgressive behaviours and sexualities – that I explore further in the remainder of the chapter.

The Vauxhall Pleasure Gardens (originally known as the New Spring Gardens) was a space of night-time leisure and entertainment, initially established in the mid-seventeenth century on a twelve-acre site in Lambeth on the south side of the river Thames. Until the building of the Regent Bridge in the early nineteenth century, most visitors arrived at the Gardens by boat and the area quickly became associated with flamboyance and excess, drinking, dancing and potential cross-class socializing.[4] Over its 200-year existence – which concurrently saw the metropolis rapidly expanding in population, geographical reach and technological advancement – the Pleasure Gardens maintained its associations with the startling, the 'exotic', and what we might consider, drawing upon the ideas of Mikhail Bakhtin, as the 'carnivalesque'.[5] All kinds of fantastical and defamiliarizing structures were erected in this space during its lifespan – artificial ruins, a grotto, a watermill and cascades, *trompe-l'œil* scenes, a Moorish tower and a Chinese pavilion – and there was much diversity and experimentation in the entertainments offered, which included musical recitals, masked balls, firework displays, tightrope- walking, ballooning competitions, horse races, large-scale battle re-enactments and performances by clowns, acrobats and ballet companies.

This 'queerness' of the Gardens in terms of defamiliarization, strangeness and challenge to hierarchies was also augmented by a queer playing with subversive and non-normative sexual behaviours. The designers of the Gardens created meandering walkways through wooded areas, which offered the possibility of romantic and sexual assignation – a situation which was quickly taken up by prostitutes working the space. As early as 1712, for example, a friend of Joseph Addison's commented, in a now-famous remark, that he would be a more regular patron of the Gardens 'if there were more Nightingales, and fewer Strumpets'.[6] Recent work by historians and geographers has also gestured towards the Gardens as a potential transgressive space for male same-sex desire, with Miles Ogborn analyzing the 'malleability of identity' associated with the Macaronis, whose 'luxurious effeminacy' sought to 'disrupt the heterosexual structuring of gazes', and Michael Chanan and Rictor Norton pointing towards examples of a molly/cross-dressing culture there.[7] While it is important to resist reading this cross-dressing transhistorically in an easy alignment with contemporary drag cultures – as Alison Oram's work has emphasized, such moments must be related to their specific sociopolitical contexts[8] – the situation nevertheless gestures towards both a history of queer transgression in this area and those fascinating concerns which the Gardens raise regarding the relationship between the sexed body and the urban space. Indeed, some of the Gardens' pathways, known as the Dark Walks, remained unlit and were particularly associated with what Penelope J. Corfield has termed 'the eroticisation of leisure' associated with spaces like Vauxhall and its Danish counterpart, the Tivoli Gardens in Copenhagen.[9] Yet by 1825, it was thought that the Vauxhall Gardens were becoming too popular in this respect and the local magistrates ordered that lighting be put in all the walkways. The culture of consumption, which had always been intricately bound up with the pleasures that the Gardens had to offer, was evidently too much for some in the early nineteenth century. Certainly, as Deborah Epstein Nord has suggested in her treatment of the complex relationship between illumination and darkness in the Gardens, Vauxhall 'seemed to epitomize, to concentrate within a circumscribed space, metropolitan pleasures, opportunities, and... dangers', and can clearly be read 'as an instance of the need for fantasy and a world turned briefly upside down'.[10]

With this commitment to subversive and transgressive practices and behaviours, the Vauxhall Pleasure Gardens constituted a 'queer' space in both the more colloquial and more recent theorized meanings of the term. In their repeated collapsing of categories – between the urban and the rural, upper and lower classes, 'reality' and artifice, and the 'civilized' and the 'debauched' – the Gardens promoted what Epstein Nord identifies as 'utopian impulses'[11] and ushered in a new concept of modern leisure. Indeed, the space can be read as both a product and enabler of modernity and, in its boundary crossings, its fluidity and its challenge to hegemonic structures and authority, as an embodiment of a specifically queer urban modernity. By the mid-1830s, however, the popularity of the Gardens was beginning to wane, despite – or maybe because of – an attempt to attract more visitors through daytime opening. In his early journalistic piece, 'Vauxhall-gardens by Day' (October 1836), for example, Charles Dickens wrote of the disappointment engendered by the space without the cover of night time and the illusory performance which the darkness provided:

We walked about, and met with a disappointment at every turn; our favourite views were mere patches of paint; the fountain that had sparkled so showily by lamp-light, presented very much the appearance of a water-pipe that had burst; all the ornaments were dingy, and all the walks gloomy.[12]

As Dickens puts it, daytime opening 'rudely and harshly disturb[ed] that veil of mystery which had hung about the property for many years'.[13] Various

FIGURE 1.1 *View of pavilion in Vauxhall Gardens. (De Agostini Picture Library/ Getty Images.)*

new incentives were trialled as the Gardens passed through different hands, but in 1848 the building of the viaduct through Vauxhall, designed to carry the railway to the new Waterloo Station, was another nail in the Gardens' coffin. The trains brought noise and soot to the vicinity and the privacy on which the Gardens had relied was seriously compromised by their being constantly overlooked. Indeed, by now, Vauxhall was frequently being referred to as 'Old Vauxhall', the epithet suggesting a sense of nostalgia, loss and the inevitable processes of change.[14] As London Zoo (recently opened to the public), the Great Exhibition of 1851 and quicker train travel to the seaside drew more customers away, Vauxhall became, in Sarah Downing's phrasing, a 'pastiche' of itself.[15] Stumbling on through the 1850s, the Gardens finally closed on 25 July 1859, the same year that Charles Darwin published his revolutionary work on evolution, *On the Origin of Species by Means of Natural Selection*. Evidently, to draw on Herbert Spencer's later Darwinian phrasing, Vauxhall Gardens was not the fittest to survive in the rapidly shifting mid-Victorian period.

Yet the queerness which the Vauxhall Pleasure Gardens could be seen to embody in its promotion of transgressive and non-normative encounter and recreation was not so easily eradicated. For within three years of the Gardens' demise, the Royal Vauxhall Tavern (RVT) was established on the site, functioning originally as a music hall. By the post-Second World War period, the RVT was being recognized as a queer venue, known particularly for its drag performances, an association which has developed across the twentieth century to the present day with key figures like Lily Savage (Paul O'Grady) having held residences there and the internationally recognized queer performance group Duckie – which showcases 'audience interactive experiences that blur the boundaries between theatre, nightclubs and arty show business' in 'the tradition of British illegitimate theatre'[16] – having run there continuously since the mid-1990s. Events like the weekly Bar Wotever, the 'Royal Queer Variety Show' with its mix of drag, burlesque, mime, spoken word, film and live music,[17] add to the celebratory status of RVT as nothing less than the oldest consistently queer venue in the UK, with its diverse experimental and challenging entertainments clearly drawing a historical link back to the original Pleasure Gardens.[18] Indeed, the Tavern's investment in LGBTQ+ identities and communities in the widest sense is particularly important in this ongoing construction of queer space. It is also particularly resonant that the arches of the same viaduct which helped kill off the original Pleasure Gardens have been used in recent decades to house the new 'pleasure gardens' of modern queer Vauxhall in clubs like Crash, Barcode and Fire; in Chariots, one of London's most popular gay men's saunas; and in the fetish club Hoist which, in its hosting of leather, rubber, uniform and other dress code nights, has enabled, as RDK Herman's theorizing about fetish spaces suggests, 'a celebration of "perversity", and of difference, consistent with many of the ideas embraced within queer politics'.[19] Through these shifts, then,

Vauxhall has maintained its status of being a space of liberty in the urban matrix and an area of potential transgression, social mixing and sexual licence. The queerness that might be lost at one time can emerge with full visibility in new sexual cartographies – even within the same space.

What is particularly interesting about this history of Vauxhall – a history to which I will return later in this chapter – is its connection with a process of changing (or constantly becoming) spatial dynamics. Its transformation from an area associated with the Pleasure Gardens to an area associated principally with queer sexualities and subcultures signals much about the overlayering of history and the shifting use of the urban space, as well as the complex relations between the built environment, spectacle, consumption and implicitly, mechanisms of control such as the law and policing. For as Kath Browne, Jason Lim and Gavin Brown usefully argue, '[i]t is this continual process of becoming that challenges essential or pre-determined bodies, identities or spaces [and which] prompts questions about how things come to be materialised and about the regulation of such materialisation'.[20] It is to these 'challenging' spaces and their 'materialisation' that I now turn.

Theorizing queer urban space

Since the publication of *Mapping Desire: Geographies of Sexualities*, edited by David Bell and Gill Valentine, in 1995, the theorization of the multiple and complex relations between sexualities and space has become a growing area of multidisciplinary, interdisciplinary and transdisciplinary concern.[21] As part of the wider 'spatial turn' in the humanities and social sciences, such theoretical work offers a number of ways through which we are able to interrogate how spaces create, promote, control or close down sexual identities, practices and communities – and how, in turn, these identities, practices and communities influence and structure particular spaces. Many commentators have emphasized the central role of the expanding urban space – and particularly the metropolis – in the history of the formation of the modern sexual subject from the mid-nineteenth century onwards, citing its size and diversity of spaces and bodies as key to the proliferation of sexual possibilities.[22] Indeed, as Lawrence Knopp has suggested in his insightful essay 'Sexuality and Urban Space: A Framework for Analysis', '[t]he city's sexuality is [often] described as an eroticisation of many of the characteristic experiences of modern urban life: anonymity, voyeurism, exhibitionism, consumption, authority (and challenges to it), tactility, motion, danger, power, navigation and restlessness'.[23] With what Knopp identifies as its 'permanent cluster of heterogeneous human beings in circulation',[24] the city can be read as both a shifting signifier of desire and the signifier of shifting desires.

Within this context, however, the construction of queer urban space is far from straight/forward. For as a number of urban theorists have emphasized, drawing upon Judith Butler's ideas of performativity, urban spaces are often produced and enacted as 'prediscursively straight'.[25] That is, a set of repeated acts, and of social and discursive conventions, here to do with 'heterosexual' behaviours, congeal over time in order to appear 'natural' in these spaces and thereby confirm that these spaces are 'naturally' heterosexual – a situation which is also reinforced by repeated patterns of regulation and control. As Gill Valentine notes:

> [t]his repetition takes the form of many acts: from heterosexual couples kissing and holding hands as they make their way down the street, to advertisements and window displays which present images of contented 'nuclear' families; and from heterosexualized conversations that permeate queues at bus stops and banks, to the piped music articulating heterosexual desires that fill shops, bars and restaurants.[26]

At the same time, however, this 'straight space' has the potential to be contested and challenged, both implicitly and explicitly.

In a significant account of queer spatial formation, the cultural geographer Affrica Taylor has offered a study of the interconnections of what she terms 'closet space', the 'symbolic community' (that which we imagine we might find in the urban matrix), and the dynamics of actual 'ghetto space'. The closet/ghetto dichotomy might appear dated now in some ways but it persists in much critical thinking and Taylor's essay, 'A Queer Geography', is effective both in its drawing out of the complexities of meaning associated with these different spaces and in its resisting any easy 'progressive' spatial narrative (that LGBTQ+ subjects are 'freed' from the entrapment and claustrophobia of the closet space by their entrance into the ghetto). For Taylor, 'closet space' is always potentially subversive since 'the closet conceals something that can at any moment be revealed' and which therefore always has the potential to disrupt seemingly established models of heteronormativity (for example, in the family home).[27] Moreover, the idea of the closeted homosexual passing for straight in public space has wider disruptive potential given that '[a]s long as anyone can successfully keep the (known) secret of homosexuality by carrying off the performance of heterosexuality, all heterosexuality can be seen as performance, all heterosexuality becomes open to question, and all spaces become sexually ambiguous'.[28] In terms of her analysis of the 'ghetto' space, Taylor emphasizes how LGBTQ+ communities are often 'imagined', in Benedict Anderson's sense of the term,[29] an idea that Marco Venturi also returns to in his chapter in this volume. For both Taylor and Venturi, the idea of a unified community is often only symbolic. While there might be embedded in it a notion of protection and cohesion, the 'ghetto' or 'village' frequently exposes the exclusions – based on gender, sex, class, ethnic, racial or national differences – that lie just beneath the surface of the concept of 'community' (a point to which the chapters by Lesley Hall, Anne Witchard, and Gemma Romain and Caroline Bressey in this collection also speak). These 'utopias of belonging', to use Taylor's phrasing, might be just that – unachievable utopias.[30] Indeed, this can certainly often be seen in Soho's 'gay village', a very different fabrication of the sexualized urban space from Vauxhall. Old Compton Street and its surrounding locale is undoubtedly important for a particular kind of queer (albeit essentially gay male) politics – one which is invested in visibility, a concept of 'safe space' (although this can also lead to targeting, as seen in the 1999 bombing of the Admiral Duncan pub), and a notion of community and solidarity (albeit, as Taylor suggests, somewhat nominal for particular groups). Yet it might also be argued that Soho's potential for more radical activism has to a degree been sacrificed to a particular kind of 'pink pound' consumerism and, increasingly, a politics of homonormativity centred predominantly on white, gay male capitalist culture.[31]

Both Taylor, and Bell and Valentine, among others, have used the notion of queer geography to transcend the limiting binary of 'straight' community/ LGBTQ+ 'ghetto' (where spaces are constructed as either/or). Instead, they argue for the potentially more radical possibility of queering *all* 'straight' space through 'fracturing and rupturing' queer acts which effectively function as moments and/or sites of resistance and transformation – for example, the lesbian couple kissing in the 'family' pub in St John's Wood; the bisexual man reconfiguring the function of the public urinal at Victoria Station; the patterns of cruising in spaces like Brompton Cemetery; or, on a larger scale, the occupation of the streets of Central London by the annual Pride march.[32] In this model, the seemingly 'restrictive, bounded and strictly coded territory' of the ghetto/village is transformed into the idea of the queer city as 'a site of open-ended difference' regarding sexualities and desires and the spaces they inhabit.[33] And this is, of course, manifestly political in its challenge to the ideological privileging of heterosexuality.

What queer thinking about space shows us, then, is the potential for all space to be in flux, unfixed and changeable, in a challenge both to heterocentric models of the urban and the potentially problematic closet/ghetto binary. At the same time, however, this politics of possibility might be overlaid and intricately bound up with a wider set of anxieties, particularly among dominant groups, concerning the ordering of the urban space and the need to police what is perceived as (un-)acceptable sexual conduct and 'morally threatening' expressions of desire. As Matt Houlbrook demonstrates, these anxieties are often part of a wider set of concerns regarding population density, crowding and anonymity in the city.[34] Subsequently, there is a keen focus on the disorderly, undisciplined body which requires policing in its assumed challenges to urban and, by extension, national order (a concern which Chris Waters sees as emerging in the nineteenth century in response to Malthusian and Darwinian ideas).[35] Individuals are therefore constantly subject to the gaze of the state and the law, as well as other members of the population who function as agents of surveillance, as part of a wider Foucauldian biopolitics of the everyday – whether this takes the form of a same-sex couple receiving offensive comments when kissing in the street or the prosecution of an individual for engaging in a sex act in public.[36] The effect of this, of course, is that policing and mechanisms of control effectively work to help *shape* the urban matrix and are testament to anxieties about boundaries, order and the 'training' of subjects to self-discipline. Certainly, in this line of thinking heteronormative space is not as secure as some might wish. For as the ongoing work on 'recovering' queer London to which I now turn attests, the 'rupturing' and 'fracturing' of the urban space through queer challenge can take many different forms.

Recovering queer London

The recovering of the spaces of historical Queer London is undoubtedly a distinctly tricky affair. How can we uncover what those spaces might have been? Where do we find the traces of London's queer past in its spatial dynamics? Documentary evidence might not have survived (if, indeed, it ever existed), and records might have been suppressed for all kinds of personal, political or legal reasons. As Simon Ofield emphasizes, the queer historian is forced to become detective, piecing clues together and trying to read codes and signals in the search for sexual/textual evidence: 'you can never be quite sure if you will find what you are looking for', Ofield maintains, 'or if you will come across something you never knew you wanted, or even knew existed'.[37] On one level, then, attempting to map queer spaces – to seek out places of queer meeting, socializing, assignation and cruising – is as much about how we 'do' queer history and how we uncover our shared pasts in ways which are politically significant as it is about challenging and revising heterosexist models of the metropolis.

Much of this recovery work concerning Queer London was undertaken in the first years of the twenty-first century, galvanized variously by developments in queer history, human geography, urban studies, literary studies and cultural studies. Matt Cook's *London and the Culture of Homosexuality, 1885–1914*, published in 2003, was one of the first of these full-scale interventions into the developing field, a text which examines the period from the introduction of the Criminal Law Amendment Act (1885) to the outbreak of the First World War and which seeks to 'counter the largely unchallenged orthodoxy' that, after the Wilde trials of 1895, 'there was renewed repression and a recession in the urban homosexual subculture'.[38] Drawing on extensive archival work, Cook traces a history of male same-sex desire in the capital from the anarchic Molly House culture of the eighteenth and early nineteenth centuries to the increased concentration of queer subcultures in the West End in the late Victorian and Edwardian periods – particularly around theatre land, on the one hand (an area which Neil McKenna has also examined in his study of the infamous cross-dressing Ernest Boulton and Frederick Park[39]), and, on the other, the burgeoning shopping areas of Regent Street, Oxford Street and Haymarket, well known in this period for female prostitutes and rent boys. Certainly, these are spaces of consumption and commodity culture in the widest sense. Cook also examines hotels, Turkish baths, gentlemen's clubs, urinals, parks and railway carriages – often spaces of transitory encounter – and considers the vibrancy and variety of gay men's London in this period through a variety of interpretive frameworks including sexology, anthropology, and contemporary debates around aestheticism, decadence and Hellenism. Unsurprisingly, these frameworks are also intricately bound up with discussions about the law and legal process, particularly with regard to a perceived 'need to control the sexual life of the growing city'.[40] For as Cook has argued elsewhere, legal process has been 'the primary means through which the state [has] attempted to regulate "morality" and people's supposedly private lives' and legal records and archives have consequently been central – if not unproblematically – to the writing of sexual histories.[41]

Published in the same year as Cook's study, Mark Turner's *Backward Glances: Cruising the Queer Streets of New York and London* reconsiders the transient nature of sexualized encounter that Cook often emphasizes by focusing on the fabrication of the figure of the cruiser from the late nineteenth century to the present. As a particular way of experiencing the modern city, Turner reads cruising as 'a counter-discourse in the literature of modernity' and 'an alternative street practice … a way of both imagining and inhabiting the spaces of the city that challenge other ways we have come to understand urban movement, in particular through the overdetermining figure of the *flâneur*'.[42] For Turner, the cruiser is particularly adept at exploiting the 'indeterminacy and fragmentation' of the modern city,[43] an exploitation which he elucidates through insightful consideration of sources as wide ranging as newspaper reports, Walt Whitman's notebooks, David Hockney's art, pornography and autobiography – a practice which itself questions the very idea of what might constitute 'evidence' in the way that Ofield suggests. *Backward Glances* significantly refuses a linear narrative of the kind which might underpin a celebratory, progressive view of queer existence, and subsequently uncovers much that is exciting and previously marginalized in the queer histories of these two major cities.

Effectively picking up where Cook's study leaves off in terms of historical positioning, Matt Houlbrook's meticulously researched and wide-ranging *Queer London: Perils and Pleasures in the Sexual Metropolis, 1918–1957* is concerned with the queer urban geographies, cultures and politics of London from the time of the 'Black Book' trial to the publication of the Wolfenden report. Like Cook, Houlbrook is keen to resist any notion of 'a unified "homosexual" experience' and rather seeks to examine 'the complex interrelationship between modern urban life and the organization of sexual and gender practices'.[44] Divided into four major parts dealing with 'Policing', Places', 'People' and 'Politics', *Queer London* draws on impressive archival research, as well as newspapers, memoirs and novels, in order to complicate the varying relations queer men had with the law and the variety of places (both public and commercial) which shaped male sexual experiences and which also often foregrounded class and economic differences. Certainly, this sense of difference is central to Houlbrook's work in his attention to the often problematic relations between the effeminate quean, the 'normal' working-class man who sought sex with men as well as women, and the 'respectable' middle-class homosexual – relations which open up the 'fragmentation and antagonisms of queer urban culture in the first half of the twentieth century'.[45] Indeed, in his consideration of the period leading up to Wolfenden and his looking forward to the 1967 Sexual Offences Act, Houlbrook shows how these 'antagonisms' would contribute to a post-war sense of the wider threat to the nation by the (criminalized) urban homosexual. For Houlbrook, then, the history of queer London in this period is both one of opportunity and one which is problematically 'exclusive and exclusionary'.[46]

What repeatedly emerges from these major studies, therefore, along with other key interventions like Morris B. Kaplan's *Sodom on the Thames* and Anthony Clayton's *Decadent London*,[47] is a sense of the plurality of queer spaces in London and the variety of ways in which they have been deployed from the mid-nineteenth century to the present. Importantly, too, these studies reveal the variety of sources which might be mobilized in the uncovering of queer London, a mobilization that Cook has taken in different directions in his more recent work on the formations of queer *domestic* space in the capital and the 'ways in which queer men orientated their sense of themselves... behind closed doors'.[48] But what might be seen to be as equally important as this recovery of 'real' material spaces to the fabrication of queer London is the place of literary and imaginative constructions. For as Sebastian Groes argues, '[o]ne particularly insightful way of understanding London is to study the lives the city is given by writers who make and remake it in their imagination' and which are therefore 'implicated in shaping our understanding of the city'.[49] Indeed, literature has been crucial to the circulation of ideas about the capital's queer spaces from Wilde's *A Picture of Dorian Gray*, with its subtle but careful mapping out of the spaces of erotic possibility for the West End gentleman, to the explicit rendering of what might constitute this urban possibility in the contemporary novels of Alan Hollinghurst (see Bart Eeckhout's chapter in this collection), Neil Bartlett (*Who Was That Man?*) and Jonathan Kemp (*London Triptych*). Moreover, as Cook and Morris B. Kaplan have emphasized, the circulation of pornographic narratives, such as the infamous late-Victorian *Sins of the Cities of the Plain, or the Recollections of a Mary-Ann* with its detailing of 'how the sin of Sodom was regularly practiced in the modern Babylon',[50] often worked to reinforce particular spaces of sexual encounter. Certainly, the awareness-raising of such literary texts, whether they are meant for mainstream publication or underground circulation, helps fabricate London in different and telling ways and clearly has strong political import in the shaping of the queer capital.

Nevertheless, what will be clear from this discussion is the fact that the recovery of 'queer London' has principally been used as a gloss for (usually white) queer men's experiences, a fact which Houlbrook flags up in his brief consideration of the different socio-economic factors which might – historically at least – affect women's relations to the urban space. As Houlbrook asserts:

> Certainly, queer men and women inhabited many of the same commercial venues, and their sense of self took shape within overlapping understandings of gender and sexuality. Yet their experiences of London were fractured by differences of gender…The association between femininity and domesticity, familial and neighbourhood surveillance, anxieties surrounding the moral status of public women, and the city's very real dangers constrained women's movements…While female sexual deviance – particularly prostitution – was inscribed within forms of surveillance that echoed the regulation of male sexualities, lesbianism remained invisible in the law and, in consequence, in the legal sources…Lesbian London deserves its own study.[51]

Houlbrook's emphasis on lesbian 'invisibility' here obviously resonates with Terry Castle's famous notion of the 'apparitional lesbian', that figure who is effectively absent from dominant culture's world view, 'never with us…but always somewhere else: in the shadows, in the margins, hidden from history'.[52] Indeed, as Laura Gowing has argued, '[s]ex and relationships between men have been culturally and legally more visible than those between women' since '[m]uch of lesbian subcultural life took place in spaces and spheres that have been largely invisible to historians'.[53] Yet while the full-length study of lesbian London that Houlbrook notes is needed has not yet been forthcoming, insightful and engaging analyses of the relations between urban space and lesbian identities and practices more generally have emerged in the work of theorists such as Sally Munt, Julie A. Podmore and Tamar Rothenberg. Munt, picking up on the earlier work of Elizabeth Wilson on the female *flâneur*, has persuasively analyzed the figure of the self-conscious lesbian *flâneur* in Brighton and New York and subsequently demonstrated how '[l]esbian identity is constructed in the temporal and linguistic mobilisation of space'.[54] Podmore has analyzed patterns of lesbian social interaction, place making and expressions of desire in the 'spaces of difference' of inner-city Montréal, while Rothenberg has challenged those theories of gentrification that erase lesbians by examining the society of Brooklyn's Park Slope and thereby drawing attention to the complexities of lesbian communities and spaces.[55] These are all important approaches for the reconsideration of what might constitute a spatial politics of queer women's London. And just as the writings of, and critical work on, the literature of Wilde, Hollinghurst, Bartlett and Kemp have invigorated the analysis of queer men's spaces in the capital, recent reassessments of the lives and literature of women as varied as the Victorian *fin-de-siècle* poets Amy Levy and 'Michael Field' (the pseudonym of collaborating aunt and niece/lovers Katherine Bradley and Edith Cooper), and later novelists Edith Lees Ellis, Virginia Woolf, Radclyffe Hall and Sarah Waters, continue to ask pressing questions about queer women's relations to both historical and contemporary spatial formations of London. The political value of such considerations, which often lay material and imaginative spatial constructions alongside one another, cannot be overestimated in the ongoing project of mapping marginalized geographies. Indeed, it might be argued that the imaginative interventions of these women have a particular radical energy precisely because our knowledge of the material spaces experienced by queer women is so slight at the side of that of queer men. As the chapters by Anne Witchard and Paulina Palmer in this collection suggest, there is much more to be considered in the complex relations between female same-sex desire and the urban matrix, just as Kayte Stokoe's chapter demonstrates there is in thinking about London's trans* spaces and Gemma Romain and Caroline Bressey's chapter demonstrates there is in relation to wider intersectionalities – those 'multiple modes of queerness' as Houlbrook terms them.[56] The recovery and analysis of London's queer spaces continues to be an exciting and dynamic project which is opening up a wide array of issues, concerns and insights. And yet, tellingly, this work is expanding at a time when these spaces are again under threat.

Disappearing spaces

I opened this chapter with a consideration of the changing spatial dynamics of Vauxhall in its shift from the site of the Pleasure Gardens to the site of the queer Royal Vauxhall Tavern and an array of (principally) queer men's clubs. Over the past few years, however, that narrative has been complicated further with a series of closures of key LGBTQ+ establishments across the geographical spread of London – including the Colherne in Earl's Court, the Joiner's Arms and the George and Dragon in East London, the Black Cap in Camden, ManBar on Charing Cross Road, the burlesque/cabaret venue Madame JoJo's in Soho and, even more problematically given the discussion above, the queer women's spaces, First Out on Tottenham Court Road and Candy Bar on Carlisle Street, Soho. Candy Bar's location adjacent to and yet separate from the main central hub of Old Compton Street, and its subsequent relocation to the basement of a predominantly gay men's bar, highlights many of the potential issues regarding spatial placing, in/visibility, economics, and the politics of assimilation and exclusion which are key to the study of queer London. Certainly, the maintenance of physical queer spaces is seemingly becoming increasingly untenable in a socio-economic climate which is witnessing higher rental costs and rapid processes of gentrification (an issue tackled by both Emma Spruce and Kayte Stokoe in their chapters in this collection). As Ben Walters has argued, '[t]he LGBT and drag scenes are the canary in the coalmine. For various reasons, not least our society's structural homophobia, the gay community tends not to actually own many of the spaces it uses, so it is relatively easily disposed of them'.[57] In addition, queer venues have witnessed the impact of an assumed acceptance of LGBTQ+ subjects in 'mainstream' society (who might now go to other venues in their leisure time), and the proliferation of geosocial networking apps like Grindr, Growlr and Findhrr. Indeed, as the chapters by Marco Venturi and Sam McBean in this collection demonstrate, the relationship of apps like Grindr and social media sites like Facebook to a spatial understanding of 'Queer London', and their impact upon queer identities, relationships and communities, is both fascinating and, potentially, highly problematic.

The Royal Vauxhall Tavern has, in many ways, been at the heart of these debates. The high-profile and widely reported buyout of the RVT in 2014 by an Austrian company which frequently acquires historical buildings for redevelopment as high-quality hotels or residences, and the subsequent battle to get the Tavern awarded Grade II listing based on a combination of its architectural significance and its historical significance for the LGBTQ+ community, is a prime example of the potential fragility of queer space.[58]

FIGURE 1.2 *Grand view of park entrance and Vauxhall Tavern at dusk. (Photo by View Pictures/UIG via Getty Images.)*

Indeed, at the time of writing, despite the RVT's being the first building in the UK to be listed for its LGBTQ+ heritage – putting it on a par with New York's Stonewall Inn being given Landmark status in 2015 – the battle for its long-term security is still ongoing. What risks being lost, of course, is both the history and the political significance that spaces like the RVT embody – a significance which might include their functioning as spaces of support both before and after the decriminalization of homosexuality, as spaces of care around moments of crisis and increased homophobia (such as the onset of AIDS in the 1980s), and as spaces of fundraising and information dissemination, as well as socializing.[59] Certainly, the current situation of venue loss points to the complex issues surrounding the establishment and maintenance of queer spaces, subject as they always are to any number of ideological, political, social, economic and cultural factors.

It is intriguing that the RVT – which might be seen as the most queer space in London in the widest sense – is now in a physical location where it could be bookended by two major Establishment buildings: the new £612 million American Embassy in Nine Elms on the one side and the British MI6 (SIS) building on the opposite side of the river. In an area which is rapidly witnessing the effects of gentrification, particularly in the massive residential building projects along the river from Vauxhall to Putney, the RVT stands as a resisting embodiment of particular kinds of queer history and their spatial formations. Yet it might be another feature of Vauxhall which sums up the spaces of queer London. For at the very heart of the area is a bus station through which buses are endlessly moving, and a constantly busy ring road that branches out in all directions. Vauxhall is fundamentally a place of transition, of flux and change, of constantly becoming. And it is this image of constant movement and encounter which seems to me to suggest both the possibilities of, and threats to, London's queer spaces.

~

The analyses, reflections and interrogations brought together in this volume derive from a range of disciplinary origins, including social and political history, literary studies, art history, sociology, ethnography and the history of science. This has been key to the project and to the agenda of queer studies more widely, which has seen much of the most fruitful work being undertaken and articulated at the intersections and permeable borders between disciplines, at the levels of multidisciplinarity, interdisciplinarity or even transdisciplinarity. As Joe Moran has argued in his discussion of the transformative potential at the heart of such work, the term 'interdisciplinary' (with which his study is particularly concerned) 'can suggest forging connections across the different disciplines; but it can also mean establishing a kind of undisciplined space in the interstices between disciplines, or even attempting to transcend disciplinary boundaries altogether'.[60] Certainly, such multi-/inter-/transdisciplinary work has the potential to organize knowledge and methodologies into new configurations and alliances, and to draw attention to the (often very problematic) politics involved in discipline boundaries. Indeed, as Moran suggests, '[i]t can form part of a more general critique of academic specialisation as a whole, and of the nature of the university as an institution which cuts itself off from the outside world in small enclaves of expertise'.[61]

This collection of essays builds upon and extends existing work in the field in a number of ways. In their focus on a wider range of subject positions, and in their consideration of a wider range of sexual practices and identities, the contributors offer a more diverse sense of the ways in which the spatial politics of London enable the creation and enactment of queer subjectivities. And as Katherine M. Graham demonstrates in her chapter, and as I have suggested in my reading of Vauxhall above, this is complicated still further by the fruitful overlayering of competing histories and perspectives. Matt Houlbrook has called for a more fluid methodology which is alert to changes both spatially *and* temporally, arguing that 'if the experience of being modern and urban is constantly shifting, then so too is the geographical and cultural organization of sexual practices and identities'.[62] We hope that the chapters in this volume – in their emphasis on the sheer complexity and diversity of what might be said to constitute 'Queer London', and in the exciting pluralism of their approaches – will be seen to have contributed towards this project.

Notes

1   Heike Bauer and Matt Cook, 'Introduction', in H. Bauer and M. Cook
     (eds), *Queer 1950s: Rethinking Sexuality in the Postwar Years* (Basingstoke:
     Palgrave Macmillan, 2012), pp. 1–12, 1. By 'homonormativity', I refer, in the
     phrasing used by Gavin Brown, Kath Browne and Jason Lim, to 'the practices
     and privileges of those gays and lesbians (in the main) who are prepared
     to assimilate on the basis of largely capitalist and heteronormative values'
     ('Introduction', in *Geographies of Sexualities: Theory, Practices and Politics*,
     Aldershot: Ashgate, 2007, pp. 1–18, 12).

2   Nikki Sullivan, *A Critical Introduction to Queer Theory* (Edinburgh:
     Edinburgh University Press, 2003), p. vi.

3   Sara Ahmed, *Queer Phenomenology: Orientations, Objects, Others* (Durham,
     NC: Duke University Press, 2006), p. 161.

4   Sarah Jane Downing notes that Vauxhall was 'never truly exclusive, allowing
     admittance to all those who could afford the entrance fee of a shilling per
     evening, except for masquerade nights' (*The English Pleasure Garden,
     1680–1860*, Oxford: Shire, 2013, p. 22).

5   Bakhtin developed his ideas around the carnivalesque in his work on Rabelais
     (translated into English in 1968 as *Rabelais and His World*). The carnivalesque
     is associated with anti-authoritarianism, inversion, the materiality of the body

and affirmative renewal. See Simon Dentith, *Bakhtinian Thought* (London: Routledge, 1995), pp. 65–87.

6   Quoted in Downing, *The English Pleasure Garden*, p. 14.

7   Miles Ogden, 'Locating the Macaroni: Luxury, Sexuality and Vision in Vauxhall Gardens', *Textual Practice* 11.3 (1997), pp. 445–61, 452, 457, 455; Michael Chanan, *From Handel to Hendrix: The Composer in the Public Sphere* (London: Verso, 1999), p. 17; Rictor Norton, 'Princess Seraphina', http://rictornorton.co.uk/eighteen/seraphin.htm (accessed 25 July 2015).

8   Alison Oram, 'Cross-Dressing and Transgender', in H.G. Cocks and Matt Houlbrook (eds), *Palgrave Advances in the Modern History of Sexuality* (Basingstoke: Palgrave Macmillan, 2006), pp. 256–85.

9   Penelope J. Corfield, *Vauxhall: Sex and Entertainment* (London: History and Social Action Publications, 2012), p. 21.

10 Deborah Epstein Nord, 'Night and Day: Illusion and Carnivalesque at Vauxhall', in Jonathan Conlin (ed.), *The Pleasure Garden, from Vauxhall to Coney Island* (Philadelphia, PA: University of Pennsylvania Press, 2013), pp. 177–94, 184, 193.

11 Ibid., p. 178.

12 Charles Dickens, *Sketches by Boz*, ed. Dennis Walder (London: Penguin, 1995), pp. 153–59, 156–57.

13 Ibid., p. 155.

14 Penelope J. Corfield, *Vauxhall and the Invention of the Urban Pleasure Gardens* (London: History and Social Action Publications, 2008), p. 5.

15 Downing, *The English Pleasure Garden*, p. 37.

16 'Duckie: About', http://www.duckie.co.uk/about (accessed 30 October 2015).

17 'Bar Wotever', http://www.vauxhalltavern.com/events/event/bar-wotever/ (accessed 30 October 2015).

18 For a fascinating piece on Duckie's 'Gay Shame' events, see Catherine Silverstone, 'Duckie's *Gay Shame*: Critiquing Pride and Selling Shame in Club Performance', *Contemporary Theatre Review* 22.1 (2012), pp. 62–78.

19 RDK Herman, 'Playing with Restraints: Space, Citizenship and BDSM', in Browne, Lim and Brown (ed.), *Geographies of Sexualities: Theory, Practices and Politics*, pp. 89–100, 92. Herman's piece points to the ways in which BDSM, and by extension other fetishes, are particularly 'spatially marginalised' (p. 94), not least because they are usually viewed as a practice rather than an identity – a distinction, Herman argues, 'that reflects the problematic nature of how sexual identities are discursively constructed and reified within the social order' (p. 89).

20 Gavin Brown, Kath Browne and Jason Lim, 'Introduction', in *Geographies of Sexualities: Theory, Practices and Politics*, pp. 1–18, 13.

21 David Bell and Gill Valentine (eds), *Mapping Desire: Geographies of Sexualities* (London and New York: Routledge, 1995).

22 See, for example, Matt Houlbrook, 'Cities', in Cocks and Houlbrook (eds), *Palgrave Advances in the Modern History of Sexuality*, pp. 133–56; and Judith R. Walkowitz, *City of Dreadful Delight: Narratives of Sexual Danger in Late-Victorian London* (Chicago, IL: University of Chicago Press, 1992).

23 Lawrence Knopp, 'Sexuality and Urban Space: A Framework for Analysis', in Bell and Valentine (eds), *Mapping Desire*, pp. 149–61, 151.

24 Ibid.

25 Bell and Valentine, 'Introduction: Orientations', in *Mapping Desire*, pp. 1–27, 19.

26 Gill Valentine, '(Re)Negotiating the "Heterosexual Street": Lesbian Productions of Space', in Nancy Duncan (ed.), *Bodyspace* (London: Routledge, 1996), pp. 146–55, 146.

27 Affrica Taylor, 'A Queer Geography', in Andy Medhurst and Sally R. Munt (eds), *Lesbian and Gay Studies: A Critical Introduction* (London and Washington: Cassell, 1997), pp. 3–19, 14.

28 Ibid., p. 15.

29 See Benedict Anderson, *Imagined Communities: Reflections on the Origin and Spread of Nationalism* (London: Verso, 1983; revised 1991, 2006).

30 Taylor, 'A Queer Geography', p. 10.

31 For an interesting discussion of this, see Jon Binnie, 'Trading Places: Consumption, Sexuality and the Production of Queer Space', in Bell and Valentine (eds), *Mapping Desire*, pp. 182–99.

32 Taylor, 'A Queer Geography', pp. 12–14; Bell and Valentine, 'Introduction: Orientations', p. 19. See also Gill Valentine's insightful reading in '(Re)Negotiating the "Heterosexual Street"'.

33 Taylor, 'A Queer Geography', p. 13.

34 Houlbrook, 'Cities', pp. 134–5.

35 Chris Waters, 'Sexology', in H.G. Cocks and Matt Houlbrook (eds), *Palgrave Advances in the Modern History of Sexuality*, pp. 41–63, 44.

36 Michel Foucault, *The History of Sexuality Volume 1: The Will to Knowledge* [1976], trans. Robert Hurley (London: Penguin, 1990). In this context, Foucault is particularly concerned with the 'numerous and diverse techniques for achieving the subjugation of bodies and the control of populations' (p. 140).

37 Simon Ofield, 'Cruising the Archive', *Journal of Visual Culture* 4.3 (2005), pp. 351–64, 357.

38 Matt Cook, *London and the Culture of Homosexuality, 1885–1914* (Cambridge: Cambridge University Press, 2003), pp. 5–6.

39 Neil McKenna, *Fanny and Stella: The Young Men Who Shocked Victorian England* (London: Faber and Faber, 2013).

40 Cook, *London and the Culture of Homosexuality*, p. 12.

41   Matt Cook, 'Law', in H.G. Cocks and Matt Houlbrook (eds), *Palgrave Advances in the Modern History of Sexuality*, pp. 64–86, 64–65.

42   Mark Turner, *Backward Glances: Cruising the Queer Streets of New York and London* (London: Reaktion, 2003), p. 7.

43   Ibid.

44   Matt Houlbrook, *Queer London: Perils and Pleasures in the Sexual Metropolis, 1918–1957* (Chicago, IL and London: University of Chicago Press, 2005), p. 11.

45   Ibid., p. 4.

46   Ibid., p. 265.

47   Morris B. Kaplan, *Sodom on the Thames: Sex, Love and Scandal in Wilde Times* (Ithaca, NY: Cornell University Press, 2005); Anthony Clayton, *Decadent London* (London: Historical Publications, 2005).

48   Matt Cook, *Queer Domesticities: Homosexuality and Home Life in Twentieth-Century London* (Basingstoke: Palgrave Macmillan, 2014), p. 3.

49   Sebastian Groes, 'Introduction', in *The Making of London: London in Contemporary Literature* (Basingstoke: Palgrave Macmillan, 2011), pp. 1–16, 1.

50   *Sins of the Cities of the Plain, or the Recollections of a Mary-Ann with Short Essays on Sodomy and Tribadism* (London: The Erotica Biblion Society, 1881), p. 90. For discussion, see Cook, *London and the Culture of Homosexuality*, pp. 18–22; and Morris B. Kaplan, 'Who's Afraid of Jack Saul?: Urban Culture and the Politics of Desire in Late Victorian London', *GLQ: A Journal of Lesbian and Gay Studies* 5.3 (1999), pp. 267–314.

51   Houlbrook, *Queer London*, p. 10.

52   Terry Castle, *The Apparitional Lesbian: Female Homosexuality and Modern Culture* (New York: Columbia University Press, 1993), p. 2.

53   Laura Gowing, 'History', in Andy Medhurst and Sally R. Munt (eds), *Lesbian and Gay Studies: A Critical Introduction*, pp. 53–66, 55, 61.

54   Sally Munt, 'The Lesbian *Flâneur*', in Bell and Valentine (ed.), *Mapping Desire*, pp. 114–25, 125.

55   Julie A. Podmore, 'Lesbians in the Crowd', *Gender, Place and Culture* 8.4 (2001), pp. 333–55, 334; Tamar Rothenberg, '"And She Told Two Friends": Lesbians Creating Urban Social Space', in Bell and Valentine (eds), *Mapping Desire*, pp. 165–81.

56   Houlbrook, 'Cities', p. 146.

57   Quoted in *Independent*, http://www.independent.co.uk/news/uk/home-news /the-black-cap-protest-queens-and-lgbt-activists-gather-to-save-iconic-london -gay-bar-from-10186891.html (accessed 20 July 2015).

58   See the Future of the Royal Vauxhall Tavern website. http://www.rvt .community/ (accessed 30 September 2015).

59 The important Pride of Place: LGBTQ Heritage Project, funded by Historic England, is working to map the UK's queer locations and 'uncover the untold queer histories of buildings and places'. See https://historicengland.org.uk/research/inclusive-heritage/lgbtq-heritage-project/ (accessed 30 July 2015).

60 Joe Moran, *Interdisciplinarity* (London: Routledge, 2nd edn, 2010), p. 14.

61 Ibid., p. 15.

62 Houlbrook, 'Cities', p. 148.

CHAPTER TWO

Queer Temporalities, Queer Londons

Katherine M. Graham

*I cannot claim that many of the 'Queer Things' treated of
in these pages are 'unknown'. It would be very queer
indeed if they were. But most of them are but
little considered and not greatly visited except
by those whose business lies that way.[1]*

I'm from Hounslow. For those who haven't visited, it's over in West
London – further out than places like Kensington and Chiswick, but before
places like Feltham and Staines. It's in zone four and bang underneath
one of the Heathrow flight paths, so everything was covered in what my
parents referred to as 'airplane poo'. I was born there, bred there and I've
'boomeranged' back repeatedly. My early queer years were spent in the
Queens Arms, a gay pub that was demolished to make way for Hounslow's
second bus station. But it turned out Hounslow didn't need a second bus
station, so the space of the pub remains, an empty space and a reminder of
that past. I worked at the 'QA' from the age of 17. I was too young to serve
pints legally so I was in charge of coats, glasses and ashtrays, which meant
I often smelt unpleasant. I learnt to DJ there, I illegally served pints there
and I broke up fights there. My entire understanding of 'queer London'
is filtered through this very particular, past space and my sociocultural
practices within it. I learnt how to *be* in a queer community, in a very
material sense, in that pub.

Now this is an anecdote, but this queer past is important in how I understand my queer present – this past structures how I act in any queer space in the present. Empty glasses left on a pub table for longer than necessary make me physically twitchy; I have to stop myself from bursting into song whenever I hear the opening strains of Aqua's 'Barbie Girl'; and I'm often disappointed that the diversity (of class and race especially) I found in the Queens Arms is not repeated in other queer venues. I start with this anecdote both to put Hounslow on London's queer map and because in this chapter I want to highlight understandings of queerness, and of London, that necessitate and encourage a concurrent understanding of the past. Such an understanding is crucial, in part, because of the temporal breadth of this volume. Thus, in this chapter, I consider the possible methodologies for bringing together such a breadth of material. As Simon Avery gestured towards at the end of his chapter, Matt Houlbrook importantly argues for the need to create 'a form of analysis that can simultaneously account for differences over time and space'.[2] This chapter is meant as a small step in that direction. Thus, I explore the term 'queer' and, in particular, I reflect on the attention that queer scholars have paid to questions around time and around history. Here, Carolyn Dinshaw's notion of a 'touch across time' becomes a productive impulse for considering and engaging with this collection and the organization of material within it.[3]

Sex, Time and Place covers work from the 1850s to the present. Our contributors reflect on Soho, Bloomsbury, Brixton, East London and St Giles, among other areas of London. They deal with art, literature, politics, journalism, geography, performance, archives, oral histories, technology and the Internet. They often offer competing and contradictory readings of particular moments or spaces. They are established and emerging scholars working in a wide range of disciplines and, as such, they work in challenging and interdisciplinary/transdisciplinary ways – as Avery has discussed in the previous chapter. Taken as a whole, this volume offers a dizzying array of material, bodies and moments, and that is the point: to create a scholarly impression of London that complicates, develops and adds to the work that has gone before. While there is, obviously and vitally, an important role for work which focuses singularly on particular subsections of London's queer communities – that is, the work which focuses on (mostly white) male–male experience – there must also be room for work which shows a breadth of material and which brings into focus communities who are not so readily recorded in the historical (and especially legal) archive. Towards the end of this volume, Sam McBean implicitly suggests that the ways in which photographs (specifically Christa Holka's) travel on the Internet might be seen to trouble, even to problematize, any notion of queer London. If we are to comprehend the implications of such an assertion, we need to understand fully the breadth of people who might be considered under the umbrella of 'queer London'. In thinking about queerness, and in thinking about touches across time, I am gesturing towards a methodology that allows us to think through and across the differing subjects, bodies and methods at play in this volume. I am aware of the temptation to read the chapters that speak to one's own research interests and to skip over the others, but I would urge the reader to read widely – here, to do so is to read inclusively.

A huge amount of work has already focused on London and the history of its sexually marginalized communities. Texts such as Matt Houlbrook's *Queer London: Perils and Pleasures in the Sexual Metropolis*, Matt Cook's *London and the Culture of Homosexuality, 1885–1914* or Mark Turner's *Backwards Glances: Cruising the Queer Street of New York and London*[4] draw on, complement and produce the work of those scholars investigating the relationship between sexuality and space that can be found in edited collections like *Mapping Desire, Geographies of Sexualities* and *Queer Cities, Queer Cultures*.[5] Historical enquiries, like Seth Koven's *Slumming*, Hugh David's *On Queer Street*, H.G. Cocks' *Nameless Offences* and Brian Lewis' edited collection *British Queer History*, extend and contextualize the field.[6] All of this work, and much much more (this list is in no way exhaustive), informs the analyses within this volume. It is necessary and important work, but this volume pushes to diversify and extend the kinds of peoples, bodies and communities that might be considered as part of a discussion of 'queer London'.[7] Amy Villarejo has recently stated, in a discussion of 'sexual and spatial practices', that much existing work offers 'wonderful guides to queer cities, but despite declarations to the contrary, [it is] not particularly interested in gender, much less women, much less transgender'.[8] Villarejo is referring explicitly to Houlbrook and George Chauncey Jr. here,[9] and while we might want to note the rhetorical force behind her words, it pays to remain aware of the exclusionary practices of some of this work. Indeed, Gemma Romain and Caroline Bressey acknowledge this in their chapter on Claude McKay here, when they remind us that not everyone was able to access the 'networks of public and commercial sociability' that Houlbrook identifies.[10] For Romain and Bressey, it is important to note that McKay's race 'made him feel … conspicuous' and thus excluded him from these networks.

Sometimes work which focuses on one subset of queers and excludes others confronts this exclusion directly, as in Hugh David's *On Queer Street* when he suggests, 'I have also consciously ignored the lesbian history of the period, except where it overlaps with my own material.'[11] But at other times the exclusion is more subtle. I am not suggesting here that this collection addresses all the lacks – it would be difficult to do so – but hopefully it represents a step towards broader representation of the communities, people and aesthetic production which might be understood as comprising 'queer London'. But firstly though, I want to consider how exactly we might be using the term 'queer' and, in doing so, to consider the importance that recent queer thinking on questions of history and temporality might have in undertaking and navigating the work on queer London.

Queer and *Queer Things About London*

This volume takes the term 'queer' as one of its organizing principles but throughout contributors use the term in various and differing ways, which is an accurate reflection of a term whose meaning is debated and disputed. Throughout this volume, it functions as an umbrella term for LGBTQ+ identities and, in a troubling of this usage, it is used to describe people who disrupt and refuse these identities, as well as to describe people for whom such a taxonomy simply is not possible, due to their historically contingent socio-cultural position. In the introduction to *Queer Cities, Queer Cultures*, Matt Cook and Jennifer Evans point out that queer 'might accommodate individuals who "disturb" categories that have become conventional',[12] and there is a nice reminder in their phrasing that identity categories, and the sociocultural positioning of them, shift constantly across time and contexts – that the conventions that we find in any given moment are the product of a temporal development and not a static given.

Queer is not just a term associated with identity categories (the inhabiting or shattering of them) and theoretical discourse. It also functions as a more colloquial term and throughout the period under consideration, the colloquial meaning of queer shifts and changes and is not always, or solely, associated with homosexuality. However, one of the most familiar uses of the term *is* when it is used, as a noun, to denote '[h]omosexual, esp. a male homosexual'.[13] Such a usage has a difficult and derogatory history, although the term has also been subject to some form of rehabilitation, as I will discuss below. *The Oxford English Dictionary* also suggests that the association between queer and homosexuality continues in its use as an adverb, where it might mean '[o]f a person: homosexual. Hence: of or relating to homosexuals or homosexuality'.[14] This use of queer to signal homosexuality is dated from the late 1800s (for its use as a noun) and from the early 1900s (for its use as an adverb). This usage of the term comes to replace, to some extent, its other possible older meanings, including its definition of '[s]trange, odd, peculiar, eccentric. Also: of questionable character; suspicious, dubious',[15] along with '[o]ut of sorts; unwell; faint, giddy',[16] uses which date from the early 1500s and the mid-eighteenth century, respectively. However, traces of these connotations might be thought to remain in the present, especially in the later theoretical development of the term.

In the late 1980s and early 1990s, the term underwent a political transformation, stemming in part, but not only, from its re-emergence and reclamation by groups like ACT UP and Queer Nation.[17] Both these groups, and others, used queer as part of overt and aggressive political campaigns, drawing on the anger around HIV/AIDS and various governments' poor responses to that crisis. During the same period in the academy, we see queer theory growing as a discourse in response to poststructuralist understandings of subjectivity, identity and meaning as constructed, contingent, indeterminate and in flux.

This 'fluidity' became an important tool for scholars considering questions of gender and sexuality. Drawing on this poststructuralist frame, Eve Kosofsky Sedgwick, in *Tendencies*, underscores the disruptive potential of the queer when she argues that 'queer can refer to: the open mesh of possibilities, gaps, overlaps, dissonances and resonances, lapses and excesses of meaning when the constituent elements of anyone's gender, of anyone's sexuality aren't made (or *can't* be made) to signify monolithically'.[18] For Sedgwick, then, queer is the effect produced when an attempt at monolithic signification fails – or when stable identity categories fail. Not all of the contributors in this volume adhere to this theoretical model of queerness, but they do all understand their subjects as occupying a position (in relation to their sexuality and/or gender and/or desire) that refuses, or eschews, the 'normal'. This understanding of queer as a relational term is an important one because, as David Halperin suggests, 'queer is by definition *whatever* is at odds with the normal, the legitimate, the dominant'.[19]

Queer theory is a body of work which has developed significantly since its critical inception in the 1990s, and as it does so its new insights and frames might be put to use. In particular, in the case of this collection, we have drawn on and been influenced by the recent investigations into questions of temporality and history. Critics such as Carolyn Dinshaw, Heather Love, Elizabeth Freeman, David Halperin, Valerie Rohy, Ann Cvetkovich, Lee Edleman, Judith Halberstam and José Esteban Muñoz have all questioned the need and desire for queer history;[20] they have questioned the role that archives play in constructing queer identities, communities and histories; they have considered how 'queer' communities might speak to each other across different historical moments; and they have even questioned the validity of privileging difference as the dominant mode of understanding the past.[21] All these scholars ask, in very different ways, what does it mean to find a 'queer' person (or to find 'queerness') in a past when those categories fundamentally cannot exist? In *Queer London*, Matt Houlbrook deploys the term 'queer' to explore how the urban space of London offered men the opportunity to engage in sexual practices in ways which destabilized any kind of monolithic heterosexuality, but which did not contribute to the constitution of a homosexual identity. In doing so, he effectively troubles the boundaries of any homo/hetero binary, and the monolithic nature of identity categories. Thus, Houlbrook is specific in his usage of the term, using 'the rubric "queer" to denote all erotic and affective interactions between men and all men who engaged in such interaction'[22] – not to denote solely homosexuality. The term then functions plurally, both describing male–male erotic contact (along with those who partake in it) and signalling a refusal of categorization and categories.

There is, then, a tension found in the term 'queer' which is associated with how its various meanings might function and also in how those meanings might be tied up with a question of history or associated with the historical. I would argue that this is also visible in the more colloquial uses of the term, and would suggest that we can see this in Charles G. Harper's 1923 book, *Queer Things About London*. Harper was a writer and illustrator who, between 1892 and 1933, produced a huge selection of travel books exploring England. Several of these focused on London; as well as *Queer Things About London*, Harper published a follow-up, *More Queer Things About London* (1924), along with *A Literary Man's London* (1926), *A Londoner's Own London* (1927) and *The City of London Guide* (1927).[23] *Queer Things About London* offers a companion guide to the city which, as the title suggests, aims to highlight the queer 'things' that might interest the reader. Indeed, the book is aimed more at the reader (and that reader's imagination) than the actual visitor, because 'the armchair is comfortable and sight-seeing is a tiring affair'.[24] In 1923, when Harper's book was first published, the term 'queer' functioned in a multi-vocal way, signalling 'strange, odd, peculiar, eccentric', or 'out of sorts', but it could also infer homosexuality.[25] When Harper uses the term, he ostensibly uses it to signal the 'strange, odd, peculiar, eccentric' elements of the London landscape. But for Harper, these strange, odd, peculiar 'things' are objects or moments from the past which irrupt into the present. Thus I want to suggest that Harper's use of queer, and the way in which he attaches it to the historic and the past, might be suggested to anticipate proleptically the attention to, and desire for, history, which we find in later queer theorists (such as those mentioned above). Thus, the term 'queer' might be read as always already being engaged with the past.

Harper's book begins with the quote with which I started this chapter: 'I cannot claim that many of the "Queer Things" treated of in these pages are "unknown." It would be very queer indeed if they were. But most of them are but little considered and not greatly visited except by those whose business lies that way.'[26] For Harper, these 'little considered' things are irruptions of the past in the present – irruptions we might not note unless we were looking in the correct fashion. He begins Chapter One with the following statement: 'Londoners do not, perhaps, notice their great city to be full of the oddest survivals, alike of strange buildings, visible relics, curious nooks and corners and customs.'[27] The language of the past abounds here and the notion of 'survivals' seems particularly resonant, but so too is the range of places where Harper expects to finds this surviving history – the 'buildings', 'relics', 'nooks' and 'corners', but also in the embodied 'customs'. The majority of the objects that Harper points towards are sites in which the past appears in, or disrupts, the present. Sometimes these are material objects – weathervanes or street tablets, for example. Sometimes these are embodied – such as the procession of Vintners made up of 'four men in short white smocks and silk hats, who swept the road with besoms, as they go' because of requirements 'in some far-off time' which '[t]he Vintners, it seems, have never forgotten'.[28] Sometimes the object is Harper himself, such as when he is discussing 'lost' bus stops with a policeman who 'looked at me as though I had re-appeared from the loom of ages ago'.[29] Each of the 'things' that Harper mentions, though, are felt to somehow disrupt the space in which they are found, disrupt it through temporal effect.

We might notice in Harper's recording of history something of the 'retrogression, delay, and the pull of the past upon the present', which Elizabeth Freeman notes when she interrogates the 'time of queer performativity'.[30] But what we find in Harper is not the same as the queer desire for history that Freeman, Love or Cvetkovich might note. Harper's references are not queer, as Sedgwick might understand the term, and they are not overtly concerned with gender or sexuality. But Harper repeatedly uses the term throughout the book, albeit colloquially, and if we read through both uses – that which signals homosexuality and that which signals peculiar or odd – then queer might always, whatever the colloquial meaning, be taken as a concern with the past, or as a trace of the past that somehow demands observation or, for Harper's armchair reader, demands imagining.

In Avery's chapter, he alludes to Sara Ahmed's entreaty in *Queer Phenomenology* that when dealing with the multiple possible meanings of queer we keep them all present, so as to allow 'us to move between sexual and social registers, without flattening them or reducing them to a single line'.[31] Here, reading through the different meanings of the term 'queer' creates strange bedfellows; suddenly the contributors of this volume are performing a similar analytic function to a turn-of-the-twentieth-century travel writer. At the very least, bringing these ideas together might, in a small way, shift our notion of the queer, and might firm up its preoccupation with the past. Certainly, though, bringing together texts and words, across different moments in time – moments at which meaning is different – generates ideas and creates productive connections in a fashion which might prove useful when approaching the material contained within this volume.

Touching across time

In 1999's *Getting Medieval*, Carolyn Dinshaw introduced the idea of a 'queer touch across time',[32] a 'beautiful image', to use Mark Jordan's phrase, which has been highly influential in work on queer historiography and queer temporality.[33] For Dinshaw, these queer touches are moments at which subjects are brought into (affective and possibly erotic) 'contact' across different time periods. The notion of this 'touch across time' allowed Dinshaw to create a historiographical method that accounted for, and responded to, a queer desire for history. It also allowed her to create queer 'communities' which functioned across time as well as allowing her to '*queer* historiography' itself.[34] As Dinshaw states, 'in my view a history that reckons in the most expansive way possible with how people exist in time, with what it feels like to be a body in time, or in multiple times, or out of time, is a *queer* history – whatever else it may be'.[35] The chapters in this book open up the possibility of a broader understanding of London's queer histories than has previously been constructed purely through their juxtaposition in this volume. But it is through the formation of connections across these chapters that these histories can come together in the way that Dinshaw suggests.

Throughout *Getting Medieval*, Dinshaw privileges the affective connections across and between times rather than the construction of linear and teleological histories. She creates this queer history of identification through the construction of a constellation of texts, moments and bodies across a range of different times and through a consideration of what is produced, or the impression created, when these connections across times are formed. Dinshaw focuses on connections between the pre- and postmodern, but the affective power of possible connections works for the period of time covered by our book nonetheless – the differences between 2015 and 1872 (for example) might not be as marked as those between the pre- and postmodern, but 'queer' in 2015 is very different to 'queer' in the 1870s. Rather than constructing a linear chronology, Dinshaw is interested in creating a queer history of identification across different texts and different times. One of the examples used to substantiate these constellations is that of John Boswell, author of *Christianity, Social Tolerance, and Homosexuality*, who received large amounts of fan mail from gay men following the publication of his book, which radically reinterpreted Christian attitudes towards homosexuality in the medieval and pre-medieval period. As Dinshaw notes, these letters 'reveal the intense, personally enabling effects of *Christianity, Social Tolerance, and Homosexuality* ... [S]ome of these letters, nominally concerning the book, provided the occasions of brief, private, supportive contact with another gay man, creating a tiny and temporary community of two'.[36] But more than this, they chart a relationship between the letter writers and the historical subjects of Boswell's book, leading one correspondent to claim, 'I had never felt – until I read your book – that I had *gay* friends across the centuries'.[37]

The community gestured towards through Dinshaw's consideration of these letters is a complicated one, not simply a 'feel-good collectivity of happy homos', but rather a 'community of the isolated, the abject, the shamed'.[38] These communities might refuse, as Dinshaw insists, to conform to the simple dichotomy of 'mimetic identification with the past or blanket alteritism'.[39] Rather, we might invest in 'partial connections, queer relations between incommensurate lives and phenomena – relations that collapse the critical and theoretical oppositions between transhistorical and alteritist accounts, between truth and pleasure, between past and present, between self and other'.[40] Or, as Ann Pellegrini productively suggests of Dinshaw's ideas,

[t]his is a queer geometry of identification, in which relation and relatedness do not unfold through mirroring, the assumed resemblances of identity, but are constituted though 'a connectedness (even across time)

of singular lives that unveil and contest normativity'. These connections between incommensurable lives and phenomena are necessarily partial.[41]

But despite being partial, these connections are productive.[42] They are evident throughout this edited collection – in the Soho that Marco Venturi identifies and Anne Witchard makes lesbian; in the queer Brixton that Emma Spruce finds few people recall and yet Matt Cook remembers; in the Cannibal Club that Silvia Antosa examines and the traces of it that appear in Lesley A. Hall's essay; they are more numerous that I can account for here and to do so would be proscriptive. They are for the reader to find. This collection, then, offers an opening out and a deepening – in the name of community and in the name of discovery – of what we have previously considered under the auspices of queer London.

Touching Oscar

Oscar Wilde's tomb in Pére Lachaise is covered in lipstick marks – much to the chagrin of Wilde's living family, but much to the delight of those who visit the graveyard to pay homage. For them, these lipstick marks are a way to make, or mark, a tangible connection with the man who is perceived by many to be a queer martyr. For Dana Luciano, these lipstick marks 'manifest the "touch across time" that Carolyn Dinshaw locates at the heart of a queer historiographic practice'.[43] As Sam McBean notes in her contribution, Luciano understands that these lipstick marks work to create a queer time and she posits this in a number of ways. Noting that the marks are often 'dismissed as unreal, transient, ephemeral',[44] Luciano argues that '[t]he lipstick kisses don't trace a timeline, a narrative of descent, between Wilde and those who made them; rather, they bend time through the location of partial affinities, pressing up against a present from the past, the present-ness of this being-otherwise'.[45] She goes on to suggest that the '[m]ournfulness [of the kisses] conveys the insufficiency of a present marked by loss and emptiness, maintaining the conviction that the present should have been otherwise, while the exultation of the outcast brings that otherwise-present into being, charging in with a mingled sense of consummation and expectation – just as a kiss can do'.[46]

What Luciano understands as a moment of queer temporality – and her application of Dinshaw's theory is a productive one – is also anchored in space; it is a concrete geographic location that facilitates this connection between Wilde and those who leave the marks. But we must read this space through its history; the connections that Luciano reads through the lipstick marks are enhanced by our knowledge that Wilde shares the grave with Robbie Ross, a man with whom he has an erotic history; that the monument once had genitalia which were removed by vandals in 1961, and briefly replaced by visual artist Leon Johnson in 2000; and our knowledge that

Wilde's family have tried to stop these kisses being left behind, through the erection of a barrier around the monument in 2011. Present in Wilde's grave, there is a complicated relationship between time and space, one that Wilde's grandson, Merlin Holland, demonstrates an anxiety about – visible in the erection of the barrier and in his claim that 'the lipstick is just the final straw. Unthinking vulgar people may have defaced Wilde's tomb forever'.[47] Holland's anxiety about this relationship between time and space, and the connections facilitated by them, is also evident in another claim he makes about his son, Wilde's great-grandson, Lucian. Lucian, like Wilde, attended Magdalen College, Oxford, and during his time there lived in accommodation in which Wilde had also resided.[48] This spatial alignment between great-grandfather and great-grandson made Holland feel, rather ominously, as though 'the similarities were getting out of hand'.[49] Thus he reports himself as saying to Lucian, 'I don't give a damn about your sexuality, but for goodness sake keep out of the courts', and added to the Guardian journalist that '[t]he *coincidences* had gone far enough'.[50] This constellation then, across times and spaces, creates an unwanted community of 'unthinking vulgar people' and unwanted connections within familial lines – not a happy community of homos, but a community nonetheless.

While Merlin Holland wishes to regulate the ability of 'vulgar people' to form a connection to Wilde, for many a connection to Wilde is something to make manifest. Accordingly, Hugh David starts his book *On Queer Street* by announcing:

> I once kissed a man who'd once been kissed by Lord Alfred Douglas. That a man now in his mid-forties is thus only two pecks away from Oscar Wilde in a fantastically apostate succession is interesting principally for the light it throws on the size of what is now commonly referred to as 'the gay community'.[51]

David goes on to use this as a way of disparaging the size of the said 'gay community', but he also uses it, I would argue, as a way of inserting himself into queer history – not just any queer history though, but queer 'royalty'. This affective force, this alignment in and across time that Wilde appears to facilitate is also evident in Jonathan Kemp's 2010 novel *London Triptych*, which reinstates that relationship between time and space (as Luciano, following Dinshaw, constructs it above) in its very fabric and structure.

In *London Triptych*, Kemp brings together a constellation of bodies and creates affective moments of connection across the three different time periods in which the novel's three different narrative strands are set – 1894–95, 1954 and 1998. The novel interrogates the relationship between gay identity and the law; gay identity and history; but also gay identity and space focusing as it does broadly on London and, more specifically, on the boundaries between the public and the private within London. The novel's play with form is clear, and the three narratives wind through history, creating striking resonances – to return to Sedgwick's language and to invoke Dinshaw's ideas – across these times and the city. To conclude this chapter, I want to focus on a specific moment in the novel which brings together the threads of my discussion. It is also a moment that uses the figure of Wilde through which to facilitate the affective potential of Dinshaw's 'touch across time'. Here the idea of Wilde and the bodies and objects that are connected to him disrupt the present through the evocation of the past and trouble any simple sense of the 'now' as a discrete and contained moment. Before I offer this analysis though, I want to acknowledge that I am focusing on white gay men in exactly the fashion I have criticized others for doing. That I do so is both a symptom of the problem and reproduces the problem. Nevertheless, I hope though to make claims about methodology which will facilitate an engagement with the rest of the material in this book – material I hope, in turn, will facilitate a move away from this subject.

The 1954 thread of Kemp's book focuses on Colin, a reclusive artist who is paying the attractive Gore to model for him. This modelling relationship is framed by certain erotic undertones, with the two men having met at a public life-drawing class and having then negotiated a private arrangement, which sees Gore model for Colin in the privacy of Colin's own home. The chapter under consideration opens ominously, with Colin informing the reader that 'I spent last night in a police cell'.[52] The cause of this event is immediately offered to the reader in the chapter's second line; 'Gore had taken me to my first queer pub'.[53] The first two sentences directly tell the reader the outcome of the chapter, so the tension is not created here by watching things unfold – we know that Colin's first trip to a gay pub will end with him in prison. This play with temporality and narrative is also a play with space, the text linking, implicitly, the space of the police cell and the space of the queer pub. But the text further plays with these links through a figure from the past, when, almost as soon as Colin and Gore are seated with drinks, they are joined by 'a grey-haired old man in an extremely tight burgundy velvet jacket and blue cravat' who has 'the fruitiest voice'.[54] This figure is Jack Rose who, in the 1894 thread of the novel, is Oscar Wilde's favourite rent boy.

The first connection that the text makes between the temporal threads is through the question of art. Jack's initial approach to Colin and Gore is through a desire to cast Gore's hands and genitals in bronze, a request Gore shrugs off. Instead he passes attention to Colin, who he describes as a 'real artist',[55] eschewing Jack's overly eroticized 'art practice'. The notion of a 'real artist' takes Jack instantly to Oscar Wilde and he claims dreamily, 'I knew a real artist once'.[56] Thus, the figure of the artist in the present – Colin – takes us to the figure of the artist in the past – Wilde – and it is worth noting that both figures are enmeshed with the law (the chapter has already told us that Colin will end up in a police cell and the 1894 narrative is, by this stage, focused on Wilde's legal troubles). Once the spectre of Wilde has been raised, Jack is 'transported' to the past, a time he narrates with both nostalgia – 'I was a beautiful boy, not ashamed to say it, a shiny ripe apple in this veritable Eden' – and anger – '[i]t's a crime what this country did to that man, a crime!'[57] Jack's nostalgia, or the 'drag' that he feels the past enact on the present, is in part for a lost community, thus he mourns that after Wilde's trial 'the inns were empty, the drag balls wiped off the face of the city like a tart's panstick. Most of the well-to-do queens had sodded off abroad'.[58] This loss is tempered with both contempt for the structures which exile Wilde – 'Lily Law',[59] as he calls it – and also through a marking of the re-emergence of a kind of queer scene: 'ever so gradually, legions of Oscars started to spring up like flowers all over London, on every street corner in town from the Dilly to Oxford Street. So many Oscars. Vivid and proud'.[60] Thus the re-emergence of homosexuality in London is figured as a re-emergence of Oscar Wilde himself – 'it was as if he had to die so as to be reincarnated not just as a person, but as a whole new century. That's how big he was', claims Jack later.[61] But this positive queer community is immediately troubled by the text, as Jack's monologue about the exciting and invigorating re-emergence of all these 'Oscars' is followed by 'a sudden burst of noise and half a dozen policemen crash[ing] through the doors'.[62] Jack leaves the scene, 'slinking off to the back room, gliding like a phantom',[63] or like a ghost from the past, but he also leaves the spectre of legal intervention into the lives of gay men in the room behind him – like a concrete manifestation of Wilde's past legal troubles. The pub therefore provides a glimpse into a past structured by law, and then it facilitates a present also structured by the law.

But this moment in the pub changes Colin, and produces for him some sense of community – even if it is a community structured in part by danger. Arrested in the police raid at the pub, Colin is then visited by the police the next day at his home, his excursion into London's queer public spaces having produced the opening and violating of his private spaces. After the police leave, Colin goes to a cottage, an act he cannot account for: 'I have no explanation for what I did next. Perhaps I needed further humiliation; perhaps I needed some reason to feel so shamed, needed to commit the crime for which I was being pursued.'[64] In the cottage, the promise of an illicit sexual encounter is negated; instead, Colin experiences a moment of homophobic violence and, as he attempts to escape from the man threatening him, he jumps into a cab. Here he finds a sympathetic cabbie who gives Colin a wink and advises '[n]ext time, just give him some money – that usually shuts them up'.[65] This moment of community, or at least connection and understanding, is slightly undercut by Colin's immediate (lonely) recollection that it is his birthday, but nonetheless it offers a glimmer, however depressing, of some sort of community.

This community, though, is brought into existence by the presence of the past in the present, through the figure of Jack and through his storytelling. I want to take a moment here to emphasize the physicality of that presence, to emphasize that Jack is a firmly corporeal character. He is introduced as a 'grey-haired old man in an extremely tight burgundy velvet jacket and blue cravat, who had been staring and blinking', and his opening line to Gore emphasizes a loaded body part: 'you *must* let me make a cast of your hands. They're divine'.[66] Present in the line is a knowing nod to Wilde's *Picture of Dorian Gray* (1890) and the use within the novel of hands as codified symbol. Jack's following line, though, explodes any need for the codification present in Wilde's novel, when he states, '[a]nd your cock too, if you'd let me'.[67] The physicality of Jack's textual presence continues throughout the scene with the text taking care to note his 'limp hand', and the 'dropping [of] the genteel accent and trowelling on the Cockney'.[68] Jack's face is also 'powdered' and he steals Gore's cigarettes and gulps from their drinks.[69] Finally, he hands Colin 'a tatty sepia photograph' on which Wilde has written '*To Jack, my favourite writing desk, O.W.*',[70] and which the reader has already seen Wilde give to Jack.

Thus, this figure, so clearly tied to the past through his angry monologues about Wilde's treatment and his theories about Wilde's resurrection, is a material one. This touch across time is manifested through this figure, through his handshake and his cherished photograph. It is also figured through the comparison between times that Kemp offers in the structure of the chapter and its inherent parallel between the role of the law in the life of Oscar Wilde and the role of the law in the 1954 present. It is the space of a queer London pub that facilitates this kind of community and makes these touches possible. Then, once this touch across time has occurred, it opens further queer spaces up for Colin, as evidenced by his visit the next day to a cottage. But it also challenges his private spaces, leaving his home open to a police visit that creates for Colin the feeling of having been 'violated, exposed, shamed, intimidated'.[71]

The text here insists that we read across times; it insists that to understand Colin in the present we must see him as part of a history that includes Wilde. But the figure of Jack insists – through both his characterization and function – that the past has not actually gone anywhere, it is not over and to understand the present requires the past. Thus our knowledge is strengthened and enhanced through a connection across time.

I have sought to give a brief indication of the potential of creating networks of connections across different moments in time and gesture towards how they may speak to the present, or speak to an understanding of the past. And I want to suggest that our methodology in putting together the material this volume goes to creating one of these constellations – forming connections across the 150+ years the book covers. We are not just aiming here then to 'find queers' in the past – although some of the individual work of the contributors does that very thing. Rather, we are aiming to create a different looking model of 'queer London', one which is wider and broader and which – through its *partial* connections – gestures towards the contradictory and fragmentary world that queers may have inhabited. There is a politics to this construction of a community, and there is a politics to refusing the exclusive and exclusionary tactics of some previous work which considers queer London. But in part, we hope that this frame of queer time allows us to consider a little more what's at stake when we discuss queer London historically and in its contemporary formations.

Notes

1   Charles G. Harper, *Queer Things About London* (London: Cecil Palmer, 1923), p. 9.

2   Matt Houlbrook, 'Cities', in H.G. Cocks and Matt Houlbrook (eds), *Palgrave Advances in the Modern History of Sexuality* (Basingstoke: Palgrave Macmillan, 2006), pp. 133–56, 148.

3   Carolyn Dinshaw, *Getting Medieval: Sexualities and Communities, Pre- and Postmodern* (Durham, NC: Duke University Press, 1999), p. 21.

4   Matt Houlbrook, *Queer London: Perils and Pleasures in the Sexual Metropolis, 1918–1927* (Chicago: University of Chicago Press, 2005); Matt Cook, *London and the Culture of Homosexuality, 1885–1914* (Cambridge: Cambridge University Press, 2003); Mark Turner, *Backwards Glances: Cruising the Queer Street of New York and London* (London: Reaktion Books, 2003).

5   David Bell and Gill Valentine (eds), *Mapping Desire: Geographies of Sexualities* (London and New York: Routledge, 1995); Kath Browne, Jason Lim and Gavin Brown (eds), *Geographies of Sexualities: Theory, Practices and Politics* (Aldershot: Ashgate, 2007); Matt Cook and Jennifer V. Evans (eds), *Queer Cities, Queer Cultures: Europe Since 1945* (London: Bloomsbury, 2014).

6   Seth Koven, *Slumming: Sexual and Social Politics in Victorian London* (Princeton, NJ: Princeton University Press, 2004); Hugh David, *On Queer Street: A Social History of British Homosexuality 1895–1995* (London: Harper Collins Publishers, 1997); H.G. Cocks, *Nameless Offences: Homosexual Desire in the Nineteenth Century* (London and New York: I.B. Tauris Publishers, 2003); Brian Lewis (ed.), *British Queer History: New Approaches and Perspectives* (Manchester: Manchester University Press, 2013).

7   The Queer London conference took place at the University of Westminster in March 2013.

8   Amy Villarejo, *Ethereal Queer: Television, Historicity, Desire* (Durham, NC: Duke University Press, 2014), p. 27.

9   See George Chauncy Jr., *Gay New York: Gender, Urban Culture, and the Making of the Gay Male World, 1890–1940* (New York: Basic Books, 1994).

10 Houlbrook, *Queer London*, p. 3.

11 David, *On Queer Street*, p. xi.

12 Cook and Evans, 'Introduction', p. 3.

13 'queer, n.2.' *OED Online*. Oxford University Press, September 2015.
http://www.oed.com/view/Entry/156235?isAdvanced=false&result=1&rskey
=RkvabD& (accessed 15 September 2015).

14 Ibid.

15 'queer, adj.1.' *OED Online*. Oxford University Press, September 2015.
http://www.oed.com/view/Entry/156237?isAdvanced=false&result=3&rskey
=RkvabD& (accessed 15 September 2015).

16 Ibid.

17 Queer Nation formed in March 1990 and ACT UP in March 1987.

18 Eve Kosofsky Sedgwick, *Tendencies* (London: Routledge, 1994), p. 8.

19 David Halperin, *Saint Foucault* (Oxford: Oxford University Press, 1995),
p. 62. However, the shaping and defining role that an idea of the 'normal'
might play has been interrogated recently by Robyn Weigman, Elizabeth A.
Wilson and the contributors to their special issue of *differences: A Journal
of Feminist Cultural Studies*, 'Queer Theory Without Antinormativity'
(26 January 2015).

20 See, especially, Dinshaw, *Getting Medieval*; Carolyn Dinshaw, Lee Edelman,
Roderick A. Ferguson, Carla Freccero, Elizabeth Freeman, Judith Halberstam,
Annamarie Jagose, Christopher Nealon and Nguyen Tan Hoang, 'Theorizing
Queer Temporalities: A Roundtable Discussion', *GLQ* 13.2–3 (2007),
pp. 177–96; Heather Love, *Feeling Backwards* (Cambridge, MA: Harvard
University Press, 2007); Elizabeth Freeman, 'Packing History, Count(er)
ing Generations', *New Literary History* 31.4 (Autumn 2000), pp. 727–44;
Elizabeth Freeman, *Time Binds: Queer Temporalities, Queer Histories*
(Durham, NC: Duke University Press, 2010); Halperin, *Saint Foucault*; Ann
Cvetkovich, *An Archive of Feelings* (Durham, NC: Duke University Press,
2003); Lee Edelman, *No Future: Queer Theory and the Death Drive* (Durham,
NC and London: Duke University Press, 2004); Judith Halberstam, *In a Queer
Time and Place* (New York: New York University Press, 2005).

21 See especially Valerie Rohy, 'Ahistorical', *GLQ* 12.1 (2006), pp. 61–83.

22 Houlbrook, 'Note on Terminology', *Queer London*.

23 Charles G. Harper, *More Queer Things About London* (London: Cecil Palmer,
1924), *A Literary Man's London* (London: Cecil Palmer, 1926), *A Londoner's
Own London* (London: Cecil Palmer, 1927) and *The City of London Guide*
(London: Charles G. Harper, 1927).

24 Harper, *Queer Things About London*, p. 10.

25 'queer, adj.1.' *OED Online*. Oxford University Press, June 2015. http://www.
oed.com/view/Entry/156237?isAdvanced=false&result=3&rskey=RkvabD&
(accessed 3 August 2015).

26 Harper, *Queer Things About London*, p. 9.

27 Ibid., p. 15.

28   Ibid., p. 226.

29   Ibid., p. 182.

30   Freeman, 'Packing History', p. 728.

31   Sara Ahmed, *Queer Phenomenology: Orientations, Objects, Others* (Durham, NC: Duke University Press, 2006), p. 161.

32   Dinshaw, *Getting Medieval*, p. 21.

33   Mark D. Jordan, 'Touching and Acting, *or* The Closet of Abjection', *Journal of the History of Sexuality* 10.2 (2001), pp. 180–4, 180.

34   Carolyn Dinshaw, 'Got Medieval?' *Journal of the History of Sexuality* 10.2 (2001), pp. 202–12, 203. Emphasis in original.

35   Dinshaw, *Getting Medieval*, p. 109.

36   Ibid., pp. 27–6.

37   Quoted in Dinshaw, *Getting Medieval*, p. 28. Emphasis in original.

38   Dinshaw, 'Got Medieval?' p. 204.

39   Dinshaw, *Getting Medieval*, p. 34.

40   Ibid., p. 35.

41   Ann Pellegrini, 'Touching the Past; or, Hanging Chad', *Journal of the History of Sexuality* 10.2 (2001), pp. 185–94, 191.

42   I would also like to point here towards Laura Doan's engaging suggestion that 'we reconsider the value of unknowability and vagueness as a way of knowing differently', as a further affirmation that the search for the partial, or here the 'vague', can be important and productive. See Laura Doan, *Disturbing Practices: History, Sexuality and Women's Experience of Modern War* (Chicago and London: University of Chicago Press, 2013), p. 140.

43   Dana Luciano, 'Nostalgia for an Age Yet to Come: *Velvet Goldmine*'s Queer Archive', in E.L. McCallum and Mikko Tuhkanen (eds), *Queer Times, Queer Becomings* (Albany, NY: State University of New York Press, 2011), pp. 121–55, 122–3, quoting Dinshaw.

44   Luciano, 'Nostalgia for an Age Yet to Come', p. 122.

45   Ibid., p. 123.

46   Ibid.

47   Quoted in Stuart Jeffries, 'Scarlet Kisses of Death for Oscar's tomb', *Guardian*, 29 October 2000. http://www.theguardian.com/world/2000/oct/29/books.booksnews (accessed 11 August 2015).

48   Stephen Moss, 'The Importance of Being Merlin', *Guardian*, 24 November 2000. http://www.theguardian.com/books/2000/nov/24/classics.oscarwilde (accessed 11 August 2015).

49   Quoted in ibid.

50   Quoted in ibid. Emphasis added.

51 David, *On Queer Street*, p. ix.

52 Jonathan Kemp, *London Triptych* (Brighton: Myriad Editions, 2010), p. 159.

53 Ibid.

54 Ibid., p. 161.

55 Ibid.

56 Ibid.

57 Ibid., pp. 161, 162.

58 Ibid., p. 162.

59 Ibid.

60 Ibid.

61 Ibid.

62 Ibid., p. 162, 163.

63 Ibid.

64 Ibid., p. 185.

65 Ibid., p. 187.

66 Ibid., p. 161.

67 Ibid.

68 Ibid.

69 Ibid., p. 162.

70 Ibid., p. 161.

71 Ibid., p. 184.

CHAPTER THREE

Mapping This Volume

Simon Avery and Katherine M. Graham

The contributors' chapters in the second and major part of this volume are not structured by theme and they do not follow chronologically. Rather, they are arranged in order to facilitate dialogue across disciplines, spaces and times, in ways that create synergies between the chapters and their topics, both thematically and ideologically. Some of these synergies may be found in the various chapters' approaches to race and ethnicity, class, gender, nation and nationality, technology, cultural production and location. The following is designed to gesture towards some of these possible synergies, but is not meant to be exhaustive. As will become clear, the interconnections are many and varied.

This section opens with Matt Cook charting the ways in which the HIV/ AIDS crisis of the 1980s shaped queer spaces and their usages across London. Cook draws attention to a wide range of different spaces – both public and private – in his analysis of 'the "gaying" of the epidemic in London',[1] and considers the alternative structures of care that developed across the capital, both personal and institutional. In particular, Cook notes the creation of a queer, alternative form of family in response to the disease,[2] and highlights the tensions and anxieties around housing and security. Towards the end of the chapter, Cook draws on the notion of haunting, a concept which returns throughout the volume in the work of a number of contributors, including Paulina Palmer and Bart Eeckhout.

Cook relies, in part, upon practices of oral history, which are also methodologically central to Emma Spruce's work. Spruce draws upon elements of ethnography and queer geography in order to investigate the problematic deployment of gay progress narratives in Brixton, South London. Spruce introduces the concept of 'bigot geography' which she describes as a 'suturing of homophobia, people and place...an imaginary mapping that works...to differentially locate, and thus value, bodies in relation to sexual modernity'.[3] In particular, Spruce discusses the ascribing of homophobic beliefs to Brixton's black and/or immigrant and/or poor communities, but she goes on to challenge this 'bigot geography' by tracing Brixton's history and emphasizing, among other things, both gay squats located in the area and a wider tolerance. Thus, for Spruce, 'memory sharing becomes a possible site of anti-racist resistance'.[4] Spruce's chapter is the first in a number of chapters that might be read as offering a challenging and at times uncomfortable picture of how race and ethnicity might play into our understanding of queer London. In doing so, she shares a focus with the work of Silvia Antosa, Carolyn Conroy, and Gemma Romain and Caroline Bressey included here.

While Spruce offers a close consideration of a particular London space, Paulina Palmer offers a broader engagement with notions of the city. In one of two chapters to address the literatures of queer London, Palmer examines the range of strategies deployed by Sarah Waters in order to interrogate the interaction between queer female identities and the urban matrix. Focusing on *Tipping the Velvet* (1998), *Affinity* (1999), *Fingersmith* (2002) and *The Night Watch* (2006), Palmer's chapter utilizes important concepts such as the *flâneur* and the carnivalesque in order to explore the texts' politics, drawing particular attention to the ways in which Waters' fiction plays with intertextual references as a means of understanding the city. As such, Palmer argues that '[b]y juxtaposing reference to the dominant culture with its marginalized counterpart, [Waters] fills in the gaps and absences relating to gender and sexuality...and fleshes out the feminine and queer areas of metropolitan life'.[5]

For Palmer, one of those marginalized counterpoints is the queer performance that she discusses in relation to *Fingersmith*. Kayte Stokoe's chapter resonates with this through its focus on the Drag King scene in London, juxtaposing the contemporary King scene with the work of Vesta Tilly in the late nineteenth and early twentieth centuries – a period which a number of contributors return to and reinvestigate. In particular, Stokoe highlights the ways in which Tilley's drag sought to move away from a 'masculine' performance, creating instead a more 'androgynous' or 'feminine' one. Stokoe proceeds to demonstrate the impact this has had on contemporary King performances and the contemporary perception of Kinging. Methodologically, the chapter approaches the material from both historical and experiential positions, using interviews with current performers alongside the historical documentation of Tilley's life and career. Throughout the chapter, Stokoe is in dialogue with the work of Marie-Hélène/Sam Bourcier and especially with the notion of *pratiques transgenres*, a queer theoretical concept which can 'facilitate a recognition of the possibilities for gender expression and gender identification outside the gender binary' through its mobilization of theories of performativity.[6]

Building upon Stokoe's exploration of twentieth-century queer experiences, as well as returning to the investigation of the tensions between queerness and race which Spruce raised, Gemma Romain and Caroline Bressey offer a rare consideration of the life of Claude McKay in London between 1919 and 1921. Using his journalism, letters and poetry as the basis for their historical analysis, they chart the racist discrimination and abuse that McKay received, sometimes in precisely those clubs which other commentators take as radical and queer spaces (see, for example, the chapter by Anne Witchard in this volume). Romain and Bressey highlight the ways in which McKay was excluded from the queer networks which other critics, such as Matt Houlbrook, have highlighted. In doing so, they argue forcefully for the 'need to examine the intersections of class and race with queer identity and radical activism', which, as they point out, 'have been little explored in the context of black interwar presence in Britain'.[7]

With the same agenda of rewriting history from a more marginal position and drawing upon archival research to facilitate this, the following chapter by Lesley A. Hall returns us to the late nineteenth century, and in so doing explores the history of the British Society for the Study of Sex Psychology (BSSSP) and its role in the changing political and social attitudes towards homosexuality. The chapter gestures towards the influence of Bloomsbury's permissive attitudes and communities on the group's work, and decisively demonstrates the effects which the organization and its members had upon later sociopolitical groups and institutions, as well as upon legislative change. In tracing the group's influence, Hall is able to show that 'thirty years after the collapse of the Society nearly all the reforms it had desired had been implemented, including homosexual law reform'.[8]

Dealing with a concurrently existing group to the BSSSP, Silvia Antosa's chapter examines the all-male Anthropological Society of London, founded in 1863 by Richard Francis Burton and James Hunt, and its inner circle, the Cannibal Club. Like Spruce, and Romain and Bressey, Antosa is particularly keen to examine the complex interrelations of the discourses of sexuality and race, but here particularly in the context of the homophobic and misogynistic mindset at the heart of both Anthropological Society and the Cannibal Club. Through a consideration of the Club's activities and publications – particularly around pornography and seemingly 'transgressive' sexual practices – Antosa suggests how this thinking about sexuality led to, and was challenged by, the work of subsequent sexologists like Havelock Ellis and Arthur Symonds. This is one of a number of chapters which show the fruitful uncovering of possibilities when reading late nineteenth-century London through a queer lens and enable us to examine what might be considered transgressive at different historical junctures.

In the first of two chapters dealing with the relationships between London and transgressive artistic practice, Dominic Janes explores the twentieth-century artist Francis Bacon and particularly the connections between his production of queer visual culture and his personal life. Janes demonstrates Bacon's self-fashioning through practices of gender indeterminacy, such as his use of make-up, before considering one of his key works, *Figure Study II* (1945–46), in relation to contemporary police photography. By reading across aesthetic practices and lived experiences, Janes highlights Bacon's interest in queer domestic spaces and perverse desires, drawing attention to the ways in which Bacon 'aestheticized violence and transgression in association with his sadomasochistic, same sex desires'.[9]

Considering an earlier artist, Carolyn Conroy examines the nineteenth-century Anglo-Jewish Simeon Solomon from the time of his conviction for attempted sodomy until his death in 1905. As Conroy documents, Solomon insisted upon living in the slum area of St Giles in ways which established crucial links between poverty, bohemianism and homosexuality. Rejecting earlier critics' readings which connect Solomon's lifestyle with mental illness, Conroy convincingly argues that St Giles offered Solomon a liberating space unconstrained by convention and dominant morality, where he could pursue 'his passion for queer "exotic vice"'.[10] As such, Solomon might be read in terms of the non-repentant homosexual identified by critics such as Richard Dellamora.

Moving from lived experiences of Queer London back to fictional representations, Bart Eeckhout re-reads three key fictions by Alan Hollinghurst – *The Swimming Pool Library* (1988), *The Line of Beauty* (2004) and *The Stranger's Child* (2011) – in order to map out a trajectory of increased queerness across Hollinghurst's work. As Eeckhout demonstrates, *The Swimming Pool Library* rewrites the tradition of the urban novel in its frequent concern with liminal spaces which are semi-public and semi-private. In Eeckhout's reading, the protagonist Will functions as an ethnographer and sexual *flâneur*, demonstrating how 'gay' spaces were constructed in London in the early 1980s. In subsequent fictional interventions, however, Hollinghurst has queered these depictions to a greater extent. Eeckhout demonstrates how, in *The Line of Beauty*, Nick queers Thatcher's heteronormative England from within, while in *The Stranger's Child* both the content and the form emphasize 'the fundamental uncontainability of sexual desires'.[11]

In line with Conroy's uncovering of aspects of a forgotten queer London, Anne Witchard's chapter, 'Sink Street: The Sapphic World of Pre-Chinatown Soho', challenges the often held assumption that there was no lesbian nightlife in early twentieth-century London. Witchard effectively exposes a lesbian scene through the 'lingering textual traces' of a variety of clubs around the West End,[12] clubs which Hall, and Romain and Bressey also reference in their chapters. Of particular concern here is the social phenomenon of the 'modern girl' and the attendant anxiety about both her sexual orientation and her challenge to 'clubland's standard demarcations of social class and propriety'.[13] Interestingly, Witchard's queer nightlife also extends to the growth of the coffee bar as a haunt for queers.

In a treatment of more recent Soho, Marco Venturi interrogates questions of 'community' in the age of the location-based app. Drawing on Benedict Anderson's idea of imagined community, Venturi traces the history of Soho as a place of assumed security for many exiled groups, before considering the implications of shifting patterns of gay male encounter. Venturi juxtaposes the material community of Soho with the recent emergence of an online male–male community, specifically on Grindr, which has the potential to fracture the area's perceived coherence. In this way, Venturi expands the notion of community which has been central to many other chapters here.

In the final chapter of the collection, Sam McBean picks up on the idea of potential community erosion explored by Venturi in her exploration of Christa Holka's 'I WAS THERE' project. McBean examines how Holka's photographs both contribute to, and constitute, an online archive of queer community, examining the complex relations between queer subjects, inclusivity and 'desires for queer historicity'.[14] Considering the kinds of effects created by these new media archival sites, McBean interrogates the ways in which Facebook and Tumblr might contribute to the erasure of specificity with regard to both space (London) and time. McBean's emphasis on the subject's desire for history therefore offers an intriguingly different view on queer historical enquiry, suggesting that it is concerned not solely with recovery of the past, but also with the shaping of the individual.

Throughout the chapters, then, the contributors have made visible previously ignored or marginalized historical moments and figures, asking us to revisit what a notion of queer London might actually mean and what is at stake when we make that enquiry. Moreover, the chapters demand that we rethink where this queer London might be situated. While most of the chapters focus on various aspects of what we might term 'central' London, occasional chapters (such as those by Graham, Eeckhout, Spruce and Cook) move further out, thereby gesturing towards that greater complexity of 'queer London' which the volume as a whole interrogates.

Notes

1   This volume, p. 51.

2   Ibid., p. 55.

3   Ibid., p. 66.

4   Ibid., p. 76.

5   Ibid., p. 83.

6   Ibid., p. 101.

7   Ibid., p. 117.

8   Ibid., p. 143.

9   Ibid., p. 170.

10   Ibid., p. 186.

11   Ibid., p. 204.

12   Ibid., p. 222.

13   Ibid., p. 224.

14   Ibid., p. 257.

Exploring Queer London

CHAPTER FOUR

London, AIDS and the 1980s

Matt Cook

Soon after I moved to London in August 1990, I met my boyfriend of fourteen years at Bang! (subsequently G-A-Y) on Charing Cross Road. Bang! was London's first big US-style gay club. It opened in 1974 and in its early years drew stars like Rod Stewart and David Bowie at a point when sexual ambiguity and bisexuality had a certain rock and pop cache.[1] By the time I danced there that night it seemed more niche: the 'gay plague' had, some felt, further entrenched the existing homo-/heterosexual dyad. That divide was also visibly apparent in the new European-style gay bars which opened in Soho in the early 1990s, cementing the area's reputation as the capital's gay village. Condoms and safer sex advice were available at each of these and there were often bucket shakers raising funds for the range of AIDS charities by then operating in the city. These bars, clubs and charities were represented at Pride in central London each July – an event I never missed then. As numbers reached over 100,000 for the Euro-pride event of 1992, *Gay Times* reported the sense of this being 'an unstoppable movement, part of a tribe that had scattered but is now reunited'.[2]

I became a buddy for Terrence Higgins Trust (THT) in 1991. I made new friends in my local buddy group in Clapham, and was partnered with men I would probably never have got to know otherwise. My boyfriend volunteered for the Immune Development Trust based in Islington, offering massage therapy to people with AIDS (PWAs as the acronym now had them). AIDS and HIV was a frequent topic of conversation in our domestic life. He was seven years older than me – a significant age difference at this historical juncture. While I had moved to London at twenty equipped with an (apparently) clear knowledge about risks, he had come out earlier in London in more uncertain times. It was his friends and former lovers he and sometimes I visited at the Middlesex Hospital in Fitzrovia and at the brand new Chelsea and Westminster (formerly St Stephen's Hospital) in Fulham Road to the west. Much less often than many men I knew, but more frequently than most people in their early twenties, I went to funerals in central London churches and the cemeteries which fringed the capital, and to memorial services at the Lighthouse in Ladbroke Grove and a former synagogue in Spitalfields. Looking back, we now know that AIDS-related deaths in the UK were peaking at around 1,000 per year in these early years of the 1990s. The vast majority of these were in London.[3]

This personal but also substantially shared geography shaped my understandings of what it meant to be gay at this time. Looking back, I realize how new this city was, how fundamentally it had been shaken and re-inflected by the AIDS epidemic, and how recently hospitals, clinics and cemeteries had entered the routine lives of gay men, young and old. Gay men and their urban 'haunts' were exposed more clearly to view in the 1980s and battle lines were re-drawn across urban spaces (and between the metropolis and provinces) as fear and homophobia faced off anger and grief, pride and shame. New solidarities were forged and fresh enmities and disaffections emerged. Familiar spaces became strange or uncomfortable, and others were newly associated with gay life (and death). Ideas of urban safety, danger and community were reappraised and reconfigured. In barely eight years, gay lives in the city had been transformed – and so too had the ways in which others thought about them.

There were a number of intersecting reasons for these shifts – among them the legacies of gay liberation and the vivid urban counter cultures of the 1970s; economic crisis and then recession; a growth in intercontinental travel; housing reform; and the emergence and development of Thatcherism and the 'new right'. However, the pace, scale and dimensions of change simply cannot be understood without taking detailed account of AIDS, its disproportionate effect on gay men in the UK and the way London became the clear epicentre of the national epidemic. In what follows I explore first the ways in which London took on this status and then look more specifically at some of the overlapping geographies which re-shaped the city for many gay men during the 1980s – geographies of support, care and treatment; of activism and socialization; of fear and insecurity; and finally of death. These ways of experiencing and understanding the city have changed again since I first engaged with them in 1990 – not least because of new treatments for HIV and the advent of the Internet. I nevertheless argue that they continue unevenly to haunt our city.

This piece is specifically about gay men in relation to AIDS and the city. There are other crucial layers of analysis which I leave for another time and which relate to intersecting yet distinct networks associated with AIDS and responses to, and of, positive women, haemophiliacs, intravenous drug users, BME individuals and communities, and those who did not identify in any of these ways. The general marginalization of these other experiences was germane to the 'gaying' of the epidemic in London and so to the dominance of gay male experience in accounts of AIDS and HIV in the UK. I am working further on the interface between diverse groups and individuals caught up in the AIDS crisis. This, though, is not the focus of my study here.

AIDS and London

Late in 1981, a 49-year-old gay man died of pneumocytis carinii pneumonia (PCP) in Brompton Hospital in west London. When AIDS was coined by the US Centre of Disease Control the following September, this man was retrospectively thought to be its first UK casualty. Over the ensuing years the death toll mounted: 29 by the end of 1983; 106 by the end of 1984; 271 by the close of 1985; 610 by year-end 1986. Initially, diagnosis and death came hard on the heels of each other, but thereafter alongside the death toll was a growing number who were becoming ill but surviving for longer.[4] By mid-1989 there were 2,000 people with AIDS in the UK, of whom 1,000 had died.[5] Over 70 per cent of cases to this date were reported within the four Thames health authority regions, most in the North West Thames area.[6] The latter included Earls Court, Notting Hill and Ladbroke Grove – all areas which had been associated subculturally and more broadly with queer life in the city in the preceding years (I use 'queer' here and at other points in this piece to include men and networks predating or not necessarily organized around or affiliated to a 'gay' identification).[7] St Mary's Hospital in Paddington, St Stephen's in Fulham and the Middlesex in Fitzrovia were leading the way in treatment and research. The first dedicated AIDS hospices in the UK – the Mildmay Mission Hospital in Shoreditch and the Lighthouse in Ladbroke Grove – opened their doors in 1988. London was also the centre of government and government action (and inaction) on AIDS. It was the base of the national media which reported on the crisis; it was where the first charities began; and it was where protest and activism was focused. All this underscored, entrenched and 'dramatized' London's position as Britain's 'AIDS capital'.[8]

London had long been closely associated with queer lives,[9] and since in the Western world AIDS seemed primarily to afflict such lives, the conjunction between the metropolis and this new syndrome appeared self-evident. London was moreover well established as Britain's global city and AIDS was understood as a 'disease' of globalization and international travel and exchange.[10] If music, dance and activist cultures from the USA had been precedent products of an international gay metropolitan circuit, AIDS seemed the latest import. In terms of a response to the epidemic, gay men, doctors and researchers in London frequently looked to New York and San Francisco for lessons in epidemiology, treatment, and models of both protest and voluntary care. Others were in turn inspired by innovations in treatment and the liberal and pragmatic health policy emerging in London.[11]

Unsurprisingly, then, AIDS was initially seen in the UK as a gay Londoners' disease. When the government began thinking harder about health education from the mid-1980s, the then chief medical officer, Donald Acheson, purportedly favoured advice to 'avoid London'.[12] Responses to the National Lesbian and Gay Survey's (NLGS) directive on 'Gay Men and Health' in 1986 meanwhile suggested that outside the capital many gay men remained relatively complacent.[13] A twenty-year-old from Birmingham, for example, garnered a sense of safety in his distance from the capital:

> I don't think we need worry ourselves about having an epidemic as large as in the United States[. W]e don't have the bath houses and the bawdy houses like the Americans do. If someone in the USA wants to have sex with 30 men in one day he can[;] in Britain he'd have to live in London, and even then he'd be very hard pushed to make 10.[14]

AIDS was often identified with particular places – in this case with New York bath houses and in the testimony of another with the Subway Club in London's Leicester Square.[15] It was sometimes places rather than acts that could seem infectious. Some of the Mass Observation project's largely heterosexual respondents to a directive on AIDS in 1987 positioned dangers away from their hometowns and districts and firmly in the capital. A 53-year-old publisher from the south-east noted that 'we had to visit London, and I have to admit that in the rush hour we felt very much aware that we might be in a hazardous zone'.[16] A common thread in Mass Observer responses related to the fate such metropolitan AIDS 'carriers' had brought upon themselves. 'For most of the country', reported the *Journal for Public Policy* in 1989, 'AIDS is something alien: a threat radiating out from the metropolis where, of course, the inhabitants are well known for their wicked ways and perverse habits'.[17]

The consequences for London and the 'scandal' of supposed preferential treatment for gay men in terms of health and housing exercised elements of the press. When Lambeth became the first local council nationally to designate homeless people with AIDS to be in priority housing need, there was 'outrage' in some quarters. Under a banner headline 'AIDS Gays to Get Council Housing', *The Express* cited the fears of a local Tory councillor that the borough would be 'turn[ed] into a Mecca for these people[,] with Lambeth being flooded by gay men claiming they have AIDS and then demanding council housing'.[18] Reaction tapped into fears about the concentration of AIDS cases in London. In 1987, the *London Evening Standard* wondered how the city would cope: 'by the year 1994', it proclaimed, 'there will be more than a million carriers of AIDS in Britain. Virtually all of these will be living in central or West London, in places like Westminster, Kensington, Chelsea, Notting Hill and Ealing'.[19] Echoing the concerns of Lambeth Tories about 'AIDS gays', this journalist worried that they would be drawn from outside London because 'almost all of the hospital and out-patient treatments are on offer only in London'.[20] Such accounts fed the fears and hyperbole that circled gay life in general and gay life in London in particular.

Gay men themselves were meanwhile experiencing the city and certain spaces within it in radically different ways. Their lives were discussed not only in the papers but in forums of health, housing and government where they had previously only received glancing attention. This new entry into public consciousness, debate and infrastructures of care is significant in terms of the development of an equalities agenda which underpinned a growing sense of rights among gay men. This laid the ground for ensuing campaigns for legislative change, as well as a gradual softening of the kind of homophobic attitudes voiced in the 1980s in sections of the press and in opinion polls.[21] The reformulation of gay life and consciousness outlined in the ensuing sections is thus important to that story of subsequent (and uneven) liberalization.

Geographies of support, care and treatment

If the 49-year-old man who died at Brompton Hospital in 1981 is thought to have been the first case, it was the death of 37-year-old Terry Higgins on 4 July 1982 at St Thomas' Hospital opposite Parliament that prompted a wider consciousness of AIDS on London's gay scene and beyond. Higgins had been subjected to double barrier nursing and had died, a nurse commented, 'in abject misery'.[22] Friends set up a trust in his name and began fundraising through London's bars and clubs (and first at the newly opened Heaven nightclub at Charing Cross). From 1983, the organization began to professionalize in its fundraising, networking and lobbying from cramped offices at Mount Pleasant and later in Grays Inn Road – both just south of Kings Cross station. That same year, THT became the first avowedly gay charity to be approved by the Charity Commission.

Just next to Kings Cross station itself, London Lesbian and Gay Switchboard was meanwhile responding to a rising volume of anxious callers. The telephone advice service was established in 1974 out of the ashes of the Gay Liberation Front (GLF).[23] It was now key in sharing what little was known about the condition and in 1983 co-convened (with the Health Education Council) the first national conference on AIDS at London's Conway Hall near Holborn. Further west, from a flat in Philbeach Gardens in Earls Court, Body Positive began operating in 1984. It brought men together who had a shared AIDS or (from 1985) HIV diagnosis in campaigning, fundraising and support work. Many of these men had known each other for years on the gay scene.[24] The initial response to AIDS emerged at this grassroots level and it was from here that awareness spread. The condition, noted *Capital Gay* in 1983, 'is the main topic of discussion in every [gay] pub and club and over dinner tables throughout London'.[25]

Given the preponderance of AIDS cases in west London, it is no coincidence that St Mary's and St Stephen's were two of the leaders in research, treatment and care. These hospitals and others began to take their place in the daily and weekly lives of gay men with AIDS-related conditions and of those supporting them. For others, there were anxious visits to attached STI (sexually transmitted infection) clinics. These were already familiar to many but from an era when visits were inconvenient rather than life changing. The clinics had to adapt rapidly in order to keep up with shifting medical knowledge, advice on 'safer sex' and conflicting ideas about whether or not to test for the virus. They drew clients from within and beyond London as gay men sought out places they felt would know most, be sympathetic and offer heightened anonymity. 'I invented a new identity and went to the special clinic of a major London hospital', wrote one National Lesbian and Gay Survey (NLGS) correspondent who lived in Leicester and was worried his HIV test might prejudice his life insurance.[26] If London was a fearful place of plague and infection to some, to others it promised the best advice and treatment. In his testimony to the NLGS in the late 1980s, Tony described spending 'half his life' in hospital in the 1980s as well as his 'luck' at having access to London's hospitals and doctors.[27] A survey of London general practitioners (GPs) in 1989 in the *British Medical Journal* indicated a higher level of awareness about the disease than elsewhere in the country, with two thirds treating at least one PWA.[28]

Traditional power and knowledge dynamics between patients and medical professionals shifted in the early years of the epidemic in these contexts as gay men actively gathered and shared information with each other and with their doctors and nurses. Journalist Oscar Moore described this as a 'fraternity of sickness'.[29] It was for him and others a new kind of London gay scene – a bush telegraph of alternative treatments, conspiracy theories and rumours from the United States and Europe. London's specialist AIDS wards and clinics developed a distinctive, informal atmosphere.[30] According to one senior social worker, the Broderip Ward at the Middlesex Hospital was alive with sex and relationship gossip and a camaraderie he had not encountered elsewhere.[31] This was in part because patients would often return repeatedly and would get to know each other and the medical staff. Many of the nurses on the wards were also gay and had experience of AIDS in both their personal and professional lives.[32] 'The ward [at St Barts hospital sandwiched between Smithfield Market and St Paul's Cathedral] is run with panache, friendly, completely informal…All smiles, laughs, intimacies', wrote film-maker Derek Jarman.[33] He and Moore found a sense of safety and respite in some of their hospital stays partly because of this.

Lighthouse, Mildmay Hospice and Landmark in Brixton (from 1990) became additional sanctuaries for many men. Aside from residential palliative care, they ran drop-in support groups and workshops – on cooking and nutrition, for example, and on camouflage make-up for those with Karposi's sarcoma (KS) lesions. These and other activities were to do with literal survival strategies in the city. 'Passing' as 'normal' had long felt important for many gay men but now passing for 'well' might be as significant. This was especially the case for those who reported stares and abuse on the streets and in bars because of visible signs of ill-health – a rather different economy of gazes from the cruising and backward glances queer Londoners had long been familiar with.

Aside from providing treatment, advice, respite and a sense of safety, London clinics, wards and hospices saw desperation and heart-breaking grief. Men described their friends waste and fade – sometimes seeming to anticipate their own illness and death. In his monochrome film *Blue* (1993), Jarman described 'a young man frail as Belsen' on his ward. 'There is death in the air here', he said. 'We are not talking about it. But I know the silence might be broken by a distraught visitor screaming, "Help, Sister! Help, Nurse!" followed by the sound of feet rushing along the corridor. Then silence.'[34] Jarman was one of the most prolific, insistent and politicized chroniclers of the disease in the city – a chronicler crucial given the much less sympathetic coverage that was emerging through sections of the media. He and others relate the sense of overload and trauma accompanying daily hospital visits, serial losses, burgeoning homophobia and intolerance, and an overall sense of being embattled.[35] They also sometimes testified to a reciprocity and generosity of spirit as family, friends, and voluntary and professional medical and support workers formed tight networks around the men they cared for. Sociologist Judith Stacey notes that the AIDS crisis 'incited gay men to perform Herculean levels of caretaking outside default family form'.[36] One HIV positive resident of the gay enclave of the Brixton Housing Co-op (BHC) described how moving there ameliorated the isolation and depression he had experienced in his flat in Limehouse, east London, where he had lived with no local support.[37] Meanwhile, the community of squatters who lived in the Brixton houses in the 1970s before they were absorbed into the BHC gathered around those of their number who became ill in the 1980s. Jamie, for example, was taken in by a former community member until his death at the age of 35 in 1985.[38]

'Coming together' and coming into view

During and in the wake of GLF activism in the early 1970s, a range of special interest groups had formed and forged new ways for gay men to 'come together'.[39] These provided a model and infrastructure for urgent activism and support networks in the context of AIDS – as we have seen in relation to Gay Switchboard, Body Positive and THT, as well as squatting communities (like the one in Brixton). Simon Watney recalls that 'many of us involved in the early days of the epidemic had known each other as young gay men on the gay scene [and from] a political culture that had revolved around the

London Lesbian and Gay Switchboard, and many other organizations and groups'.[40] ACT UP (from 1987) and Outrage! (1990) made their mark with zaps (direct action protests) in the city. Gay men, lesbians and their allies also came together in other voluntary capacities – as buddies in groups across the capital, in kitchens organized by Food Chain (whose first Christmas meal went out from the Metropolitan Community Church in Camden in 1988), as advisors on welfare and the law, and in fundraising in pubs, bars and clubs.

These were new configurations, engendering differently focused friendships, relationships and ways of socializing. There were fresh solidarities and frictions in these contexts of care and campaigning. There were tensions, for example, between THTers and other London-based groups and organizations (the Immune Development Trust, Body Positive and GMFA in particular). This related not least to the way THT was seen to be 'cosying up to government' and becoming complicit in dominant treatment models and what was seen by some to be the de-gaying of AIDS.[41] Stonewall (from 1989), ACT UP and Outrage clashed over campaign tactics and goals – even though many within these groups worked together and recognized the value of a pincer movement of lobbying and direct action. Despite the tensions, there was nevertheless a growing sense of collectivism and community in fundraising, care, pride and protest in the city. Political fractures between some gay men and lesbians in the 1970s and early 1980s had not all healed, but there was now more joint organizing. One woman observed that 'it was AIDS that changed the schism between lesbians and gay men…particularly with the anti-AIDS backlash…[P]eople started to come back together again as men and women, lesbians and gay men'.[42]

The 1980s also saw a burgeoning and defiant lesbian and gay cultural scene which was very much part of the London I entered into in 1990. The Lesbian and Gay Film Festival became an annual feature of the National Film Theatre's calendar from 1986 (building on earlier one-off events in 1977 and 1981). The Drill Hall (just off Tottenham Court Road) staged gay-themed plays and hosted tours of companies like Gay Sweatshop and Bloolips from 1984. The Lesbian and Gay Centre (1985–91) on Cowcross Street near Kings Cross was a key if short-lived community hub. HIV and AIDS were writ large in the plays, films and events screened and staged in these contexts.

New monitoring projects, activist and charity work, and renewed media interest further exposed the queer dimensions of the city. The Gay Monitoring and Archive Project (initiated by the campaign for Homosexual Equality in 1980) tracked media coverage of both AIDS and London (often in the same pieces). From 1982, GALOP (the gay and lesbian police monitoring group) recorded and mapped homophobic crime and police response (or lack thereof). Activists floated helium-filled condoms carrying safer sex information over the walls of Pentonville Prison in London to highlight the catastrophe of HIV and AIDS among inmates. The media frequently hooked into human interest stories in their reporting of AIDS, reporting which usually centred on London. *Operation Cottage*, a BBC documentary screened in 1988, revealed the dynamics and extent of the rent boy scene around Victoria Station, for example (apparently resulting in a 'dramatic fall off in trade').[43] This and other railway stations emerged more clearly as part of a queer map of the city in such coverage and also through charity and sexual health work. CLASH (the Central London Action on Street Health), for example, worked from 1987 to 1990 to address the gap in provision existing between London's drug, homeless and HIV charities – and highlighted the intersections of these three factors for some involved in the capital's queer life. CLASH volunteers distributed condoms and advice to both male and female sex workers and kept careful records. These reveal different geographies for men and women. Female prostitutes commonly worked circuits taking in Kings Cross, Euston, and then north to Finsbury Park and Stamford Hill. Male prostitutes worked more exclusively in central London – around Piccadilly, Victoria, Euston and Kings Cross.[44] This focus on central London for rent boys marked a continuation of long existing trends. But there were now new vulnerabilities. According to CLASH, only 36 per cent of these men were using condoms compared to 74 per cent of the women.[45] An NLGS correspondent who commuted in and out of London via Victoria Station each day felt that the rent boys there 'simply refuse to think about AIDS so long as the money is still coming in'. 'Is it beyond the wit of society to devise some method of helping these boys?' he asked.[46] Responses to HIV and AIDS were variable and deeply contingent – a truism which we need to hold on to alongside the narrative of collective action and community that is frequently told about the gay reaction to the epidemic in the 1980s.

City of fear and insecurity

Even a city known intimately and previously navigated confidently could feel disorientating in the context of ill-health. Jarman's regular trips across the Charing Cross Road from his studio flat on one side to the bars and cafes on the other became taxing as he lost his strength and sight.[47] Housing, rarely easy in London, could become even more problematic in the context of the epidemic. One report noted that there was a 'remarkably high correlation between HIV and housing need'.[48] Young men, sometimes new to London, at a distance from familial support and with limited resources, could find themselves in accommodation ill-suited to conditions associated with AIDS.[49] One London council reported that even as a priority 40 per cent of people with AIDS died before being permanently housed.[50]

'Home' in the city was not necessarily the most comfortable or safest place to be. This had been true for gay men before,[51] but there were now additional dimensions to those feelings of insecurity. Jarman had shit posted through his letterbox. Stallholders of the market in Islington shouted 'AIDS' at 'Rupert' when he passed by to get to and from his flat.[52] Proposals for the Lighthouse, in 1986 were met with 'angry protests' from 200 local residents at a public meeting. There were threats to withdraw children from a local school and to stage a rent and rates strike at the arrival of what the *London Evening Standard* erroneously dubbed an 'AIDS Hostel'.[53] Though this area had been known for vibrant precedent queer cultures and counter-cultural crossovers,[54] anti-Lighthouse campaigners determinedly reclaimed it for 'the family' (narrowly reconceived). It was apparently unsuited to these gay outsiders in ill-health. For my interviewee Angus, the comfortable and often erotic connections he experienced in the area in the 1970s ceased in the early 1980s. This rather queer milieu separated out: 'all my friends were gay from then on; straight men – perhaps especially those who'd slept with gay men in the 1970s – were frightened'.[55] They quickly stepped away. If the 1980s was marked for many gay men by support from sometimes unexpected quarters, these other responses and rejections exacerbated a sense of separation and feelings of embattled isolation and loneliness. This could engender a felt need to keep diagnosis secret or to reveal it to strangers at a distance from everyday life. One gay and HIV positive Mass Observer wrote in 1987: 'only one or two friends know. I did go along to a disco organised by Body Positive [in London]. I opened up to a stranger and had a good cry which was beneficial'.[56]

In the early years of the epidemic, PWAs encountered prejudice within as well as beyond hospitals.[57] A doctor at the Middlesex remembers that 'one night I was sitting in a patient's room, and this hand came round the door with a tray with food on it and just dumped it. I laughed with the patient, who said "it happens all the time". Within five minutes a bunch of flowers flew across the room – whoosh! That time I didn't even see the hand!'[58] Thirteen London GPs reported patients complaining that PWAs were being treated in the same surgery as themselves.[59] The Conservatives for the Family campaign called for the exclusion of PWAs from certain workplaces while others were unhappy about sharing swimming pools or hairdressers with them.[60] Spurious notions of risk endured despite the availability of clear information about transmission routes and this affected the daily lives of people well beyond the gay 'community' as well as those who had gay family, friends and neighbours.[61] The lines between gay and straight and the ways in which these divisions mapped onto the urban landscape were thus reappraised in the context of the early years of the epidemic. The homophobic insistence on separation and exclusion by some paradoxically redoubled an insistence by many gay and lesbian Londoners on a visible presence. The consequent growth of awareness is apparent in the uneven attitudinal change which ensued.[62] As Denis Altman convincingly argues, AIDS paradoxically began to legitimize homosexuality despite the homophobia it also unleashed.[63]

Hauntings

An NLGS correspondent wrote in the early 1990s that 'the friends and friends of friends that I have lost to AIDS are about to reach three figures'.[64] Ken became 'a professional funeral goer': 'there were three in one day once', he said.[65] Some of the city's cemeteries – Abney Park in Stoke Newington and Brompton near Earls Court most notoriously – had long been on the queer map of the city as cruising grounds. Now it was death not sex that as often took gay men to such places – though largely to the newer sites established on the peripheries of the city in the late nineteenth and early twentieth centuries (Mortlake, Isleworth and West Norwood cemeteries, for example). Ceremonies took place there and were also performed in other venues – at churches, in favourite pubs, in homes and community centres across the city. Fear underpinned early exclusions by some undertakers and funeral venues. Others gained a reputation for dealing sensitively and professionally with the partners, friends and family of those who had died and catered flexibly as funereal ritual became more individualized.[66]

Many PWAs carefully pre-planned their funerals with particular music, readings and acts of remembrance, often beyond and in defiance of tradition. David Ruffell felt that for him it was a way of 'taking control' in circumstances in which he felt powerless.[67] Other funerals remained conventional: established ritual could provide a certain familiarity and comfort. Funeral and memorial services often brought together divergent aspects of a man's life. As often, though, they brought a sense of exclusion as friends felt alienated from events organized by family – and vice versa. Watney eloquently described the funeral of his friend Bruno in 1986 and the trauma of his parents who felt 'condemned to silence, to euphemism… in this the most devastating moment of their lives as parents'. For Watney himself, there was a painful tension in crossing from central London into this other world of a family funeral which did not reflect the life of the man he had known: 'The irony of the difference between the suffocating life of the suburbs where we found ourselves, and our knowledge of the world in which Bruno had actually lived, as a magnificently affirmative and life-enhancing gay man, was all but unbearable.'[68] Watney's account underscores the idea of a reinscription of some classic gay/straight divisions – between friends and family and between the city and suburbs. It indicates too, though, how those divisions could be breached at such moments.

For those left behind, the city was haunted by the friends and lovers who lived and died there. Places of socialization or sex could also be places of remembrance. Journeys through the city might be punctuated with sudden reminders or chilling absences. It is striking how geographically specific Jarman is when he remembered lost friends in his polemic *At Your Own Risk* (1992). The book gives a vivid sense of how the city was indelibly marked for him. Describing the moment when his friend Howard told him in 1984 that he had AIDS, Jarman wrote: 'As we walked along he rolled up his shirt sleeves to show me his Kaposi; this was the first time I'd seen symptoms. We said goodbye at Cambridge Circus and never saw each other again.' After this, he went on, 'it rollercoastered':

> The next month I met a film-maker in his early twenties…He pulled me over and said, 'Derek, please help me. The doctor told me I have six months to live. I've been walking the streets ever since. I haven't been home. I don't know what to do. Can you help me tell my lover and parents?' I spent an anguished night with him making telephone calls. Eventually, after I had taken him home, I walked back across London in a cold dawn. Slowly but surely every conversation and every encounter was stalked by the shadow of the virus; a terrible impotence overwhelmed us – there was nothing to do.[69]

Jarman's writing evokes specific places and also the broader 'shadow' spreading across the capital in the early and mid-eighties. These are the kinds of hauntings philosopher Michel de Certeau describes shaping our urban lives and the way we navigate, negotiate and experience the city.[70] They are highly individualized and they shape shift and also recede. Jarman took these particular experiences to his own grave in February 1994, leaving their residues in his published writing and in the memories of his partner and friends. They are picked up and mobilized differently now (by me here, by others elsewhere) but many of these ghosts are largely unseen by a subsequent generation of gay men who now much more frequently live – or see their friends live – with HIV than die of AIDS-related illnesses. They inhabit a different gay London again, reinflected by medical advance, the 'normalization' of HIV (despite the ongoing health crisis and rising infections rates), a shifting commercial and cultural scene, growing liberalism (and neoliberalism), the inception of the Internet and a profoundly changed politics. Yet in this chapter I have suggested how the changing contours of gay London in the 1980s set out some of the terrain on which this later city was understood. Gay men in the 1980s traversed the city in new ways and took in new places there. Burgeoning activism and Pride marches forcefully articulated the right to be and the right to be in urban space. The city's gay life was exposed afresh to a broader public in salacious and sometimes more measured reporting. Some of the city's apparently straighter places were queered in the process and discussion of gay men entered council chambers and meetings rooms of a wide range of organizations across the capital. This all left social, cultural and political legacies for the London I got to know in the 1990s – in terms especially of visibility, a sense of rights and equality, feelings of difference, and proliferating intersections, integrations and cross-overs with the so-called mainstream. These things were identifiable strands of queer life before the 1980s (and especially in the wake of GLF activism) but they gained impetus and substance during that decade because of responses to the AIDS crisis in London and then beyond.

In terms of those ghosts, meanwhile, the losses of the 1980s and early 1990s are well within the living memory of a generation of men jolted into engaging with the city in new ways by the health crisis. They experienced the kind of trauma which, in sociologist Karl Manheim's words, 'uniquely cuts off a generation from its past and separates it from its future'.[71] This intense, isolating, but in some respects unifying experience is inevitably drawn forward unevenly into the everyday lives of the men who survived and those they share their lives with. The multiple horrors and pleasures of 1980s queer London haunt the city's gay social, cultural and political life. And they live on in this deeply personal interlacing of past and present.

Notes

1 Alkarim Jivani, *It's Not Unusual: A History of Lesbian and Gay Britain in the Twentieth Century* (London: Michael O'Mara, 1997), p. 175.

2 *Gay Times*, August 1992, p. 4.

3 Patricia Day and Rudolf Klein, 'Interpreting the Unexpected: The Case of AIDS Policy Making in Britain', *Journal of Public Policy* 9.3 (1989), pp. 337–53, 344.

4 Between 1984 and 1986 the median survival time for people diagnosed with AIDS in the UK was 9–10 months; from 1987 to 1995 the median survival time was 20 months. See Eddy Beck, 'The Cost of Hospital Care for HIV Patients', in David Fitzsimons, Vanessa Hardy and Keith Tolley (eds), *The Economic and Social Impact of AIDS in Europe* (London: Cassell, 1995), pp. 90–8.

5 Virginia Berridge, *AIDS in the UK: The Making of a Policy, 1981–1994* (Oxford: Oxford University Press, 1996), p. 1.

6 Day and Klein, 'Interpreting the Unexpected', p. 344.

7 See Matt Cook, *Queer Domesticities: Homosexuality and Home Life in Twentieth Century London* (Basingstoke: Palgrave Macmillan, 2014), chap. 5.

8 Day and Klein, 'Interpreting the Unexpected', p. 366.

9 On this point, see Matt Houlbrook, *Queer London: Perils and Pleasures in the Sexual Metropolis, 1918–1957* (Chicago: University of Chicago Press, 2005); Matt Cook, *London and the Culture of Homosexuality, 1885–1914* (Cambridge: Cambridge University Press, 2003).

10 See Dennis Altman, 'Globalisation, Political Economy and HIV/AIDS', *Theory and Society* 28.4 (1999), pp. 559–84.

11 On this liberal health policy, see Berridge, *AIDS in the UK*, chap. 1.

12 Ibid., p. 75.

13 National Lesbian and Gay Survey, *Proust, Cole Porter, Michelangelo, Marc Almond and Me: Writings by Gay Men on Their Lives and Lifestyles from the Archives of the National Lesbian and Gay Survey* (London: Routledge, 1993), pp. 162, 166, 173.

14 Respondent 106, National Lesbian and Gay Survey (NLGS), The Keep East Sussex Record Office, Brighton, Box 1, Directive B: Gay Men and Health.

15 Clare Summerskill, *Gateway to Heaven: Fifty Years of Lesbian and Gay Oral History* (London: Tollington, 2013), p. 201.

16 Mass Observer D1974, Mass Observation project archive (MO), The Keep East Sussex Record Office, Box: Spring 1987 (2) D-E.

17 Cited in Day and Klein, 'Interpreting the Unexpected', p. 344.

18 'AIDS Gays to Get Council Housing', *Daily Express*, 10 December 1985. See also 'Move to House AIDS Victims', *Glasgow Herald*, 11 December 1985.

19 'Can London Cope', *London Evening Standard*, 7 January 1987.

20 Ibid.

21 On opinion polls, see Yvette Rocheron and Olga Linne, 'Aids, Moral Panic and Opinion Polls', *European Journal of Communication* 4 (1989), pp. 409–34.

22 Berridge, *AIDS in the UK*, p. 15.

23 Ibid., p. 17; for an account of GLF legacies, see especially Lisa Power, *No Bath but Plenty of Bubbles: An Oral History of the Gay Liberation Front, 1970– 1973* (London: Cassell, 1995).

24 Berridge, *AIDS in the UK*, p. 22.

25 Cited in ibid., p. 17.

26 Respondent 114, NLGS, Directive: Gay Men and Health, Box 1.

27 National Lesbian and Gay Survey, *Proust, Cole Porter, Michelangelo, Marc Almond and Me*, p. 162.

28 Michael B. King, 'Psychological and Social Problems in HIV Infection: Interviews with general practitioners in London', *British Medical Journal* 299 (16 September 1989), pp. 713–16.

29 Oscar Moore, *PWA: Looking AIDS in the Face* (London: Picador, 1996), p. 62.

30 Berridge, *AIDS in the UK*, pp. 6, 9.

31 Interview with Malcolm Williams, 2008.

32 Berridge, *AIDS in the UK*, p. 60.

33 Derek Jarman, *Modern Nature: The Journals of Derek Jarman* (London: Century, 1991), p. 261.

34 Jarman, *Blue* (1993).

35 Aside from Jarman, see, for example, Adam Mars Jones, *Monopolies of Loss* (London: Faber, 1992); Moore, *PWA*.

36 Judith Stacey, 'The Families of Man: Gay Male Intimacy and Kinship in a Global Metropolis', *Signs: Journal of Women in Culture and Society* 30.3 (2005), pp. 1911–35, 1914.

37 'Jonathan', interview with Matt Cook, 2009.

38 Cook, *Queer Domesticities*, p. 223.

39 'Come Together' was the GLF newsletter. For an oral history of the GLF, see Power, *No Bath but Plenty of Bubbles*.

40 Simon Watney, *Imagine Hope: AIDS and Gay Identity* (New York: Routledge, 2000), p. 6.

41 Berridge, *AIDS in the UK*, pp. 76–77.

42 Summerskill, *Gateway to Heaven*, p. 207.

43 Tim Rhodes, *Hard to Reach or out of Reach? An Evaluation of an Innovative Model of HIV Outreach Health Education* (London: Tufnell, 1991), p. 107.

44 Ibid., p. 105.

45 Ibid., p. 114.

46 Respondent 183, NLGS, Box 1, Directive B: Gay Men and Health.

47 Jarman, *Blue*.

48 Chris Yates, *Building for Immunity: Housing People with HIV Disease and AIDS* (London: National Federation of Housing Associations, 1991), p. 4.

49 Nick Raynsford, *Housing Is an AIDS Issue* (London: National AIDS Trust, 1989), p. 7.

50 Ibid., p. 8.

51 Cook, *Queer Domesticities*, sec. III.

52 Stephen Mayes and Lyndall Stein (eds), *Positive Lives: Responses to HIV: A Photodocumentary* (London: Cassell, 1993), p. 76.

53 'Protest at AIDS hostel', *London Evening Standard*, 14 August 1986.

54 Cook, *Queer Domesticities*, pp. 160–63; see also Mort, *Capital Affairs* (New Haven, CT: Yale University Press, 2010).

55 Angus, interview April 2012.

56 Respondent B1106, MOA, Folder: Spring 1987 (2), A–B.

57 Simon Garfield, *The End of Innocence: Britain in the Time of AIDS* (London: Faber, 1994), p. 71.

58 Ibid.

59 King, 'Psychological and Social Problems in HIV Infection', p. 715.

60 Conservatives for the Family Campaign, *HIV Infected Citizens: Charter of Responsibility* (27 September 1990).

61 Simon Watney, *Policing Desire* (London: Comedia, 1986), p. 46. See also Matt Cook, 'AIDS, Mass Observation and the Permissive Turn' (forthcoming).

62 Jeffrey Weeks makes this argument in *The World We Have Won: The Remaking of Erotic and Intimate Life* (London: Routledge, 2007).

63 Denis Altman, 'Legitimisation Through Disaster', in E. Fee and D.M. Fox (eds), *AIDS: The Burdens of History* (Berkeley: University of California Press, 1988), pp. 301–16.

64 National Lesbian and Gay Survey, *Proust, Cole Porter, Michelangelo, Marc Almond and Me*, p. 175.

65 Mayes and Stein, *Positive Lives*, p. 77.

66 Margaret Holloway *et al.*, ' "Funerals Aren't Nice but It Couldn't Have Been Nicer": The Makings of a Good Funeral', *Mortality* 18.1 (2013), pp. 30–53.

67 Hall Carpenter Archives. Gay Men's Oral History Group, *Walking After Midnight*, p. 109.

68 Watney, *Policing*, p. 7.

69 Derek Jarman, *At Your Own Risk: A Saint's Testimony* (London: Hutchinson, 1992), p. 115.

70 Michel de Certeau, *The Practice of Everyday Life* (Oakland: University of California Press, 1984), pp. 91–110.

71 Karl Mannheum, 'The Problem of Generations', *Psychoanalytic Review* 57.3 (1963), pp. 4–38, 7.

CHAPTER FIVE

Bigot Geography: Queering Geopolitics in Brixton

Emma Spruce

Despite the radical egalitarian rhetoric often espoused by gay liberationist and gay rights movements, many of the strategies adopted in the name of 'gay progress' seem to have rejuvenated and sustained structures of inequality and exclusion. The twenty-first-century neologism 'homonormativity' builds on critiques expressed throughout gay political history to name this complicity between gay identity and inequality, arguing that, rather than being inherently deviant, homosexual identities and practices can also perpetuate normativity.[1] As a working definition, 'gay progress narratives' group together accounts of positive change for LGBTQ people that are structured according to chronological and evolutionary logics. These narratives span from individual coming out stories to national accounts of increasing social tolerance, and sharing (in) them constitutes a central feature of gay identity.[2] Without negating examples of positive change, foundational queer theorist Judith Butler has cautioned against an uncritical endorsement of this rhetoric of gay progress, arguing that 'certain notions of relevant geopolitical space – including the spatial boundedness of minority communities – are circumscribed by this story of a progressive modernity'.[3] Progress narratives function as a technique of modernity, therefore, because they have been used to construct and define the relations between different places and people according to a set of binaries: modern or backwards; out or repressed; civilized or barbaric; liberal or prejudiced.

As has been well documented, the dominant narrative of progress for gay rights has typically been mapped as either emerging from the city, gradually seeping out into the suburban and finally finding a place in rural contexts; or – at the international scale – emerging in 'the West', diffusing into other countries in the Global North and eventually being taken up by countries in the Global South.[4] This positions those places that emerge last in the narrative as repressed, barbaric and prejudiced, while those that are represented as the defenders of sexual rights have the capacity and obligation to bring the stragglers 'into modernity'. From proposals of aid embargos to Uganda following anti-gay legislation, to declarations around being a safe haven for LGBT asylum seekers fleeing persecution, it is clear where in the gay progress narrative the UK imagines itself to be. The assonance between the contemporary language that positions the UK as an enforcer of sexual modernity and the paternalistic defence that underwrote colonial occupation is stark.[5] It is the suturing of homophobia, people and place that I am identifying here as *bigot geography*: an imaginary mapping that works through gay progress narratives to differentially locate, and thus value, bodies in relation to sexual modernity.

Although troubling traditional understandings of space has occurred in a broader context of postmodern critiques and is thus not particular to a queer analytic, Larry Knopp nonetheless argues that deconstructing spatial ontologies represents a key strategy for queer agendas.[6] 'Queer geography' or a 'queer approach to space' has been proposed to develop anti-essentialist perspectives on sexuality and space.[7] Among other possibilities, this queered approach allows critiques that are typically constrained to different scales to be newly read alongside one another. Concretely, by putting homonationalism and gay gentrification into dialogue in my research, displacement and stigmatization emerge as central features of sexual modernity from the local to the (inter)national.[8]

In this chapter, I follow the critique of the stigmatizing and exclusionary effects of gay progress narratives to argue that a queer intervention into the contemporary spatial politics of London might be particularly fruitful. Drawing on empirical work conducted for a larger research project that traces the relationship between notions of progress, LGBT narratives and the inclusions and exclusions generated through the spatio-temporal delimitations of 'sexual modernity', I explore bigot geography in the context of the rapidly gentrifying South London district of Brixton.[9] Bigot geography's projection of homophobia is counteracted by evidence of past and present LGBTQ existences that occur both in parallel to, and within, those immigrant and/or black and/or poor communities that are presumed to be inherently homophobic and 'sexually backwards'. This evidencing of gay lives constitutes another reason to explore gay progress narratives through the accounts of some of Brixton's LGBT residents. The final section explores how remembering Brixton might represent one strategy for challenging the violence of bigot geography. Queering, I propose, suggests researching the practices and products of homonormativity *across* sites and *between* analytic scales, examining the imbrication of time and space in the techniques of modernity.

Gay progress and urban change

Generally, city spaces have a complicated but deeply invested relationship with gay identity politics as they come to represent the most viable place for people with non-normative sexualities to live 'freely'.[10] This relationship is evidenced in critiques pointing to the displacement of poor and non-white communities as a direct result of practices of LGBTQ spatial concentration (gay gentrification). It is also apparent in the more recently observed link between visible gay residents and urban reinvestment. This latter correlation of LGBT presence and the regeneration of urban districts with poor reputations has been intensified through the wide dissemination of Richard Florida's work.[11] Beyond these generic links between LGBT-identified people and the contemporary city, there are some reasons, perhaps, that can be advanced for approaching London in particular through a queered lens.

In response to the fixing of 'out' LGBT sexualities in the capital cities of the Global North by dominant gay progress narratives, recent sexuality studies have consciously pushed towards recognizing and researching sexualities in the less-attended-to spaces of the rural, suburban and Global South.[12] Despite this valuable diversification of research sites within academia, however, the key cities of Western Europe and North America remain overwhelmingly storied at the forefront of global gay politics and sexual liberation.[13] London, as 'progressive' England's capital city, must secure its position at the forefront of sexual modernity in order for the UK to maintain its geopolitical authority. This conceptualization of London as a leading example for gay equality was evident in accounts of global flows of homophobia among the LGBT people living in Brixton that I interviewed. Kate, for example, suggested that:

> In theory, for a metropolitan London gay, everything is pretty much sorted; but this is one of the five gayest cities in the world. If it is still bad in parts of London, never mind Uganda or Moscow, it's not even good in Hull. (Kate, white, British, journalist)

Although she implicitly troubles London as an LGBT utopia by noting that particular areas might be less gay friendly, the capital city is nevertheless represented by Kate as a benchmark against which Hull (in the north-east of the UK), Uganda and Moscow can be plotted. This is consistent with the positioning of capital cities as spaces of sexual freedom, and the UK at the forefront of global gay rights in British political discourse more broadly. The entrenched association between progressive (Western) sexuality and the progressive (Western) capital city constitutes, therefore, one of the reasons that London appears a site of sexual modernity *par excellence*.

Of course, multiple narratives compete to tell the story of a place and London is not just figured as a precocious reflection of the rest of the UK's progress narrative, but also serves as a space where anxieties about the future are voiced. The hysteria that a supposedly 'migrant-laden' London provokes can be seen in the frenzied tenor of responses to the publication of the 2011 census data revealing that, for the first time, less than half of London residents identified as white British.[14] Extrapolating in part from this data, a link has been made between increased reports of hate crimes – with those against LGBTQ peoples frequently highlighted – and the increased presence of 'Other' cultures in London. An example of this was a blog published by The Spectator which asked, 'Is London's "diversity" to blame for its "unprogressive" views on homosexuality?'[15] The framing of an association between hatecrime and immigration sticks an (imagined) 'backwards' temporality to the non-white resident by association with other places.[16]

Unlike in the majority of sites in the Global South where, at least in the media and politics of the Global North, changes to sexual cultures are attributed to external factors (from colonial legacies to international gay advocacy), gay progress in London is figured as endogenic. That is to say, progressive changes are narrated as the naturalized story of London and any deviation from this plotline is attributed to the 'foreign' cultures and religious beliefs imported by migrants. Given meaning through the racialized and spatially framed backstory of homophobia, migrant and/or non-white communities are located as yet to accede to sexual modernity.[17] The ubiquitous representation of what demographic change means in terms of gay experience shores up the essentialization of culture and codifies the impression of hard boundaries between groups, thus obfuscating more complex and dynamic situations. One pernicious result of this is that the black or migrant homosexual is only imagined as an exile.[18]

While London features as a haven for homosexuals fleeing less tolerant places in its first figuration, then, the second representation of increasing homophobia within the city emphasizes the fragility of this positioning. This purported vulnerability of London's gay progress narrative to the imagined 'sexual backwardness' of migrants then justifies the hardening of xenophobic and racist politics. This hardening happens not only in explicit political projects, but also through the bigot geographies that are used to attach homophobia to areas within London that are associated with particular immigrant communities, rendering it difficult to oppose the 'civilizing' practices of gentrification that are seen to displace the 'problem'.

Brixton

As is clear from this brief discussion of the tension between representations of gay friendliness and homophobia in London, places often contain and are generated through seemingly incompatible narratives. Brixton is a rich site in which to explore the boundary work of gay progress narratives, then, because of the existent palimpsest of sexual politics, race politics and the dynamics of immigration. Tracing the temporal and spatial dynamics of Brixton begins to explain how bigot geography works, through attachments to sexual modernity, to stigmatize migrant and non-white populations living in the urban centres of the Global North, as well as to fix relationships between entire geographic regions. Simply put, the logic of bigot geography means that Brixton's dominant representation as immigrant, black and poor will lead to its positioning within London as an area of likely homophobia.

In accounts about Brixton in the 1970s to the 2000s, the area is positioned as spatially outside the normative juridical, cultural and social space of the metropolis. Representative of the imbricated figurative and physical separation of Brixton from other districts in London, one of the most frequently occurring anecdotes of Brixton-past is that of the taxi that refused to take you home. Pat moved to Brixton in the late 1980s and remembers:

> If you would get in a cab [to go] home, they wouldn't take you. And the racism, the things these cab drivers would come out with ... they wouldn't take you further than Stockwell, and they'd be really, really rude. (Pat, white, British, artist)

The repetition of this story serves to underline the way that systemic racism and a reputation as a violent area marked Brixton as off the map in ways that had material effects on the experience of space. This difference from other parts of London is frequently attributed to its non-white population. Brixton has been linked in particular to the English-speaking Caribbean territories since Caribbean migrants began living in the area in the late 1940s. Although the diasporas and heritages represented in this district of South London constitute much more of a tapestry, Brixton does remain related to the Caribbean through residential concentration, cultural importance, marketing and memory. This is illustrated from central Brixton's 'Windrush Square', named after the boat which carried immigrants from the Caribbean in 1948, to the flags which fly omnipresent on Jamaican Independence Day, and the plethora of cafes – from 'Bickles Caribbean Takeaway' to 'Fish, Wings and Tings' – that make reference to the Caribbean. Although in other parts of London the commodification of difference has led to 'ethnoscapes' being viewed positively as places of consumption that stimulate local development, in Brixton this has not historically been the case.[19] Instead, combining the racist evolutionary stereotyping that legitimated colonialism with the recognition of past racism that helps to mark the contemporary moment as more tolerant, Brixton's Caribbean-heritage population emerges as the reason that Brixton lagged behind, or was held back from, the economic prosperity and property booms experienced in many other parts of central London during the 1980s.[20]

Today, this (hi)story of Brixton as a no-go zone stuck in a different temporality to the rest of London is interrupted by progress narratives of urban renewal. The estate agent paraphernalia represents Brixton as centrally located and accessible,[21] and – described as 'smack bang in the centre of south London' in 2015 – *Time Out* now names Brixton 'a go-to haunt for foodies, clubbers, artists and rockers alike'.[22] Despite this repositioning of the district to lie within the boundaries of desirable London, many of the residents I spoke to continue to reference perceptions of Brixton as distant, disproportionate to its geographical location. In exploring this perception, it became clear that Brixton's difference is marked not only negatively ('not like' other parts of London), but also through the active drawing of lines between Brixton and other places.

This technique of spatialization is apparent if we turn to a fictionalized account of Brixton in the 1980s. In Richard Dyer's novel *The Colour of Memory*, the protagonist describes walking down a main road in Brixton:

> When we turned into Railton Road it was as if we had accidentally strayed into a paramilitary coup. Suddenly we were surrounded by a renegade army of guerrillas...'What the fuck's going on?' said Steranko. 'It's the Rats, that big security outfit,' I said quietly. 'I've heard of them but I've never seen them before.' 'It's like we're in Angola or Guatemala or something.'[23]

In its description, this scene seems to reference implicitly the 1981 uprisings/ riots in Brixton.[24] Likened to a 'paramilitary coup', the reader is directed towards 'Angola' and 'Guatemala' to make sense of the scene. Later in the novel, when the protagonist goes to Lambeth Country Fair (an annual event held in Brockwell Park just on the borders of Brixton), the reader is again directed elsewhere on the map:

> By the side of the stage a giant video screen the size of a terraced house showed close-ups of the musicians and dancers...The video looked more real, more authentic than the people on stage. The dancers and musicians looked as if they were playing at the Country Fair in Brockwell Park; the pictures on the video screen looked as if they were being broadcast live by satellite from Harare or Lagos.[25]

It is apparent from the references to 'Harare' and 'Lagos' that the musicians and dancers are racialized as non-white and the protagonist appears to be struggling with the juxtaposition of black bodies and the British locale: the white narrator experiences the live-screened close-ups as more authentic than the unmediated direct view of the stage. That it is in these two specific moments – of racialized militarism and the (white) consumption of (black) entertainment – that Brixton's blackness is centralized in the novel is not coincidental, but instead reflects the limited figuration of blackness in dominant British discourse. The excerpts exemplify what Sara Ahmed describes as the 'stickiness' which metonymically fixes (imagined) culture to bodies, writing that 'we can think of stickiness … *as an effect of the histories of contact between bodies, objects, and signs'*.[26] Racialized Brixton residents are made legible by the white narrator (and to a presumably white audience) through citation of the tropes that have a long history of underwriting racist divisions: of ungovernable, violent black masculinity, or the framing of depoliticized blackness as cultural cool.[27]

One of the reasons for the enduring ambiguity over Brixton's spatial relationship to central London is precisely that the narratives of the past have not dissolved, but instead sediment and constitute the possibilities of the present. While the representations above emerge in a fictionalized narrative, it is clear that the racist and racializing logic within them continues to enforce a stigmatizing boundary around Brixton. What is clear from an analysis of Brixton is that this works not only at the level of the nation and the migrant, but also at temporally attenuated and spatially localized levels. Naledi, for example, recounted that at university in the 2010s:

> [People] would ask where my mum lived, and I would say she is an hour from Brixton, and they went 'Brixton?! Fucking hell!' They were petrified. I think maybe it's this remembrance of the riots … it happened before we were even born, so there was no reason, the second lot of riots hadn't happened. They were petrified! (Naledi, black, British, dancer)

Naledi's account emphasizes the flexibility of both time and space in the sticking of cultures to bodies. Despite both her and her peers being born after these first 'riots', and her family home being an hour away, the white students that she is speaking to remain petrified by this evocation of Brixton.[28] The characterization of Brixton through racialized progress narratives also has particular implications for reading homophobia in Brixton. Asked whether people thought of Brixton as gay friendly, Naledi continued:

> No … because it's black … [and] I don't think the current media shit … interacting with people's internalised racism will allow any black place to be presumed to be gay friendly, whether it's Brixton, Uganda, Peckham … I think if you've got a black majority, the presumption is it will be homophobic. (Naledi, black, British, dancer)

Just like in *The Colour of Memory*, in this response Naledi foregrounds Brixton's 'blackness' through references to other places; however, this time the link being drawn is not one of inherent culture or imperialist divisions, but of systemic racism and the way that this bigot geography locates homophobia in 'Brixton, Uganda [or] Peckham'.

Although perceptions of Brixton's gay friendliness varied dramatically according to different research participants, the diminishment of homophobia

was repeatedly correlated to racialized and classed demographic change.[29]
For example, when asked if Brixton was gay friendly, Linford responded:

> I don't know that [people] … would say that. As I say, at the moment, it is
> still very much not fully gone through the transformation … I don't know
> that [Brixton] will be getting the Pride parade going down the street.
> (Linford, black, British, doctor)

In this account, Brixton and its gay friendliness are undergoing a process
of transformation. The terminology of 'transformation' and the emphasis
on 'not fully' aligns diminishing homophobia to a narrative of progress
and binds together the need for a continuation in the existent direction
in order to secure the space as a friendly one for gay people. Throughout
his interview, Linford reiterated that the potential benefits he saw coming
from gentrification in Brixton for gay friendliness were weighed against the
erasure of black and poor local culture. Reflecting further on change in
Brixton, Linford continued:

> the other day I was in Brixton Village and there was 'Champagne and
> Fromage', and I thought, 'Why is that there?' I don't want those places
> to start replacing the Atlantic Bakery and those sorts of things. (Linford,
> black, British, doctor)

Atlantic Bakery is an established unit serving low-cost food primarily
to Caribbean and Black clientele, while the arrival of Champagne and
Fromage – a high-end café serving affluent white people – has been the
focus of a lot of anger about the 'yuppification' of the market. Linford
narrates the relative positioning of a black presence and a gay presence as
a necessary relationship; gay friendliness can only increase *as* the blackness
of the space is diluted by middle-class whiteness. This narrative of progress
for gay friendliness in Brixton thus substantiates bigot geography, locating
homophobia in those groups – black and/or migrant and/or poor – who
are understood to be displaced by gentrification, while sexual modernity
(both minority sexualities and the tolerance of them) continues to be
located firmly within the bounds of the privileged and/or white agents of
gentrification.

Brixton's characterization as a black space, while dominant in local
narratives of place, was not unchallenged. As Maz stressed:

> actually the case for everywhere that is seen as black or Asian, or
> whatever … because those people are different from what we expect
> as the norm, they stand out, but it's not actually their space. There is
> nowhere in all of England and Britain that I would say is a truly black
> area. It just doesn't exist. (Maz, black, British, poet)

Maz went on to emphasize the white solipsism of describing areas in the UK as 'black or asian', pointing not only to the physical presence of white bodies in these places but also to the structural whiteness of the UK. Although it provides only a limited challenge to bigot geography, the emphasis on whiteness and racism as constitutive of Brixton does potentially puncture the projection of it as homophobic *because* it is black.

The potential of these fracturing representations of the homogeneity or blackness of the space to disturb bigot geography was undermined, however, by the reiterated trope of discrete and oppositional groups inhabiting Brixton. Symptomatic of this representation of diversity within Brixton, one review of Dyer's novel describes the setting as 'a slightly seedy, multi-ethnic district of London populated by immigrants and artistic types who live uneasily side by side'.[30] The implication here is that white bohemians and non-white immigrants constitute two parallel communities. Indeed, recalling her experiences of living in Brixton in the 1990s, Sarah's description of Brixton was that:

> there was a turf war going on; there was definitely a feeling of black youngsters fronting up, like 'this is our turf, fuck off queers'. (Sarah, white, British, journalist)

Although she did suggest that this hostility emerged in part because of disruptive queer practices, including large Pride celebrations, Sarah's description of Brixton presents a divided neighbourhood: black and straight versus white and queer. The drastically simplified narrative of two communities 'liv[ing] uneasily side by side', combined with Sarah's memory of 'turf war' and Linford's mixed feelings about neighbourhood change, therefore continues to erase more complicated, overlapping accounts of the histories and presents of working-class LGBT and black LGBT in the area, as well as more positive recollections of proximate lives.

Troubling bigot geography

In Brixton – unlike London's Soho or Manchester's Canal Street – same-sex sexuality is neither obviously coded through the retail and social spaces nor clearly represented in public art or regeneration policy. It is nevertheless possible to construct an alternative sexual history of Brixton and this historiographic reclamation constitutes an established strategy for sexual minority movements. When I posited a link between the blackness of the area and the perception of homophobia, a number of participants who had resided in the area for longer amounts of time, in particular, were explicitly resistant. Following their cue, here I weave together individual story-telling/memory sharing and archival/historicist work to suggest narratives around LGBTQ Brixton that might be less easily incorporated into a bigot geography.

In the late nineteenth century, Brixton was well known as a regional centre for entertainment, the locus for a number of music halls as well as boarding houses for the West End. The association between theatricality and homosexuality is firmly established (whether it stands up to examination or not) and bleeds into popular interpretations of place. This was reflected by Sarah, who explained the LGBT presence in Brixton today partly through reference to a queer history that is:

> very old, *because* it was a dormitory town for the West End palaces of entertainment. (Sarah, white, British, journalist; my emphasis)

Indicative of the processes of sedimentation that constitute place, this association between queer lives and theatrical Brixton is referenced in Sarah Waters's popular lesbian novel, *Tipping the Velvet* (1998). Set in the 1890s, the novel depicts Nan moving to London to pursue work as a 'male impersonator' and living, for a period of time, in Brixton. Electric Avenue (a street in the centre of Brixton) is described to her as 'a place so full…of music-hall people and actors that they call it "Grease-Paint Avenue"'.[31] Relating to the same time period, one of the few physical traces of a queer history to be found in Brixton is a small blue plaque commemorating the residence of Henry Havelock Ellis. The prominent sexologist is credited as being a driving force behind the eventual legalization of homosexuality and popularized the term 'homosexual' itself. Further to this, Havelock Ellis was married to women's rights activist Edith Lees, and his writings about his wife's 'inversion' (retrospectively cast as lesbianism) constitute their own queer archival trace.[32]

From these glimpses, we might jump a century forwards to what could be described, in direct contestation to the narrative of new sexual possibilities brought to Brixton by gentrification, as Brixton's gay heyday. In 1974, the South London Gay Community Centre was opened on Railton Road. The Brixton Faeries, a gay theatre group associated with the Gay Liberation Front, put on shows in community centres and small theatres.[33] Local properties were squatted during this period and experiments in communal living emerged, a number of which were organized around sexuality and sexual politics.[34] In 1993 and 1994, London's Pride celebration – established in the 1970s – was held in Brockwell Park. As well as the squats and a number of recreational spaces, there was also a lively cruising culture that endured into the 1990s.

Although these histories also tended to recreate an image of multiple, rarely overlapping LGBTQ communities in Brixton, there were also occasions during my research when distinct racialized boundaries seemed slightly less impermeable. One physical space that served as the locus for a number of memories was a gay 'shebeen' (unlicensed bar), run from the 1970s in a basement on Railton Road by a woman called Pearl Alcock. This space was fondly remembered by Simon as:

> always heaving … a space this sort of size [50m²] packed with people dancing, and there would be a bar at the end selling Heineken or cocktail type stuff, martinis and so on … there were only one or two women there, about 80% black men, 20% white I suppose … Of the black guys that would go to Pearl's … maybe half of them would be in a relationship with a white person, and half would be in a relationship with a black person. (Simon, white, British, unemployed)

Simon himself was in a relationship with a black Guyanese man during the 1980s and, while he acknowledged racism among the white gay community towards his partner and black friends, his social and sexual practices do seem to evidence that there was more interaction than is often reflected in both 'straight' and 'queer' histories of Brixton. Many of the descriptions of Brixton's lively cruising scene also attest to sexual encounters across classed and racialized boundaries.[35] In an unfinished film, the photographer Ajamu X, a well-known Brixton resident and co-founder of 'rukus Federation' (a black LGBT initiative that brings together artists, activists and cultural producers), wanders round Brixton pointing to places 'where some of the guys would pick guys up and have sex … get fucked or whatever'. This, he concludes, 'is like the secret history of Brixton, in a strange kind of way'.[36]

In his research of the 1970s gay squats on Railton/Mayall Road, the historian Matt Cook found evidence of 'generally cordial relations between the squatters and the local Afro-Caribbean community'.[37] Although perhaps undermined by the seemingly limited dialogue between these gay (middle-class, white and male) squats that occupy the majority of archival space and existing attention, and the neighbouring women's and anti-racist squats and centres, there is also some evidence of attempts at political solidarity. Sally remembered coming to Brixton for 'Rock Against Racism' in 1978 and being surprised to see:

> all these queens on the roofs [of Railton Road] with … wedding dresses and stuff on … they had … bunting across the street, and it was like … wow, you know. (Sally, white, British, artist and bus driver)

While for Sally this encounter was affirmative, without gathering more testimonies it is difficult to know whether this act of civil and gendered disobedience was experienced by black residents more as an expression of white spatial privilege at a time when black youth were being harassed by the police for merely being there.

Conclusion

This chapter has sought to illustrate the argument that 'queer' is most usefully deployed as a catalyst to destabilize orthodox correlations of research question and analytical site. Simultaneously opening up academic agendas while also pushing us to recognize knowledge production as inherently situated and partial, queering thus contributes to important feminist, critical race and post-colonial critiques that have drawn attention to the sexism, racism and Occidentalism of epistemological convention. An approach that brings 'queer' and 'geopolitics' to an analysis of London thus stresses the imbrication of the transnational, the national and the local in the study of the capital. Moreover, although some have called for the extraction of queer from the field of LGBT studies,[38] queering geopolitics specifically emphasizes LGBT sexualities as a site through which global patterns of inequality are sustained, with material and localized effects.

The central target of this chapter – bigot geography – is colonialist shorthand. Through a narrow inscription of progress narratives and sexual modernity, it sustains global power relations that are expressed both at the level of the nation and the local. Challenging bigot geography entails the recognition of our continued political investment in colonialism and pushing against the desire for condensed taxonomies that quickly fix people and places into positions according to gay progressive narratives. As discussed, a number of Brixton's LGBTQ residents drew on the personal recollection and retelling of memories to contest dominant stories of Brixton's gay (tolerance) progress narrative as chronologically linear, and so attached to the racialized and classed displacements of gentrification. In these moments, intergenerational LGBTQ memory sharing becomes a possible site of anti-racist resistance and it becomes apparent that a queer geopolitics can work through a queer approach to history. This points to the imbrication of temporality and spatiality and demonstrates the need for interdisciplinary research. Although it is clear that there were extremely racialized, classed and gendered divisions and hierarchies operating to segregate the spaces of Brixton, it remains crucial to pay attention to – and theorize from – those moments and practices where these exclusions break down. Although many of the more recent arrivals had no knowledge of any LGBTQ Brixton past, the maintenance of archives means that there are materials that can, and should, be returned to. As part of a queered geopolitics, this represents a vital avenue for interrogating the exclusions and violence of both domestic and internationalized gay progress narratives. If the narrative in gay communities that the classed and racialized displacements of gentrification are key to feeling safer is left unchallenged, it feeds racism and classism in the UK. Further, it closes down the space for coalitional politics between minority groups that might secure less exclusionary modes of change.

Notes

1   Lisa Duggan, *The Twilight of Equality? Neoliberalism, Cultural Politics, and the Attack on Democracy* (Boston: Beacon, 2003), pp. 43–66.

2   Although each has a more specific set of characteristics, progress narratives, developmental narratives and evolutionary narratives have all been identified as significant to the constitution and understanding of gendered and sexual identities. The more recent uptake of progress narratives as an analytic node is indebted to earlier works, notably Teresa de Lauretis, *Alice Doesn't: Feminism, Semiotics, Cinema* (Bloomington: Indiana University Press, 1984) and Ken Plummer, *Telling Sexual Stories: Power, Change and Social Worlds* (London: Routledge, 1995).

3   Judith Butler, 'Sexual Politics, Torture, and Secular Time', *The British Journal of Sociology* 59 (2008), pp. 1–23, 2. Cf. Jasbir Puar, 'Israel's Gay Propaganda War', *The Guardian*, 1 July 2010. http://www.theguardian.com/commentisfree/2010/jul/01/israels-gay-propaganda-war (accessed 7 July 2010); Jasbir Puar and Amit Rai, 'Monster, Terrorist, Fag: The War on Terrorism and the Production of Docile Patriots', *Social Text* 20 (2002), pp. 117–48; Jasbir Puar, 'Queer Times, Queer Assemblages,' *Social Text* 23 (2005), pp. 121–39; and Jasbir Puar, *Terrorist Assemblages: Homonationalism in Queer Times* (Durham, NC: Duke University Press, 2007). See also the discussion in Amar Wahab, 'Homophobia as the State of Reason: The Case of Postcolonial Trinidad and Tobago', *GLQ: A Journal of Lesbian and Gay Studies* 18.4 (2012), pp. 481–505.

4   The terms 'Global South' and 'Global North' are (overly simplistic but useful) categorizations that reference both position on the development index (according, primarily, to the United Nations Development Programme (UNDP)) and geographical location. 'Global South' is commonly used in development discourse to describe 'developing' countries primarily located in the Southern Hemisphere.

5   Neville Hoad, 'Arrested Development or the Queerness of Savages: Resisting Evolutionary Narratives of Difference', *Postcolonial Studies* 3.2 (2000), pp. 133–158.

6   Larry Knopp, 'On the Relationship Between Queer and Feminist Geographies', *The Professional Geographer* 59.1 (2007), pp. 47–55, 49. See also Jon Binnie, 'Coming Out of Geography: Towards a Queer Epistemology?' *Environment and Planning D: Society and Space* 15 (1997), pp. 223–37, 231; and Claudio Minca, 'Postmodernism/Postmodern Geography', in Rob Kitchin and Nigel Thrift (eds), *International Encyclopaedia of Human Geography* (Oxford: Elsevier, 2009), p. 368.

7   Larry Knopp, 'From Lesbian and Gay to Queer Geographies: Pasts, Prospects and Possibilities', in Kath Browne, Jason Lim and Gavin Brown (eds), *Geographies of Sexualities: Theory, Practices and Politics* (Aldershot: Ashgate, 2007), pp. 21–28; Natalie Oswin, 'Critical Geographies and the Uses of Sexuality: Deconstructing Queer Space', *Progress in Human Geography* 32.1 (2008), pp. 89–103.

8   In an article that returns to the themes elucidated in *Terrorist Assemblages* and the ways in which homonationalism has been taken up, Puar describes homonationalism as a 'conceptual frame ... for understanding the complexities of how "acceptance" and "tolerance" for gay and lesbian subjects have become a barometer by which the right to and capacity for national sovereignty is evaluated'. J. K. Puar, 'Rethinking Homonationalism', *International Journal of Middle Eastern Studies* 45 (2013), pp. 336–9, 336. For a comprehensive definition of gentrification, see Tom Slater, 'The Eviction of Critical Perspectives from Gentrification Research', *International Journal of Urban and Regional Research* 30.4 (2006), pp. 737–57. The role of residential concentration in community formation, the development of gay identity and the possibility of gay politics have been explored in the North American context in particular. See Manuel Castells, *The City and the Grassroots: A Cross-Cultural Theory of Urban Social Movements* (Berkeley: University of California Press, 1983); Tami Rothenberg, '"And She Told Two Friends": Lesbians Creating Urban Social Space', in David Bell and Gill Valentine (eds), *Mapping Desire: Geographies of Sexualities* (London: Routledge 1995), pp. 150–65; and Larry Knopp, 'Some Theoretical Implications of Gay Involvement in an Urban Land Market', *Political Geography Quarterly* 9.4 (1990), pp. 337–52.

9   The research on which this chapter draws comprised of three years of residence and auto-ethnography in Brixton, nineteen semi-structured interviews with LGBTQ residents, participation in a large number of local events, archival work, online research and multiple informal dialogues. The interview material used here was collected, and has been anonymized, in accordance with research ethics guidelines.

10   This representation happens partly through the figuration of the city in LGBTQ literature, films and the cultural imagination. As such, these texts represent an underexplored site of analysis for sexual geographers.

11   Richard Florida, *The Rise of The Creative Class: And How It's Transforming Work, Leisure, Community and Everyday Life* (New York: Basic Books, 2002), p. 256. See also Florida, *The Rise of The Creative Class: Revisited* (New York: Basic Books, 2012). For a critique, see Jamie Peck, 'Struggling with Creative Class', *International Journal of Urban and Regional Research* 29.4 (2005), pp. 740–70.

12   See Glen Elder, 'Of Moffies, Kaffirs and Perverts', in Bell and Valentine (ed.), *Mapping Desire*, pp. 50–58; Michael Brown and Larry Knopp, 'Queer Diffusions', *Environment and Planning D: Society and Space* 21 (2003), pp. 409–24; Jerry Lee Kramer, 'Bachelor Farmers and Spinsters: Gay and Lesbian Identities and Communities in Rural North Dakota', in Bell and Valentine, *Mapping Desire*, pp. 182–94; Martin Manalansan, *Global Divas: Filipino Gay Men in the Diaspora* (Durham, NC: Duke University Press, 2003); and Alison J. Murray, 'Let Them Take Ecstasy: Class and Jakarta Lesbians', *Journal of Homosexuality* 40 (2001), pp. 165–84.

13   The progress of gay identity politics is often presented as analogous to sexual liberation. This limits the scope of earlier sexual liberation calls for de-essentialized gender, anti-racist and anti-capitalist dimensions as necessary components.

14 Hugo Gye, '"British Whites" are the Minority in London for the First Time as Census Shows Number of UK Immigrants has Jumped by 3 million in 10 Years', *Daily Mail*, 11 December 2012. http://www.dailymail.co.uk/news /article-2246288/Census-2011-UK-immigrant-population-jumps-THREE -MILLION-10-years.html (accessed 10 April 2014).

15 Douglas Murray, 'Is London's "diversity" to Blame for Its "Unprogressive" Views on Homosexuality?' *The Spectator*, 19 March 2015. http://blogs .spectator.co.uk/douglas-murray/2015/03/is-londons-diversity-to-blame-for-its -unprogressive-views-on-homosexuality/ (accessed 13 June 2015).

16 'Country of origin' is applied and given significance in ways which invariably erase more complicated relationships between the individual and their national heritage. It is even a stretchy enough association to exceed actuality, with people born in the UK and holding only British citizenship still forcibly attached to other places on a map.

17 Butler, 'Sexual Politics', pp. 3–5.

18 Although there is not space to discuss this at length, the violence that this enacts is pointed to in David A.B. Murray, 'The (not so) Straight Story: Queering Migration Narratives of Sexual Orientation and Gendered Identity Refugee Claimants', *Sexualities* 17.4 (2014), pp. 451–71.

19 Stephen J. Shaw, 'Marketing Ethnoscapes as Places of Consumption: "Banglatown – London's Curry Capital"', *Journal of Town and City Management* 1.4 (2011), pp. 381–95.

20 See George Mavrommatis, 'A Racial Archaeology of Space: A Journey Through the Political Imaginings of Brixton and Brick Lane, London', *Journal of Ethnic and Migration Studies* 36.4 (2010), pp. 561–79; and Mavrommatis, 'Stories from Brixton: Gentrification and Different Differences', *Sociological Research Online* 16.2 (2011), pp. 1–10.

21 For example, an eagle-eye photo of London was included in the initial advertising for a block of flats developed by Barratt London, with three markers pointing to the development of 'Brixton Square', Westminster and the Shard. This very clearly implies a knitting together of these locations, both spatially and, I would suggest, in terms of a shared temporality and significance.

22 'Brixton Area Guide', *Time Out*, 7 January 2015. http://www.timeout.com /london/things-to-do/brixton-area-guide (accessed 15 June 2015).

23 G. Dyer, *The Colour of Memory* (Edinburgh and London: Canongate, 1989), p. 212.

24 The uprisings/riots are now widely understood to have been catalysed by the racist policing of black bodies in London.

25 Dyer, *The Colour of Memory*, p. 239.

26 Sara Ahmed, *The Cultural Politics of Emotion* (New York and London: Routledge, 2004), p. 90.

27 bell hooks, *Black Looks: Race and Representation* (London: Turnaround, 1992); Franz Fanon, *Black Skin, White Masks* (new edn., London: Pluto Press, 2008).

28   Naledi previously described her university as 'middle England, upper middle class' and recounted that she 'was often the first black person they had met'.

29   Unfortunately there is not space here to discuss fully the operation of class and gender in Brixton and the gay narratives of progress. This is undertaken in a forthcoming work.

30   Kirkus Reviews, *The Colour of Memory*, 16 March 2014, https://www .kirkusreviews.com/book-reviews/geoff-dyer/colour-of-memory/ (accessed 13 February 2014).

31   Sarah Waters, *Tipping the Velvet* (London: Virago, 2012 [1998]), p. 61.

32   Henry Havelock Ellis, *My Life* (London: Heinemann, 1940).

33   There is an evocative mixture of memory and images at http://www.urban75 .org/blog/the-brixton-fairies-and-the-south-london-gay-community-centre -brixton-1974-6/comment-page-1/ (accessed 1 January 2014). Cf. http:// www.unfinishedhistories.com/history/companies/brixton-faeries/ (accessed 1 June 2015).

34   Matt Cook, ' "Gay Times": Identity, Locality, Memory, and the Brixton Squats in 1970s London', *Twentieth Century British History* 24.1 (2013), pp. 84–109; and Taha Hassan's documentary, *Brixton Fairies: Made Possible by Squatting* (2014). Although there is significantly less archival evidence than that of the gay male squats, during my research I regularly spoke to people who remembered, and lived in, lesbian and women-only squats in Brixton.

35   The inclusion of cruising in an exploration of LGBTQ histories points to further reflection that is needed on the relative violence of naming histories as LGBTQ if the subjects of them do not identify as LGBTQ, and of excluding working-class and black histories because of the classed and racialized conditions of gay identity. Cf. Steve Valocchi, 'The Class-Inflected Nature of Gay Identity', *Social Problems* 46.2 (1999), pp. 207–24.

36   'Brixton Recreation with Ajamu', dir. Danny Solle, filming date unknown, posted to https://www.youtube.com/watch?v=4dRva4Va0qE on 18th February 2014 (accessed 4 February 2015). rukus! Federation has also worked to gather an archive to document black LGBTQ lives, now being held at London Metropolitan Archives. The website states: 'The rukus! Archive, launched in 2005, generates, collects, preserves and makes available to the public historical, cultural and artistic materials relating to our lived experience in the UK': http://rukus.org.uk/introduction/ (accessed 10 July 2015).

37   Cook, 'Gay Times', p. 97.

38   Cf. Noreen Giffney, 'Denormatizing Queer Theory: More Than (Simply) Lesbian and Gay Studies', *Feminist Theory* 5 (2004), pp. 73–78.

CHAPTER SIX

Representations of Queer London in the Fiction of Sarah Waters

Paulina Palmer

I had learned that London was even stranger and more
various than I had ever thought it; but I had learned too
that not all its great variety was visible to the casual eye.[1]

Reference to London locations and the opportunities they furnish for queer sexual exploration and experimentation serve as a unifying feature in Sarah Waters's three neo-Victorian novels, *Tipping the Velvet* (1998), *Affinity* (1999) and *Fingersmith* (2002), different though the three texts are in theme and narrative structure. They also assume prominence in her subsequently published *The Night Watch* (2006), set in the later period, 1941–47. As suits the latter novel's wartime context, Waters vividly depicts the bomb-damaged streets of the metropolis and the terror of the air raids while foregrounding the opportunities for forming unorthodox relationships that the social changes occurring in the period offered people, both heterosexual and queer. My aim in this chapter is to explore the roles that the representation of London locations and topics relating to the city play in Waters's fiction, especially in relation to her treatment of queer sexuality. The term 'queer' is multifaceted in meaning for, while employed in academia in relation

For the queer community in Cambridge.

to contemporary queer theory to challenge the concept of a stable sexual orientation and problematize the binary division homosexual/heterosexual, it is alternatively used as a shorthand to encompass the categories lesbian, gay and, on occasion, transgender.[2] I employ it in both ways in this chapter, with the context indicating its significance.

In depicting London as the location of queer sexualities (both lesbian and male gay), Waters develops in fictional form the writing of sociologists and historians who have investigated the relation between an urban environment and queer subcultures. Considering from a sociological viewpoint the influence of a metropolitan environment on the lives of women who, until the Industrial Revolution separated the workplace from the home, frequently spent their lives in a familial environment, Elizabeth Wilson describes the lesbian as 'the inhabitant of the great cities', citing as evidence the growth of lesbian enclaves in nineteenth-century London and Paris.[3] The lesbian's relationship with the metropolis, foregrounded by Wilson in 1986, has received analysis by theorists and critics writing recently in queer contexts. Gill Valentine examines the lesbian's role in the sexual politics of the street,[4] while Sally Munt, elaborating the ideas of Walter Benjamin, introduces the concept of 'the lesbian *flâneur*' who, by appropriating the male prerogative of the gaze, reclaims the urban space for women.[5] These approaches, as well as those of other theorists and critics to whom I refer, furnish a context for discussing Waters's representation of London as the setting for her female characters' experience of same-sex relationships and cross-dressing, as well as their interaction with male homosexual characters.

In addition to describing the metropolis as furnishing a site for the development of lesbian identity and culture, Wilson associates it with the carnivalesque. The concept of carnivalesque is associated with the writing of Mikhail Bakhtin who relates the liberation that carnival festivity offers from socio-sexual conventions to forms of literature that similarly transgress convention.[6] Arguing that a metropolitan existence 'normalises the carnivalesque aspects of life',[7] Wilson observes that, despite the mundane routine of work and travel that it frequently involves, 'at every turn the city dweller is also offered the opposite – pleasure, deviation, disruption'.[8] These experiences are especially in evidence, she argues, in the lives of the city's female residents. Though acknowledging the dangers of poverty, physical assault and prostitution that an urban context holds, she nonetheless regards it as potentially signifying 'a place of liberation for women'[9] since it gives them the opportunity to escape the constraints of family life, achieve a degree of anonymity and pursue, to a degree, their own ambitions and desires.

Waters likewise explores in her fiction the carnivalesque dimension of metropolitan life, depicting the elements of misrule, shifts of fortune and contradictions with which it can confront the city dweller. Whereas carnivalesque themes are obviously to the fore in *Tipping the Velvet*, with its focus on the music hall and the licence for cross-dressing that the theatre permits the female actor, they also indirectly inform her later novels. This is apparent in the unorthodox sexualities and gender roles on which she focuses.

These include, in addition to same-sex desire and male impersonation, reference to the way in which roles traditionally regarded as the prerogative of men, such as the *flâneur* and the pleasures of the gaze he enjoys, can be appropriated by women. In *Affinity, Fingersmith* and *The Night Watch*, however, in contrast to *Tipping the Velvet*, these topics frequently carry connotations of danger and assume, like the labyrinthine London streets that form their context, uncanny associations. Emphasis is placed less on 'the new outlook on the world' which, as Bakhtin writes, carnival promotes but on the instability and fragmentation of both the urban environment and the psyche.[10] London, Waters reminds us, in addition to offering opportunities for pleasure and self-fulfilment, provides a context for loneliness, acts of violence and the concealing of secrets, both social and sexual.

The narrative strategies Waters employs in her fiction echo her representation of London as an arena of carnivalesque misrule and sexual exploration. In exploiting devices of postmodern parody and recasting in her neo-Victorian novels storylines and scenarios from the works of nineteenth-century writers such as Charles Dickens and Wilkie Collins, she herself engages in a form of carnivalesque inversion and misrule. Inverting the perspectives and value-schemes of these male writers, she represents Victorian London from female and queer viewpoints. By juxtaposing reference to the dominant culture with its marginalized counterpart, she fills in the gaps and absences relating to gender and sexuality in their texts and fleshes out the feminine and queer areas of metropolitan life at which they merely hint. Her description of London locations contributes to this. Dickens's description of Fagin's den in the neighbourhood of Field Lane in *Oliver Twist* (1838) is transformed in *Fingersmith* into the headquarters of the gang of thieves in Lant Street controlled by the baby-farmer Mrs Sucksby, while Walter Hartright's uncanny meeting with Anne Catherick on the road to London in Collins's *The Woman in White* (1860) is echoed in Margaret Prior's eerie meeting with 'the spooky girl' Selina Dawes whom she encounters in Mill Bank Prison.[11] In addition, Elizabeth Bowen's descriptions of bomb-damaged London in her stories 'I Hear You Say So' and 'The Demon Lover' (1945) are recast in *The Night Watch* to furnish a setting for the lovers Julia and Helen when they stroll together through the war-torn metropolis at night and enjoy their first kiss. *Tipping the Velvet* is similarly rich in intertextual reference, alluding to a variety of texts both comic and serious, including George Leybourne's music-hall songs and the works of Eleanor Marx.[12] It is the first of Waters's novels to appear in print and, as we shall see, is notably rich in references to queer London.

Tipping the Velvet: Music hall and masquerade

The London locations that form the context for the picaresque trajectory of Nan King, the oyster seller from Whitstable who partners the music-hall performer Kitty on the music hall stage in *Tipping the Velvet*, are highly relevant to Waters's interest in queer sexuality and gender since she associates each with a different form. The narrative, having opened in the Brixton lodging-house where Nan and Kitty commence their love affair and the Star theatre where they perform on stage, moves in the central section to the streets and parks of the metropolis. Here Nan, having given up her stage career as a result of Kitty jilting her, disguises herself as a boy and engages in what she expressively terms 'the curious gaslit career' of servicing men seeking homosexual sex.[13] The action then moves to the interior of the affluent residence in St John's Wood owned by the upper-class sapphist Diana Lethaby, who employs Nan as her tart, before eventually concluding romantically in the humble Stratford home of the suffragist Florence, with whom she falls in love.

In describing Kitty's and Nan's performance in the music-hall production at the Star, Waters focuses attention on their joint act of male impersonation. Performances of this kind were of especial interest in the 1880s and 1890s since there occurred at this time an unprecedented influx of women as both audience and performers into the London musical hall.[14] Basing her account of Nan and Kitty's theatrical act on the career of Nellie Power and other Victorian female performers, Waters explores both the thrills and problematic aspects of male impersonation. In addition to describing Nan's 'pleasure in performance, display and disguise' and the audience's enjoyment of her act,[15] she examines the risks it involved for the female actor. By mimicking the male role, the actor implicitly questions the 'naturalness' of masculinity by exposing it as an artifice that a woman can perform as successfully as a man.[16] Kitty's theatrical agent, Walter Bliss, it is interesting to note, takes measures to prevent this. On perceiving that Nan's performance of masculinity is too lifelike, that 'she looks like a *real* boy' rather than an imitation,[17] he makes efforts to tone it down. He alters her make-up to appear more feminine, puts tucks inside her jacket to accentuate her waist and replaces her masculine-looking boots with dainty shoes. In consequence she makes her debut on stage, as she ironically remarks, 'clad not exactly as a boy but, rather confusingly, as the boy I would have been, had I been more of a girl'.[18]

A more serious problem that the male impersonator could encounter on stage was the accusation of deviancy, resulting in her being stigmatized as sexually perverse.[19] This is, of course, especially pertinent to Nan and Kitty since they are lovers. Kitty makes an effort to protect Nan and herself from scandal by striving to keep their relationship secret. Her efforts, however, prove futile. Waters describes how one evening in a shabby theatre in Islington, a drunken spectator accuses them of being 'a couple of *toms*',[20] forcing them to retire from the stage amid jeers.

Waters continues her investigation into the sexual politics of female cross-dressing in the second half of the novel in which Nan, on learning to her distress that Kitty has deserted her to marry Bliss, retires from the stage. Masquerading as a boy in a guardsman's uniform that she salvaged from the theatre, she discovers in Soho and the West End a world of sexual secrets whose existence she never suspected. Here she survives financially by servicing men seeking homosexual sex by performing acts of *fellatio*. In addition to introducing the reader to the male homosexual dimension of London and the sex-trade catering for it, Waters foregrounds the connections between the occupations of actor and sex worker. She portrays Nan humorously, observing '[m]y only contact with the theatre now was a renter'[21] while regretting the absence of an audience to acclaim her 'marvellous performances' of masculinity.[22] Nan engages in yet another form of male masquerade when, on catching the eye of the upper-class Diana Lethaby who sees through her pretence of masculinity, she agrees to accompany her to her residence in St John's Wood to service her sexually. On finding Nan's preference for drag erotically titillating, Diana purchases her a sumptuous wardrobe of suits. Theatrical allusions again abound, with Nan describing the selecting of her costumes as 'quite like dressing for the halls again'.[23]

The theatrical references that litter these episodes, in addition to creating a link with Nan's former music-hall life, alert attention to the performative dimension of gender. According to Judith Butler, gender, rather than being authentic and the effect of some inner essence, takes the form of 'a set of repeated acts within a highly rigid regulatory frame that congeal over time to produce the appearance of substance, of a natural sort of being'.[24] Nan in fact comes to regard it in a similar way. On first venturing abroad into Berwick Street dressed as a boy, she quite expects her disguise to be penetrated and 'the cry to be let up: "A girl! There is a girl, here, in boy's clothing"'.[25] When no such cry occurs, she congratulates herself on 'the success of that first performance'[26] and soon becomes accustomed to identifying as male. She even starts to experience confusion about her own sex, confessing that, like the proprietor of the knocking-shop where she changes her costume who 'was never quite sure whether I were a girl come to her house to pull on a pair of trousers, or a boy arrived to change out of his frock, sometimes, I was not sure myself'.[27]

The role of *flâneur* is also relevant to Nan's experience of metropolitan life. Although Walter Benjamin initially envisaged the role as male, Sally Munt draws attention to its significance as 'a vessel to be filled by a lesbian narrative' and suggests that 'the *flâneur* could be a cross-dressed lesbian'.[28] Waters inventively develops these ideas. She portrays Nan initially adopting masculine dress because she is tired of enduring male scrutiny, of being, as she describes, 'a solitary girl…in a city where girls walked only to be gazed at'.[29] However, although she pleasurably discovers that, dressed as a boy, she enjoys the licence to participate in the urban ritual of 'walking and watching',[30] she finds, as I suggested above, that she can be as much the object of the gaze as she was when wearing feminine attire. She also experiences other problems with the role of *flâneur*. When she eventually has the good fortune to encounter the feminist activist Florence, a woman to whom she is attracted and who she wishes to impress, she is ironically wearing the wrong clothes. She sheepishly recalls how 'I smiled and gave a little bow. My stays creaked; it felt all wrong being a gallant in a skirt, and I had a sudden fear that she might take me not for an impertinent *voyeur*, but for a fool.'[31] Waters's references to the figure of the *flâneur* therefore illustrate the varied nature of London life and the diversity of roles that Nan performs in the city.

Affinity: Spiritualism and prison cells

Affinity, as suits the novel's emphasis on frustrated female passion, offers the reader a notably bleaker image of Victorian London than *Tipping the Velvet*. The contrast is reflected visually in the different colours brought to the fore in the two novels. Instead of the red of the guardsman's uniform that Nan wears on stage and the 'belt of amber beads' of the lights fringing the Thames,[32] *Affinity* is pervaded by the dark shape of Millbank prison, the brown of the female prisoners' uniforms and the grey of the fog-bound streets. Interior, rather than exterior, locations also achieve prominence. Margaret Prior moves to and fro between her claustrophobic upper-class home in Cheyne Walk and the confining corridors and cells of Millbank Prison, described by an official as 'quite a little city',[33] where Selina, the beautiful spiritualist with whom she falls in love, is entrapped. The narrative structure of *Affinity* also differs from that of *Tipping the Velvet*. Instead of focusing on the picaresque adventures of a single protagonist, it interweaves two storylines, the one recounted by the working-class medium Selina Dawes and the other by the upper-class prison-visitor Margaret Prior.

The spiritualist movement, as Alex Owen describes in *The Darkened Room*, flourished in London in the 1860s and 1870s.[34] Since séances frequently took place in the home and the role of medium required emotional sensitivity, a quality typecast as feminine, it attracted the interest of women. Though provoking controversy and even scandal, it provided a vehicle for female members of the working class to achieve upward mobility and, on occasion, celebrity. However, these prizes came at the price of significant dangers. The medium was vulnerable to accusations of charlatanism or hysteria and, as a result, risked confinement in a prison or mental institution. Historical material of this kind forms the basis of Waters's fictional account of the working-class Selina Dawes. Emphasizing Selina's speedy social ascent, Waters portrays her moving from a humble abode in Bethnal Green to operating as a medium in the affluent Clerkenwell residence of Mrs Brink who, crediting her uncanny powers, invites her to live with her. Here, with the help of the house-maid Ruth who becomes her lover, Selina enacts a performance of communicating with the dead and making physical phenomena materialize. As the reader discovers, it is, in fact, Ruth, acting as Selina's spirit-control Peter Quick, who manages this web of deceit, her near invisibility in the text parodying the invisibility of the maid in the Victorian household.[35] When Selina's luck runs out and, as the result of the death of Mrs Brink, she is confined in Millbank Prison, her skills of dissimulation continue to assist her. They enable her, again with the help of the quick-witted Ruth, to deceive the prison visitor Margaret into believing that she loves her and persuading her to hand over her fortune to promote her flight.

Margaret, on learning from Selina that she works as a medium, refers to spiritualism – ironically, considering Selina's sexual relationship with Ruth – as 'her queer career'.[36] Although Margaret employs the adjective 'queer' in the commonplace sense of 'strange' or 'odd', Victorian spiritualism did in fact have a queer sexual dimension since, as Waters's portrayal of Ruth and Selina's partnership illustrates, the séance furnished the medium and spirit guide with the opportunity to enjoy erotic relations both with one another and with their clients. As a result, though the séances Ruth and Selina hold are fraudulent as a means of contacting the dead, their role as a vehicle to express same-sex erotic desire is authentic. As Tatiana Kontou perceptively writes, '[t]ricks allow desires to be realized ... There is a psychical reality in deceit.'[37] Viewed from a sexual perspective, Selina's role as a medium is not a form of fakery but, as Kontou describes, 'a way of expressing or, more accurately, *performing*, her passion for Ruth'.[38] Spiritualism also gives Ruth, in the guise of the dashing spirit-control Peter Quick, the opportunity to flirt with and fondle the female visitors to the séance since, in a spiritualist context, the sex of the spirit is irrelevant. As Selina explains to the puzzled Mrs Brink, 'This spirit was a gentleman on earth & is now obliged to visit me in that form.'[39]

Ruth, in addition to acting as Selina's spirit-control, exploits the freedom that her office as maid allows her to achieve – that is, to access, under the pseudonym 'Vigers', Margaret's home in Cheyne Walk. She surreptitiously conveys there locks of Selina's hair which Margaret believes to be transported by supernatural means. Ruth's trickery, in addition to illustrating the power that the working-class lesbian or 'tom' could wield, sheds light on the potentially disruptive role that the maid could play in family life. Jane Gallop depicts the maid as a 'threshold figure' who, living physically inside the family though socially outside it, exemplifies the threat of anarchy that the Victorian bourgeoisie associated with the working class.[40] Waters's portrayal of the maid Ruth/Vigers vividly reworks this concept. The maid, as a figure characterized by her hushed, behind-the-scenes role in the running of the Victorian household, also assumed metaphorical connotations of spectrality. Selina, remarking approvingly on how 'quietly' Vigers performs her duties in Mrs Brink's household, in fact compares her to 'a ghost'.[41] This connects Vigers with the figures of the prisoner and spinster who, due to their social invisibility, Waters also describes in spectral imagery.

The motif of the lesbian *flâneur*, performed by Nan in a carnivalesque context in *Tipping the Velvet*, also features unexpectedly in *Affinity* in the grim setting of Millbank Prison. The prison was constructed on the model of a panopticon, the architectural design that Michel Foucault associates with state surveillance, with the central tower permitting the spectator a view of the interior of the building.[42] As Margaret watches the female prisoners returning from the exercise yard, the governor, intuiting her same-sex desires, pointedly remarks, 'You like to look at them'.[43] Her remark heralds the role of lesbian *flâneur* that Margaret subsequently plays. The doors to the cells housing the female prisoners contain spy-holes, colloquially known as 'eyes'.[44] They enable her, while walking along the corridor, to gaze at the inmates and objectify the beautiful Selina aesthetically and erotically. Rebecca Pohl, in discussing the roles that walking plays in the novel, describes how 'Margaret performs her desire [for Selina] through the practice of walking the corridors of Millbank', while returning constantly to Selina's cell.[45] Here Waters problematizes the role of *flâneur*. Rather than associating it with the lively outdoor world of the city streets, she situates it in the claustrophobic location of a prison. In addition, the pleasures that the gaze permits Margaret, though she enjoys them, do not empower her but give rise to her sexual entrapment. She becomes sexually obsessed with Selina and, in assisting her to escape from Millbank Prison, brings about her own ruin.

Fingersmith: Interplay between London and provincial locations

In *Affinity*, as illustrated above, Waters creates a double narrative, utilizing both Margaret and Selina as narrators and skilfully interweaving their storylines. She subsequently develops this structure in *Fingersmith*. However here, in addition to employing Sue Trinder and Maud Lilly as narrators and interrelating their stories, she associates each with a different location: Sue with London and Maud with the provinces. Utilizing this pastoral structure gives her the opportunity to explore features of the metropolis which she does not treat elsewhere. Describing London from the contrary viewpoints of urban and country residents, she reworks the debate about the pros and cons of metropolitan and rural life which was to the fore in the 1860s and 1870s.[46] She also examines, in relation to Maud's life, the trade in erotic literature that operated between London and provincial areas.

In constructing *Fingersmith* on the interrelation between city and country, Waters appropriately imitates the structure of two famous Victorian novels by London-based writers that employ a similar design: Wilkie Collins's *The Woman in White* and Dickens's *Bleak House* (1853). For example, the journeys that Sue Trinder makes in *Fingersmith* between the thieves' den in London operated by Mrs Sucksby and the country house of Briar, where Richard Rivers courts Maud Lilley in an attempt to obtain her inheritance, rework those that the characters in *The Woman in White* make between London and rural Blackwater Park, where Sir Percival Glyde attempts to coerce his wife Laura into signing away her fortune. There are also other intertextual connections between the two novels. Sue Trinder's imprisonment in an asylum for the insane in *Fingersmith* echoes the similar incarceration that Laura suffers in *The Women in White*, while the sexual relationship that develops between Sue and Maud in Waters's novel recalls the close attachment, with its homoerotic resonances, between Marian Halcombe and Laura Fairlie in Collins's text. However, Sue is not Maud's half-sister but, on the contrary, her maid. This, in turn, echoes the emotionally intense relationship that develops between Lady Dedlock and her two personal maids, the pretty naïve Rosa and the passionate Hortense, that Dickens portrays in *Bleak House*. However, in contrast to Dickens, Waters foregrounds the sexual nature of Sue's and Maud's relationship and makes it central to her novel.

In the debate about the merits of urban and rural environments that flourished in Victorian England, some people, influenced by the association of the city with poverty and vice, championed a rural location, whereas others, arguing that a metropolitan context promoted social interaction and access to culture, endorsed the latter. Waters reworks the debate in relation to the lifestyles of the London-based pickpocket Sue and the provincial Maud who lives as a lady at the rural estate of Briar. The Londoner Sue prefers city life. Waters humorously portrays her, on stepping from the train onto the station in the rural vicinity of Briar, appalled by the absence of 'coffee-stalls and milk-stalls and a pastry-cook's shop'.[47] In addition to disliking the silence of the countryside, relieved, as she despondently describes, only by the occasional bird song and 'the very mournful sound' of a bell,[48] she prefers what she regards as the blatant crime of the metropolis (to which she herself contributed as a pickpocket) to the penny-pinching dishonesty typifying life on a country estate. As she scornfully remarks, 'At Briar, they were all on the dodge in one way or another, but all over sneaking little matters that would have put a real thief to the blush'.[49] Her passion for London is vividly illustrated in the episode in which, after escaping from the provincial asylum in which Richard Rivers had her imprisoned, she makes the trek home. On glimpsing with relief the interplay of light and dark on the horizon, she ironically welcomes the signs of pollution since they indicate that she is nearing the city. She impressionistically describes how '[t]he chimneys grew taller...the threads of smoke more thick; until at last, at the further point of all, they made a smudge, a stain...a darkness that was broken, here and there, where the sun caught panes of glass and golden tips of domes and steeples, with glittering points of light'. She concludes with the rapturous exclamation, 'London...Oh, London!'[50] On entering the metropolis, she puts her street-wise skills as a city dweller to good use and quickly locates the route to Lant Street. As she confidently observes, 'That part of London was strange to me, but I found I knew my way alright.'[51]

Maud, on the contrary, having been raised as a lady in rural isolation, is described succumbing to panic when, having escaped from Mrs Sucksby's control in Lant Street, she finds herself adrift in the maze of London alleys. Passers-by, intrigued by her upper-class attire, subject her to scrutiny. The topic of the gaze that features in Waters's earlier novels with reference to the figure of the *flâneur* is again foregrounded, though here emphasis is placed on its threatening aspect. Maud perceives with alarm that 'Everybody stares – men, women, children – even here, where the road is busy again, they stare.'[52] On experiencing male ridicule, she wearily thinks, 'On, on, I go. I think boys run beside me, for a time – two boys or three – shrieking to see me stagger.'[53] Men working in a nearby warehouse, on noting her uncovered head, mistake her for a prostitute and whistle at her. When a gentleman offers her a lift in his carriage, she misinterprets his invitation as an act of kindness, recognizing only in the nick of time that it signifies an attempt at seduction.

In contrast, the metropolitan Sue, instead of being dominated by the gaze of other people, is portrayed controlling it. When Maud is imprisoned by Mrs Sucksby, eager to obtain the fortune that she thinks she owns, Sue stares longingly at her through the window of the house. She describes how 'Maud turned her head and seemed to look at me, to hold my gaze across the dusty street'.[54] Here the gaze, signifying the desire that the two women feel for one another, appears to Sue to be mutual. It metaphorically heralds in this respect the two women's eventual reunion.

The interplay between London and the provinces on which *Fingersmith* is structured is achieved not only by the journeys that the characters undertake but also, reflecting Waters's focus on sexual politics and the sociocultural interests relating to it, by the trade in erotic literature that flourished in Victorian London. Maud's tyrannical guardian, Christopher Lilly, is engaged in compiling a 'Universal Bibliography' of erotica,[55] and Waters portrays him coercing Maud into copying passages and reciting them to gentlemen visitors. The latter include the bookseller Mr Hawtrey who travels from London to sell Lilly new texts. Rivers, too, initially gains access to Briar under the pretext of inspecting Lilly's collection. The transactions that occur between Lilly and his visitors signal Maud's role as sexual commodity. Obsessed by copying and reading passages from his books, she begins to envisage herself as one. Referring to the plate pasted on each volume to indicate his ownership, she thinks, 'Sometimes I suppose such a plate must be pasted on my own flesh – that I have been ticketed, and noted and shelved – so nearly do I resemble one of my uncle's books.'[56] The image of 'a phallus, wound about with a stem of briar at the root'[57] inscribed on the plate indicates his ownership of her.

Waters bases Lilly's collection of erotica on that of the London textile trader Henry Spencer Ashbee, now housed in the British Museum.[58] She describes Lilly's books, like Ashbee's, as referring to queer material as well as heterosexual, including male 'sodomitical matter' and descriptions of 'the means a woman may employ to pleasure another'.[59] On making love with Sue, Maud finds her view of the latter topic changing. Lying in Sue's arms and comparing life with fiction, she wonders, 'May a lady taste the fingers of her maid? She may, in my uncle's books, – The thought makes me colour.'[60] Reference to erotic literature, and to London as the hub of its production and sale, recurs when, after having escaped from Mrs Sucksby's house, she seeks out Mr Hawtrey's book shop in Holywell Street in the hope that he will give her refuge. However, shocked by her sudden appearance in the capital and the unembarrassed interest that she shows in his books, their content familiar to her from her life at Briar, he insists that she leave the premises.

A more intimate viewpoint on erotica and its production is represented in the novel's concluding episode. It portrays Maud, sitting alone at Briar, engaged in writing a text of this kind. With her guardian Lilly now deceased and having discovered that it is Sue, not herself as she had assumed, who is in fact the heiress, she now gains a living by producing and selling erotic texts. When Sue – who, impelled by desire, has followed her there – expresses astonishment at the unladylike nature of her occupation, she explains that it is the only kind of work she knows. She also confesses that the passage she is writing has personal import since '[i]t is filled with all the words for how I want you'.[61] The episode recalls Waters's observation in a radio interview that women living in the Victorian era may possibly have read and even produced erotic material.[62] It also has topical interest since it reminds readers of the heated debate that the production of publications of this kind by women who identify as lesbian – such as the magazine *Quim* – has provoked in the lesbian feminist community.[63] In addition to alerting the reader to London's connection with the production of erotica, Waters draws attention to the topic's relevance to women and the controversies relating to it.

The Night Watch: London in war and peace

The strategy of chronologically inverting her characters' storylines that Waters employs in *The Night Watch* – commencing the novel in the context of the post-war year 1947 and concluding it in 1941 in the period of the London blitz – has more than merely stylistic interest. It enables the reader, by travelling back in time, to recognize the changes in the sociopolitical climate that contribute to the formation of their subjectivities and perspectives. The experience of living through the London bombing raids, which all the key characters in the novel share, is of major importance here.

In order to give historical resonance to her representation of the bomb-damaged metropolis, Waters introduces intertextual reference to works of fiction produced by writers working in the period of the war, and Elizabeth Bowen in particular. Her description of the partially demolished houses with their 'phantom staircases'[64] echoes Bowen's reference to 'the terraces that were still nailed up, blind, uninhabitable' in 'I Hear You Say So'.[65] In 'Mysterious Kor', Bowen portrays Londoners, accustomed to the darkness of the unlit streets and the partial protection from bombing that it furnished, regarding the way 'the moonlight drenched the city and searched it' as 'remorseless' and fearing that 'the polished roads and streets ... sent a ghostly unbroken reflection up'.[66] Waters similarly describes how 'when the moon was so bright, surfaces were lit up, white against black. It made you feel vulnerable, exposed'.[67]

Leo Mellor describes Bowen's utilization of spectral imagery as accentuating the eerie atmosphere of wartime London,[68] and Waters employs imagery of this kind in a similar way. She also imaginatively develops Bowen's reference to the city's 'unfamiliar queerness',[69] in the sense of 'strange' and 'uncanny', to refer to her characters' queer sexualities. Like Bowen, who portrays her female protagonist in 'The Demon Lover' associating the ghostly appearance of the bomb-damaged buildings with the 'spectral' visage of her deceased lover,[70] Waters portrays Helen moving from contemplating 'the ghost of a road', reduced to rubble by the blitz, to thoughts of her absent partner, Kay, that are haunting her.[71] Kay, a member of an ambulance crew that works at night, is unaware of the fact that, while she is occupied tending the victims of the bombing raids, Helen is secretly engaging in a romantic stroll with Julia. When the latter two eventually surrender to the imperative of desire and kiss, the darkness, as Julia observes, has the effect of rendering them 'invisible', their physical invisibility evoking their social invisibility as lesbians.[72] As Terry Castle, commenting on the sociocultural effacement of the lesbian, describes, she 'has been effectively ghosted – or made to seem invisible – by culture itself' since 'Western civilization has for centuries been haunted by fear of women indifferent or resistant to male desire'.[73]

It is not only the darkness furnished by the unlit streets that renders Helen and Julia invisible, sheltering them from observation. The partial relaxing of conventional gender roles and dress codes that the wartime culture promoted has a similar effect. When Helen expresses fear of discovery, Julia reassuringly observes that, on account of the heavy coat and cap she herself is wearing, an onlooker 'would probably take us for a boy and his girl'.[74] With the ending of the war, however, these freedoms diminish. Julia, whose reputation as a writer of detective fiction is on the ascent, feels compelled, in order to assume a feminine image, to obey the dictates of fashion and wear a skirt, stockings and make-up. Kay, on the contrary, despite the fact that the ambulance unit in which she worked has been disbanded, refuses to accommodate to feminine fashion. As a result, on visiting the local bakers, she is greeted by the mocking question, 'Don't you know the War's over?'[75] It is provoked, she perceives, by her trousers and 'masculine' haircut.

A distinctive feature of *The Night Watch* is that, in contrast to Waters's earlier neo-Victorian novels, it explores the queer sexualities of male characters as well as female. Duncan, imprisoned in Wormwood Scrubs on the charge of attempted suicide, finds himself sharing a cell with Fraser who is there as the result of identifying as a conscientious objector. Though insisting that he is in no way 'homosexual' and fiercely criticizing the behaviour of the 'effeminate' homosexuals with their camp behaviour who he encounters in the gaol, Duncan establishes a warm emotional attachment to his cellmate. On one occasion, when the noise of the bombing is especially loud, he succeeds in overcoming his fear of male physical contact and permits Fraser, who admits to being scared, to share his bunk. He is aware that, according to heterosexual convention, '[i]t ought to have been strange, to be pressed so close to another [male] person; but it wasn't strange'. Waters describes how, when the bombing ceased, '[t]he two men moved closer together, not further apart'.[76] In addition to illustrating the lack of bomb-shelter facilities in prisons during the war, the episode interrogates the binary division 'heterosexual'/'homosexual', signalling the queer mobility of sexuality.

As illustrated above, London features in Waters's fiction in numerous different roles and guises. Represented in terms of the contradictions of rich and poor, genteel and shabby, light and dark, it signifies, on the one hand, a site of carnivalesque pleasure and masquerade and, on the other, a labyrinthine world carrying connotations of danger. The role that the metropolis plays as the site of queer sexualities and subcultures is illustrated in a variety of ways, with urban locations furnishing the setting for the female characters' same-sex relationships and their encounters with men with homosexual lifestyles. Examples of cross-dressing are also in evidence, as illustrated by Nan's careers as a music hall artiste and 'renter' in *Tipping the Velvet* and Ruth's performance as the spirit-guide Peter Quick in *Affinity*. The two novels also introduce inventive variations on the role of the lesbian *flâneur*, illustrating both the pleasures and problematic aspects of her appropriation of the gaze. In *Fingersmith*, Waters develops the motif of the gaze and its significance. In addition to employing it to evoke Sue's and Maud's romantic attachment, she describes Maud experiencing the oppressive effect of the male gaze when subjected to ridicule in the London streets.

Representations of male sexuality in the context of London life, though by no means central to Waters's fiction, nonetheless play a contributory part in it. The importance of London as the hub of the trade in erotica and the different roles that the bibliographer Christopher Lilly and the bookseller Hawtrey play in it are described in *Fingersmith* in relation to both Maud's sexual education in the rural location of Briar and her subsequent adventures in the metropolis when she visits Hawtrey's bookshop. *The Night Watch*, in contrast, movingly explores the homoerotic attachment that develops between Duncan and his cellmate Fraser while the two men are imprisoned in Wormwood Scrubs during the war. These episodes contribute, with the others discussed in this chapter, to the rich array of perspectives on sexuality and gender that Waters describes in representing London and its sociocultural significance.

Notes

1   Sarah Waters, *Tipping the Velvet* (London: Virago, 1998), p. 200.

2   Annamarie Jagose, *Queer Theory* (Melbourne: Melbourne University Press, 1996), pp. 72–74.

3   Elizabeth Wilson, *Hidden Agendas: Theory, Politics and Experience in the Women's Movement* (London: Tavistock, 1986), p. 169.

4   Gill Valentine, '(Re)negotiating the "Heterosexual Street": Lesbian Productions of Space', in Nancy Duncan (ed.), *Body Space: Destabilizing Geographies of Gender and Sexuality* (London: Routledge, 1996), pp. 146–55.

5   Sally Munt, 'The Lesbian *Flâneur*', in David Bell and Gill Valentine (eds), *Mapping Desire: Geographies of Sexualities* (London: Routledge, 1995), pp. 114–25.

6   Mikhail Bakhtin, *Rabelais and His World*, trans. Helene Iswolsky (Bloomington: Indiana University Press, 1984), pp. 12–20.

7   Elizabeth Wilson, *The Sphinx in the City: Urban Life, the Control of Disorder, and Women* (London: Virago, 1991), p. 7.

8   Ibid.

9   Ibid.

10   Bakhtin, *Rabelais*, p. 34.

11   Sarah Waters, *Affinity* (London: Virago, 1999), p. 109.

12   Waters, *Tipping*, pp. 109, 386.

13   Waters, *Tipping*, p. 218.

14   J.S. Bratton, 'Jenny Hill: Sex and Sexism in the Victorian Music Hall', in J.S. Bratton (ed.), *Music Hall: Performance and Style* (New York: Taylor and Francis, 1997), pp. 92–110, 92, 103–4; and Peter Bailey, *Music Hall: The Business of Pleasure* (Milton Keynes: Open University Press, 1986), p. xvii.

15   Waters, *Tipping*, p. 126.

16   Kristina Straub, 'The Guilty Pleasures of Female Theatrical Cross-Dressing and the Autobiography of Charlotte Clarke', in Julia Epstein and Kristina Straub (eds), *Body Guards: Cultural Politics and Gender Ambiguity* (London: Routledge, 1991), pp. 142–66, 146–7.

17   Waters, *Tipping*, p. 118.

18   Ibid., p. 120.

19   Straub, 'Guilty Pleasures', pp. 147–50.

20   Waters, *Tipping*, p. 140.

21   Ibid., p. 207.

22   Ibid., p. 206.

23   Ibid., p. 264.

24 Judith Butler, *Gender Trouble: Feminism and the Subversion of Identity* (London: Routledge, 1990), p. 33.

25 Waters, *Tipping*, p. 194.

26 Ibid., p. 195.

27 Ibid.

28 Munt, 'Lesbian *Flâneur*', p. 117.

29 Waters, *Tipping*, p. 191.

30 Ibid., p. 201.

31 Ibid., p. 223.

32 Ibid., p. 101.

33 Waters, *Affinity*, p. 9.

34 Alex Owen, *The Darkened Room: Women, Power and Spiritualism in Late Nineteenth Century England* (London: Virago, 1989), pp. 1–10.

35 Tatiana Kontou, *Spiritualism and Women's Writing: From the Fin-de-Siècle to the Neo-Victorian* (London: Palgrave, 2009), p. 190.

36 Waters, *Affinity*, p. 162.

37 Kontou, *Spiritualism*, p. 194.

38 Ibid., p. 195.

39 Waters, *Affinity*, p. 191.

40 Jane Gallop, *Feminism and Psychoanalysis: The Daughter's Seduction* (London: Macmillan, 1982), p. 146.

41 Waters, *Affinity*, p. 119.

42 Rosa Ainley, 'Watching the Detectors: Control and the Panopticon', in Rosa Ainley (ed.), *New Frontiers of Space, Bodies and Gender* (London: Routledge: 1998), pp. 88–100, 89.

43 Waters, *Affinity*, p. 17.

44 Ibid., p. 23.

45 Rebecca Pohl, 'Sexing the Labyrinth', in Kaye Mitchell (ed.), *Sarah Waters: Contemporary Critical Perspectives* (London: Bloomsbury, 2013), p. 37.

46 Wilson, *Sphinx*, pp. 27–8.

47 Sarah Waters, *Fingersmith* (London: Virago, 2002), p. 53.

48 Ibid., p. 56.

49 Ibid., p. 91.

50 Ibid., p. 467.

51 Ibid., p. 469.

52 Ibid., p. 371.

53 Ibid., p. 370.

54 Ibid., p. 475.

55 Ibid., p. 201.

56 Ibid., p. 218.

57 Ibid.

58 Lisa Jardine, 'Sarah Waters: Sex and the Victorian City'. Interview with Sarah Waters, BBC2, 4 May 2005.

59 Waters, *Fingersmith*, pp. 201, 279.

60 Ibid., p. 256.

61 Ibid., p. 547.

62 Jardine, 'Sarah Waters'.

63 Paulina Palmer, '"She began to show me the words she had written one by one": Lesbian Reading and Writing Practices in the Fiction of Sarah Waters', *Women: A Cultural Review* 19.1 (2008), pp. 69–86, 78–9.

64 Sarah Waters, *The Night Watch* (London: Virago, 2006), p. 7.

65 Elizabeth Bowen, *Collected Stories* (London: Vintage, 1999), p. 752.

66 Ibid., p. 728.

67 Waters, *The Night Watch*, p. 360.

68 Leo Mellor, *Reading the Ruins: Modernism, Bombsites and British Culture* (Cambridge: Cambridge University Press, 2011), pp. 159–63.

69 Elizabeth Bowen, 'The Demon Lover', in *Collected Stories*, p. 661.

70 Ibid., p. 668.

71 Waters, *The Night Watch*, p. 337.

72 Ibid., p. 349.

73 Terry Castle, *The Apparitional Lesbian: Female Homosexuality and Modern Culture* (New York: Columbia University Press, 1993), pp. 4–5.

74 Waters, *The Night Watch*, p. 339.

75 Ibid., p. 94.

76 Ibid., p. 411.

CHAPTER SEVEN

Are Drag Kings Still Too Queer for London? From the Nineteenth-Century Impersonator to the Drag King of Today

Kayte Stokoe

This chapter examines London as a locus both of male impersonation in the late nineteenth and early twentieth centuries, and of Drag King performance today. I explore the relationship between these performances and the space/s they occupy, focusing on the male impersonator Vesta Tilley, who performed between 1870 and 1920 on the Music Hall stage, before concentrating on the way in which twenty-first-century London creates a thought-provoking, particularized context for Drag King events and performance. These discussions enable me to offer some preliminary answers to the question, 'Are Drag Kings still too queer for London?'[1] It is pertinent to clarify my use of 'queer' in this chapter. While I rely primarily on the definition established by queer theoretical approaches – that is, queer in the sense of troubling definitions, pushing boundaries and challenging assumptions[2] – I equally employ 'queer' to gesture towards stances of fluidity, collectivity and anti-normativity,[3] both within and outside the context of LGBTQIA practices. Further, I recognize that, perhaps appropriately, the meaning of queer is subject to temporal and cultural shifts, and does not refer monolithically to a single identity or practice. I equally believe that it would be reductive to suggest that any individual practice is necessarily subversive or challenging, irrespective of any association with LGBTQIA subcultures and strategies.[4]

This chapter presents an interdisciplinary investigation of male impersonation on the Music Hall stage around the turn of the century, and of London's Drag King scene, exploring the atmosphere which pervades Drag King communities and events. In terms of methodology, the chapter aims to balance historical analysis with a more subjective analysis of contemporary Drag King spaces. The latter focuses on the material gleaned during my interviews with Drag King performers, including Jen Powell and Lenna Cumberbatch,[5] and explores material garnered in my experience of Drag King spaces. I bring these disparate methodologies together in a comparative analysis, placing the data found in dialogue with Marie-Hélène/Sam Bourcier's concept of Drag King performance as within the rubric of 'pratiques transgenres' ('trans* practices').[6]

Vesta Tilley, the Music Hall and nineteenth- and twentieth-century male impersonators

Matilda Powles – henceforth addressed by her stage name, 'Vesta Tilley' – whose celebrity and longevity surpassed that of many other British male impersonators, began performing masculinity onstage in 1870, at the age of six.[7] While Tilley was developing a career as one of the British Music Hall's first male impersonators, Annie Hindle and Ella Wesner were becoming celebrities in American Vaudeville.[8] However, their portrayals of masculinity were very different to Tilley's. As Gillian Rodger demonstrates, the masculinity performed by first-generation male impersonators such as Hindle, whose peak of popularity was during the 1870s and 1880s, thrived on theatrical realism, stereotypically 'masculine' gestures and attributes, and the resignification of male-coded behaviours. These impersonators

> often had masculine facial features and plump or thickset bodies and could
> have passed as male off the stage if dressed in men's clothing...These
> women rarely if ever appeared in women's clothing: onstage they
> embodied masculinity. They did not just play the role of a man, speaking
> lines written by somebody else; rather, they used song to transform
> themselves into the character about whom they sang.[9]

Contrariwise, later generations of male impersonators, including Tilley, incorporated elements of femininity and androgyny into their performances.[10] Tilley's performance of androgyny – the inclusion of elements of femininity, boyish presentation and 'refinement'[11] – was a central factor in her popularity as W.R. Titterton's glowing testimony suggests: 'all the while, for all her truth to the masculine type, you get a sense of the feminine, not as with

FIGURE 7.1 *Actress Vesta Tilley and her bicycle pose for a publicity postcard circa 1910 in London, England. (Photo by Transcendental Graphics/Getty Images.)*

those clumsy imitators of hers who are giggling women in thin disguise, but just so much that the truth of the male gesture is made the more piquant by that hint of curving shape'.[12]

Here, readers perceive the significance of femininity in Tilley's image: this affectation of 'refinement' and delicacy, combined with a deliberate replication of childish innocence, makes the image of the male impersonator distinctly less threatening to stereotypical gender roles.[13] Further, Tilley deliberately frames her decision to perform masculinity as stemming from a lack of variety in women's acting roles, thereby suggesting that it was the pleasures of variety and excitement that she sought in first donning a frock coat, rather than the privileges allotted to masculinity and maleness.[14]

Whether stemming from her personal dislike of 'realistic' masculinity or from perceptive marketing, Tilley's mobilization of androgyny places her within the realms of heteronormativity. That is, this emphasis allows audiences to appreciate the performance of masculinity without posing significant challenges to the assumption of masculinity as naturally adhering to a cissexual man. The deliberate manipulation of Tilley's image to cater to specific mores – the adoption of an image which Rodger describes as 'astutely managed by [Tilley's] father'[15] – is present throughout her career. Rather than embrace unconventional masculinity offstage, echoing the gender presentation of figures such as Annie Hindle, Tilley sought to emphasize a marked distinction between her 'proper', feminine, private life, and her onstage persona.[16] I suggest that Tilley's performance of (cishet) normativity is manifested in three distinct ways: through the performance of femininity onstage, particularly in terms of the singing voice employed; as a result of her marriage and subsequent class mobility; and, finally, through her repudiation of 'mannishness' and homosexuality.

Tilley's vocal femininity seemingly played a significant role in her androgynous image. Contemporary Drag Kings employ a range of vocal techniques when they sing: the majority choose songs which underline their masculinity and subject position, while many employ low contralto singing voices to accentuate their masculine song choices. Key examples are 'Heart Shaped Box', the dark, velvety Nirvana anthem as performed by Danny von Sleaze, and Michael Bublé's 'Mrs Jones', crooned softly by Adam All. Tilley, however, limited her masculinity to her subject position and physical gestures, singing in a distinctly feminine voice: high, close to soprano and delicate.[17]

The second evident layer of conservative propriety lies in Tilley's marriage to her one-time manager, Walter de Frece, who would later be knighted.[18] I do not suggest that this marriage was entered into solely for reasons of propriety or media approval. Nevertheless, it must be acknowledged that Tilley's marriage altered the class sphere in which she moved: from a relatively modest, working-class, musical background, through the status of respectable married woman, to the titled status of Lady de Frece. While respectability and 'refinement' had marked Tilley's career from her youth, her marriage certainly presented a further step in this regard: the 'respectable' status of wife absolved Tilley of any suspicion of impropriety that might have been allotted to her as an actress at that time.[19] Further, Tilley's regular appearances in hyper-feminine garments and on the arm of her highly reputable consort acted to draw a further sharp line between her onstage masculinity and her 'proper' private life.[20] The final, and highly significant, aspect of the heteronormative, upper-middle-class 'wifeliness' enacted by Tilley lies in her vehement repudiation of offstage female masculinity and of homosexual desire. As Rodger explains, Tilley was the first male impersonator to 'exhibit any defensiveness about "mannish" women': Tilley refused to be associated with impersonators who performed masculinity in their quotidian gender expression, or those whose identity included masculinity.[21]

While Tilley certainly displayed an astute awareness of audience response and public mores, and while this may render her queer in the sense of producing her own popularizing narrative, readers can easily discern her investment in the normative. While many local towns underlined their connection to Tilley,[22] her first performances in London presented a significant step in her career.[23] It is perhaps unsurprising that Tilley's image earned her particular favour in London: Tilley positioned herself as the centre of male impersonation, thereby mirroring London's status as capital city. Furthermore, both Tilley and her central locus can be seen as necessarily constructed, as presenting a particular façade and as presenting a heterogeneous mix of the 'refined' and the working class. The importance of pantomime, as well as Music Hall theatre, to London's population harmonized with Tilley's performance style and facilitated her desire for celebrity status: she could attract customers as the image of the desirable principal boy, while equally gaining further popularity.

The perception of Drag King performance strategies through the lens of *pratiques transgenres* (trans* practices) was pioneered by leading French queer theorist Marie-Hélène/Sam Bourcier in 'Des *"Femmes travesties"* aux pratiques transgenres: repenser et queeriser le travestissement'.[24] Bourcier began participating in queer theory in the 1990s, working with Beatriz Preciado, translating works by Teresa de Lauretis and Monique Wittig, and acting as the *animatrice* – facilitator and animating spirit – of the French queer activist and academic group Le Zoo.[25] In addition to playing a significant role in bringing queer theory to France, Bourcier has focused particularly on Judith Butler's theorizations of gender performativity, developing this first in 'Des *"Femmes travesties"'*,[26] and critiquing the implications of non-agential performativity for trans* people in 'F*** the Politics of Disempowerment in the Second Butler'.[27]

Bourcier's mobilization of performativity is particularly useful here, as *pratiques transgenres* employs 'the valuable resources of performance and performativity' to engage with drag while including trans* performers.[28] As Bourcier demonstrates, positioning Drag King performance within 'trans* practices' acts to separate it from terms such as 'cross dressing', which lack a nuanced awareness of the complexity of gender performance and which rely on a binary model of two fixed genders to cross between.[29] Situating Drag King performance and techniques within *pratiques transgenres* can facilitate a recognition of the possibilities for gender expression and gender identification outside the gender binary.

Although the term *'pratiques'* (practices) emphasizes performance and performativity, Bourcier centres identity alongside performance in his work. That is, *pratiques transgenres* includes 'the range of acts and signs which constitute gender performance (the factors remarked on by Marjorie Garber: dressing, naming, performance and acting out)',[30] while also directing attention towards the fact that *'femmes travesties'* may not account for the identities of those it purports to describe.[31] Focusing on agency, queer community practices and self-determination,[32] Bourcier's lens enables readers to perceive that gender presentation is not necessarily a fixed conclusion, but can instead constitute a continual process of interrogation and exploration.[33] This flexibility allows theorists, readers and activists to explore drag in a way which may not have been possible previously.

In many ways, Tilley's prolonged romance with heteronormativity renders her an unsuitable candidate for an analysis of her performances as *pratiques transgenres*: she does not appear to be engaging in identity work or seeking to expand the categories 'male' and 'female'. Nevertheless, *'pratiques transgenres'* may shed further light on Tilley's presentation and self-positioning. Tilley's androgyny, with touches of 'boyish' playfulness and 'feminine' innocence, arguably echoes the gender expression of some genderfluid and/or genderqueer people.[34] However, Tilley *performs*, rather than identifies with, this androgynous image. In keeping with Bourcier's concept of a self-aware performance style, including '*l'habillement, la nomination, la performance et l'acting out*',[35] Tilley seems to have held an awareness of which boundaries were acceptable to flout, and to have tapped into her childhood performances of feminine roles to expand her characterization. In addition to capitalizing on audience desires and fantasies, Tilley skilfully tailored her performances to suit the country's mood. Prior to the First World War, Tilley included sketches of military masculinity among her performances, presenting an image of '[t]he bumptious and swaggering Tommy'.[36] During the war, however, Tilley clearly positioned the soldier as a hero, not a figure of fun. Indeed, in her autobiography, Tilley proudly emphasizes the plaudits she received from Horatio Bottomley for boosting recruitment.[37] Through its meticulous emphasis on Drag King performance as a composite form, '*pratiques transgenres*' draws further attention to Tilley's savvy self-positioning, which operated on- and offstage to create a popular public image. Further, exploring Tilley's work through Bourcier's lens enables one to question the extent to which '*pratiques transgenres*' can elucidate performances by conservative or even homophobic and/or transphobic performers.

What on earth is a Drag King?

Turning to my exploration of the contemporary Drag King scene, I first outline a central obstacle facing current performers – a lack of mainstream understanding – which constitutes a sharp contrast to the popularity of Music Hall impersonators in London in the early twentieth century. Even the term 'Drag King' is not widely understood. Two London Drag Kings whom I have interviewed – Adam All (Jen Powell) and Leon Da Luvva (Lenna Cumberbatch) – discussed the bemused reactions of friends on encountering the idea of Drag King performance.

In my first interview with her, Jen, who started performing in 2008, discussed the comparative popularity of Drag Kings and Drag Queens in London and elsewhere: 'Drag Kings are much less popular; it doesn't seem to matter where you go'. As Jen explained, Drag Kings, unlike Drag Queens, are often hired for women's nights – rather than LGBTQ+ nights more generally – which limits them to a specific market. Jen partially attributes this contingency to the limited mainstream understanding of Drag King performance. When discussing her performances with friends or acquaintances, Jen has not only encountered those who are unaware of Drag King performance, but has equally met with the assumption that a Drag King must be a form of Drag Queen.

Jen argues that many audience members fail to realize that Drag King performance is, or can be, a 'massive exaggeration of a gender stereotype'. Jen suggests that audience members may therefore not appreciate the comedic dimension of Drag King performance, expecting instead that performers will be 'very sexy and maybe strip even'. Further, Jen recently emphasized a perceived expectation that Drag Kings will perform a flawless, 'passable' masculinity, potentially presenting a difference in standards applied to Drag Kings than to Drag Queens.[38] Consequently, some audience members are surprised and unsettled by a Drag King performance which plays with hyperbole and stereotypical masculinity; 'comedy...with music...with costumes and flashing lights and silly things like that which are a massive exaggeration, cock jokes and everything'.[39]

This lack of comprehension provokes multiple questions. First, one questions whether Drag Kings are generally recognized as the counterpart of Drag Queens. That is, if audiences expect excess and exaggeration from Drag Queens, why is this not the case for Drag Kings?[40] Can one argue that there is a clear image of what a Drag Queen is and should be, whereas no comparable image exists for King performance? Second, if audiences expect Drag Kings to be sexy, on what basis is that expectation drawn? Is it possible that the androgyny and titillating femininity, performed by male impersonators such as Vesta Tilley, has created a legacy which twenty-first-century Drag Kings are expected to follow? Third, to what extent does systemic sexism inform the perception of Drag King performance? How much does the perception of masculinity as 'natural' inform and/or impede the understanding of performances of masculinity?[41] This lack of understanding of Drag King performance in London spaces seems particularly curious in the light of London's rich history of non-normative masculinities and male impersonation. While male impersonation was once common enough to be featured in popular crime fiction[42] – albeit as a means of concealing criminal intentions – London today has only recently begun to wake up to the concept of King performance.

Kinging in London

This section first turns to a further analysis of contemporary Drag King performance styles and their resonances with Bourcier's *pratiques transgenres*. As noted above, *pratiques transgenres* draws attention to performance style, character development and personal constructions of gender.[43] Adam All has a clear core personality – naïve, awkward and loveable – which is communicated to the audience through exuberant gestures, facial expressions and, as in the case of male impersonators such as Hindle, the formation of character through song choice.[44] Further, by appearing in diverse costumes – with at least one new costume at each 'Boi Box' Drag King cabaret night[45] – and by interacting with other performers, Adam presents a character which constantly develops. Thus, as bell hooks notes of particular drag performances, Adam's character and performance is 'capable of construction, invention, change'.[46]

Adam's core personality builds on elements of celebrated queer masculinity, as present in Freddy Mercury for example, yet also incorporates, rewrites and illuminates working-class masculinities – such as those of young men that Jen encountered while working in construction, who, when interacting in groups, modified their behaviour to engage in misogynistic 'banter'. Jen's performance of Adam allows her to critique normative, narrow constructions of masculinity: Adam constantly strives for macho-masculinity and suave self-presentation yet always fails in producing this archetype as his own fears become visible. The macho mask slips further during Adam's endearing encounters with Apple, 'his first ever girlfriend', for whom he evidently feels a mix of pride, desire, lust and fear. Consider the 'General Erection' medley performed by Adam and Apple.[47] When celebrating his growing political popularity, Adam preened and flexed, with Apple gazing longingly at him before waving graciously to an imagined electorate, yet later, realizing that his 'first lady' is about to hear the news of his sexual impropriety, Adam's face falls, he covers his head with his hands, and cowers, diminished.

Lenna Cumberbatch performs two distinct Drag King personalities: the sleek, handsome ladies' man Leon, and the sleazy, dodgy Uncle Lenny. Both characters can be analysed according to Bourcier's concept; the very decision to perform these separate yet interlocking characters is an immediate invitation to multiplicity and construction. Leon's suave masculinity, his open flirting and cheekiness sit comfortably on Lenna's own female masculinity. Judith Jack Halberstam praises this capacity to perform two distinct forms of masculinity, positioning it as a specific Kinging technique: 'layering'.[48] Equally, Lenna's performances resonate with the concept of *pratiques transgenres*, as these performances engage critically with stereotypical, cissexist ideas of masculinity. One revealing aspect of Lenna's performance of strong black masculinity occurs offstage, in the response she encounters from strangers while travelling in costume. Lenna reports that, when strangers code her as male, eyes are immediately turned away; strangers change their poses, and look behind them. This not only demonstrates the accuracy of Lenna's portrayal but also attests to a common reaction to strong black masculinity.[49]

Additionally, there is the exuberant, ridiculous hilarity of Juan Kerr, whose attraction lies partially in his refusal to perform suavity, and his open offer of exaggerated, masculine autoeroticism; and the cocky, voluble bravado of LoUis CYfer, who teasingly invites audience participation, making audience members ready and willing to respond and to interrogate boundaries between on- and offstage. These masculinities are queered, opened up and placed squarely in the bracket of *pratiques transgenres*, while the gazes that respond are equally complex and layered.[50]

My emphasis on recent improvements in the Drag King scene may appear incongruous in the light of the above discussion of a mainstream lack of understanding of performance techniques. However, I suggest that this lack of understanding acts as a backdrop on which these improvements play out. While the contemporary scene is progressing and while audiences are beginning to understand Drag King performance, the current and former lack of mainstream awareness of Drag King performance necessarily affects the position in which Drag Kings find themselves.[51] Further, as I stress in the final section of this chapter, London's contemporary climate affects its drag scene as a whole so that the growing popularity of Drag Kings plays out on a potentially precarious backdrop.

The current improvements in London's Drag King scene seem to me to occur across three categories: the proliferation of Drag King nights and performances; the growing publicity surrounding Drag Kings; and the developing links between Drag King performers and other drag performers. While remaining less celebrated than its Drag Queen counterpart, London's Drag King scene continues to develop, including two regular performance nights in Soho: 'Boi Box', the Drag King Cabaret Night hosted by Adam All and Apple Derrières; and 'WTF! Wednesdays' held by LoUis CYfer.[52] These events present valuable queer spaces, adding to London's rich subcultural life. In addition to hosting talented established performers, 'Boi Box' provides a platform for burgeoning Drag King performers through their open mic sessions. For example, both Romeo De La Cruz and Richard Von Wilde began performing on the 'Boi Box' stage and have now undertaken successful performances elsewhere.[53] This supportive atmosphere, fostered by 'Boi Box' and by events such as 'Bar Wotever's Female Masculinity Appreciation Society', acts to enrich the King scene while equally providing a safe space for LGBTQIA people to experiment with their gender expression.[54]

In addition to 'Boi Box' and 'WTF! Wednesdays', London's scene includes workshops, Drag King competitions and performance collectives.[55] This diversity may play a role in the growing attraction of London's scene for the mainstream press. Summer 2015 witnessed the BBC Newsbeat documentary *Drag Kings of the UK* (featuring Adam All, Richard Von Wilde and Jack the Lad),[56] the publication of '8 Drag Kings That Will Leave You Feeling All A-Quiver' on news-site Buzzfeed,[57] and the inclusion of Drag King performances and events at London Pride.[58] While performers and audience members are yet to witness the full impact of this publicity, summer 2015 seemed to be an exciting time for the Drag King scene as a whole.

However, as both Lenna and Jen have pointed out, Drag Kings in London tend to experience peaks and troughs of popularity.[59] Committed members of the scene are frequently unable to push Drag King performance into the mainstream due to the cost and difficulty of running and maintaining Drag King events. While it is possible that the current activity may only be a short-lived peak, I contend that the links forged through and across contemporary drag scenes may allow King performance to progress further. The inclusivity offered by nights such as 'Boi Box', 'FMAS' and 'King of the Castle' – in terms of centring marginalized performers and audience members through factors such as price scales and accessibility – creates a sense of the Drag King scene as a community which represents a form of queer intersectional politics. Equally, the growing connections between Drag Kings and Drag Queen, Drag Queer and Burlesque performers augur well for Drag King popularity while presenting a necessary step towards a queer performance community. I suggest that such a community is more necessary now than ever due to the contemporary neoliberal climate and its effect on performance venues. This sense of community is further evinced in links across Drag King scenes. From the launch of Drag King bar 'Kings' in Blackpool to the mutual hosting of nights between London and Manchester-Kings,[60] these connections facilitate a sense of community and enable more people to take part in the Drag King scene.

Cutting the scene

The current climate in the UK, featuring governmental cuts to welfare, the rise of the neoliberal academy and widespread gentrification, necessarily affects LGBTQIA Londoners, particularly those who face intersecting forms of oppression.[61] Thus, improvements to the Drag King scene can be seen to occur in the context of a general sense of precariousness for the drag scene as a whole. On one level, the Drag Queen scene appears to be encountering a peak of mainstream popularity; 2014 saw the hit TV show *Drag Queens of London*, while May 2015 saw the search for RuPaul's Drag Race UK Ambassador with the finals attended by celebrity judges.[62] Equally, however, the rising rents in London have contributed to the loss of multiple drag venues, including the historic venues Madame Jojo's, The Joiners' Arms and The Black Cap.[63] The Royal Vauxhall Tavern, a space of particular importance for queer and trans* patrons, may also be threatened with closure due to a change in ownership.[64] The disparity in popularity between Drag Queens and Drag Kings may mean that venue losses will have a disproportionate impact on the Drag King scene; competition for residencies will be fierce, and managers may hire the performers that they feel are most likely to provide revenue. Further, as Drag King performance remains connected to queer women's scenes, the issue of affordability and rising prices may also disproportionately affect the Drag King scene. Lenna Cumberbatch eloquently elucidated this point, emphasizing the costs of running and/or attending Drag King events and stressing the fact that black and minority ethnic women – whose job opportunities and pay are frequently less than those available to white women – are disproportionately likely to suffer as a result of 'hidden' costs. As Lenna argued, these difficulties are also likely to be exacerbated as a result of intersecting forms of prejudice and oppression relating to disability, cultural context and trans* status. While disabled patrons and trans* patrons may incur further expenses in order to ensure their attendance and safety, these expenses are likely to be disproportionately greater due to the cost of living and price hikes present in London.

Conclusion

Beginning this chapter with an exploration of Music Hall impersonation has enabled me to illustrate elements of the historical legacy of Drag King performance, while equally demonstrating that male impersonation is not inherently queer, even as it outlines aspects of masculinity which may be rendered invisible elsewhere.[65] As demonstrated here, Vesta Tilley astutely balanced apparent challenges to norms with a politics of respectability, and tailored her performances to popular taste – as in the case of her wartime performances of soldierly masculinity.[66] This chapter has equally emphasized the correlation between Tilley's savvy self-positioning and celebrity, and the popular appreciation of pantomime and Music Hall theatre in late nineteenth- and early twentieth-century London.

These questions of taste and of correlation permeate the chapter as a whole, playing a significant role in my analysis of contemporary Drag King performance. While Tilley could capitalize on the popularity of 'male impersonation' during the 'great age of Music Hall',[67] London's contemporary Drag Kings face the two obstacles mapped here: a lack of mainstream understanding, and the current climate of rising costs and venue closures. Equally, London's size may present an obstacle to the mainstreaming of Drag King performance therein. While some individuals may continue to feel that their area offers a strong sense of queer community, they may be unable or unwilling to travel outside their particular area. Such unwillingness could stem from the cost of public transport, the difficulty of returning home safely, and/or the cost of outfits and the price of drinks at a particular night. Moreover, in the current climate, the cost of living may prevent people from attending nights that they might otherwise enjoy. At the same time, however, some of the problems faced by LGBTQIA people in contemporary London – rising rent costs, the loss of established venues, etc. – have prompted drag performers and queer activists to band together as a community.[68]

Overall, I suggest that the contemporary moment includes at least two interlocking dimensions relating to, or affecting, Drag King popularity in London. On the one hand, the irruption of drag into the mainstream, through series such as RuPaul's Drag Race, the recent BBC Newsbeat documentary *Drag Kings of the UK* and the performances of Drag Kings on the Cabaret Stage at London Pride 2015, seems to suggest that Drag Kings are steadily gaining in mainstream popularity in London. On the other hand, however, Drag Kings continue to receive substantially less pay for their performances than Drag Queens, performance residencies are difficult to retain, the rising property prices have affected performers, audiences, and venues alike, and London's LGBTQIA community has lost at least three Cabaret venues in the last year.[69] These potentially conflicting circumstances may mean that, while the Drag King scene is developing, it is unlikely to ascend quickly to the popularity of male impersonation on the Music Hall stage. In this way, one might argue that Drag Kings are indeed too queer for London.

To conclude on a positive note, however, the discussion of contemporary Drag Kings and of Marie-Hélène/Sam Bourcier's *pratiques transgenres* has demonstrated that contemporary performances can continue to play with and (de)construct stereotypical notions of gender, thereby opening up possibilities for a wider understanding of masculinity and femininity. Further, the Drag King scene is progressing – if slowly – thereby suggesting that Drag community spaces will be available to a wider range of people, que(e)rying gender, one King at a time.

Notes

1   Here, the 'still' in my title references two circumstances: first, that despite its long history, Drag King performance has not yet achieved the success of Drag Queen performance; and second, to reflect the fact that I first posed this question in a paper given at the 'Queer London' conference at the early stages of my research.

2   In her introductory piece on queer theory, Annamarie Jagose writes:

> While the mobilization of queer in its most recent sense cannot be dated exactly, it is generally understood to have been popularly adopted in the early 1990s. Queer is a product of specific cultural and theoretical pressures which increasingly structured debates (both within and outside the academy) about questions of lesbian and gay identity. Perhaps most significant in this regard has been the problematizing by post-structuralism of gay liberationist and lesbian feminist understandings of identity and the operations of power.

Annamarie Jagose, *Queer Theory: An Introduction* (New York: New York University Press, 1996), p. 76.

3   Todd R. Ramlow suggests that to be 'anti-normative in all regards' is to be 'anti-racist, anti-homophobic, anti-neoliberalism, anti-ableism' ('Queering, Cripping', in *The Ashgate Research Companion to Queer Theory* (Farnham: Ashgate Publishing, 2012), p. 130).

4   Here, 'individual practice' refers to performance practices (such as Drag King performance) or sexual practices.

5   I would like to thank these performers for their kind help and invaluable insights. My first interviews with Jen Powell and Lenna Cumberbatch, two London-based Drag Kings, took place in January 2013 and August 2013, respectively. I have also had the pleasure of several informal discussions with Jen, whose monthly Drag King night 'Boi Box' will be discussed here. While Lenna performs less frequently now than she did during the early stages of my research, I have chosen to centre her work alongside that of Jen Powell in this analysis as both of these performers interrogate hegemonic models

of masculinity in their performances. Equally, both Lenna and Jen offer particularly perceptive insights into the complexities and issues at work in London drag scenes.

6   Marie-Hélène/Sam Bourcier introduces *'pratiques transgenres'* in 'Des "Femmes travesties": Repenser et queeriser le travestissement', in *Queer Zones: Politique des identités sexuelles et des savoirs* (Paris: Editions Amsterdam, 2006), p. 130. This text was published under the name Marie-Hélène Bourcier.

7   Sarah Maitland, *Vesta Tilley* (London: Virago, 1986), p. ix. Tilley's exceptional success is testified by Maitland's remarks that Tilley constituted 'the highest-earning woman in Britain in the 1880s; the woman who could "fill any Hall anywhere"' (p. 5), as well as by the praise offered by W. R. Titterton in *From Theatre to Music Hall* (London: Stephen Swift & Co., 1912). Maitland also testifies to the longevity of Tilley's career, remarking on the fortuitous fact that 'the years of her career' coincided with the 'great age of Music Hall' (p. 11) in Britain.

8   Gillian Rodger, '"He Isn't a Marrying Man": Gender and Sexuality in the Repertoire of Male Impersonators, 1870–1930', in Sophie Fuller and Lloyd Whitesell (eds), *Queer Episodes in Music and Modern Identity* (Chicago: University of Illinois Press, 2002), p. 109.

9   Ibid.

10   Ibid.

11   Ibid.

12   Titterton, in Maitland, *Vesta Tilley*, p. 3.

13   Titterton, in particular, values the image of childish innocence as portrayed by Tilley: 'yet her soul is that of a boy – or perhaps, shall I say, of a girl at the age when girls and boys are very much alike. She is and always will be a naïve child' (Titterton, *From Theatre to Music Hall*, p. 145 in Maitland, *Vesta Tilley*, p. 3).

14   Lady Mattilda de Frece, *Recollections of Vesta Tilley* (London: Hutchinson and Co., 1934), p. 25.

15   Rodger, '"He Isn't a Marrying Man"', p. 119.

16   Gillian Rodger, who stresses the distinct opposition between onstage masculinity and offstage feminine respectability, notes that, in an article written by Tilley, '[s]he is also careful to distinguish her onstage "business" from her offstage "private" life, and invokes late nineteenth-century middle-class constructions in which women properly belong in the home, or private sphere, while men occupy the public sphere' (ibid., p. 122).

17   These vocals are clearly audible in recordings of Tilley's performances. One example can be found on YouTube: http://www.youtube.com /watch?v=pf3LsGQPxSU (accessed 20 May 2015).

18   de Frece, *Recollections*, p. 248.

19   As Tracy C. Davis writes, 'the popular association between actresses and prostitutes and belief in actresses' inappropriate conduct endured

throughout the nineteenth century'. 'Actresses and Prostitutes in Victorian London', *Theatre Research International* 13.3, http://dx.doi.org/10.1017/ S0307883300005794 (accessed 20 May 2015).

20   J.S. Bratton underlines Tilley's femininity in a somewhat scathing manner: 'Tilley undercut any challenge she made by a parade of essential womanliness; she was most definitely not a dissenter in her public and private life off stage, acting as "The Lady Bountiful of the Music Halls" whose husband became a Tory MP' ('Irrational Dress', in Viv Gardner and Susan Rutherford (eds), *The New Woman and Her Sisters* (Hemel Hempstead: Harvester Wheatsheaf, 1992), p. 79).

21   Rodger, '"He Isn't a Marrying Man"', p. 121.

22   de Frece, *Recollections*, p. 19.

23   Ibid., pp. 45–6.

24   Marie-Hélène/Sam Bourcier, 'Des "*Femmes travesties*" aux pratiques transgenres: repenser et queeriser le travestissement', in *Queer Zones: Politique des identités sexuelles et des savoirs* (Paris: Amsterdam, 2006).

25   Genres Pluriels, 'Visiblté des personnes aux genres fluides, trans* et intersexe: Accueil, Publications, AuteurEs', http://www.genrespluriels.be/Marie-Helene-Bourcier?lang=fr (accessed 25 May 2015).

26   Bourcier, 'Des "Femmes travesties"', pp. 129–31.

27   Marie-Hélène/Sam Bourcier, 'F*** the Politics of Disempowerment in the Second Butler', *Paragraph* 35.2 (2012), pp. 235–40.

28   Ibid., pp. 239–40.

29   Bourcier writes: 'L'expression même de travestissement, outre qu'elle oblige à focaliser sur le vêtement, présuppose qu'il existe une vérité du genre: celle-là même que l'on travestirait. Or, cette affirmation ne peut se comprendre que d'un point de vue hétérocentré, dans le cadre du système de relation sexe/genre imposé par le régime hétérosexuel' ('Des "*Femmes travesties*"', p. 128). I translate this as follows: 'As well as obliging a focus on clothing, the expression "cross dressing" presupposes that there is a truth of gender; that which one crosses. That is, this affirmation can only be understood from a heterocentric point of view, along the lines of an assumed relationship between sex and gender as imposed by the heterosexual system.'

30   The above is my translation. The original quote runs as follows: 'l'ensemble des actes et des signes qui participent de la performance du genre (les opérations répertoriées par Marjorie Garber: l'habillement, la nomination, la performance et l'acting-out)'. Ibid., p. 130.

31   Bourcier stresses the fact that some individuals positioned as '*femmes travesties*', such as Brandon Teena and Billy Tipton, seemingly identified outside the category 'woman' and could potentially be seen as transgender. Ibid., p. 127.

32   Ibid., pp. 127–34.

33   Ibid., pp. 131–2.

34 Significantly, genderfluid and genderqueer people have a range of gender expressions and are not necessarily 'androgynous' in the sense indicated above.

35 Bourcier, 'Des "*Femmes travesties*"', p. 130.

36 Maitland, *Vesta Tilley*, p. 117.

37 de Frece, *Recollections*, p. 143.

38 Jen made this point in a telephone conversation on 25 May 2015, contrasting this expectation to the acceptance of Drag Queens who do not perform 'passable' or 'realistic' femininity.

39 As I have seen at Drag King Cabaret night 'Boi Box', this surprise can be followed by delight, excitement and laughter. However, as Jen noted in the telephone call referenced above, some audience members have questioned why 'cock jokes' are necessary in a Drag King performance.

40 The expectation that Drag Queen performance will be excessive and exaggerated may be linked to the close relationship between drag and camp, described by Esther Newton in *Mother Camp: Female Impersonators in America* (Chicago, IL: University of Chicago Press, 1979), pp. 105–7.

41 Judith Jack Halberstam underlines the naturalization of masculinity in *Female Masculinity* (Durham, NC and London: Duke University, 1999), p. 238–41 and in *In a Queer Time and Place* (New York and London: New York University Press, 2005), p. 126. While agreeing with Halberstam's assertion that Drag Kings can interrogate this naturalization of masculinity (pp. 126–7), I equally question how this naturalization affects audience's understanding of Drag King performance.

42 Agatha Christie, *The Mystery of the Blue Train* (London: Harper Collins, 2001), pp. 340–1, 364–5.

43 Bourcier, 'Des "*Femmes travesties*"', pp. 128–32. Bourcier emphasizes the idea of gender as personally constructed through references to queer and trans* community practices, focusing on the way in which experience and subjectivity shape gender.

44 In the same way that male impersonators such as Hindle embodied masculinity onstage through song (Rodger, '"He's Not a Marrying Man"', p. 109), Adam All and Apple Derrières perform medleys which tell stories, taking on the characteristics and emotions expressed by the songs in question.

45 Drag King Cabaret Night 'Boi Box' is a monthly event hosted by Adam All and Apple Derrières at SHE Soho. For more information, see http://dragkingadamall.wix.com/adam-all#!boi-box/c1ait (accessed 1 May 2015).

46 bell hooks, 'Is Paris Burning?' in *Reel to Real: Race, Class, and Sex at the Movies* (New York: Routledge, 1996), p. 276.

47 This performance occurred at 'Boi Box' on 6 May 2015.

48 Judith Halberstam, *Female Masculinity* (Durham, NC and London: Duke University Press, 1998), pp. 260–1.

49 Following Amy André, who discusses her experiences of hostile reactions to black masculinity in 'And Then You Cut Your Hair: Genderfucking on the

Femme Side of the Spectrum', I suggest that these reactions constitute an example of institutionalized racism (Amy André and Sandy Chang, 'And Then You Cut Your Hair: Genderfucking on the Femme Side of the Spectrum', in *Nobody Passes: Rejecting the Rules of Gender and Conformity* (Berkeley, CA: Seal Press, 2006), pp. 254–69, 262–3).

50 Participating in *pratiques transgenres* can facilitate the development of one's own understanding of gender and allow one to challenge cisheterosexist assumptions about gender (Bourcier, 'Des "femmes travesties"', pp. 130–1). Significantly, however, I am in no way suggesting that participating in *pratiques transgenres* necessarily alters one's gender status.

51 While some individual Drag Kings continue to encounter a lack of understanding, the lack of mainstream awareness equally means that, although the scene is growing, Kings may continue to be perceived as 'niche', while certain Drag Queens are perceived as relatively mainstream in comparison.

52 'WTF! Wednesdays' are held at the Admiral Duncan on Old Compton Street; http://www.the1440.co.uk/(S(xhd1dhd2zpria4ddccmsf20x))/Venue/Whats-On /admiral-duncan#T [accessed 31 May 2015].

53 Romeo De La Cruz performed at the sixth and seventh 'Barelesque' events at the Royal Vauxhall Tavern in 2014 (http://www.barelesque.com/events/ (accessed 31 May 2015)), while Richard Von Wilde appeared at 'King of the Fringe' at Brighton's Marlborough Theatre on 8 May 2015 (http://boxoffice. brightonfringe.org/cabaret/9560/king-of-the-fringe (accessed 31 May 2015)).

54 The 'Wotever Manifesto' explicitly states its aim to be a 'safer space for the LBGTQ community' and stresses its acceptance of diverse gender identities; http://wotever.pragmative.net/wotever-manifesto/ (accessed 31 May 2015). Equally, as discussed in our conversation of 25 May 2015, Jen has received compliments about the status of 'Boi Box' as a safe space for gender expression and gender play.

55 'The Pecs' are a Drag King collective performing in London and elsewhere: http://www.pecsdragkings.com/new-page/ (accessed 31 May 2015). Additionally, East London drag venue The Glory now hosts a vibrant, popular Drag King competition named 'Man Up', which is composed of six heats and offers a prize of £1,000 to the winning contestant. For more details about this event, see http://www.theglory.co/man-up/ (accessed 27 May 2016).

56 'Drag Kings of the UK' can be viewed at http://www.bbc.co.uk/newsbeat /article/32764145/drag-kings-of-the-uk-the-women-who-perform-as-men (accessed 31 May 2015).

57 http://www.buzzfeed.com/jamestreacher/8-drag-kings-that-will-send-you-all-a -quiver-1gacv#.ky80GKWQ9p (accessed 31 May 2015).

58 The official Pride Cabaret stage included a performance by Adam All and Apple Derrières (http://prideinlondon.org/wardour/ (accessed 31 May 2015)), while Pride-related events included performances by 'The Pecs' (http://www .pecsdragkings.com/summer-tour (accessed 31 May 2015)).

59 Lenna made this comment in our interview of August 2013.

60   Kings Bar Blackpool held its promotional launch at Blackpool Pride, 13–
14 June 2015; http://www.kingsbarblackpool.co.uk/# (accessed 31 May 2015).
'The Drag King' Lydia Bernsmeier-Rullow hosts Manchester's Drag King
night 'Boi Zone' and made her London debut at 'Boi Box Fools' in April 2015.
Adam All appeared at 'Boi Zone' in July 2014. For more information on 'Boi
Zone', see https://www.facebook.com/TheBoiZone (accessed 31 May 2015).

61   Ian Silvera discusses the Conservative government's proposed welfare cuts in
the following article: http://www.ibtimes.co.uk/tory-welfare-policy-questioned
-after-no-child-benefit-cuts-promise-1503862 (accessed 1 June 2015). Hugo
Radice offers one account of neoliberalism in the UK university system: H.
Radice, 'How We Got Here: UK Higher Education Under Neoliberalism',
ACME: An International E Journal for Critical Geographies 12.3 (2013),
pp. 407–18, http://www.acme-journal.org/vol12/Radice2013.pdf (accessed
2 June 2015). Writing in *The Londonist*, Shehzad Raj stresses the impact
of gentrification on the LGBTQIA, cabaret and alternative communities,
noting that the losses of venues have been experienced by some as a loss of
community: http://londonist.com/2015/02/londons-lgbt-and-alternative
-scenes-are-fighting-gentrification.php (accessed 2 June 2015). While separate,
these phenomena act together in terms of their cumulative effect on London's
population.

62   *Drag Queens of London*, first broadcast in April 2014, is available to watch
online at London Live: http://www.londonlive.co.uk/programmes/drag-queens
-of-london/e5ad2975 (accessed 2 June 2015). *The Londonist*'s article on the
search for a UK ambassador for RuPaul's drag race is as follows: https://
londonist.com/2015/06/rupaul-sashays-into-london-to-handpick-her-uk-
ambassador.php (accessed 2 June 2015).

63   Michael Segalov discusses the closure of these historic venues in *Vice*:
https://www.vice.com/en_uk/read/photos-from-this-weekends-protest-to-save
-the-black-cap-in-camden (accessed 2 June 2015).

64   Ibid.

65   This chapter does not aim to provide an overall history of the development
of male impersonation and Drag King performance. Such an account would
be difficult in the space available. Further, there is reason to suggest that Drag
King performance did not develop on a smooth line from male impersonation
on the vaudeville stage. Significantly, some male impersonators, such as
Stormé DeLarverié, who performed between 1955 and 1969, continued to
perform in theatrical contexts after the 1930s (Elizabeth Drorbaugh, 'Stormé
DeLarverié and The Jewel Box Revue', in Leslie Ferris (ed.), *Crossing the Stage:
Controversies on Cross-Dressing* (London: Routledge, 1993), pp. 120–43).
Nevertheless, as Drorbaugh suggests, 'gender impersonation' generally faded
from the mainstream stage after the decline of vaudeville (ibid., p. 124), while
'by 1933…the feared conflation of (homo)sexuality with gender impersonation
caused male impersonation seemingly to evaporate and female impersonation
to go underground' (ibid., p. 124). Thus, while performers like Stormé and
the theatrical group Split Britches – who began performing in the late 1970s;
https://splitbritches.wordpress.com/about/splitbritches (accessed 3 June 2015) –
continued the tradition of male impersonation, it seemingly continued in a

fragmented, underground manner rather than operating on a clear, continuous line which culminates in Drag King performance as practised today.

66　Maitland, *Vesta Tilley*, pp. 117–18.

67　Ibid., p. 11.

68　Consider, for example, the protests held after the unexpected closure of the Black Cap (https://www.vice.com/en_uk/read/photos-from-this-weekends -protest-to-save-the-black-cap-in-camden (accessed 3 June 2015)), and the subsequent creation of the 'We Are The Black Cap' group, which is aiming to ensure that the Black Cap remains an LGBTQIA venue; https://www .facebook.com/groups/weareblackcap/ (accessed 3 June 2015). Additionally, the group 'Camden Queer Punx 4eva' are now occupying the Black Cap, protesting against gentrification in Camden; http://www.nottelevision.net /inside-the-squatted-black-cap/ (accessed 8 June 2015).

69　In terms of the impact of property prices on LGBTQIA venues, Ben Walters writes: 'Now the soaring London property market makes many sites vulnerable to commercial and residential redevelopment when leases end'; 'Closing time for gay pubs – a new victim of London's soaring property prices', *Guardian*, 4 February 2015, http://www.theguardian. com/society/2015/feb/04/closing-time-gay-pubs-lgbt-venues-property-prices (accessed 3 June 2015).

CHAPTER EIGHT

Claude McKay: Queering Spaces of Black Radicalism in Interwar London

Gemma Romain and Caroline Bressey

Between the two world wars, London served as a challenging, engaging and cosmopolitan space for individuals from the African and Asian diasporas, including students, writers, political activists and artists. For some, as Maroula Joannou has observed, 'inter-war London acted as a mecca for a varied assortment of radical subaltern networks in which the Indian student might exchange ideas informally with the Jamaican sailor or the Somali visitor converse with the politician from Kenya, or the exile from the Gold Coast'.[1] Within this cultural space, queer black artists, writers and activists lived, worked and socialized. This chapter explores the experiences of one such queer black activist, the Jamaican poet and activist Claude McKay, who lived in London between 1919 and 1921 as he worked to complete the publication of a collection of poetry. The chapter concentrates specifically on the formation and expressions of his cosmopolitan literary, radical, queer and political identities. Though known primarily for his contributions to America's Harlem Renaissance, Claude McKay's sojourn in London provides a lens through which to examine moments of cultural exchange, in spaces such as art galleries, the newspaper office and the political club, and places of cultural exchange, including cafes and jazz clubs. During his stay in London, McKay spent time in the British Museum reading room researching Marx's writings, carrying out research on African sculpture, and meeting writers including George Bernard Shaw. He also worked with

FIGURE 8.1 *Jamaican writer and poet Claude McKay (1889–1948), 1926. (Photo by Berenice Abbott/Getty Images.)*

the Suffrage campaigner Sylvia Pankhurst, the painter Frank Budgen, and Charles Kay Ogden, the polymath who edited McKay's collection of poems.

McKay identified within himself a 'mania for wandering'; he had always wanted to visit Europe, especially England, a desire he recorded in an early poem 'Old England', but McKay's experiences in London were marred by racism.[2] McKay's queer identity was a constituent of his life as an internationalist, a radical and freethinker. As Josh Gosciak argues:

> for McKay as a sexual rebel, internationalism crosses over into the twentieth century not as ideology, but as a vast social network of pacifists and feminists, renegades and vagabonds, quirky intellectuals and assorted political rogues, and spills out disruptively onto the modern dance floors of Pittsburgh, Philadelphia, Cardiff, Liverpool, Marseilles, and Tangier.[3]

Like characters highlighted in Judith Walkowitz's *Nights Out* (though he was in London during an earlier period), McKay found in Soho an engaging and multi-cultural, though complex and at times alienating, social life where he met activists, writers, artists, sailors and boxers.[4] In his personal letters written during his time in London, as well as his 1937 autobiography *A Long Way From Home*, he reported suffering verbal abuse in the Soho-based 1917 club, violence in East London and racial discrimination when trying to find accommodation in Bloomsbury. Without access to venues such as the International Socialist Club (ISC) in the East End or friends he met at the Drury Lane club for 'colored' colonial soldiers, McKay believed he would not have survived his London residence. However, even at the ISC he experienced racism from one member. Although McKay experienced complex and varied intellectual, social and cultural experiences, the city did not provide the same opportunity to engage or freely enjoy 'networks of public and commercial sociability' as it did for many of the men identified in Matt Houlbrook's *Queer London*, when his 'colour alone' made him feel so conspicuous.[5] Exploring McKay's London life experiences, this chapter argues that there is a need to examine the intersections of class and race with queer identity and radical activism, which have been little explored in the context of the black interwar presence in Britain. As Gary Edward Holcomb states, McKay's political activism 'cannot be disentangled from his queer resistance'.[6] Inspired by Holcomb's pioneering work on McKay's queer identity, this chapter considers the multiplicity of McKay's London through a lens of queer black spaces. It does so by focusing on published and unpublished writings, including his London poems which formed part of *Harlem Shadows* (1922), and his 1919–20 publications in the *Workers' Dreadnought*.

McKay's poetry and letters provide us with a first-hand account of some of his London-based experiences. *A Long Way From Home* was shaped by years of oppressive surveillance by the British and US governments for his political beliefs as well as his eventual move away from communism. His memoirs, representing his identity seventeen years after his time in London, served, as Holcomb reflects, to 'not so much conceal his sexual difference and black anarchism as wrap up these features of his past in a picturesque, carefree form of bohemianism' whereby 'elements of his personal history do not infect his present'.[7] The texture and diverse experiences of his London living are somewhat obscured in his 1937 autobiography; as Wayne Cooper reflects, to write an autobiography that fully detailed his associations with the Workers' Socialist Federation and his friendship with Sylvia Pankhurst and other members of the British Left would have meant structuring his memoir around an entirely different emphasis.[8] From a reading of his personal correspondence and publications in *The Workers' Dreadnought*, it is clear that, as Cooper has argued, McKay's personal experiences of England were more intense than his memoirs revealed. In a 1966 interview, McKay's London friends, Frank and Francine Budgen, remembered McKay was 'openly homosexual'.[9] However, in exploring 'evidence' of a queer black life or history, Holcomb's work is instructive in suggesting that to understand queer identities such as McKay's, we must not solely seek to look for 'evidence' of queerness in relation to McKay's sexual relationships; queer black histories cannot just be examined by declared mentions and moments of same-sex sexuality. How McKay's queer identity surfaced and was performed is more complex. McKay's writing, which commented upon his identity or the 'queer' way in which he viewed the world and lived his life, was often implicit and subtle. As Holcomb states,

> [i]f we read his writings with a methodology calculated to *divulge* the gay or bisexual constituent, to decode closeted signs of the *life*, then we pursue an incomplete study. When it comes to considering McKay's life and labor in the 1920s and 1930s, *queer* is the ideal terminology. In the genealogy of queer, one may trace a subject agency that refuses to submit itself tractably to questionings of identity.[10]

In line with Holcomb's theories, a focus on Nadia Ellis' important work in exploring post-war queer black life in Britain is particularly instructive; Ellis found that 'visibility could only be an ambivalent political imperative for the Caribbean queer subject in post-war Britain. To be visible is to be vulnerable to surveillance. As such, evidence as to a subject's sexuality, his or her class, race and national identification is often muted and complexly coded'.[11] In addition, McKay's documenting of other people's radical and nonconformist sexual and social lived experiences appears in his fictional work and this literary identity is one of the most significant aspects of his queer life; as Holcomb states, 'the current language of queer counterhegemony may be traced to its origins in the 1920s' and 'some of the earliest expressions of queer counterspeech are present in McKay's black radical leftist writings'.[12]

Political, queer and creative beginnings

McKay was born in 1890 in the Clarendon Parish of Jamaica, the youngest child of a small farming family. In his childhood, McKay lived for several years with his brother Uriah Theodore, a schoolteacher who became responsible for his education. McKay developed an interest in reading literature, particularly English literature, including works by Charles Dickens, Walter Scott and William Shakespeare, as well as the writings of freethinkers such as Annie Besant.[13] McKay began to write poetry, though initially his career was coupled to a trade scholarship which was to be spent in Kingston. He was unable to continue his education when the school was destroyed in the 1907 earthquake and instead McKay apprenticed himself to a tradesman in Brown's Town, where he stayed for two years.[14] Particularly inspired by everyday life and people in Jamaica, his 1909 poem 'Hard Times' explored Jamaica's poverty and exploitation. This was included in his 1912 book *Songs of Jamaica*.[15]

Throughout his apprenticeship, McKay continued writing poetry and it was at the tradesman's shop that he met Walter Jekyll, an English migrant who helped arrange the publication of *Songs of Jamaica*.[16] Jekyll had a deep interest in the folk cultures of Jamaica and England. When he met McKay, Jekyll had just published his edited collection *Jamaican Song and Story: Annancy Stories, Digging Sings, Ring Tunes and Dancing Tunes*, with the Folk-lore Society.[17] Jekyll and McKay began to correspond about poetry through which a friendship developed. For a short time McKay moved to Kingston and joined the police force, a career he disliked but one which enabled him to live in the city. Here McKay studied in Jekyll's library, reading works by Shelley, Keats, Dante, Leopardi and Baudelaire.[18] Gosciak has recently explored how McKay's admiration for Victorian writers has been neglected in historical analyses of his work and life. One result of this absence is that the particularities of McKay's life in a British colony, British colonialism, and its intersections with literary 'Englishness' have often been marginalized.[19] This is a reminder that writing about 'queer London' includes writing about, and researching beyond, the boundaries (lived and archival) of London; for London includes those whose lives were influenced by and lived within empires, diasporas, political communities – at city, transregional and transnational scales. Londoners were not bounded in their personal geographies. This transnational identity proved to be one of the main reasons for the deep disappointment McKay later experienced when living in London, where he was confronted with the reality of his racialized existence as a black person in the imperial metropole, as opposed to the romantic imaginative geographies of England shaped by his reading of English literature in Jamaica.

Soon after leaving the police, McKay published his first books of poetry, *Songs of Jamaica* and *Constab Ballads* (both 1912).[20] Cooper argues that 'these early poems can be read today as autobiography, as social documents of historical value, and as linguistic and artistic creations of pioneering importance in the development of modern West Indian literature'.[21] These works reached an international audience and were celebrated within Jamaica; in December 1912, the Board of Governors of the Jamaica Institute awarded 'the Musgrave Medal to Mr. Claude McKay for his verses in native dialect'.[22] *Songs of Jamaica* contained fifty poems reflecting the political and socio-economic experiences of the everyday lives of Jamaicans, while *Constab Ballads* reflected on McKay's experiences as a policeman.[23] These books built upon his earlier poems published in Jamaican periodicals, primarily in the *Gleaner*. McKay's use of creole in his early poetry, starting from the 1909 'Hard Times', was something he decided to pursue more often after discussions with Jekyll. He recalled Jekyll saying, 'this is the real thing. The Jamaica dialect has never been put into literary form except in my Annancy stories. Now is your chance as a native boy to put the Jamaica dialect into literary language. I am sure your poems will sell out'. McKay recalled being initially 'not very enthusiastic' about Jekyll's statement because the Colonial education in Jamaica had designated the 'Jamaican dialect' as 'vulgar', but then he began seriously thinking about it and 'as I knew so many pieces in the dialect, which were based on our local songs of the draymen, the sugar mills, and the farm lands, I decided to do some poems in dialect', and so 'I had the consolation of having done my share in helping to preserve the dialect in written form'.[24]

The relationship between Jekyll and McKay was a complex one, which can be characterized as a queer friendship. Their relationship, based on literature and a love of horticulture, surfaced in homosocial affection and in their participating in non-heteronormative intellectual spaces. Cooper argues that McKay 'once indirectly suggest[ed] that Jekyll introduced him to the reality and to the moral legitimacy of homosexual love'.[25] In a 1918 essay in *Pearson's Magazine*, McKay reflected upon Jekyll's influence on his career and the various authors they read and discussed; as Cooper observes, 'he significantly grouped together Oscar Wilde, Edward Carpenter, and Walt Whitman'.[26] During this time, McKay's poetry speaks to an imagined or experienced queer romantic homosocial/homosexual intimacy with Bennie, a police officer colleague. This intense queer relationship between Bennie and McKay (or McKay's fictional narrator) is told within three poems published in 1912: two in *Constab Ballads* and one in *Songs of Jamaica*. In *Songs of Jamaica*, the poem 'To Bennie (In Answer to a Letter)' promises his love 'burns as of old' and nothing can sever their friendship.[27] In *Constab Ballads*, 'Bennie's Departure', described by William J. Maxwell as 'McKay's most pointedly homoerotic poem', tells the story of their meeting, working together, the narrator's love for Bennie and his pain at Bennie leaving the police depot. This poem was then followed with 'Consolation' where he again reflected on the pain of Bennie's leaving.[28]

McKay left Jamaica in 1912, aged 21, to study agriculture in the United States, but instead continued with poetry and carried out a number of short-term low-paid jobs before moving to New York. McKay initially lived in the South where he experienced the shocking racism of Jim Crow. While studying in Kansas, his political ideas, present in his Jamaican poetry, developed into something more radical, influenced by W.E.B. Du Bois's *The Souls of Black Folk* (1903), which he read at Topeka Public Library. At the end of his time in Kansas, McKay received a gift of a few thousand dollars, probably from Jekyll.[29] With this McKay moved to New York and married his Jamaican girlfriend, Eulalie Imelda Lewars, during a time when, according to Cooper, 'McKay had yet to come to terms with himself, his ambitions, and his personal sexual inclinations.'[30] He soon separated from his wife and Lewars moved back to Jamaica where she gave birth to their child, Rhue Hope McKay.[31]

New York, in particular Harlem, had a significant effect on McKay. During this time he joined the black socialist organization, the African Blood Brotherhood, and explored his queer sexuality, having 'brief but passionate affairs' with men and women.[32] He continued writing and though he did not want to be defined as a poet who dealt only with race, his poems on race were a significant articulation of his identity, reflecting on racism, colonialism, and the experiences of being a person of African heritage living in countries saturated with racial discrimination.[33] By 1917, he was published in *Seven Arts*, using the pseudonym Eli Edwards.[34] McKay's poem 'The Harlem Dancer' was, as Gosciak argues, one of the first poems to explore Harlem 'as a geographic site of cultural performance and oppression.'[35] In 1918, *Pearson's Magazine* published five of his poems with an autobiographical section on McKay's life and career. In this, McKay expressed his opposition to the war and in 1920 he reflected 'perhaps ten years hence the white peoples will realize what the war has done to their civilization'.[36]

Throughout 1919, before his arrival in London, McKay worked on the railroads, living through racialized insecurities and fears heightened by the racist riots which broke out in the United States (and Britain) that year.[37] Working as a waiter on the railroads and travelling through different cities, McKay remembered the intense fear he and others felt. That year, the *Liberator* published seven poems of McKay's, which included the influential 'If We Must Die'.[38] The poem was, and is, cited by many as articulating the pain and feelings of black people being targeted by racist violence, and concludes: 'Like men we'll face the murderous, cowardly pack / Pressed to the wall, dying, but fighting back!'[39] McKay's time on the railroads also initiated his personal identifications with a global geography of black, international working-class men; these homosocial bonds of black transnational community have been analysed by Michelle Stephens.[40]

Politics and the 'colour bar' in London

McKay moved to London through a chance opportunity but with a specific aim to publish a book of poetry.[41] His experiences in the city were complex; he contributed to literary and political radical writing and publishing in London. He also formed a number of friendships, perhaps the most significant being with Charles Kay Ogden, a Cambridge academic, linguist, editor and writer, who was one of the 'Heretics'. Ogden founded the society as an undergraduate and it developed into a dynamic intellectual forum.[42] Ogden also worked in assisting the publication of McKay's next book of poetry.[43] They wrote to one another frequently during this time on subjects including linguistics and art, and they visited the British Museum together and attended classical concerts and exhibitions including the Chelsea Book Club Negro Art exhibition of 1920.[44] The pair also attended the 1917 Club, located close to Ogden's Soho flat. McKay's ideas on England, however, radically altered after experiencing the realities of British racism, including the colour bar in many of London's hotels and social clubs. In his memoirs, McKay painfully recalled the colour bar preventing him finding accommodation near to the British Museum; he had wanted to stay close to the Museum's reading room where he spent much of his time reading and drafting work.

Though eventually exasperated by the paper, much of his London experience centred on working alongside the radical activist Sylvia Pankhurst on her socialist newspaper *The Workers' Dreadnought*. He joined the Workers' Socialist Federation, which produced the newspaper, and helped edit and run the paper along with contributing his own articles. His April 1920 article, 'A Black Man Replies', was a refutation of the sexual racism of E.D. Morel's 'Horrors on the Rhine' article published in George Lansbury's newspaper the *Daily Herald*.[45] Morel's article 'Black Scourge in Europe: Sexual Horror Let Loose', was a racist polemic on black soldiers being stationed in post-war Germany, filled with racist ideas of the sexual 'savagery' and 'primitivism' of Africans. McKay asked in his reply, 'why all this obscene, maniacal outburst about the sex vitality of black men in a proletarian paper?'[46] Other articles focused on subjects including the experiences of dockers – of all ethnicities – as well as socialism, racism and Garveyism, the movement founded by Jamaican Marcus Garvey. In a January 1920 *Dreadnought* article entitled 'Socialism and the Negro', published under his own name, McKay considered racism, capitalism and black nationalism alongside W.E.B. Du Bois and the NAACP (National Association for the Advancement of Colored People), arguing that '[i]f our Negro professionals are not blindly ignorant they should realise that there will never be any hope – no sound material place in the economic life of the world for them until the Negro masses are industrially independent.'[47] These articles were based on meeting a wide range of activists as well as dock workers in East London. One article he helped to publish, penned by a Royal Navy sailor called Springhall under the pseudonym S.000 (Gunner) and called 'Discontent on the Lower Deck', prompted a police raid on the *Dreadnought*'s offices. Pankhurst, who refused to name McKay as being involved in the publication or reveal that he was the author of the 'The Yellow Peril and the Dockers' (another piece targeted by the police), was convicted of publishing seditious articles and sentenced to imprisonment.[48]

McKay also published poetry in the *Dreadnought*, the first, published before he began working there, being reprints from the *Liberator*, including 'If We Must Die'.[49] Thereafter he published, under various pseudonyms, fiercely political, radical poems in the *Dreadnought* on the experiences of the marginalized, on racism, capitalism, and struggles against oppression. These included the poem 'Battle', published under his pseudonym Hugh Hope, where he wrote about a dream of his demise and mused on the fight against imperial power.[50] His activities tied to the paper, including the people he met while working there and those he interviewed for stories, were a significant constituent of his political and social life during his time in Britain. His radical poems and articles are generally, with the exception of his reply to E.D. Morel and his article on 'Socialism and the Negro', published using pseudonyms. His non-political poems, however, including the poem 'Summer Morn in New Hampshire', were published in the *Dreadnought* using his own name.[51] This division represents the careful way in which he negotiated his newly formed career in London-based radical Communism with his career as a poet. However, his radicalism and poetry cannot and were not completely divorced from one another and he did not seek this division. But as he feared, the *Dreadnought* was subject to police surveillance and so McKay's radicalism became more potentially dangerous and in need of protection during his short London stay.

Though not a Garveyite, McKay also wrote articles for Garvey's publication *Negro World* while in London. In the early 1920s, he supported the movement's radical politics as representing a transitional phase to Communism, stating in a January 1920 edition of the *Workers' Dreadnought* that 'although an international Socialist, I am supporting the movement, for I believe that for subject peoples, at least, Nationalism is the open door to Communism'.[52] In later years, Garvey condemned McKay's novel *Home to Harlem*, in the *Negro World*, including it within a general criticism of work arising from the Harlem Renaissance as 'under the direction of the white man...show[ing] up the worst traits of our people'.[53] *Home to Harlem* focused on black proletariat characters and stories of their sexual activity and sexuality in a manner much opposed by socially conservative intellectuals such as Du Bois, who wanted to celebrate and promote 'respectable' blackness. In a 1928 review of the book in *The Crisis*, Du Bois explained that he found the novel nauseating 'and after the dirtiest parts of its filth I feel distinctly like taking a bath'.[54] McKay's political radicalism was tied to his affinity with working class life in all its diversity – a long-standing public commitment which began with his early Jamaican poems about the lives of Jamaican working people and social, racial and economic inequality.

Poetry, friendship and the politics of race

On Gerrard Street, Soho, the 1917 Club was the haunt of various intellectuals, activists and writers.[55] Jane Marcus has argued, though 'the 1917 Club was a political haven for the Woolfs and other socialist members of Bloomsbury, it was not mixed racially and had none of the international camaraderie of the colored clubs McKay enjoyed'.[56] McKay sought to respond by organizing an exhibition at the 1917 of the works of his friend, the artist and anarchist Henry Bernard, but an incident at the club marred the possibilities for McKay. McKay reflected in a letter to Ogden, 'I thought it was rather embarrassing for you & Miss Olivier; for myself I didn't care – for I am always coming up against his type and worse – in America & also here, so I'm used to it. My colour alone makes me so conspicuous; I must reconcile myself to such things.'[57]

McKay's trip to London was in part supported by McKay's Dutch friend J.L.J.F. Ezerman, who financed the publication of *Spring in New Hampshire*. McKay met Ezerman in New York, where he had hired McKay to carry out research at the New York Public Library on 'the Negro'. The relationship between McKay and both Ezerman and Ogden, exhibited through their correspondence, was, as Gosciak argues, 'clearly homosexual in the coded patterns of the early twentieth century'.[58] Ezerman closely followed McKay's poetry and Gosciak maintains that 'Ezerman, like Walter Jekyll, was particularly taken with McKay's "sex-passion" sonnets, modeled on the earlier *Constab Ballads* and written in a suggestive style that was popular among the *fin-de-siècle* decadents.'[59] In a letter to Ogden, McKay recalled Ezerman's views on *Spring in New Hampshire*, writing '[m]y first letter referring to the book came from my friend in Holland and he is very, very pleased – although he regrets the exclusion of his double 4 sonnets! Being a powerfully sexed person who is ashamed of his passion he has sentimentalised ideas about that sort of stuff.'[60]

McKay's love poems, while not overtly political, were radical in several ways. His poetry was published in an environment of sexualized racism against black men, and McKay was explicitly exploring and sharing expressions of love to the wider world as a man of African-Caribbean heritage. McKay commented on the sexualized racism he and others had to contend with as a result of being a poet of African heritage who wished to write and talk about love, implicitly referencing Morel's sexualized racism. McKay recalled in his autobiography that a review of *Spring in New Hampshire* in the *Spectator* stated that 'Mr. Claude McKay never offends our sensibilities. His love poetry is clear of the hint which would put our racial instinct against him, whether we would or not.' 'So there it is again', McKay responded. He continued, 'As it was among the élite of the class-conscious working class, so it was among the aristocracy of the upper class: the bugaboo of sex – the African's sex, whether he is a poet or pugilist. Why should a Negro's love poetry be offensive to the white man, who prides himself on being modern and civilized?'[61] McKay's poems were radical in their discussions, musings and declarations of love, including queer love and 'transgressive' love. His love poem 'One Year After', published in *Harlem Shadows* a year after his return to the United States from London, can be read, as A.B. Christa Schwarz argues, 'as depicting the consequences of not only an acceptance but also an espousal of the powerful force that transgressive sexuality in a racial and/or homosexual context constitutes'.[62] In this poem, Howard J. Booth argues that 'as well as addressing race, [in] the references to "illicit wine" and life beyond "the bound of laws", we can see McKay using a language developed during the Renaissance for male-female love that fell foul of strong social and legal interdictions to address illegal homosexual sex'.[63]

Politics, friendship and radicalism

McKay's work with the *The Workers' Dreadnought* saw him document the lives of those affected by global capitalism, particularly sailors and soldiers from across the globe living and working in London's East End. These were the individuals McKay chose to socialize with and his friendships were built upon not just common kinship but also an internationalist identity of workers' struggles. McKay wrote about these friendships in articles he produced for the *Dreadnought*. In 'The Yellow Peril and the Dockers', which explores the effects of racism against Chinese dockworkers, he started by recalling his own experiences of the East End:

> A fortnight ago, three friends and I went down to visit a ship that had just arrived from the Argentine…We were met at the gate by an old pal who took us down to the hold of his ship, where we had breakfast à la creole, rice and corn meal and flour dumplings swimming in cocoanut oil, and thick, coarse, unadulterated cocoa made in native style with the fat floating on the top. It was a great meal, for years I had not tasted one like it; but it turned bitter in my mouth when I thought of the despairing crowd of men outside. Even the wretched life of my swarthy friends in the ships' bottoms was better than gnawing starvation ashore.[64]

McKay's two main haunts in London were the International Socialist Club and the Drury Lane Club, the latter a club for 'colored soldiers'. Reflecting on his time in London, McKay did not think that he could have survived his time in the capital without the 'freedom' provided by these two spaces – though having exposed the racist paternalism of the woman who ran the Drury Lane club in the *Negro World*, he spent most of his time at the International Socialist Club. This he described as a space 'full of excitement, with its dogmatists and doctrinaires of radical left ideas: Socialists, Communists, anarchists, syndicalists, one-big-unionists and trade unionists, soap-boxers, poetasters, scribblers, editors of little radical sheets which flourish in London'.[65] The International Socialist club was located in the East End, a significant space of interwar cosmopolitanism which was home to Eastern European Jewish and Irish migrants and many of the interwar London black working class who were employed in seaport trades. In *A Long Way From Home*, McKay reflects upon the men (he mentions no women) who he introduced to the International Socialist Club in Shoreditch:

> a mulatto sailor from Limehouse, a West Indian student from Oxford, a young black minister of the Anglican church, who was ambitious to have a colored congregation in London, a young West Indian doctor from Dulwich, three soldiers from the Drury lane club and a couple of boxers. The minister and the doctor did not make a second visit, but the others did.[66]

These same dockers, sailors and 'vagabonds' appear in his novels, though usually in locales such as France and the United States. *Home to Harlem*, however, does include reference to London docking life. In the first part of the novel, the protagonist, Jake, before travelling back to Harlem, works as a docker in the East End of London where 'he found friends. He found a woman. He was happy in the East End'; but Jake also witnessed the 1919 anti-black riots, where he 'saw a big battle staged between the colored and white men of London's East End. For three days his woman would not let him out-of-doors.'[67] Though women feature less prominently in his novels, there are several central women characters within them. McKay also socialized with women and Gosciak mentions his connections with radical lesbian women.[68]

McKay and Ogden both spent time at the ICS and McKay mentioned the club in a number of their letters. Before they arranged their first meeting to start work on McKay's book, McKay suggested the ISC as a meeting place, which was open between 12 pm and 12 am, but it was also 'quite a sordid place & there are no conveniences for private talk'.[69] Though he found good friends at the ISC and it became an important space for him, McKay experienced a painful episode of racism there too. He wrote to his friend Francine (who would marry his artist friend Frank Budgen) about the incident and that he would have to meet him 'in Committee about the charges I have made against him for trying to stir up race prejudice in the club'.[70] Later, in his autobiography, he reflected on the fear of surveillance at the club towards the end of his stay, and that 'the secretary showed me an anonymous letter he had received, accusing me of being a spy. I declare that I felt sick and was seized with a crazy craving to get quickly out of that atmosphere and far away from London.'[71]

For McKay, the East End of London, though providing a refuge from the elite bohemian space of the 1917, also had a geography of isolation and fear. He experienced overt racist violence in East London, both against himself and against others who worked in the shipping industry, as he documented in *The Workers' Dreadnought*. In a letter to Ogden, explaining why he missed an invitation to the British Museum, he recalled the direct violence he experienced, though also the moments of solidarity he experienced through friendship:

Were it not for some white friends I should have been badly mauled in Limehouse a fortnight ago & last Monday I was the chief actor in a near tragedy at the Old St. tube station. I was walking home from the Socialist Club with a young Serbian & just as we said goodbye a drunken South African soldier (discharged) came up to me and asked whether I came from Basutoland or some other place. I answered no & tried to pass but he held me up, got hold of my tie, & was rather threatening. Of course I know what the average S.A. white thinks of the blacks & what was evidently working in his sodden brain so I thought quickly & sent him sprawling to the street. Instantly a little mob gathered round me, but some friends of mine from the club came along & two policeman who perceived what was happening so drove them off. Had there been no help they wouldn't have reached me though as I would have dived into the tube immediately after hitting out. One must always be on one's guard. Since then, until to-night, I have been sleeping with a friend over West; so the incident is really the cause of my missing your letter & interesting afternoon with you. So soon as I can find a suitable place I will move back to the West side for its a little safer there.[72]

Black histories of queer London

McKay's time in London was complex; alongside surveillance, fear, racism and violence, he established significant and positive friendships and achieved his aim of publishing a collection of poetry while maintaining and developing his interest in radical left wing politics. Unpacking how these experiences intersected with his understanding of his sexualized identity holds many of the complexities of coded and opaque readings of archival works with which many of those researching queer London contend. However, if we are to unpack the 'freedom' that bohemian and queer spaces, such as central London clubs or working-class spaces in the East End, held for McKay, his sexual identity cannot be uncoupled from his experiences of racism in the city which had held so much promise for him before he arrived. However, the geographies of identity of the black men with whom McKay socialized remain, for now, deeply embedded within the archive. Were the black soldiers, boxers and colonial soldiers to whom he refers part of a black queer network 'of public and commercial sociability', providing an opportunity for McKay to tap into sites of 'vibrant, extensive and diverse queer urban culture'?[73] What might their stories be and how might geographies of black queer London differ and overlap with those of other queer communities in inter-war London with sensitivity to how 'race' made queer blackness visible in certain spaces in ways other queer communities were not? And what of black lesbian women? How are their many and undoubtedly diverse stories to be uncovered and integrated into the histories of queer London? It is ironic that McKay's feeling of conspicuousness in regards to race and also, perhaps, queerness, is obscured in the archives. However, as with uncovering many diverse or marginal experiences in the archives, a reading 'against the grain' provides us with an understanding of the way in which McKay's queer black life was experienced, formed and articulated, even if we do not have access to all the biographical details of this queer black life.

Notes

1   Maroula Joannou, 'Nancy Cunard's English Journey', *Feminist Review* 78 (2004), pp. 141–63, 151.

2   Claude McKay to C.K. Ogden, 25 February 1920, The Charles Kay Ogden Archive, McMaster University. See Winston James's exploration of the symbolism and meaning behind McKay's poem 'Old England' in Winston James, *A Fierce Hatred of Injustice: Claude McKay's Jamaica and His Poetry of Rebellion* (London: Verso, 2000), pp. 95–6.

3   Josh Gosciak, *The Shadowed Country: Claude McKay and the Romance of the Victorians* (New Brunswick, NJ: Rutgers University Press, 2006), p. 14.

4   Judith Walkowitz, *Nights Out: Life in Cosmopolitan London* (New Haven, CT: Yale University Press, 2012).

5   Matt Houlbrook, *Queer London: Perils and Pleasures in the Sexual Metropolis, 1918–1957* (Chicago, IL: Chicago University Press, 2005), p. 3; Claude McKay to C.K. Ogden, 2 April 1920, Charles Kay Ogden Archive, McMaster University. Letter from Claude McKay to C.K. Ogden, 2 April 1920 is used with the permission of the Literary Estate for the Works of Claude McKay.

6   Gary Edward Holcomb, *Claude McKay, Code Name Sasha: Queer Black Marxism and the Harlem Renaissance* (Gainesville: University Press of Florida, 2007), p. 12.

7   Ibid., p. 33.

8   Wayne F. Cooper, *Claude McKay: Rebel Sojourner in the Harlem Renaissance: A Biography* (Baton Rouge, LA: Louisiana State University Press, 1987; paperback 1996).

9   Cited in ibid., p. 129.

10 Holcomb, *Claude McKay*, p. 12, original emphasis.

11 Nadia Ellis, 'Black Migrants, White Queers and the Archive of Inclusion in Postwar London', *Interventions: International Journal of Postcolonial Studies* 17.6 (2015), pp. 893–915.

12 Ibid., p. 12.

13 Biographical information on McKay comes from Cooper, *Claude McKay*, p. 15.

14 Ibid., p. 22.

15 Gosciak, *The Shadowed Country*, pp. 59–60. The first verse of 'Hard Times' states 'De mo-me wuk, de mo' time hard, I don't know what fe do; I ben' me knee an' pray to Gahd, Yet t'ings same as befo'. In Claude McKay and William J. Maxwell, *Complete Poems* (Urbana: University of Illinois Press, 2004; paperback 2008), p. 41.

16 Cooper, *Claude McKay*, p. 24.

17 *Jamaican Song and Story: Annancy Stories, Digging Sings, Ring Tunes and Dancing Tunes, Collected and Edited by Walter Jekyll* (London: Pub. for the Folk-lore Society by D. Nutt, 1907).

18 Claude McKay, *A Long Way from Home* (London: Pluto Press, 1985), p. 13.

19 Gosciak, *The Shadowed Country*, pp. 17–18.

20 Cooper, *Claude McKay*, p. 35.

21 Ibid., p. 36.

22 *The Gleaner*, 7 December 1912, p. 13. This medal was named after Sir Anthony Musgrave, a former governor of Jamaica and the founder of the Institute of Jamaica for the Encouragement of Literature, Science and Art in Jamaica.

23 Cooper, *Claude McKay*, p. 36.

24 Claude McKay, 'Boyhood in Jamaica', *Phylon* 14.2 (1953), pp.134–45, 142; and Claude McKay to C. K. Ogden, 12 March 1920, Charles Kay Ogden Archive, McMaster University.

25 Cooper, *Claude McKay*, p. 30.

26 Ibid., p. 30.

27 McKay and Maxwell, *Complete Poems*, p. 82.

28 Ibid., p. 296.

29 Cooper, *Claude McKay*, p. 70.

30 Ibid., p. 70–1.

31 Ibid., p. 73.

32 Ibid., p. 75.

33 Ibid., p. 78.

34 This pseudonym was based on his mother's name. See Cooper, *Claude McKay*, pp. 81–2.

35 Gosciak, *The Shadowed Country*, p. 11.

36 McKay to Ogden, 25 February 1920, The Charles Kay Ogden Archive, McMaster University.

37 On the 1919 race riots in Britain, see Jacqueline Jenkinson, *Black 1919: Riots, Racism and Resistance in Imperial Britain* (Liverpool: Liverpool University Press, 2009).

38 Cooper, *Claude McKay*, p. 99.

39 McKay and Maxwell, *Complete Poems*, pp. 177–8.

40 Michelle Stephens cited in Nadia Ellis, 'The Eclectic Generation: Caribbean Literary Criticism at the Turn of the Twenty-First Century', in Michael Bucknor and Alison Donnell (eds), *The Routledge Companion to Anglophone Caribbean Literature* (Abingdon, Oxon: Routledge, 2011), p. 140. See Michelle A. Stephens, *Black Empire: The Masculine Global Imaginary of*

Caribbean Intellectuals in the United States, 1914–1962 (Durham, NC: Duke University Press, 2005).

41   Claude McKay to C.K. Ogden, 18 February 1920, Charles Kay Ogden Archive, McMaster University.

42   John Forrester explains that 'The Heretics Society was founded in Cambridge by undergraduate C. K. Ogden in 1909 and soon developed into the most adventurous forum for intellectual debate in Cambridge until its demise in 1930. The Cambridge Magazine was started in 1912 by Ogden as an extension of the Heretics.' John Forrester, 'The English Freud: W.H.R. Rivers, Dreaming, and the Making of the Early Twentieth-Century Human Sciences', in Sally Alexander and Barbara Taylor (eds), *History and Psyche: Culture, Psychoanalysis, and the Past* (New York: Palgrave Macmillan, 2012), p. 78.

43   Claude McKay, *Spring in New Hampshire and Other Poems* (London: Grant Richards, 1920).

44   Jane Marcus, *Hearts of Darkness: White Women Write Race* (New Brunswick, NJ: Rutgers University Press, 2004), p. 54.

45   Winston James, 'A Race Outcast from an Outcast Class: Claude McKay's experience and analysis of Britain', in Bill Schwarz (ed.), *West Indian Intellectuals in Britain* (Manchester: Manchester University Press, 2003), pp. 71–92.

46   Claude McKay, 'A Black Man Replies', *The Workers' Dreadnought*, 24 April 1920. On this see Letter from George Lansbury to Maude Royden, 16 April 1920, papers of Agnes Maude Royden Women's Library Collection and Wayne Cooper and Robert C. Reinders. 'A Black Briton Comes "Home": Claude McKay in England, 1920', *Race & Class* 9.1 (1967): 67–83.

47   Claude McKay, 'Socialism and the Negro', *The Workers' Dreadnought*, 31 January 1920.

48   Barbara Winslow, *Sylvia Pankhurst: Sexual Politics and Political Activism* (London: Routledge, 2004; first published 1996), pp. 128–30.

49   Gosciak, *The Shadowed Country*, pp. 105–6.

50   Hugh Hope (pseudonym for Claude McKay), 'Battle', *The Workers' Dreadnought*, 9 October 1920, p. 5.

51   Claude McKay, 'Summer Morn in New Hampshire', *The Workers' Dreadnought*, 21 July 1920.

52   McKay, 'Socialism and the Negro'.

53   Cited in Robert A. Hill (ed.), General Introduction to The Marcus Garvey and UNIA papers, Volume 1, p. iv.

54   Cited in William J. Maxwell, 'Banjo Meets the Dark Princess: Claude McKay, W.E.B. Du Bois, and the transnational novel of the Harlem Renaissance', in *The Cambridge Companion to the Harlem Renaissance* (Cambridge: Cambridge University Press, 2007), pp. 170–83, 170.

55   Jean Mills, 'The Writer, the Prince and the Scholar: Virginia Woolf, D. S. Mirsky, and Jane Harrison's Translation from Russian of *The Life of the Archpriest Avvakum, by Himself* – a Revaluation of the Radical Politics of

the Hogarth Press', in Helen Southworth (ed.), *Leonard and Virginia Woolf, the Hogarth Press and the Networks of Modernism* (Edinburgh: Edinburgh University Press, 2010), p. 160.

56 Marcus, *Hearts of Darkness*, pp. 54–5.

57 Claude McKay to C.K. Ogden, 2 April 1920, Charles Kay Ogden Archive, McMasterUniversity.

58 Gosciak, *The Shadowed Country*, p. 118.

59 Ibid., pp. 117–18. Gosciak states that these sonnets, termed 'sex-passion' by Ezerman in a letter from him to McKay on 18 June 1920, 'might have been poems written about Exerman or homoerotic pieces in *Constab Ballads*'. Ibid., p. 178, n. 92.

60 Claude McKay to C.K. Ogden, 9 October 1920, The Charles Kay Ogden Archive, McMaster University.

61 McKay, *A Long Way From Home*, pp. 88–9.

62 A. B. Christa Schwarz, *Gay Voices of the Harlem Renaissance* (Bloomington: Indiana University Press, 2003), p. 95.

63 Howard J. Booth, 'Claude McKay in Britain: Race, Sexuality and Poetry', in Len Platt (ed.), *Modernism and Race* (Cambridge: Cambridge University Press, 2011), pp. 137–55, 147.

64 Leon Lopez (pseudonym for Claude McKay), 'The Yellow Peril and the Dockers', *The Workers' Dreadnought*, 16 October 1920.

65 McKay, *A Long Way From Home*, p. 68.

66 Ibid., p. 70.

67 Claude McKay, *Home to Harlem* (Boston: Northeastern University Press, 1987; first published 1927), pp. 6–7.

68 Gosciak, *The Shadowed Country*, p. 106. Presently, we do not know the names of these women.

69 Claude McKay to C. K. Ogden, 25 February 1920, Charles Kay Ogden Archive, McMaster University.

70 Cooper, *Claude McKay*, pp. 130–1.

71 McKay, *A Long Way from Home*, pp. 86–7.

72 Claude McKay to C.K. Ogden, 2 April 1920, Charles Kay Ogden Archive, McMaster University.

73 Houlbrook, *Queer London*, p. 3. Research for this chapter was undertaken as part of 'Drawing over the Colour Line: Geographies of art and cosmopolitan politics in London 1919 – 1939' funded by the AHRC AH/I027371/1.

CHAPTER NINE

The British Society of the Study of Sex Psychology: 'Advocating the Culture of Unnatural and Criminal Practices'?

Lesley A. Hall

A meeting at the Hotel Cecil in the Strand in Central London on 12 August 1913, chaired by the German sexologist Magnus Hirschfeld, brought together an all-male group interested in homosexual law reform, and informally inaugurated what became the British Society for the Study of Sex Psychology (BSSSP). This set out to advance an agenda based on the writings of Edward Carpenter and Havelock Ellis, and the inspiration of continental writers and activists such as Hirschfeld. Several historians have explored London as a metropolitan site facilitating the development of a covert subculture of illicit male sexual interactions, but it was also a place, one of the few, where the claims for changes in the law and social attitudes being discussed at this meeting could be openly articulated. It is highly improbable that such a group could have come together anywhere else than London, or an equivalently large and metropolitan, even cosmopolitan, city. A conurbation needs to reach a certain critical mass for there to be enough people who are interested in a marginalized subject regarded as morally dubious to form a viable group, and to have the kinds of spaces available to provide a meeting place for such groups. The anonymity of a large city also more readily enables the establishment of associations with interests which the majority may regard with some suspicion: there is less chance of being identified by one's next-door neighbour going to and from meetings if those meetings are a good bus, tram or tube ride away from home. There were provincial members of the BSSSP, but the correspondence it received from them, and the endeavours to set up local groups, suggest that, however supportive of its aims, they felt a little short-changed.[1]

This chapter considers the role of the BSSSP in changing attitudes towards homosexuality in the UK before the Second World War, a period during which homosexuality was illegal and the laws against it, which paid no regard to mitigating circumstances of privacy, consent or legal adulthood, were considered a 'blackmailer's charter'. Being homosexual was widely stigmatized and alluded to in derogatory terms. In this pervasively hostile ambience it was eccentric, to say the least, to suggest that the homosexual was not an evil degenerate and sinner. It was a considerable risk even to suggest that he might be deserving of humane treatment. However, as John Stuart Mill famously observed, 'the crotchet of to-day, the crotchet of one generation, becomes the truth of the next and the truism of the one after'.[2]

The Society itself may appear peripheral and obscure, and its members were perceived, and may even have perceived themselves, as weirdo eccentrics. Lytton Strachey, after attending a meeting of the Society, described them to Virginia Woolf as having the appearance of 'a third variety of human being'. 'Hairless perverts with twitching lips', fumed American educational psychologist Homer Lane, an invited speaker.[3] Gilbert Murray was alleged to have 'gibed that sex reform seems to be "a sort of disinterested enthusiasm for sexual misconduct in all its forms, from obscene language to unnatural vice"'.[4] Nonetheless, more than a few of the Society's members made a mark in various fields, and several feature in standard works of reference such as the *Oxford Dictionary of National Biography* – see, for example, the entry on George Ives.[5] Cranky eccentrics they may have been, but they cannot be dismissed as a bunch of seedy losers.

It can be considered a 'queer' organization in more than just its homophile agenda. The Society itself and the kind of person who belonged to it were also perceived as 'queer' in the contemporary colloquial meaning of peculiar, eccentric, failing to conform to current standards of conventionality. It was a (relatively) open organization for both sexes, enabling frank debates that the public might attend. This engendered a 'queering' approach to the discussion of sexuality by destabilizing existing assumptions about who might talk about sexual questions, in what context, and how they might do it. Possibly its juxtaposition of topics apparently dissimilar but sharing in perceptions of being 'unnatural' and controversial also served this purpose. The attitude was very much one of enquiry and investigation rather than authority and certainty: the Australian doctor Norman Haire, who joined in 1920, was disappointed to discover that 'most of the people were enquirers on the same plane as myself', not figures 'at whose feet I might sit and drink in wisdom'.[6]

Group discussion of sexual matters taking a scientific approach was not entirely new but had previously been part of a male homosocial culture emphasizing discretion beyond the cohesive in-group. A body such as the Cannibal Club, the inner circle of the Anthropological Society, a dining club founded by Sir Richard Burton, was a members-only purlieu of elite males. Lisa Sigel has characterized the members' interests as combining 'imperialism, sadism, and sexism'. While using the rhetoric of science to legitimize their interests, they constituted a closed coterie within which it was possible to explore the liminal space between scientific study and pornography, in particular pruriently observing the racialized Other. They had no commitment to openness or generating wider debate: their publications appeared under pseudonyms (for fear of prosecution under the obscenity laws) or in limited editions, and the club kept no records.[7]

Tentative discussions of homosexuality took place among British psychiatrists in the later nineteenth century. However, these occurred within clearly demarcated professional environments and were regarded as unsuited for a general audience. In fact, Ivan Crozier, in his analysis of these discussions, characterizes the general approach as 'cautious, conservative and internalist'. Even though British psychiatrists might be reading the works of Continental sexologists, unlike them they were not, it seems, intersecting with the work of reformers or engaging with self-aware homosexuals who did not necessarily define themselves within terms of pathologization.[8] Their deliberations seem remote from the activities of the rather marginalized group of medical men (and others) who were trying more generally during the later nineteenth century to investigate the mysteries of sex and elucidate its problems.[9] The more general attitude within the British medical profession was delineated by Dr Ethilda Meakin Herford (who would go on to have significant connections with the BSSSP). She had discovered during her early years as a doctor that 'subjects and conditions causing the profoundest misery in married life' were absent from the medical curriculum and never discussed. However, when attending the social events associated with medical congresses, at which women were still rare, she was astounded by 'the prominent place given to these matters as a subject of laughter and jest'.[10]

Countering this mindset was indeed subversive, and during the early decades of the twentieth century there arose certain spaces within which productive interactions between homophile reformers and members of the medical profession, mainly in the area of psychiatry, could occur. These, unlike the closeted case-presentations of elite psychiatrists, the smutty homosociality of the Cannibal Club, or the bawdy jesting of unbuttoned doctors, had a significant and growing influence on increasing societal toleration towards homosexuality, and even some impact on ameliorating the rigours of legal policy prior to actual law reform.

A number of individual writers had set the ball of reform rolling during the later decades of the nineteenth century. As early as 1883, John Addington Symonds had produced a limited edition pamphlet for private circulation on *A Problem in Greek Ethics* (invoking the cultural respect for classical antiquity), followed in 1890 by *A Problem in Modern Ethics*. In 1892, Havelock Ellis wrote to his friend Edward Carpenter concerning his projected work on *Sexual Inversion* in collaboration with Symonds, stating that 'We want to obtain sympathetic recognition for sexual inversion as a psychic abnormality which may be regarded as the highest ideal, and to clear away many vulgar errors – preparing the way, if possible, for a change in the law.'[11] Carpenter was engaged in a similar project with his own essay on homogenic love in a free society, his inclusion of a chapter on same-sex relationships in the later editions of his influential book *Love's Coming of Age* (1896), his study *The Intermediate Sex* (1909), and the anthology *Iolaus: An Anthology of Friendship* (1902).

These pioneering steps took place at a time when the problem had burst upon public knowledge through the medium of the Cleveland Street Scandal of 1889–90, and the media circus of the successive trials of Oscar Wilde in 1895. Of the latter, a despairing correspondent wrote to Edward Carpenter that 'the late miserable trial resulted in an expression of most horrible opinion all over London…it seems as if the whole affair had set the world back fifty years'.[12] Carpenter himself wrote to Havelock Ellis in more optimistic vein, claiming that 'I find all this stir has roused up the Urning community and pulled it tog[ethe]r. a good deal.'[13] However, later the same year Carpenter's publisher, after a period of vacillation, refused to publish Carpenter's volume on sex: 'I think there is no doubt that the H.L. [Homogenic Love] pamphlet upset his applecart – and I daresay he has heard talk going on at the clubs wh[ich] alarmed him.'[14]

These works provided great inspiration and encouragement to those who identified themselves as among the group being described, as well as providing more general enlightenment.[15] Ellis wrote to Carpenter in 1918, commenting on the effects of their writings over a period of some twenty years:

> The process of evangelising intermediate folk seems to go on regularly and steadily. At almost regular intervals they write or call mysteriously and unexpectedly. Either they read your book and want mine, or they read mine and of course I put them on to yours…I heard from a man of nearly 40 who has only just now found the clue to his mystery by reading your book.[16]

Besides these virtual relationships mediated through texts and correspondence, George Ives founded the homophile Order of Chaeronea during the 1890s, but this was a secretive organization specifically for homosexuals, about which little information survives even among Ives's own papers.

A perhaps overlooked precursor for the British Society for the Study of Sex Psychology was the radical and shocking feminist journal *The*

Freewoman, published during 1912 before it mutated into the literary periodical *The Egoist*, to which a number of the eventual founders and early members of the BSSSP had contributed. As contributor and eventual editor Rebecca West remarked, 'the greatest service' it performed was 'through its unblushingness', mentioning 'sex loudly and clearly and repeatedly, and in the worst possible taste', and 'shatter[ing] the romantic conception of woman'. It 'even mentioned the existence of abnormalities of instinct'.[17] A Freewoman Discussion Circle began to meet in London to take the debates that had begun in the pages of the journal, especially in the vigorous exchanges in its correspondence columns, into a more immediate form. Besides the general meetings, which were controversial enough, on topics such as divorce and birth control, a smaller group came together for the more informal exchange of ideas on 'Sex Oppression and the Way Out' (in an artist's studio in Chelsea, another area associated with bohemian artists and intellectuals).[18] It was probably as a result of the impact of *The Freewoman* that Laurence Housman was able to claim to his friend Janet Ashbee in 1913 that '[i]t is wonderful how open to a free discussion of everything I now find women – suffragist women I mean...even in the last two years the advance has been immense; and between now and six years ago it is as if a century had intervened'.[19]

Situating a space for queer conversations

There was something particularly significant about the specific urban spaces within the wider context of the metropolis with which the BSSSP was identified. As with most large cities, specific areas had distinctive characters of their own. Many of the Society's meetings were held in Bloomsbury and its office and library were finally established in Bloomsbury Square, which seems peculiarly appropriate to the organization's aims and self-positioning. The Society intended to facilitate discussion and interrogation rather than engage in lobbying. Its activities were envisaged as 'the reading of papers in agreement with the general objects' and the issue of occasional pamphlets, while collecting data 'on matters within the scope of the Society'. The image aimed for, according to Carpenter's good friend E.B. Lloyd, was 'serious stodgy [and] scientific':[20] a base in bohemian Soho or Fitzrovia would have had quite unsuitably raffish connotations. Although the 1917 Club, the politically radical club named for the advent of revolution in Russia with 'all [its] little girls...who used to run about talking about libidos and orgasm', found its home in Gerrard Street in the heart of Soho, this would not have done for the BSSSP.[21] Bloomsbury, home to numerous academic institutions and societies, struck the right note of seriousness, while also being central and accessible. At the period in question, it had probably not yet acquired the associations generated by the network of intricately connected friends and lovers who became known as 'the Bloomsbury Group', but it is significant that the individuals who became part of this coterie were based there and already breaking down their inherited Victorian taboos on what might be discussed between the sexes and how in conversation with one another. A subsidiary base of operations for the Society was Hampstead, an area already strongly associated with a liberal-minded intelligentsia, as well as the pioneering experiment in urban development for class diversity, Hampstead Garden Suburb. It was a frequent location for committee meetings in members' homes.

The Society's stated aims were to promote 'the consideration of problems and questions connected with sexual psychology from their medical, juridical and sociological aspects', especially '(1) The Evils of Prostitution (2) Inversion (3) Sexual Ignorance (4) Disease (5) Aberrations of various kinds'. Men and women members and officers would work 'together for a common understanding' upon 'matters which vitally concern both sexes'.[22] The inaugural general meeting of the Society on 8 July 1914 had the 'distinguished magistrate' Cecil Chapman in the chair, and an audience of sixty members and guests beside the ten committee members. George Ives recorded his 'joy [at] hearing a stipendiary magistrate…denounce the senselessness and cruelty of the sentences passed on inverts…Taboos, though the most terrible things to question, once really attacked must go down in the end. The difficulty is to *begin* the assault'.[23]

The Society produced an occasional series of pamphlets between 1914 and 1934, a fairly significant number of which dealt with topics relating to homosexuality: *The Social Problem of Sexual Inversion*, an abridged translation (by Cicely Hamilton) of a German treatise; *The Relation of Fellow-Feeling to Sex* by Laurence Housman; *The Morbid, the Abnormal and the Personal* by Harold Picton; *Psychological Causes of Homoerotism and Inversion* by H.D. Jennings White; Edward Carpenter's study of *Some Friends of Walt Whitman*; and Cecil Reddie's obituary tribute to Carpenter himself. These sold well and had considerable circulation, disseminating the Society's ideas well beyond its membership and bringing its very existence to the notice of interested individuals.[24] However, the project of founding a journal never got off the ground.[25]

Although homosexual rights were clearly of significant interest to the original founding members, from the outset the Society positioned the issue within a much broader reconceptualization of sexuality. On one hand, this could be taken as a strategic device and a means by which to construct potentially valuable alliances. Alternatively, it suggests a holistic perception that the stigma against homosexuality in contemporary society was profoundly imbricated within a range of other negative attitudes towards sexuality and gender prejudices, given that a man could admit that he shrank from the use of artificial contraception 'as from sodomy'.[26]

This vision was adumbrated in particular by the poet, novelist, dramatist, pacifist and male supporter of female suffrage, Laurence Housman.[27] He gently chided his friend and colleague George Ives in 1920 for being sometimes reluctant to see your friends striking against social injustice when it does not seem immediately to affect the Cause [i.e the cause of homosexual law reform]. But, as I see it, all injustice affects the cause: because where there is injustice there is not love: and love through all the community is the remedy, and would put an end to our wrong.[28]

This was clearly a continuing debate: a few years later, Housman wrote again to Ives about the problems of a single-issue approach, arguing that the difficulty with Ives' Order of Chaeronea, composed mainly, if not entirely, 'of those who are H.S.', was that it was 'necessarily secretive'. There was a danger that membership would tend to 'the curious and the specially affected', while the secretive and ritualistic nature of the Society would tend to deter 'many who are serving the cause'.[29]

It has been suggested that 'the concerns of male homosexuals' always dominated the Society, and among contemporaries there was a persistent impression that it 'concerned itself almost exclusively with the homosexual question'.[30] In fact, there was recurrent anxiety over too close an identification with homosexuality: a 1921 'publication' including the BSSSP among 'addresses...used as "rendezvous" by homosexuals' caused the committee distress. For example, an offer to include an account of the Society's work in Hirschfeld's *Jahrbuch für Sexuelle Zwischenstufen* in 1923 appeared to the committee 'to be in a list of societies interested in homosexuality'. They did not desire this, 'but would be pleased to be included in a list of those interested in Sex Psychology'.[31]

Members were aware that their enterprise could be regarded as dubious, leading to anxieties about becoming a 'happy hunting ground for Mayfair in search of "thrills"' ('Mayfair' here represented another aspect of London, that of sensation-loving 'high society'), or the prey of gutter journalists ('Fleet Street', yet another specific London site). There was worry about how to safeguard the Society from undesirables, and some committee members were even averse to the publication of their own names. '[G]roundless fears concerning "spies" and similar obsessions', and the subjection of candidates for membership to 'vexatious inquisition' persisted well up to the 1930s, irritating E. Lonsdale Deighton, the then Secretary, to the point of threatened resignation.[32] He wrote a long letter to fellow committee member Harold Clare Booth expressing his views:

[I]t is legitimate to press for modifications in the laws which at present bear unfairly on the invert. Such a course, however, need not be secret and unavowed – on the contrary, I think it most necessary that it should be entirely above board...I think you would be in agreement with me that the law needs amendment to bring it into conformity with present day knowledge of the innate condition of inversion.

... I decline to be a party to the Society being used in a subversive way to advance this matter otherwise than scientifically, impersonally and honestly.[33]

George Ives continued to fear that 'sensational journalist[s]' could damage the Society, when 'lectures of Dr X and old Dr G' had even 'surprised the committee'.[34] Other members, however, claimed to the contrary that '[t]wenty years ago the subject was much more tabu [sic]' and that this situation had eased.[35]

After the Society had been going for a decade or so, there was a perception that attitudes were changing, though even dedicated members were cautious in attributing this to the Society's own activities. Laurence Housman could not

> decide, in my own mind, how far the B.S.S.P. [sic] has itself been instrumental in helping to form a new public opinion...or whether it only started at the psychological moment. Anyway, it is quite certain that, *since* it started, the attitude toward sex-problems has greatly changed and improved: that what the B.S.S.P. set itself to do, as a *ventilator*, has actually been done: words and things are no longer taboo.[36]

Even the rather less sanguine Ives considered that things were improving: in 1928, he confided to his diary, 'But we *have* moved: Radclyffe Hall's book cd not have been even published 40 years back...Now a magistrate has called the book...obscene but it has many defenders.'[37]

Housman also perceived that 'freedom of discussion among the young, and the growing freedom from prejudice, are very marked'. While he doubted that the laws on homosexuality would be reformed in his lifetime (although he did survive, possibly the only founder member of the Society to do so, to see the publication of the Wolfenden Report, he died before the 1967 Act), he envisaged them becoming a dead letter except in cases of overt indiscretion:[38] 'on all sides...[there are] signs that the shackles are loosening'. He was also 'by correspondence and in other ways, peacefully penetrating certain minds – men of influence – in the matter of individual sex-freedom'.[39] Ives gained some cheer from the appearance of the word 'homosexual' in the supplement to the *Oxford English Dictionary*, writing to Havelock Ellis that '[t]his shows some progress in the popular attitude to the question. Formerly...we had only indecent words and associations for it.'[40]

The BSSSP seldom engaged in activism, consistent with its agenda of combining 'insistent investigation' with 'suspension of judgement'. However, in 1931, along with a great number of other individuals and groups, it protested against the severe sentence passed on Augustine Hull, the 'Liverpool man-woman'. Hull, a young working-class man who had been living as a woman since early adolescence and who would probably now be identified as trans rather than homosexual, had been sentenced to eighteen months hard labour under the laws relating to indecency between males, largely on evidence from another young man who had lived with Hull for six months but had not, he claimed, realized Hull's biological sex. The initial agitation against the 'iniquitous state of the law' this revealed originated with the barrister John Stevenson writing in *The Weekend Review* but the Society, and individuals within it, strongly supported protests to the Home Secretary and held a large meeting on the issue. The Home Secretary, however, seems to have been unmoved.[41] Ives was unsurprised: 'It will be a long road to obtain justice and freedom; strong and obvious as the case is. But we must keep on educating, and breaking the Taboo'. He was cynical about the petition, 'except that it calls attention to the problem'.[42]

Moving towards the mainstream

Another much more mainstream initiative occurred in the wake of the Hull case: the establishment of an Institute for the Scientific Treatment of Delinquency by a group of doctors, psychologists and psychoanalysts who believed that there were many instances (including homosexuality) in which existing punitive methods were ineffective, inhumane and counterproductive. This body was initially based within the West End Hospital for Nervous Diseases in Welbeck Street in Marylebone: if not actually in Harley Street, within its penumbra of medical respectability. In 1937, the Institute moved to independent premises in nearby Manchester Street and established its 'Psychopathic Clinic' in Portman Square.[43] This was therefore geographically a very different proposition to a talking shop in Bloomsbury. Unlike the BSSSP with its fears of 'Mayfair', the Institute undertook significant efforts to acquire aristocratic, distinguished and all-round respectable patrons. A Ladies Committee was established to undertake appeal work and organize charitable events. So reputable was the Institute that it even managed to get a radio appeal for support broadcast by the BBC, at that date under the puritanical rule of Director-General Lord Reith.[44]

While this body may at first simply appear to be a manifestation of the replacement of criminalization of homosexuality by its medicalization, and certainly the Institute was anxious to appear a reputable and medically sound organization, we may note that Havelock Ellis was a signatory of the initial letters to the press proposing its establishment, and Laurence Housman featured among its vice presidents.[45] Many of the doctors, psychoanalysts and others involved with it had had at least some connection with the BSSSP, and the attitude of the Institute towards the older, smaller and possibly rather less reputable organization does not suggest that they were anxious to repudiate this connection. Although in 1939 the Institute agreed 'not to cooperate' with the Society's desire for a speaker at a planned meeting in Caxton Hall, Westminster (another site strongly associated with progressive causes), this was specifically 'on this occasion' rather than as an issue of general principle:[46] Dr E.T. Jensen, the Chairman of the Institute, had chaired at least one of the Society's lectures, in 1932.[47]

It is arguable that the Society, by providing a space for discussion and meeting between committed reformers and those in the medical professions, had enabled productive interactions with a significant influence on the development of moves in the direction of more humane attitudes towards the homosexual, and strategies to ameliorate his situation, even if they fell short of actual legal reform. Several names which appear in the Scientific Committee minutes of the Institute listed below had varying degrees of association with the Society,[48] and additionally suggest other possible networks through which its influence may have been disseminated.

A number of figures who were active in psychoanalytical circles were represented in this cross-over group (British psychoanalysis was itself heavily London-based, with its headquarters also in the Harley Street area). Barbara Low, one of the founders of the British Psycho-Analytical Society, had joined the BSSSP in 1917 (having formerly been a participant in *The Freewoman* and its circle) and became active in the Sex Education Study Group.[49] She addressed the April 1920 Quarterly Meeting on 'Some considerations of sex from the psycho-analytic viewpoint',[50] and served briefly as a member of the Executive Committee.[51] Adrian and Karin Stephen (Virginia Woolf's brother and sister-in-law, early British disciples of Freud) had briefly been members of the Society from 1919 to 1920.[52] The psychoanalyst Harold D. Jennings White had a long-standing history of involvement in the BSSSP, having joined the Society in 1919,[53] and actively participated in the discussions of the 'Heterosexuality' Study Group.[54] He was the secretary of the literature subcommittee,[55] and was elected to the Executive Committee in 1922,[56] on which he served until around 1931. Although he appears to have left the committee around the middle of that year, he remained involved to the point of offering to lead the proposed revived 'Inversion' Study Group.[57] He lectured to the Society on 'The Incest Problem' in June 1923,[58] and on 'Some Psychological Causes of Sexual Inversion' in October 1925.[59] The latter presumably turned into his pamphlet published under the Society's auspices, *Psychological Causes of Homoeroticism and Inversion* (1925). Dr Sybille Yates joined the British Sexology Society, as it had been renamed, in 1932,[60] and was suggested as a possible speaker in 1933.[61] Although James Glover had been more active in the BSSSP before his early death in 1926,[62] his brother Edward Glover knew of it and had been invited to be a speaker.[63] Dr Grace Pailthorpe and John Rickman were not members, but had attended the occasional meeting,[64] and Pailthorpe had also had some personal contacts with George Ives.[65] The Jungian analyst Godwin Baynes had addressed the Society and also solicited copies of such of their publications as were available to non-members.[66]

Other medical individuals were similarly associated with both bodies. The woman doctor Mrs Meakin Herford, who had been a member of the Society since 1918,[67] and spoken to it on at least one occasion,[68] was mentioned as being involved with one of the Institute's provincial facilities in Reading in 1939.[69] The psychiatrist Dr Emmanuel Miller does not appear to have been a member, but he had attended meetings and addressed the Society.[70] Dr Morris Robb, another psychiatrist, wrote to the Society asking for a batch of tickets for himself, friends and pupils to the lecture by Georg Groddeck which it was organizing, and expressed interest in joining.[71] Norwood East, of the Prison Medical Service, although he does not seem to have interacted with the Society as such, in 1938 at the time of his retirement wrote to Havelock Ellis thanking him for 'the help and insight into sex deviations which I have obtained from your writings and which have assisted me in dealing with sex offenders'.[72] Others involved with the Institute at least had some knowledge of the Society's existence and passing contacts. George Ives reported in 1944 that the Institute 'contains several members of the old Sexological'.[73]

The Institute apparently repudiated the suggestion that it should 'concern itself with questions of penal reform' when contacted in 1938 by the psychologist and psychoanalyst Professor J.C. Flugel – who had joined the BSSSP as early as 1915 and was still an active member in the early 1930s[74] – about his concerns over sentences imposed in homosexual cases during the previous year.[75] Nonetheless, it did work closely with the judicial system, providing medical reports, organizing seminars for probation officers, and circularizing magistrates. In spite of denying its interest in reforming the law, the Institute was invited to be represented on Home Office committees and had discussions with MPs about relevant clauses in penal reform bills.[76] This rather suggests it was well-embedded in metropolitan circles of influence, if not the actual corridors of power.

Queerly subtle influence?

In 1944, George Ives noted that the Institute 'seems very much alive', whereas the BSSSP was 'hibernating'.[77] By the end of the war, the latter body appears to have been defunct, whereas the Institute continued to thrive and its successors are still in existence. The contemporary impact of the BSSSP in terms of reform of laws, or even moderating more than a small corner of public opinion, was apparently minimal. Nonetheless, thirty years after the collapse of the Society nearly all the reforms it had desired had been implemented, including homosexual law reform. This apparent posthumous success may have resulted from wider changes in society as a whole, proceeding irrespective of its activities, in reaction to broader social and economic factors. The Society may simply have been ahead of changing public opinion, as implied by its 'General Aims' of 1914: to support 'the direction pointed by science' by a 'greater weight of public opinion'.[78]

However, it might be claimed that the Society did have a subtle and hard-to-trace influence on the development of changes in attitude. It has been demonstrated that there was a considerable degree of overlap with the much more mainstream and respectable Institute for the Scientific Treatment of Delinquency, with its greater impact on medico-legal attitudes and policies, and that its connection with a number of other networks could be traced. The Society also arguably influenced in their youth individuals who by the 1960s had risen to positions of power, most prominently Gerald Gardiner, Lord Chancellor of the reforming Labour government of the 1960s.[79]

We can compare this with many other social reforms which began with small groups regarded as dubious radical eccentrics, whose views gradually gained wider degrees of acceptance until the point when they became, if not universal, the majority opinion within society. But as with other campaigns, for example anti-slavery and women's suffrage, reforms do not just happen: they require the original derided pioneers who begin the long process of changing hearts and minds which eventually changes actual laws. The queer space in Bloomsbury created by the BSSSP during its brief queer moment of shaking up established ideas and generating unexpected contacts was certainly one contribution to that process.

Notes

1   BSS 'Misc: Minutes', Vol. [1], 3rd AGM, 7 July 1917; Minutes Vol. 2, 110th Meeting, 12 April 1923; Vol. 3, 127–128th Meetings, 6 November, 4 December 1924; 'Letters Received', R. C. Klaheven, 17 May 1936; 'Misc' Letters of Enquiry, W. Young, n.d.

2   John Stuart Mill, 'The Westminster Election of 1865', in John M. Robson and Bruce L. Kinzer (eds), *The Collected Works of John Stuart Mill, Volume XXVIII: Public and Parliamentary Speeches Part I November 1850– November 1868* (Toronto: University of Toronto Press, 1988); http://oll .libertyfund.org/titles/262 (accessed 30 April 2015).

3   *The Diary of Virginia Woolf Volume 1: 1915–19* (London: Penguin, 1979), p. 110, 21 January 1918 (I am indebted to Hermione Lee for this reference); British Sexological Society archives at the Harry Ransom Humanities Research Center, University of Texas at Austin (BSS): 'Misc', Minutes Vol. [1], Quarterly Meeting, 18 January 1918; W.D. Wills, *Homer Lane: A Biography* (London: Allen and Unwin 1964), pp. 200–201. Lane's lecture, 'The Suppression of Children as it Affects the Sexual Instincts', took place on 30 April 1919.

4   BSS 'Misc': Lecture lists; (Reginald Wellbye) 'A Constructive View of Sex Psychology as a Humanistic Study' (given 27 March 1930).

5   Matt Cook, 'Ives, George Cecil (1867–1950)', *Oxford Dictionary of National Biography* (Oxford: Oxford University Press, May 2006), online edn, October 2007. http://0-www.oxforddnb.com.catalogue.wellcomelibrary.org /view/article/57683 (accessed 19 March 2014).

6   Norman Haire to Havelock Ellis, 20 August 1923, Havelock Ellis papers in the British Library Department of Manuscripts, Additional Manuscript 70540.

7   Lisa Z. Sigel, *Governing Pleasures: Pornography and Social Change in England, 1815–1914* (New Brunswick, NJ: Rutgers University Press, 2002), pp. 50–55.

8   Ivan Crozier, 'Nineteenth-Century British Psychiatric Writing About Homosexuality Before Havelock Ellis: The Missing Story', *Journal of the History of Medicine and Allied Sciences* 63 (2008), pp. 65–102.

9   Lesley A. Hall, '"The English have hot-water bottles": The Morganatic Marriage between the British Medical Profession and Sexology Since William Acton', in Roy Porter and Mikulas Teich (eds), *Sexual Knowledge, Sexual Science: The History of Attitudes to Sexuality* (Cambridge: Cambridge University Press, 1994), pp. 350–66.

10   E.B. Meakin Herford to the Secretary, Medical Women's Federation, 23 March 1928, in 'Co-Education' File, Medical Women's Federation Archives in the Wellcome Library, SA/MWF/D.9/2.

11   Havelock Ellis to Edward Carpenter, 17 December 1892, Carpenter papers in Sheffield City Archives Ms 357/5.

12   R. Thurman to Carpenter, 15 September 1895, Carpenter papers, Sheffield, Ms 386/58.

13   Carpenter to Ellis, 28 June 1895, Harry Ransom Humanities Research Center, University of Texas at Austin (HRC).

14   Carpenter to Ellis, 14 October 1895, HRC.

15   See, for example, C. Langdon Everard to Carpenter, 29 April 1908; S. Cruwys Sharland to Carpenter, 4 July 1910, Carpenter papers, Sheffield, Mss 386/156, 384/9.

16   Ellis to Carpenter, 17 February 1918, Carpenter papers, Sheffield, Ms 357/32.

17   Rebecca West, 'The Freewoman', first published in *Time and Tide*, 16 July 1926, reprinted in *Time and Tide Wait for No Man*, ed. Dale Spender (London: Pandora, 1984), p. 66; Lucy Bland, *Banishing the Beast: Feminism, Sex, and Morality* (London: Penguin, 1995), pp. 265–87.

18   'A Discussion Circle', *The Freewoman*, 28 March 1912, p. 373; 'The Discussion Circle', *The Freewoman*, 2 May 1912, p. 464; F. W. S. Browne, '"The Freewoman" Discussion Circle', *The Freewoman*, 12 September 1912, p. 327; '"The Freewoman" Discussion Circle', *The Freewoman*, 26 September 1912, p. 371; 'Notes on Two Meetings of the Discussion Circle by B. Low' (1912), Dora Marsden papers, Princeton University Library, C0283, Box 2/10.

19   Laurence Housman to Janet Ashbee, 7 December 1913, Ashbee Journals Vol. 25, King's College Cambridge Library.

20   BSS 'Misc': Minutes Vol. [1], Preliminary Meeting, 12 August 1913; 2nd Meeting, 12 October 1913; 3rd Meeting, 3 November 1913, 5th Meeting, 10 January 1914; 10th Meeting, 19 May 1914; E. B. Lloyd to Edward Carpenter, 4 March 1914. Carpenter papers, Sheffield, Ms 368/5.

21   Douglas Goldring, *The Nineteen Twenties: A General Survey and Some Personal Memories* (London: Nicholson and Watson, 1945), pp. 183–51;

Goldring to Jane Burr, 12 July 1949, Jane Burr papers in the Sophia Smith Collection, Smith College, Northampton MA.

22　British Society for the Study of Sex Psychology Publication no. 1: *Policy and Principles: General Aims* (London, 1914) – 'General Aims' Based on Laurence Housman's Address at the Inaugural Meeting; F.W.S. Browne, 'A New Psychological Society', *International Journal of Ethics* 28 (1917–1918), pp. 266–9; BSS 'Misc': Minutes of 10th and 12th Meetings, 19 May, 1 July 1914.

23　George Ives, diary entry for 9 July 1914, 'Notebooks and Various Writings' LVI, HRC.

24　Constant discussions on printing, reprinting, distribution, etc. in BSS Minutes: 5th Meeting of Executive Committee, 10 January 1914 mentions Hamilton's translation, BSS Misc.

25　E.B. Lloyd to Carpenter, 17 December 1920, Sheffield Ms 368/38; Minutes 1920–1921 sporadic mentions, BSS Misc.

26　Mr A to Marie Stopes, 1918, 'ML [Married Love]-Gen[eral]', correspondence in the Wellcome Library, PP/MCS/A.15.

27　Katharine Cockin, 'Housman, Laurence (1865–1959)', *Oxford Dictionary of National Biography* (Oxford: Oxford University Press, 2004) http://0-www .oxforddnb.com.catalogue.wellcomelibrary.org/view/article/34014 (accessed 19 March 2014).

28　BSS 'Misc': Housman to Ives, 6 August 2258/1920.

29　BSS 'Misc': Housman to Ives, 22 July 2262/1924.

30　Sheila Jeffreys, *The Spinster and Her Enemies: Feminism and Sexuality, 1880–1930* (London: Pandora Press, 1985), p. 156; BSS 'Misc': Minutes Vol. [5], 198th Meeting, 9 April 1931.

31　BSS Minutes Vol. 2, 93rd Meeting, 17 November 1921; Vol. [3], 129th Meeting, 8 January 1925; Vol. [5], 204th Meeting, 2 December 1931; correspondence between H.C. Booth and Deighton, November 1931; George Ives: 'Notes and Various Writings Vol. XCVI 1931', 24 November 1931.

32　BSS 'Misc': Minutes of 204th Meeting of Executive Committee, 2 December 1931; BSS Letters received: Harold Clare Booth (National Physical Laboratory, Molesey) to E. Lonsdale Deighton, 10 November 1931.

33　BSS 'Misc': Deighton to Booth, 30 November 1931.

34　BSS 'Misc': Stella Browne to Janet Carson, 27 March 1919, 28 April 1920; Minutes Vol. 2, 71st Meeting, 16 April 1920; Minutes, Vol. [5], 204th Meeting, 2 December 1931; Harold Clare Booth (National Physical Laboratory, Molesey) to E. Lonsdale Deighton, 10 November 1931.

35　BSS 'Misc': Booth to Deighton, 10 November 1921.

36　BSS 'Misc': Housman to Ives, 6 November 2265/1927.

37　George Ives, diary entry, 18 November 1928, 'Notes and Various Writings' no XCIII 1928. O of C 2266.

38 BSS 'Misc': Housman to Ives, 10 January 2268/1930.

39 BSS 'Misc': Housman to Ives, 22 August 2268/1930.

40 George Ives to Havelock Ellis, c.1934/35, Ellis papers, British Library Additional Manuscripts 70566.

41 BSS 'Misc': Minutes Vol. [5], 204–206th Meetings, December 1931– February 1932, 209th Meeting, 3 May 1932; Hull, Augustine Joseph, papers concerning his conviction and imprisonment 1931–1932; 'Letters Received': Margaret Lowenfeld, 8 December 1931, Charles Ross (a prison chaplain), 7 January 1913; 'Letters Out': Deighton to Lowenfeld, 8 December 1932, Deighton to Ives, 11 January 1932; 'Misc': J.A.C. Braun to Ives, 11 October 1932.

42 BSS 'Misc': George Ives, letters to E. Lonsdale Deighton 1930–1932; 24 November 1930, 12 January 1932.

43 Edward Glover, *The Diagnosis and Treatment of Delinquency: Being a Clinical Report on the Work of the Institute During the Five Years 1937 to 1941* (London: Institute for the Scientific Treatment of Delinquency, 1944).

44 Institute for the Scientific Treatment of Delinquency (ISTD) Development Subcommittee Minutes, November 1936–March 1939. I am grateful to the Centre for Crime and Justice Studies, Kings College London, for allowing me to consult their predecessor's archives, which they retain.

45 ISTD, volume of newspaper cuttings.

46 ISTD, Director's Minutes, 25 February 1939.

47 BSS 'Misc': Lectures to the BSS.

48 Names of individuals were extracted from ISTD, Scientific Committee minutes, October 1936–March 1939, *passim*, and other records of the Institute.

49 BSS 'Misc': Minutes of 3rd AGM, 7 July 1917.

50 BSS 'Misc': Minutes of Quarterly Meeting, 16 April 1920.

51 BSS 'Misc': Minutes of 6th AGM, 14 July 1920; Minutes of 94th Meeting of Executive Committee, 12 December 1921.

52 BSS 'Misc': Minutes of 61st Meeting of Executive Committee, 14 June 1919; Minutes of 78th Meeting of Executive Committee, 27 October 1920.

53 BSS 'Misc': Minutes of 63rd Meeting of Executive Committee, 5 August 1919.

54 BSS 'Misc': BSSSP Study Group III (Heterosexuality) Minutes.

55 BSS 'Misc': Minutes of 99th Meeting of Executive Committee, 11 May 1922.

56 BSS 'Misc': Minutes of 8th AGM, 17 July 1922.

57 BSS 'Misc': Minutes of 202nd Meeting of Executive Committee, 8 October 1931.

58 BSS 'Misc': Lectures to the BSS.

59 BSS 'Misc': Minutes of 11th Annual Meeting, 15 October 1925.

60 BSS 'Misc': Minutes of 208th Meeting of Executive Committee, 6 April 1932.

61   BSS 'Misc': Rough Notes for Minutes of 221st Meeting of Executive
     Committee, 9 November 1933.

62   BSS 'Misc': Minutes of 38th, 74th, 148th Meetings of Executive Committee,
     25 April 1917, 3 June 1920, 2 September 1926, George Ives (Essay on the
     BSS) 1928.

63   BSS 'Misc': Minutes of 188th Meeting of the Executive Committee,
     1 May 1930.

64   BSS 'Misc': BSSSP Attendance Books: Members and Visitors Attending
     Meetings, 1925–1940.

65   BSS 'Misc': G.W. Pailthorpe to Ives, 27 October 1924.

66   BSS 'Letters Received': H.G. Baynes to the BSSSP, 14 December 1926;
     BSS 'Misc': Minutes of 152nd Meeting of the Executive Committee,
     6 January 1927.

67   BSS 'Misc': Minutes of 46th Meeting of the Executive Committee,
     13 February 1918.

68   BSS 'Letters Received': Mrs Meakin Herford to BSSSP, 25 January 1927.

69   ISTD, Director's Minutes, 27 November 1939.

70   BSS 'Misc': BSSSP Attendance Books: Members and Visitors Attending
     Meetings, 1925–1931; Rough Notes for Minutes of 221st Meeting of
     Executive Committee, 9 November 1933.

71   BSS 'Misc': BSS Letters Received: Morris Robb to BSS, 14 March 1932.

72   Norwood East to Ellis, 1938, British Library Department of Manuscripts,
     Additional Manuscript 70556.

73   George Ives, 'Notes and Various Writings' CXII, 2 May 1944.

74   BSS 'Misc': Minutes of 18th Meeting of Executive Committee,
     21 January 1915; Minutes of 217th Meeting of the Executive Committee,
     (4 April) 1933.

75   ISTD, Scientific Committee Minutes, 17 March 1938, responding to a letter
     from J.C. Flugel concerning recent sentencing in homosexual cases.

76   ISTD, Scientific Committee Minutes October 1936–March 1939, Director's
     Minutes October 1936–March 1948, *passim*.

77   George Ives, 'Notes and Various Writings', CXII, 2 May 1944.

78   'General Aims'; Goldring, *The Nineteen Twenties*, p. 152.

79   BSS 'Letters out': to G. Gardiner; BSS 'Misc': Gardiner's comments on whether
     Rockstro's *A Plain Talk on Sex Difficulties* would be liable to prosecution;
     transcript of Gardiner's chairman's introduction to paper by Margaret
     Lowenfeld and comments on it, 16 February 1933. Muriel Box (his second
     wife), *Rebel Advocate: A Biography of Gerald Gardiner* (London: David
     and Charles, 1983), details his achievements in social reform but omits his
     connection with the BSSSP.

CHAPTER TEN

Cannibal London: Racial Discourses, Pornography and Male–Male Desire in Late-Victorian Britain

Silvia Antosa

In late-Victorian Britain, the boundaries between homosexuality, homosociality, close friendship and intergenerational bonds were porous and unstable.[1] It would therefore be more accurate to speak of a relational and undefined sexual spectrum that ranged from hetero- to homosexuality. As critics have noted, it would be anachronistic to apply the modern category of 'homosexual' to mid- and late nineteenth-century subjects. Male homosexual identities came into discourse after 1869 and were shaped largely after the Wilde Trials in 1895.[2] Assuming a post-Foucaultian perspective, I take the view that sex is formed through interaction, and can only be understood in its sociocultural and historical contexts. I nonetheless use the word 'homosexual' for convenience, with an awareness that the temporal span dealt with in this article covers decades which saw significant changes in the definition of this term. In the second half of the nineteenth century, discourses around same-sex desire were in flux. Between the 1880s and the 1890s, there was an important shift from the notion of the sodomite, whose acts were perceived as a 'temporary aberration', to quote Michel Foucault,[3] to the 'homosexual', who was constructed as belonging to a separate species.[4] Therefore, sexual acts and desires became constitutive elements of individual identity. Still, this shift was neither instantaneous nor all-pervasive; harbingers of change had been in the air for decades. Indeed, as Eve Sedgwick has argued, 'issues of modern homo/heterosexual definition are structured not by the supersession of one model and the consequent withering away of another, but instead by the relations enabled by the ... coexistence of different models during the times they do exist'.[5]

Two related nineteenth-century contexts which were particularly animated by tensions between competing models of sexuality were the Anthropological Society of London, founded by Richard Francis Burton and James Hunt in 1863, and the influential Cannibal Club, which constituted its inner circle and was established around the same time. In this chapter, I analyse debates and activities fostered by these two associations in the light of Sedgwick's theories on queer. According to the American scholar, queer is an 'open mesh of possibilities'[6] which are enabled by non-normative and multiple understandings and practices of gender and sexuality, and is something which goes 'outward along dimensions that can't be subsumed under gender and sexuality...: the ways that race, ethnicity ... nationality criss-cross with these and other identity-constituting, identity-fracturing discourses'.[7] I discuss the influence exercised by the two associations in shaping and establishing coexisting discourses around male homosocial bonding, male–male desire and male homosexuality in mid- and late-Victorian London. Moreover, I argue that the queer, competing models of sexuality discussed within them were profoundly influenced by nineteenth-century discourses of race and by late-Victorian society's interest in the pornographic, especially in the informal gatherings of the 'Cannibals'. So far, only a few works have emphasized the mutual construction of race and homosexuality.[8] Even fewer works have outlined the connection between pornography and the development of new understandings of sexuality.[9] I show how the mutual construction of race and gender carried out in the official space of the Society paved the way for more transgressive (homo) sexual readings of pornography in the Club.

Male bonding did not have a clear subversive social role in that period. Rather, drawing on Sedgwick's study of male homosocial bonds in England, I understand it as central to the maintenance of heterosexual culture through its stigmatization of male same-sex relationships. In Sedgwick's words, '"obligatory heterosexuality" is built into male-dominated kinship systems, [and] homophobia is a *necessary* consequence of such patriarchal institutions as heterosexual marriage'.[10] Male homosocial bonds permeated a whole range of relationships between men, which were characterized by varying degrees of fear and hatred of male same-sex desire.[11] They were thus central to the maintenance of masculine sociocultural privileges in the patriarchal heterosexual system. Sedgwick has pointed out that such a system was also founded on a triangulation of desire between men and women, as male relational dynamics hinge on relationships that exclude women. My contention is that the homophobic and misogynistic nature of the Victorian patriarchal heterosexual structure is at the heart of both the Anthropological Society and the Cannibal Club, which were two male-dominated institutions. In addition, as most of their members were Tories from well-established backgrounds who travelled in the countries of the British Empire, they were influenced by what Robert Aldrich has called 'the ethos of the colonial world',[12] which was intrinsically masculine and misogynistic.

As Aldrich has convincingly demonstrated, in the nineteenth century '[t]he colonies provided many possibilities of homoeroticism, homosociality and homosexuality – a variety of perspectives and experiences by which men expressed attraction to other men (or male youths)…The gendered nature of expansion…created situations congenial to intimate male bonding.'[13] In a similar vein, other scholars have emphasized the crucial role played by same-sex sexuality in British colonial politics. For Edward Said, the appeal of the Orient was tied to the possibility of having 'a sexual experience unobtainable in Europe';[14] Joseph A. Boone has explicitly linked this possibility with the fact that '*sexual contact with and between men* underwrites and at times even explains the historical appeal of orientalism as an occidental mode of male perception, appropriation, and control'.[15] The fantasy – or alternatively the spectre – of the encounter with the colonized did not call into question the British belief in dominion and control. Rather, it consolidated the British sense of entitlement, as long as it was kept in a secret and private sphere. I argue that Sedgwick's definition of male homosociality as both emphasizing masculine privileges and stigmatizing women and male homosexual relations is pertinent to the activities of the Anthropological Society and the Cannibal Club. These organizations fostered debates that opened up a discursive space about male (homo)sexuality, even if in ambiguous and contradictory ways, as they distanced themselves from this topic by assuming objective, 'scientific' viewpoints and by projecting same-sex practices onto the 'other', exotic cultures of the colonized countries.

The 'Anthropologicals'

Richard Burton and James Hunt founded the Anthropological Society to provide a space for intellectual exchange on topics which, in their view, were forbidden in other official contexts. Burton was an explorer, a member of the Royal Geographical Society, and British consul abroad; Hunt was an anthropologist and a scientific reformer. They formed an institution where they could present their own theories on race and sexuality without censorship or fear of repudiation. In addition to its declared intent of opposing any form of social ignorance, the Society raised questions about the difficulty of generalizing about 'man' in a scientific or a sociocultural context. As one member put it, '[h]uman nature is, or appears to be, very different in China or America…*Would not a Londoner be quite as good a subject for study as twenty different races*, for the purpose of knowing what

is and what is not human nature?'[16] Quite significantly, the self-reflexive
tone of the discussion on different races and sexualities required on the
anthropologists' part an active participation in contemporary political
and economic debates, especially when they concerned British imperial
politics.[17] Such varied interests are reflected in the disciplinary specialisms
of the London-based Society's members: historians, geographers, explorers
and writers.[18]

   The Anthropological Society emerged from a schism from the more liberal
and middle-class Ethnological Society, founded by James Cowles Prichard
in the 1840s.[19] Unlike the latter, which advanced the theory of the organic
mutability and the biological unity of the human species,[20] Burton and Hunt's
Society supported the largely discredited theory of polygenesis, arguing that
different races descended from separate biological sources and are physically
and anthropomorphically different. Moreover, they opposed Pritchard's
philological view of race, which relied on a model of racial difference
which presumed common origins. Instead, they supported a physiological
approach informed by the measurements of physical differences called
anthropometry and comparative anatomy. Burton and Hunt believed in the
inherent inequality between races and in the impossibility of adaptation to
different environmental and sociocultural circumstances. Such racist views
were used to justify the 'necessity' of colonialism and slavery. Moreover,
unlike the Ethnological Society, the anthropologists excluded women from
participating in their meetings: indeed, this seems to be the reason why Hunt
decided to leave the Ethnological Society, where he had been a secretary
from 1859 to 1862.[21] The exclusion of women and the urgency of creating
a male-only environment seem to confirm Sedgwick's view that male
homosocial bonds hinge on relationships between men that isolate women.

   The scientific methods of comparative anatomy were adopted by the
members of the Society to articulate discourses on gender and sexuality.[22]
Their research was premised on the conviction that there was a biological
and irreducible sexual difference between peoples. The categories of race
and sexuality became mutually dependent in their work. According to Lisa
Z. Sigel, '[their] writings insisted that truths about nature – inherent and
unchanging – could be found in the body through the study of sexuality and
sexual organs.'[23] The main target of the anthropologists' research was to
find evidence of prevailing theories about the supremacy of the British race,
gender dissymmetry and sexual 'abnormalities', mostly sought in 'other',
exotic cultures. The technique of comparative anatomy they employed
in their research anticipated and intersected with the emerging medical
and sexological literature, which was embedded within contemporary
racial and gender ideologies and held a substantial definitional power in the
field of sexuality.

   During the eight years in which the Society was active,[24] its members
produced numerous works and papers on the subject of sexuality. Their
research entered public debate in 1860s and 1870s London. Most of the

papers delivered at the Society's meeting rooms at 4 St Martin's Place, Trafalgar Square, dealt with the study of gender roles and sexual practices in the colonized countries. Among them, it is worth mentioning Charles Staniland Wake's 'Social Condition of Woman as Affected by Civilisation', 'Sacred Prostitution' and 'Cannibalism'; Dr Charnock's 'Facts Relating to Polyandry'; A.L. Lewis's 'Notes on Polygamy'; Burton's 'Notes on Scalping' and 'Notes on an Hermaphrodite'; and Edward Sellon's 'On Phallic Worship in India' and 'Some Remarks on Indian Gnosticism, or the Worship of Female Powers'.[25] As these indicative titles make clear, the members of the Anthropological Society devoted themselves to cataloguing various 'exotic' sexual practices, from human copulation with animals to incest, clitoridectomy, polyandry, polygamy, hermaphroditism, prostitution and phallic worship, which constituted one of the most debated subjects.

The work of classification undertaken by the anthropologists responded to a widespread labelling zeal which was taking hold in the second half of the century. In addition, their taxonomical approach to sexual matters reflected a distancing strategy that tried to separate scientific interest from mere prurience and to conceal any form of personal involvement. As Sigel notes, 'to make the case that their works were not obscene or pornographic ... these authors stressed the scientific nature of their bibliographic, physiological and folkloric studies of sexuality'.[26] In so doing, they also anticipated some of the problems inherent in early sexology, including attitudes towards same-sex behaviours.[27] According to Jeffrey Weeks, '[t]he nascent science of sexology ... was centrally implicated in all the debates about gender and sexuality, weaving a web of meaning around the body and its desires through its descriptions, categorisations, definitions, neologisms, and theoretical speculations.'[28] Such speculations were founded on racial paradigms and models of gender, according to which sexual practices were located and analysed. Bodies began to be scrutinized for proof of innate constitutional deficiency as well as for physical evidence of 'abnormal' proclivities that could determine unusual sexual practices and link perverse desires to innate biological conditions.

Cannibal London

In the Cannibal Club, things were different. It was a radical dining club founded by Burton in 1863, and constituted the inner circle of the Anthropological Society. Burton dubbed the Club as 'Cannibal' to emphasize its subversive role. Its members could freely and informally discuss some of the issues that were presented in the Society. Meetings usually took place at Bertolini's, an Italian and French restaurant on St Martin's Lane, just off Leicester Square. Like the Anthropological Society, the Cannibal Club was an all-male group whose focus on male–male desire largely centred on the overlapping issues of homoeroticism, homosociality and homosexuality.

It provided an excellent opportunity for its members to investigate several forms of homosocial relational bonds, falling along a sexual spectrum that ranged from hetero- to homosexuality, including flagellation and masochism.

The Cannibal Club had closed membership and members called each other 'brother'. The idea of the brotherhood underlines the homosocial nature of the club, its elitist self-representation and its emphasis on the symbolic importance of blood relationships. Moreover, it marks an evolution in the very notion of brotherhood, which in the early-Victorian phase was shaped on the anachronistic model of celibate, 'desexualized' monastic communities, to respond to the need to articulate male anxieties about the process of construction of bourgeois masculinity in a world dominated by industrial and social change.[29] The idealization of celibate life within an enclosed all-male world raised a number of tensions, especially between the homosocial and the heterosexual. According to Herbert Sussman, 'the monastery as a sacralised, celibate all-male society *safely distanced in time* provide[d] a figure through which they could express in covert form, or as an *open secret*, their attraction to a world of chaste masculine bonding from which the female has been magically eliminated'.[30] However, even if women were excluded from the male social and symbolic spaces of the Cannibal Club, the tensions between homosexual and heterosexual were transposed to a different level. Rather than sublimating celibacy as a form of regulation of male sexual energy, the Cannibals celebrated the powers of sexual drives – by 'safely' projecting them, to paraphrase Sussman, not into a distant time but into a remote, exotic space. Therefore, the ideal of celibate monks symbolizing a disciplined masculinity gave way to a new model, which was influenced by late-Victorian pseudoscientific discourses on race: the cannibal. Consequently, the troubled boundary between the heterosexual, the homosocial and the homosexual could no longer be negotiated within the safe space of the monastery: the new arena in which British masculinity needed to prove itself was imperial space.[31]

The Cannibal Club was populated by several somewhat eccentric personalities of the time: along with Richard Burton, vice president of the Anthropological Society, founder of the Club and one of the most famous translators of pornographic Oriental literature of his time,[32] members included Edward Sellon, captain in the Indian army, pornographic writer and translator of (homo)erotic books;[33] James Campbell Reddie, an officer, consul and author of pornographic works, including homosexual narratives such as *Adventures of a Schoolboy or the Freaks of Youthful Passion* (1866), with illustrations by Edward Sellon; Richard Monckton Milnes, owner of the Fryston Library, nicknamed Aphrodisiopolis because it contained the largest collection of erotic and illegal works in Britain;[34] J. Frederick Collingwood, the assistant secretary of the Anthropological Society; Thomas Bendyshe, vice president of the Society and Senior Fellow of King's College, London; Frederick Hankey, a sadist and illegal trader of erotica; and Henry Spencer Ashbee, one of the greatest bibliographers of British pornography in the nineteenth century.[35] Ashbee was also a member of Philobiblon, a society of collectors established by Milnes, and was himself author of several pornographic works under the pseudonym of Pisanus Fraxi. Other members included Charles Duncan Cameron, an officer and consul; the poet Charles Algernon Swinburne; General Studholme John Hodgson; and Simeon Solomon, a homosexual painter involved in the Pre-Raphaelite movement, who was condemned for sodomy in 1873. These men were drawn together by their shared interests in homoerotic bonding, pornographic writing, and the collecting and illegal trading of erotic works, together with debates on extreme sexual practices such as masochism and flagellation. In their pornographic production, they explored the possibilities of sex. As Sigel has remarked, '[p]ornography is not tied to the tangible ... but to the imaginable.' Yet, even though it is connected to the realm of possibilities, pornography 'is caught in an intimate relationship with the broader society'.[36] The pornographic work produced by the Cannibals – mostly anonymously or using pseudonyms – was inspired by and, in turn influenced, their ethnographic work and their elitist social background.[37] It is no accident that most of their titles were translations or had to do with Oriental sexual practices and were addressed to a small powerful elite. The exploration of masculine sexuality became a privileged activity written by men for men.

The symbol of the Club was a mace in the shape of an African head gnawing on a human thighbone.[38] The name of the Club and its symbol are clear references to the imperial construction of the monstrous and barbarian non-European black savage, which constituted the anthropologists' main field of interest. As H.L. Malchow has emphasized, 'cannibalism as a racial image conveniently served to invert reality by encoding as appetite those whom the European sought to incorporate ... [I]ts rhetorical manipulation as an alien racial characteristic is a rich source of information about the social fears and cultural obsessions of Europeans'.[39] And sodomy was one of its fears. Cannibalism became part of a 'stockpile of representations' available for Europeans to draw upon in their own struggles – in particular those concerning their sexual identity.[40] In the late-Victorian period, cannibal depravity became analogous with sexual depravity: the 'unnatural' appetite of the cannibals was equated with 'deviant' homosexual intercourse, as the domination of the cannibal over his victim merged with that of the aggressive sodomite over his passive object. Cannibalism, then, joined together two cultural taboos – miscegenation and homosexuality – because of their 'abnormal' sexual object choice. As J.H. Malchow writes, '[b]oth cannibalism and homosexuality were often represented in the nineteenth century as acts, like masturbation, that became addictive'.[41] Racial and sexual discourses converged in a set of representations that codified 'unnatural' desire as physical perversion. On this point, C.J. Rawson has written that '[t]here is a recurrent close connection in literary texts between the normally prohibited form of eating and the "forbidden" or "abnormal" forms of sexual activity.'[42] Such a connection is made clear, for example, by Burton himself, who, on several occasions, made explicit the link between same-sex desire and cannibalism. For example, in discussing the religious significance of eunuchry, he writes: 'hence too we have an explanation of *sotadic love* [love between men] in its second stage, when it became, *like cannibalism*, a matter of superstition'.[43] In a section on the diffusion of what he calls 'the vice' in America, he reflects: 'In many parts of the New World *this perversion* was accompanied by another *depravity* of taste – confirmed cannibalism.'[44]

This connection projected the threatening homosexual outside the confines of the home country and turned homosexuality into an exotic phenomenon. Once again, this involved a process of distancing and dis-identification: like the cannibal, the sodomite had to be projected into an exotic and unfamiliar space. The term 'cannibalism' eventually came to function as a shorthand for male–male desire within the group. On this point, Deborah Lutz has emphasized that:

> among cannibals, love and sex between men existed on a secret plane…Perhaps Burton set [cannibalism and male-male desire] side by side because they were *practises seriously tabooed* in his world. Or possibly *the idea of like consuming like, of taking another's flesh into oneself*, seemed to give them a certain kinship. To name his group the Cannibal Club was a way to point to radical 'tastes', to refer…to men loving and sharing their kind. These men came together for mutual consumption.[45]

In ambiguously joining together the taboo of cannibalism and the illegal practice of male–male sex, Burton created a coded discursive space charged with semantic layers and evocative meanings. In the Club, cannibals could experience free interaction and 'mutual consumption', with ostensible sexual implications. In particular, the idea of 'like consuming like' and 'taking another's flesh into oneself' evoked by cannibalism was a clear reference to anal sex. It also pointed to the reciprocal interaction of Eros and Thanatos, love and death, life instinct and death drive.

This connection is strengthened by the choice of the topics of discussion among the Cannibals, which included Walt Whitman's collection of poems, *Leaves of Grass*, and phallic worship. Both subjects inspired general reflection on the sociocultural and literary significance of male–male desire. In 1860, Whitman published a third edition of his collection and added a group of poems, *Calamus*, which explicitly referred to manly love between comrades. The work of the American poet focused on the physical concreteness of male comradeship; alongside 'amativeness', or heterosexual love, he proposed 'adhesiveness', or love between men.[46] Discussions of *Leaves of Grass* led to considerations of the literary inspiration provided by manly love and homosocial bonds. Talking about Whitman became a linguistic code to deal with homosexuality without openly articulating it, and his poetry inspired debates about the possibility of expressing a 'pure' form of love through art and lyricism.[47] Algernon Swinburne was particularly enthusiastic about Whitman's poetry and celebrated it both during informal gatherings and in more official contexts.[48]

The Cannibals also wrote extensively about phallic worship. The debate was stimulated by the publication of several works, such as the 1865 reprinted version of Richard Payne Knight's *A Discourse on the Worship of the Priapus* (1786) and John Davenport's long section on phallic worship in his *Aphrodisiacs and Anti-Aphrodisiacs: Three Essays on the Power of Reproduction* (1869). Edward Sellon produced a paper on the topic, 'On the Linga Puja, or Phallic Worship in India',[49] which caused controversial responses in the Society and a more open debate among the Cannibals.[50] The latter pondered the symbolic and artistic fecundity of intimacy between men which, from the Greek and Roman tradition, had extended to the East and many other countries. Significantly, Sellon concluded his essay by remarking that 'the *Culte de Phallus* prevailed not only amongst the Hindus, Assyrians, Babylonians, Mexicans, Etruscans, Greeks, and Romans in ancient times, but … it still forms an integral part of the worship of India, Thibet, China, Siam, Japan, and Southern Africa, and possibly further researches will prove, in *numerous other countries also*'.[51] Similarly, in his account of the expedition to the reign of Dahome, Burton provides a detailed description of the Priapus and its diffusion in the world:

> The Dahoman Priapus is a clay figure of any size between a giant and the pigmy, crouched upon the ground as if contemplating its own Attributes. The head is sometimes a wooden block rudely carved, more often dried mud, and the eyes and teeth are supplied by cowries. A huge penis, like the section of a broom-stick, rudely carved as the Japanese articles which I have lately been permitted to inspect, projects horizontally from the middle. I could have carried off a donkey's load *had I been aware of the rapidly rising value of Phallic specimens amongst the collectors of Europe*. The Tree of Life is anointed with palm-oil, which drips into a pot or a shard placed below it … There is another Phallic god named 'Bo', the guardian of warriors and the protector of markets.[52]

The motif of phallicism and its 'rapidly rising value among the collectors of Europe' confirms the rapid expansion of interest in Western countries, to which Burton openly refers. Such an interest seemed to reflect the world of late-Victorian construction of masculinity and male sexuality, by celebrating the model of British male activity through history, art and religion. Moreover, it implies that the British projection of male–male desire to the colonies is a cover strategy that aims at concealing its diffusion in Europe and England. Burton made explicit the connection between priapism and male–male desire in other works, too, as in his 1890 translation of *Priapeia* which is still considered the most explicit book about sodomy published in *fin-de-siècle* Britain.[53]

Parodic references to Priapus abounded in the private correspondence among the Cannibals with explicit references to male–male desire. For example, Swinburne began a letter to Monckton Milnes with the salutation: 'Salus in X Priapo et Ecclesia / Sub invocatione Beatissimi Donatiani De Sade (Salvation in Christ, Priapus and His Church / by the Intercession of the most blessed De Sade).'[54] Other recurring expressions in the letters written between the Cannibals were 'swishing', which was used as a slang word for effeminate and a disparaging term for homosexual. It was also used with double reference to flagellation and homosexuality.[55] The irreverent inversion of religious symbols like the Holy Trinity and the mocking devotional references to De Sade were frequent. For example, in a letter to Swinburne, E. Villine wrote '*Un petit mot par charité s'il vous plait* my dear brother and we shall bless you in the name of Voltaire, Sade – and the Devil into the bargain.'[56] Voltaire, Sade and the Devil made up the blasphemous and irreverent Cannibal Holy Trinity.[57]

Cannibal sexology

The connections between male same-sex desire, Orientalism and pornography fostered by both Society and Club had an impact on the development of contemporary scientific, literary and social queer life in mid- and late nineteenth-century London. Research produced by the anthropologists and artistic work written by the Cannibals were influential in creating a subterranean network between scholars and thinkers on sexuality. This, in turn, paved the way for the creation of a scientific community of sexologists such as Havelock Ellis who, thanks to their work on a number of cases based in London, developed ground-breaking theories on male–male desire and helped to subvert late-Victorian prudish orthodoxy.

As mentioned earlier, Whitman's 'masculine' and regenerative poetic language inspired the formation of a coded counter-culture among the Cannibals and facilitated links between influential figures such as John Addington Symonds, a fellow of the Anthropological Society since 1865 and a peripheral member of the Cannibal Club, the sexologist Havelock Ellis, and Edward Carpenter, a poet and social reformer. Symonds had a twenty-year correspondence with Whitman, and Ellis devoted an article to the poet in his *The New Spirit* (1889). Jeffrey Weeks has pointed out that 'Whitman's work was the catalyst which brought all these strands together and facilitated collaboration between Symonds and Havelock Ellis'.[58] The two thinkers co-authored the first edition of the ground-breaking second volume of Ellis's *Studies in the Psychology of Sex: Sexual Inversion*. Earlier in the 1880s, Whitman's work also provided the occasion for collaboration between Ellis and Edward Carpenter, who wrote a long poem inspired by Whitman, *Towards Democracy* (1885).

In addition, the Anthropologicals' scientific discourses on race and fears of miscegenation influenced early sexologists by giving them a theoretical template on which they could articulate emerging models of homosexuality. As Siobhan Somerville has emphasized, '[t]he beginnings of sexology, then, were related to and perhaps even dependent on a pervasive climate of eugenicist and anti-miscegenation sentiment and legislation. Even at the level of nomenclature, anxieties about miscegenation shaped sexologists' attempts to find an appropriate and scientific name for the newly visible object of their study.'[59] Cultural anxieties about racial and etymological origins reflect most of the issues explored by key Cannibal figures such as Burton, who published a 'Terminal Essay' appended to his translation of *The Arabian Nights* in 1885. In his essay, he tackled the issue of homosexuality, which he called 'pederasty', 'vice' and 'inversion', even though he probably knew the word 'homosexual' had been coined in 1869 by German sexologist Karl Maria Kertbeny.[60] Burton's essay was one of the pioneering works which openly dealt with the subject and, as I suggest, was to influence Ellis's investigation. It also reflected the contradictions that permeated the debates of the Anthropological Society and the Cannibal Club and their imperialistic view of the world. In his sexual colonial map, he identified an area in the East in which, he argued, pederasty was widespread. In this way, he divided the zones where pederasty and other forms of sexual perversion were thought to be common practice from those 'civilized' countries, such as England, where it was considered an immoral perversion. But his map was geographically and sexually incoherent. Burton described pederasty as something exotic and distant in space and time. In order to explain its diffusion, he tried to invoke climatic theories which, however, often led to contradictory arguments. He also engaged in a critical confrontation with other scholars, such as Paolo Mantegazza, Meier and Karl Heinrich Ulrichs.

Burton's contradictory hypotheses on the causes of pederasty as first physiological, and then historical and cultural, questioned some of the main points which were being pursued by contemporary early sexologists such as Ellis, Symonds and Carpenter. In *A Problem of Modern Ethics* (1891), Symonds discussed Burton's climatic theory and argued that the phenomenon of sexual inversion could not be regarded as geographical and climatic, because it was spread across the globe. In his opinion, the 'problem' was social. He also observed that Burton's knowledge of pederasty was limited because it was confined to the Orient.[61] He nonetheless acknowledged the innovative aspect of Burton's theories, which considered the 'vice' of pederasty as a natural phenomenon rather than being 'against nature'.[62] Symonds and Ellis's 1897 edition of *Sexual Inversion* cited Burton's theory of the Sotadic Zone as an important contribution to the debate on same-sex desire. According to Lutz, '*Sexual Inversion* keeps up a steady stream of dialogue – and some refutation – with Burton and the writers and artists associated with Cannibal and Aesthetic Circles.'[63] They thought that Burton's theories were 'interesting',[64] but they also criticized his ignorance of emerging ideas about sexology. Moreover, while they acknowledged the importance of Burton's investigations, they contested his projection of sodomy onto an Oriental space as it failed to account for homosexual desire in the West and particularly Britain.

Burton's work shows that the Cannibals had been trying to project homosexual desire onto a distant, Oriental Other, by using a coded language full of racist references. Ellis' and Symonds' work brought same-sex desire back into Britain by demystifying the kind of language that the Cannibals – and Burton – were using. However, in their attempt to build a London-based discourse, Ellis and Symonds adopted the very method of comparative anatomy that had been developed by the Cannibals, applying biological determinism to the study of sexual characteristics. Coming back to my initial point, 'cannibalism' was something of a coded difference. It testified to the porousness of male homosexual/homoerotic/homosocial identities, and bespoke a complex process of queer identification and dis-identification which ran across elitism, racism, exoticism and homo-eroticism. The activities of the Anthropological Society and the meetings of the Cannibal brotherhood confirm the co-existence of different sexual models in the same period, and crucially – even if ambiguously – underline how their queer intersection with race, ethnicity and gender as suggested by Sedgwick contributed to creating a discursive context which formed a backdrop for the evolving sexological and sociocultural discourses that developed in late-Victorian London.

Notes

1   Robert Aldrich, *Colonialism and Homosexuality* (London and New York: Routledge, 2003). See also Matt Cook, *London and the Culture of Homosexuality, 1885–1914* (Cambridge: Cambridge University Press, 2008) and Sean Brady, *Masculinity and Male Homosexuality, 1861–1913* (Basingstoke: Palgrave, 2005).

2   Havelock Ellis wrote that the Wilde trials seemed 'to have generally contributed to give definitiveness and self-consciousness to the manifestations of homosexuality, and to have aroused inverts to take up a definitive stand' (*Studies in the Psychology of Sex. Vol. 2: Sexual Inversion*, New York: Random House, 1936, p. 253). See also Ed Cohen, *Talk on the Wilde Side: Toward a Genealogy of a Discourse on Male Sexualities* (New York and London: Routledge, 1993), especially pp. 91–3.

3   *The History of Sexuality. Volume 1: The Will to Knowledge* (Harmondsworth: Penguin, 1978), p. 43.

4   See Eve Kosofsky Sedgwick's 'Introduction: Axiomatic', in *Epistemology of the Closet* (Berkeley: University of California Press, 1990), pp. 1–63.

5   Sedgwick, *Epistemology of the Closet*, p. 47.

6 Sedgwick, *Tendencies* (London: Routledge, 1994), p. 7.

7 Ibid., p. 9.

8 David Halperin has remarked that 'all scientific inquiries into the aetiology of sexual orientation, after all, spring from a more or less implicit theory of sexual races' ('Homosexuality: A Cultural Construct', in *One Hundred Years of Homosexuality: And Other Essays on Greek Love*, New York: Routledge, 1990, p. 50). Other works that investigate this connection include Abdul R. JanMohamed, 'Sexuality on/of the Racial Border: Foucault, Wright, and the Articulation of "Racialised Sexuality"', in Domna C. Stanton (ed.), *Discourses of Sexuality: From Aristotle to AIDS* (Ann Arbor: University of Michigan, 1992), pp. 94–116; Jennifer Terry, 'Anxious Slippages between "Us" and "Them": A Brief History of the Scientific Search for Homosexual Bodies', in Jennifer Terry and Jacqueline Urla (eds), *Deviant Bodies: Critical Perspectives on Difference in Science and Popular Culture* (Bloomington: Indiana University Press, 1995), pp. 129–69; Siobhan B. Somerville, 'Scientific Racism and the Invention of the Homosexual Body', in Laura Doan and Lucy Bland (eds), *Sexology in Culture: Labelling Bodies and Desires* (Cambridge: Polity Press, 1998), pp. 60–76.

9 See, for example, Lisa Z. Sigel, *Governing Pleasures: Pornography and Social Change in England, 1815–1914* (New Brunswick, NJ: Rutgers University Press, 2002).

10 *Between Men. English Literature and Male Homosocial Desire* (New York: Columbia University Press, 1985), p. 3; emphasis in the text.

11 See Jeffrey Weeks, *Coming Out: Homosexual Politics in Britain from the Nineteenth Century to the Present* (London: Quartet Books, 1990 [1977]), pp. 1–137; Ed Cohen, 'Legislating the Norm: From Sodomy to Gross Indecency', *South Atlantic Quarterly* 88 (Winter 1989), pp. 181–215; and Louis Crompton, *Byron and Greek Love: Homophobia in Nineteenth-Century England* (Berkeley: University of California Press, 1985).

12 Aldrich, *Colonialism and Homosexuality*, p. 10.

13 Ibid., p. 3.

14 Edward Said, *Orientalism* (Harmondsworth: Penguin, 1978), p. 190.

15 Joseph A. Boone, 'Vacation Cruises; Or, the Homoerotics of Orientalism', *PMLA* (Special Topic: Colonialism and the Postcolonial Condition) 110.1 (January 1995), pp. 89–107, 90, my italics.

16 E. Villin, 'Discussion' (of 'On Phallic Worship'), *Anthropological Review* 8 (1870), p. cxliii, my italics.

17 On this point, see James Hunt, 'Anniversary Address to the Anthropological Society of London', *Journal of the Anthropological Society of London* 5 (1867), pp. lxi–lxii; and 'President's Address' (1864), p. xciii; Richard Lee, 'The Extinction of Races', *Journal of the Anthropological Society of London* 2 (1864), p. xcviii; 'The Chairman [Lord Stanley] at Farewell Dinner for Captain [R.F.] Burton', *Anthropological Review* 3.9 (1865), p. 169; John Beddoe, 'Discussion' (of 'The Manchester Anthropological Society'),

Anthropological Review 5 (1867), p. 20; Joseph Kaines, 'The Ultimate Object of Anthropological Study' and 'Western Anthropologists and Extra Western Communities', *Anthropologia* 1 (1873), pp. 34, 226, 229.

18　The founding members included Rajah Sir James Brooke of Sarawak; the Governor Eyre of Jamaica; George Selwyn; the prehistorian William Pengelly; the poet Algernon Charles Swinburne; Alfred Wallace; and F. W. Farrar. See J. W. Burrow, 'Evolution and Anthropology in the 1860s: The Anthropological Society of London, 1863–71', *Victorian Studies* 7.2 (December 1963), pp. 137–54, 146.

19　Burrow notes that the society was 'founded in 1843, [but] it did not begin to publish its proceedings regularly until 1848'; ibid., p. 144.

20　James Cowles Prichard, *Researches into the Physical History of Mankind*, 3rd edn, 5 vols. (London: Sherwood, Gilbert and Piper), pp. 1836–47.

21　On the controversies between the Ethnological Society and the Anthropological Society, see J. W. Burrow, 'Evolution and Anthropology in the 1860s', pp. 137–54; Ronald Rainger, 'Race, Politics and Science: The Anthropological Society of London in the 1860s', *Victorian Studies* 22.1 (Autumn 1978), pp. 51–70; and George W. Stocking, *Victorian Anthropology* (New York: Macmillan, 1987).

22　See Somerville, 'Scientific Racism and the Invention of the Homosexual Body', pp. 60–76.

23　Sigel, *Governing Pleasures*, p. 60.

24　After years of controversies, The Anthropological Society merged with the Ethnological Society into the Anthropological Institute in 1871.

25　*Anthropologia: In Which Are Included the Proceedings of the London Anthropological Society: 1873–1875*, vol. 1 (London: Baillière, Tindall & Cox, 1875), pp. 78–88, 157–64, 571–8, 165–72.

26　Sigel, *Governing Pleasures*, p. 62.

27　Significantly, they undertook their research in the decades following the 1861 Offences Against the Person Act, which removed the death penalty for buggery. In this way, they seemed to respond to a widespread attempt which was taking place in the medical field to classify different forms of male same-sex practices.

28　Jeffrey Weeks, *Making Sexual History* (London: Polity Press, 2000), pp. 236–7.

29　Male communities shaped on the 'monastic' model included the Tractarians, who started a religious fraternity in the 1840s, and the Pre-Raphaelites, who formed a secular Brotherhood devoted to the celebration of art.

30　Herbert Sussman, *Victorian Masculinities: Manhood and Masculine Poetics in Early Victorian Literature and Art* (Cambridge: Cambridge University Press, 1995), p. 5, my italics.

31　Elaine Showalter acknowledges that the drive towards masculinization was also constructed in response to perceived threats to stable masculine identity;

among them, the effects of 'British imperialism and fears of manly decline' (*Sexual Anarchy: Gender and Culture at the Fin de Siècle*, New York: Viking, 1990, p. 83).

32 Burton translated several Indian and Arabic erotic works in unabridged form, such as *The Kama Sutra of Vatsyayana* (1883), *The Perfumed Garden of the Cheikh Nefzaoui* (1884), and the *Ananga Ranga (Stage of the Bodiless One); or, The Hindu Art of Love* (1885). See Silvia Antosa, *Richard Francis Burton: Victorian Explorer and Translator* (Bern, Oxford and New York: Peter Lang, 2012), pp. 155–90.

33 His works include *New Ladies Tickler, or the Adventures of Lady Lovesport and the Audacious Harry* (1866), *The New Epicurean* (1865), *The Merry Order of St. Bridget, Personal Recollections of the Use of the Rod* (1868), and his erotic autobiography *The Ups and Downs of Life* (1867).

34 See James Pope-Hennessey, *Monckton Milnes: The Flight of Youth 1851–1885* (London: Constable, 1951), pp. 108–26.

35 Ashbee wrote a three-volume encyclopaedia which aimed at cataloguing all existing pornographic work in England: *Index Librorum Prohibitorum: Being Notes Bio-Biblio Icono-Graphical and Critical in Curious and Uncommon Books* (1877); *Centuria Librorum Absconditorum* (1879); and *Catena Librorum Tacendorum* (1885).

36 Sigel, *Governing Pleasures*, pp. 2–3.

37 Their works range from exoticism to phallicism, flagellation and hermaphroditism. See, for example, John Davenport's *Aphrodisiacs and Anti-aphrodisiacs* (1869), *Curiositates Eroticae Physiologie* (1875) and *Esoteric Physiology Sexagima* (1888); Ashbee's *Bibliotheca Arcana* (1884), *The Library Illustrative of Social Progress* (1860–1873) and *Fashionable Lectures: Composed and Delivered with Birch Discipline* (1873).

38 Deborah Lutz, *Pleasure Bound: Victorian Sex Rebels and the New Eroticism* (New York and London: W.W. Norton & Company, 2011), p. 75; and Stocking, *Victorian Anthropology*, p. 252.

39 H.L. Malchow, *Gothic Images of Race in Nineteenth-Century Britain* (Stanford, CA: Stanford University Press, 1996), p. 42.

40 Stephen Greenblatt, *Marvelous Possessions: The Wonder of the New World* (Chicago, IL: University of Chicago Press, 1991), p. 6.

41 Malchow, *Gothic Images of Race*, p. 100.

42 'Cannibalism and Fiction II: The Sexual Metaphor', *Genre* 11.2 (1978), pp. 227–34.

43 *The Book of the Thousand Nights and a Night. A Plain and Literal Translation of the Arabian Nights' Entertainments*, vol. 10 (London and Benares: Kama Shastra Society, 1885), p. 227. The adjective 'Sotadic' came from Sotades, a Greek poet who dealt with homosexual themes (ibid., pp. 206–7).

44 Ibid., p. 240, my italics.

45   Lutz, *Pleasure Bound*, p. 153, my italics.

46   In a note in the 1892 edition, Whitman acknowledged that 'comradeship' refers to male homosexuality, or 'adhesive love'. The use of the term 'comrade' is a clear political reference that joins together adhesive love to a masculine and militaristic idea (see *Leaves of Grass and Other Writings*, New York: Norton, 2002, p. 771).

47   On Whitman's influence in England see Sedgwick, *Between Men*, pp. 201–17; M. Wynn Thomas, *Transatlantic Connections: Whitman U.S., Whitman U.K.* (Iowa City: Iowa University Press, 2005); and Michael Robertson, *Worshipping Whitman: The Whitman Disciples* (Princeton, NJ: Princeton University Press, 2010).

48   Arthur Munby wrote that Swinburne usually 'kept up a long and earnest talk, or rather declamation, about the merits of Walt Whitman' (Arthur Munby, diary entry, 2 December 1867, in Derek Hudson, *Munby: Man of Two Worlds. The Life and Diaries of Arthur J. Munby, 1828–1910*, London: John Murray, 1972, p. 246). Swinburne wrote that Whitman was the 'passionate preacher of sexual or political freedom' (Swinburne, *William Blake (1868)*, reprinted in Edmund Gosse and Thomas James Wise (eds), *The Complete Works of Swinburne*, vol. VI, London: William Heinemann, 1926, p. 342).

49   *Memoirs Read Before the Anthropological Society of London* (London: Trübner, 1865), pp. 327–34.

50   See the *Journal of the Anthropological Society of London* 3 (1865), pp. cxiv–cxxi.

51   'On the Linga Puja, or Phallic Worship in India', p. 334, my italics.

52   Burton, 'Notes Connected with the Dahoman', in *Memoirs Read Before the Anthropological Society of London*, vol. 1, pp. 308–21, 320, my italics.

53   Burton translated other works on homosexuality, such as *Il Pentamerone* (1893) and *The Carmina of Caius Valerius Catullus* (1894). Before his death, he was revising one of his previous translations, *The Perfumed Garden*, which was entitled *The Scented Garden*. In his new version, he wanted to explore the issue of male homosexuality in the twenty-first chapter. His wife's burning of his annotations after his death prevented the circulation of his work. See Antosa, *Richard Francis Burton*, pp. 24–37.

54   Frank Fane (Swinburne) to Richard Monckton Milnes, 27 December 1862 (*The Swinburne Letters*, ed. Cecil Y. Lang, New Haven, CT: Yale University Press, 1959–62, vol. 1, p. 41).

55   See Sigel, *Governing Pleasures*, p. 53.

56   Letter to Swinburne from Villine, 1871, found in *The Cannibal Catechism* (London: printed for private circulation, 1913), copy held at Northwestern University.

57   Anti-religious and anti-missionary ideas fervently animated the Cannibals. During their meetings, they displayed in their front window a skeleton of a savage in order to provoke the reaction of the Christian Union, whose

headquarters were just across the street (see 'Farewell Dinner to Captain R.F. Burton', *Anthropological Review* 3.9, May 1865, p. 175).

58 Weeks, *Coming Out*, p. 59.

59 Somerville, 'Scientific Racism and the Invention of the Homosexual Body', p. 68. In acknowledging that the word 'homosexual' had entered common use, Symonds and Ellis criticized its impure origins by stating that '"homosexual" is a barbarously hybrid word' (1897, p. 1). In another edition, Ellis further explained that 'it has, philologically, the awkward disadvantage of being a *bastard term* compounded of Greek and Latin elements' (*Sexual Inversion*, 1915, p. 2, my italics).

60 It was introduced into English through the 1892 English translation of Richard von Krafft-Ebing's *Psychopatia Sexualis*.

61 Ibid., p. 78.

62 *A Problem in Modern Ethics* (London: Charles R. Dawes Ex Libris, 1896), p. 183.

63 Lutz, *Pleasure Bound*, p. 251.

64 Ellis wrote: 'The theory of the Sotadic Zone is interesting, but... Burton was wholly unacquainted with the recent psychological investigations into sexual inversion which had, indeed, scarcely begun in his day' (*Sexual Inversion*, 1906, p. 28, n. 5).

CHAPTER ELEVEN

'Famous for the paint she put on her face': London's Painted Poofs and the Self-Fashioning of Francis Bacon

Dominic Janes

The landscape inhabited by lesbians and gay men in contemporary London is haunted by past traumas from the pillory to AIDS. The term 'gay' explicitly attempts to assert the possibilities of pleasure and happiness, whereas the term 'queer' represents an appropriation of a word that originally was disdainfully employed with reference to those whom society found peculiar and perverse. This chapter will be looking at a time when 'gay' was not widely used to mean homosexual and lives of sexual deviance were extensively criminalized. Francis Bacon (1909–92) worked for most of his career in London and came to be closely associated with drinking and gambling scenes in the city's West End. He openly embraced the pleasures and experiences of London's high life and low life and his work created queerly transgressive blendings of the two. The word 'queer' is a powerful descriptor for Bacon's art because it is often used in 'queer theory' to apply to circumstances in which normativity is put under pressure and transgressed in relation not only to sexuality but also to other aspects of cultural life, including gender.[1] In this chapter I will be looking at Bacon's work as queer visual culture and reading it in its geographical and sexual context.[2] In particular, I will be seeking to contribute to recent trends in scholarship that contest earlier narratives that Bacon's art should be studied separately from what used to be seen, and in some quarters still are seen, as sordid aspects of his personal life. Bacon's sadomasochism, let alone his homosexuality, was little discussed in his lifetime in the critical literature. It was often treated as sensational biographical material in the years after his death.[3] But queer desire has begun to be read in certain quarters as central to his artistic practices such that the energy with which he painted the male nude has increasingly been seen as indicative of libidinal engagement rather than being evocative of nihilism and existential despair. Appreciating Bacon as a masochist similarly allows his fascination with brutality to be reinterpreted as a product of desire rather than of fear.[4] However, such work has not placed his art in the context of homosexual urban subcultures that were invested in transgressions of both normative sexuality and gender performance.

I will argue that it is through engagement with practices of gender indeterminacy that we can reach enhanced understandings of the self-fashioning of Francis Bacon seen in the context of his metropolitan milieu. This is not the same thing as reclaiming him for gay pride. It has recently been suggested, for instance, that a photograph dated to c.1945 by Bacon's friend John Deakin is not an 'unknown woman' but the artist cross-dressed (Figure 11.1).[5] The caption provided at the time of writing by Getty Images

FIGURE 11.1 *Caption provided by Getty Images: 'Portrait of an unidentified transvestite, possibly the artist Francis Bacon in drag, England pre-1945. The cleavage raises questions, but may be the result of photo manipulation.' (Photo by The John Deakin Archive/Getty Images.)*

is fascinating in itself: 'portrait of an unidentified transvestite, possibly the artist Francis Bacon in drag, England pre-1945. The cleavage raises questions, but may be the result of photo manipulation'. The key question raised by that cleavage is not so much whether it was 'real' or not but, more broadly, what role gender transgression played both in Bacon's self-fashioning and in our reception of those practices after his death. It is notable, whether this attribution is correct or not, that what seems to connect the *style* of this image to that of Bacon is its unhappy tawdriness rather than any obvious beauty or glamour. For Bacon's extraordinary talent enabled him to explore the deeper significance of what the conventional world viewed as ugly and shameful.

Rather than framing my argument around an extensive selection of paintings, I will juxtapose an example of his artistic work with a photograph taken in an interwar police raid. The aim of this is to disrupt expectations that studies of Bacon must be art historical. My aim here is not to present a new reading of his paintings, although I believe that attention paid to gender performance might be productive of just that, but to see them as artefacts of queer visual culture. Few of Bacon's works from the 1930s survive and therefore the painting from 1945 to 1946, *Figure Study II* (Figure 11.2), around which I will be framing my argument, can be identified as coming from the first period of his artistic fame. This was a time when many of London's homes were literally open to the skies because of bomb damage and this opening of private space to the public gaze can be seen as emblematic of the many ways in which the war had disrupted the boundaries of privacy with which bourgeois family life had been sustained. Bacon's work of this period has most often been understood as a response to violent trauma. Thus, to take one example, it has been pointed out that Bacon was inspired both by Roman Catholic imagery and by Nazi photography to create images of contemporary agony.[6] So powerful indeed was the impact of one particular work, *Three Studies for Figures at the Base of a Crucifixion* (c.1944), that it led to other work of this time, including *Figure Study II*, being read using the same interpretative reference to the profanation of the sacred. Thus this latter work, which has been described as a 'strange figure of indeterminate sex', came frequently and erroneously to be referred to as *The Magdalene*.[7] I will be arguing that in these works Bacon enacted queer transgressions through targeting the public gaze onto perverse, private desires that were sexual rather than spiritual.

This strategy can be compared with the disciplinary gaze of the police as they sought to enforce public standards of morality in London's bodily and domestic interiors. Notably, Bacon's interest in the inner city's domestic interiors as places of moral transgression echoed the well-entrenched understandings of English legal practice. Thus one of the key pieces of legislation employed against brothels and queer clubs alike during the first decades of the twentieth century by the Metropolitan Police was the Disorderly Houses Act (1751).[8] Disorderly houses were, in the words

FIGURE 11.2 *Francis Bacon*, Figure Study II *(1945–46), oil on canvas, 145 × 128.5 cm. Huddersfield Art Gallery, reproduced courtesy of the estate of Francis Bacon, all rights reserved, DACS 201x, photographed by Prudence Cuming Associates Ltd.*

of the judge presiding over the trial of those arrested at a private party in Fitzroy Square, London, in 1927, places that were 'not regulated by the restraints of morality'.[9] From the point of view of the 'respectable' opinion of the time, sodomy was a disgusting act of bodily violation. Therefore, when comparing the views of the police and those of homosexual men on scenes of perceived immorality, it is important to remember the potential for the eroticization of abject acts and spaces on the part of the latter. Crucially, it is important to stress that Bacon aestheticized violence and transgression in association with his sadomasochistic, same-sex desires. He was, if anything, erotically thrilled that men during the Second World War were often meat for the grinder.[10] Bacon's disorderly houses, therefore, were not isolated locales within a city of decency, but expressions of what he felt, ultimately, to be universal human drives. However, the manner in which Bacon approached his artistic challenge needs to be situated within the specific conditions of London in the mid-twentieth century and the subculture of the painted poof.

London's painted poofs

Gender transgression was one of the ways in which homosexuals made themselves visible to each other and the use of effeminate gestures, dress and make-up was, therefore, scrutinized by the police in their efforts to control sex between men. It has been widely noted that Francis Bacon did not only paint pictures; he also painted his own face with cosmetics. Moreover, he told the art historian Michael Peppiatt that the connection was forcibly brought home to him one day when he walked into a bar when he was starting to become well-known, probably in the immediate post-war years, and he heard a camp man say loudly, 'as for *her*, when we knew *her*, she was more famous for the paint she put on her face than for the paint she put on canvas'.[11] Bacon was hugely amused thereby to be compared to a vulgar, female street-walker. Make-up was used by a minority of men in mid-twentieth-century London and among its functions was not only to improve appearance but to send the signal that one was open to same-sex advances, or even that one was a male prostitute.[12] Some of those men simply added make-up to otherwise masculine self-presentation, while others, of whom Quentin Crisp (1908–99) was to become the most famous example, projected a more overtly androgynous self-image. Crisp similarly identified the post-war period – 1948 to be precise – as a time when art met artifice since it was in that year that he changed his hair dye from henna to blue and entered, evoking Picasso, his 'blue period'.[13]

At a time of rising public and police concern over the 'problem' of homosexuality, such behaviours became of intense interest to the authorities.[14] As Matt Houlbrook has revealed, the 'man with the powder puff' became an object of both erotic and phobic fascination in interwar London.[15] As he explains, such men 'were an integral and startling part of metropolitan modernity, embodying the nagging fear that the city offered queer men an affirmative space, where their desires were no longer abhorrent and depraved'.[16] In the nineteenth century cosmetics had been widely associated with the arts of ageing prostitutes and were seen as unfit for respectable women let alone men. Yet at least the first of these beliefs was starting to come to seem old-fashioned during the Edwardian period. And when cheap powder puffs and other items of the cosmetic arts appeared after the end of the First World War, they were seized on with enthusiasm by a new generation of women.[17] Houlbrook has emphasized the role of the spread of consumerism in working-class urban culture and the guarded degree of toleration that some in these communities might accord to men who presented themselves as feminine.[18] While the behaviour of such 'quaens' made some men careful to weed out indications of personal effeminacy, their example encouraged certain middle-class boys such as the young Crisp (then Dennis Pratt) to flee the conformist suburbs in search of opportunities for self-expression in the inner city.[19] Francis Bacon came from a wealthy, upper-middle class family which had been part of the Anglo-Irish ascendency. However, certain members of the British upper classes had been interested since the later nineteenth century in 'slumming' among the lower classes.[20] So when Bacon's father sent his seemingly effeminate son away to encounter some manly influences in metropolitan England and Germany, the results were not at all what he had intended.

Bacon entered with enthusiasm into the opportunities offered by the nightlife of the 1920s and became a 'man with a powder-puff' in Berlin, Paris and London, during which time he not only used his appearance to attract sexual partners but, probably, also to generate an income. Bacon's use of make-up predated his practices of painting on canvas and it seems the former influenced the latter, bearing in mind that he did not receive a formal training as an artist. Moreover, he not merely applied paint onto the rough side of the canvas but he also practised swirling make-up onto his own stubbled visage.[21] The implication of this is that the faces in Bacon's paintings need to be considered in relation to his own. His anonymous men, in particular, even when they seem muscular and lacking in the signs of androgyny, are queered by their being 'made-up' in this way from the viewpoint and discipline of a man with a powder-puff who self-consciously played games with the presentation of gender. Bacon's bodily performances, therefore, like those of many other self-consciously anti-bourgeois 'modern' artists, were part of a continuum between his art and his life.[22]

Christian morality before the twentieth century took the subject of cosmetics seriously. For instance, as Patricia Phillippy has pointed out in *Painting Women: Cosmetics, Canvases, and Early Modern Culture* (2006), the way in which women used make-up during the Renaissance was held to be an important moral subject for the (male) artist to explore. Furthermore, the concern that make-up was an art of deception had a tendency to reflect back on the authority of the artist's supposed mission toward the revelation of moral truths.[23] Since Bacon was characteristically emphatic that his work was not concerned with constructing elaborate codes of meaning that had to be decoded but was aimed at evoking intense emotional reactions to shared human truths (such as the universality of pain and desire), it would seem that he subscribed to the notion of what might be termed the truth of cosmetics; that is to say, the decadent position espoused by Oscar Wilde, among others, that masks reveal who we really are.

In his introduction to the catalogue for the exhibition 'Francis Bacon: Paintings from the 1950s' (University of East Anglia, Norwich 2006; Milwaukee Art Museum 2007; and Albright-Knox Art Gallery, Buffalo

2007), Michael Peppiatt begins by talking about Bacon's eyes. In his youth, says Peppiatt, the painter's eyes were wide with curiosity, but they slowly became wary and hardened: 'Later they will grow old in a young face. The smooth cheeks, the carefully tousled hair will continue to proclaim Bacon's uncanny youth, defying a lifetime of every excess. But like the portrait of Dorian Gray, the eyes will continue to absorb and record.'[24] I am engaged in a practice of reading back and forth between Bacon's perceptions and his self-projections and thinking about the way in which these processes can be understood in relation to the evolution of wider cultural practices over time. On the one hand, the painter should be carefully positioned in relation to historical contexts as being, or having been, a 'west end [of London] poof', as described by the lawyer Travers Humphreys in 1927.[25] Yet, just as Bacon and Crisp continued to embody aspects of this phenomenon late into the twentieth century, so the man with the powder puff did not jump ready formed from his powder compact. As can be seen from the historical definitions given in the *Oxford English Dictionary*, a sodomitical meaning for the word 'poof' can be traced back in London to the first half of the nineteenth century when, on 11 April 1833, it was attested during a trial at the Old Bailey that 'there was a gentleman who gave a great deal of money for boys...[and] there was a [another] gentleman in the City, too, that was one of these *poofs*, as he called them...I never heard the word *poofs* before'. By around 1855, the *Yokel's Perceptor* was pointing out to those who were, at least supposedly, innocent of the ways of the big city the existence of 'these monsters in the shape of men, commonly designated Margeries, Pooffs, &c'.[26]

In order to appreciate the cultural landscape inhabited by Bacon, it is important to appreciate that it had long, and complex, antecedents. Sodomitical subcultures of London, as far back as they can be identified, were implicated in transgressions of gender performance. Ever since the publication of Rictor Norton's *Mother Clap's Molly House: The Gay Subculture in England, 1700–1830* (1992), the precursors of modern patterns of gender-bending have come to wider attention in Britain.[27] It is perhaps the only gay history book that has been made into a play (by Mark Ravenhill), which debuted in September 2001 at the National Theatre in London. The play was directed by Nicholas Hytner at the very time when it was announced that he was to be appointed as director of the National Theatre itself. But like many another study of same-sex desire in history, Norton's work needs to be considered as a product of its own times, notably in relation to the progress of gay liberation and the contemporary AIDS crisis. In particular, Norton's naming of the subculture that he had researched as being 'gay' has been seen as highly problematic in so far as that term was not to come into widespread use in Britain with a sexual signification until the 1970s. However, part of Norton's argument was that similarities of desire could be found between those very different historical periods and with them certain similar problems, such as how to tell who was interested in a same-sex advance and who not; who was merely staring and who was doing so with sexual intent. Thus it is important to stress that the culture of London's mollies of the eighteenth century was not the same as that of its poofs in the nineteenth and twentieth centuries but there were, nevertheless, significant elements of continuity and similarity.

Female attributes such as items of dress or nicknames were employed by small networks of men in early eighteenth-century London who shared interests that at the time would have been referred to as sodomitical.[28] The very use of a woman's name, 'Molly', indicated interests in attributes of femininity which were by no means implicit in the word 'sodomite'. In fact, eighteenth-century London saw the coining of dozens of words for groups of men thought to be characterized as effeminate, such as 'fops', 'fribbles' and 'macaronis'.[29] Whatever understandings such men themselves may have had of their own behaviour and sexual tastes, there was clearly considerable public confusion over whether, and if so in what way, transgressions of gendered behaviour were coterminous with sexual deviance. While the word 'molly' did survive into the nineteenth century, along with descriptions of behaviours similar to those practised in molly houses of the previous century (such as sham marriages and births), such accounts may represent little more than the survival of satirical tropes.[30] Newspaper reports of Victorian sodomy trials make it quite clear, however, that the issue of effeminacy in men, and associated elements of gender transgression, continued to be seen as important throughout the nineteenth century. Indeed, one of the most important of such trials, that of Ernest Boulton and Frederick William Park in 1871, centred on exactly this issue of whether transgressions of gendered appearance (including both clothing and make-up) were directly to be understood as evidences of sodomitical desire.[31] In the course of the trial, the Beadle of the Burlington Arcade, George Smith, attested that he regularly saw these two men powdered and rouged, sometimes cross-dressed and sometimes not. He testified that the accused 'caused much commotion', that 'everybody was looking at them' and that this behaviour was, in effect, understood to be related to male prostitution.[32]

In the ensuing years, it came to public notice that young men of various classes were thought to be displaying the visual evidences of effeminacy more extensively than hitherto. Thus, in 1893 the periodical *Hearth and Home* denounced 'young men who are got up'. It was not simply a matter of bangles, high-pitched voices and waving lily-white hands; it was reported that 'it is an absolute fact that a large number of young men get themselves up. The rouge-pot and the powder-puff find a place on their toilet table. Their eyebrows are darkened; their hair is often crimped or curled, and sometimes even dyed; and their figures are trained and artificially improved'.[33] That there was a sexual significance to such fears is indicated by the enthusiasm on the part of artistic and decadent circles associated with Oscar Wilde for colourful and artificial transgressions of natural appearances. Thus Max Beerbohm's essay, 'A Defense of Cosmetics' (reprinted as 'The Pervasion of Rouge'), which appeared in *The Yellow Book* in April 1894, may have been written tongue-in-cheek but it engendered a remarkable public outcry among those who took seriously his claims for the delights of artifice and of face-paint as the original form of art.[34] Beerbohm was writing about the use of cosmetics by women but, twenty years later, cosmetics could be employed, not simply by the queer urban subculture, but also by middle-class young men in a spirit of rebellion and individualism. This appears to have been how they were employed by Cecil Beaton when he attended Harrow School from 1918. On 25 January 1926, after he had come down from Cambridge without a degree, Beaton wrote that:

> I wondered why I had painted my face [at Harrow]. I always used to powder and put red stuff on my lips. It's so idiotic to think that people don't notice it...Now I squirm to see a man powdered. I must have been rather awful at Harrow and I used to think I was so marvelous, so witty and bright and subtle and interesting.[35]

What is fascinating about this comment is that it was only in the mid-1920s, when he was emerging into the homosexual party-circuit of London's West End, that Beaton felt revulsion against the use of cosmetics. Perhaps it was because it was at this time that, finally, make-up on men became fixed in terms of public opinion, as opposed to sub-cultural practice, as clear evidence of same-sex desire.[36]

Because of criminalization the police were keen to ask the question 'what does a homosexual look and behave like?' The desire to bracket off such people from everyone else who was 'normal' has inspired all manner of answers. Thus one recent academic writer, E. Patrick Johnson, recounted on visiting his grandmother who lived in North Carolina that she was concerned that there was a homosexual in her care home: '"Well how do you know the man's a homosexual, Grandmama?" She paused, rubbed her leg, narrowed her eyes and responded, "Well, he gardens, bakes pies, and keeps a clean house."'[37] She would, on those grounds, presumably never have identified the notoriously dust-ignoring Quentin Crisp.[38] He first came to widespread notice as a result of the TV film of his autobiography, *The Naked Civil Servant* (1968).[39] Andy Medhurst recalled that, as a sixteen-year-old, 'its celebration of Quentin Crisp's unrepentant queenliness filled me with an elated, vertiginous sense of identification, belonging and defiant pride...I had seen the future – and it minced'.[40] Yet Crisp's life and beliefs were not the product of the gay liberation movement of the 1970s and he was not proud in the way that came to be expected by men of Medhurst's generation. Crisp felt ashamed of his effeminacy which, he felt, was a form of disfigurement that he could never conceal.[41] His autobiography provides eloquent testimony to the years of verbal and physical abuse that he suffered as the price not only for sexual opportunities but also for being himself.[42] Bacon, by contrast, enthusiastically pursued abusive sexual encounters, and created works in which blurred figures are deliberately denied their individuality. The issue of 'gay shame' has received considerable scholarly attention.[43] I will now go on to explore some of the ways in which the abject shame of the painted sodomite provided part of the erotic impetus for his processes of artistic creation.

The visual culture of Francis Bacon

Francis Bacon's *Figure Study II* (1945–46) (Figure 11.2) shows a room in which there is a half-draped, bloated form, the face of which is ruptured into a scream. This image evokes a powerful sense of embodied shame centred on bodily concealment and revelation which I would argue was related to Bacon's queer sexuality. Since sexual acts between men of any age were illegal in England and Wales until the passing of the Sexual Offences Act (1967), this meant that a room in which two or more men had sex together was the scene of a crime. This was something that seems to have fascinated Bacon since he made several references to crime scenes or even to the concept of a 'bed of crime'.[44] He would have been well aware, moving in the circles he did, of the constant threats of police raids and blackmail. In the eyes of the police, the basement flat at 25 Fitzroy Square that they testified to raiding in the case of *Rex v. Britt and Others* (1927) was a disorderly house which was the resort of what Chief Inspector Robert Sygrove described as '"Nancy Boys"'.[45] Cross-dressing was observed as part of the police surveillance prior to the raid and several items of female attire were duly presented as evidence in court.[46] In a photograph taken by the police photographer during the raid, a certain Mrs Carré, who said she was Britt's wife, stares at the camera in resigned amusement. The men, however, look away. Britt himself sits bare-chested and wearing what the police claimed to have been a transparent skirt (Figure 11.3).[47] The red-painted room behind housed a bed with rumpled covers and was dimly lit by a lamp concealed behind an umbrella.[48] Red lamps, it should be noted, were associated with prostitution and one of these was placed over the entrance to the flat. This scene, when juxtaposed with Britt's exposed person, evoked, for the police, a narrative of sodomitical shame. In *Figure Study II*, a pale figure bellows its shame (a detail which Peppiatt connects to the state of orgasm) against a red-orange background, conjuring the thought of bending over and being buggered.[49] Bacon's own sexual tastes were for violent, working-class, masculine men. The figure in Bacon's painting, executed when the artist himself was reaching middle age, may also be channelling enhanced self-disgust at the thought that he would soon become a flabby, aged poof.[50]

FIGURE 11.3 *Fitzroy Square group. Evidence presented at the Central Criminal Court,* Rex v. Britt and Others, *1927, CRIM 1/387, reproduced courtesy of the National Archives, London.*

The above example shows that private parties were by no means places of safety for homosexuals while those who put on make-up and went out onto the streets faced a potential barrage of verbal and physical abuse. While Crisp, as I have indicated, seems to have faced this with defiance, Bacon appears to have revelled in it and actively sought physical abuse both from strangers and from long-term sexual partners. Such behaviour, and indeed the very terms 'sadism' and 'masochism', was first classified as forms of sexual perversion in the late-nineteenth century by the same cadre of doctors and psychologists who were busy identifying and naming homosexuality.[51] Sexuality theorists have hotly debated whether sadism and masochism should be seen as separate phenomena from BDSM or S/M and whether they can operate as liberatory practices. Thus Leo Bersani has argued that S/M is 'profoundly conservative in that its imagination of pleasure is almost entirely defined by the dominant culture to which it thinks of itself as giving "a stinging slap in the face"'.[52] This is so because, he would argue, it involves the worship of conventional masculinity.[53] John

Noyes, however, among many others, has argued against this by advancing his view of masochism as a radical practice:

> masochism is not the love of submissiveness. It is not the pursuit of unpleasure or humiliation. It is a complex set of practices for transforming submissiveness, pain, and unpleasure, into sexual pleasure. But over and above this, it is the appropriation of the technologies that our culture uses in order to perpetuate submissiveness.[54]

Another way to look at this situation is to argue that masochistic desires are indeed based on a fatalistic capitulation to existing power structures but one which optimizes the benefits to the self from that state of subjection.[55] Seen from this point of view, queer, masochistic effeminacy acquiesced in the misogynistic abjection of femininity as the inevitable corollary of being a self-identified homosexual. The same reading back and forth between body and art that can be made in relation to Bacon's uses of make-up and paint can also be deployed in relation to his violent sexual practices and the canvases at which he slashed and gouged.[56] The reward for Bacon as masochist was both erotic satisfaction and a sense of superiority over those closeted men who were in denial about the effeminacy that was believed to be an inherent aspect of the homosexual condition.

It is interesting to compare such practices of painful self-expression with those highlighted in one of the first openly gay plays to run in New York, Robert Patrick's *The Haunted Host* (1964). Its mood of gloomy camp appears to put it in the same category as Mart Crowley's (in)famously maudlin *The Boys in the Band* (opened 1968, film directed by William Friedkin, 1970). In Patrick's play, the lead character, Jay, is an overtly feminine man whose lover has just committed suicide. Yet by using his self-assured wit, Jay is able to dominate and master a straight-acting man and thereby, in Darren Patrick Blaney's view, through 'envisioning an alternative ending for the tragic queen archetype, the play enacts a critique of homosexual identities by offering a vision in which the stereotypical power dynamic between the gay man and the straight man is inverted'.[57] In a similar manner, Bacon used his wit, and his wealth, to enable himself to survive events such as the suicide of his lover, George Dyer. And just as Patrick's play should be seen against the backdrop of an interwar heritage of queer theatre (the previous age of openly flagrant theatrics in New York was in the 1920s with the plays of Mae West), so Bacon honed his strategies of effeminate survival, and gained his foundational artistic inspirations, in the same interwar period.[58]

Interest in such strategies of self-construction from positions of weakness has risen in recent years with the appearance of a new level of appreciation for the queerness of states of failure; witness Judith Halberstam's acknowledgement of Quentin Crisp's comment that 'if at first you don't succeed, failure may be your style' as a key inspiration for her own study of the 'queer art of failure'.[59] Yet if Bacon had failed to be a real man, the effect of his art was to establish swirls of make-up – incomplete swirls that deliberately evoke interior emptiness – as the visual form for both femmes and butches. This implies that painted poofs should be seen not simply as a sub-category of 'effeminate' homosexual men, but as a partially empowered group of people able to make a variety of radical statements about the human condition, including on the advantages of eroticizing its own abject failure to live up to contemporary ideals of gender. It is not surprising, therefore, that the Metropolitan Police spent so much energy scrutinizing London's painted poofs since the latter not only embodied a state of queer transgression but also took its spirit out of their disorderly houses and onto the streets of Britain's capital city. This case study has focused on a single painting by Francis Bacon but it is intended to contribute to a process of wider engagement with re-viewing his work as having emerged from queer subcultures of London in the mid-twentieth century that were engaged in transgressions not only of sexual but also of gender norms. This means re-evaluating the world of the painted poof as containing within it counter-cultural bravery and the potential for remarkable acts of artistic self-expression.

Notes

1   Leo Bersani, *Homos* (Cambridge, MA: Harvard University Press, 1995), p. 71.

2   This discussion develops key aspects of material that I have previously explored with a different focus in Dominic Janes, *Picturing the Closet: Male Secrecy and Homosexual Visibility in Britain* (Oxford: Oxford University Press, 2015), pp. 139–61. Two important examples of the visual culture approach that I am advancing here are Simon Ofield, 'Wrestling with Francis Bacon', *Oxford Art Journal* 24.1 (2001), pp. 115–30, and Richard Hornsey, 'Francis Bacon at the Photobooth: Facing the Homosexual in Post-War Britain', *Visual Culture in Britain* 8.2 (2007), pp. 83–103. (For a different version of this, see Richard Hornsey, *The Spiv and the Architect: Unruly Life in Postwar London*, Minneapolis: University of Minnesota Press, 2010, pp. 117–62.)

3   Emmanuel Cooper, 'Queer Spectacles', in Peter Horne and Reina Lewis (eds), *Outlooks: Lesbian and Gay Sexualities and Visual Cultures* (London: Routledge, 1996), pp. 13–27, 22–26.

4   Compare Daniel Farson, *The Gilded Gutter Life of Francis Bacon* (London: Century, 1993) and more recent scholarship such as Rina Arya, 'Constructions of Homosexuality in the Art of Francis Bacon', *Journal for Cultural Research* 16.1 (2012), pp. 43–61; Nicholas Chare, *After Francis Bacon: Synaesthesia and Sex in Paint* (Farnham: Ashgate, 2012); and John H. Hatch, 'Seeing and Seen: Acts of the Voyeur in the Works of Francis Bacon', in Rina Arya (ed.), *Francis Bacon: Critical and Theoretical Perspectives* (Bern: Peter Lang, 2012), pp. 35–48.

5   Gordon Comstock, 'CIA Facial Software Uncovers the Artist Francis Bacon – In Drag', *Guardian*, 16 June 2014. http://www.theguardian.com /artanddesign/2014/jun/16/cia-software-unveils-francis-bacon-in-drag (accessed 1 May 2015).

6   Martin Hammer and Chris Stephens, '"Seeing the story of one's time": Appropriations from Nazi Photography in the Work of Francis Bacon', *Visual Culture in Britain* 10.3 (2009), pp. 315–51.

7   Jean H. Duffy, *Reading Between the Lines: Claude Simon and the Visual Arts* (Liverpool: Liverpool University Press, 1998), p. 130; Ronald Alley, *Francis Bacon* (London: Thames and Hudson, 1964), p. 11; and Kent Brintnall, *Ecce Homo: The Male-Body-in-Pain as Redemptive Figure* (Chicago, IL: University of Chicago Press, 2011), p. 150, n. 70.

8   Bob Harris, *Politics and the Nation: Britain in the Mid-Eighteenth Century* (Oxford: Oxford University Press, 2002), p. 300; and Jane Rendell, '"Serpentine allurements": Disorderly Bodies/Disorderly Spaces', in Iain Borden and Jane Rendell (eds), *Intersections: Architectural Histories and Critical Theories* (London: Routledge, 2000), pp. 247–68, 257.

9   Transcript *Rex v. Britt and Others*, Central Criminal Court, 18 February 1927 (CRIM 1/387), National Archives, London.

10 Quoted in Alistair O'Neill, *London: After a Fashion* (London: Reaktion, 2007), p. 114.

11 Michael Peppiatt, *Francis Bacon: Anatomy of an Enigma* (London: Constable and Robinson, 2008), p. 69.

12 Ibid., p. 60. See also Jeffrey Weeks, 'Inverts, Perverts and Mary-Annes: Male Prostitution and the Regulation of Homosexuality in England in the Nineteenth and Early Twentieth Centuries', *Journal of Homosexuality* 6.1–2 (1980–1), pp. 113–34; and Paula Bartley, *Prostitution: Prevention and Reform in England, 1860–1914* (London: Routledge, 2000), pp. 25, 30, 157.

13 Nigel Kelly, *Quentin Crisp: The Profession of Being* (Jefferson, NC: McFarland, 2011), p. 60.

14 Leslie J. Moran and Derek McGhee, 'Perverting London: The Cartographic Practices of Law', in Carl F. Stychin and Didi Herman (eds), *Sexuality in the Legal Arena* (London: Athlone Press, 2000), pp. 104–6.

15 Matt Houlbrook, 'The Man with the Powder Puff in Interwar London', *Historical Journal* 50.1 (2007), pp. 145–71, 170.

16 Matt Houlbrook, '"Lady Austin's camp boys": Constituting the Queer Subject in 1930s London', *Gender and History* 14.1 (2002), pp. 31–61, 39.

17 Houlbrook, 'The Man with the Powder Puff', p. 157.

18 Justin Bengry, 'Courting the Pink Pound: *Men Only* and the Queer Consumer, 1935–39', *History Workshop Journal* 68.1 (2009), pp. 122–48, 131.

19 Matt Houlbrook, *Queer London: Perils and Pleasures in the Sexual Metropolis, 1918–57* (Chicago, IL: University of Chicago Press, 2005), p. 149.

20   Angus McLaren, 'Smoke and Mirrors: Willy Clarkson and the Role of
     Disguises in Inter-War England', *Journal of Social History* 40.3 (2007),
     pp. 597–618, 597. See also Seth Koven, *Slumming: Sexual and Social Politics
     in Victorian London* (Princeton, NJ: Princeton University Press, 2004),
     pp. 25–87; and Scott Herring, *Queering the Underworld: Slumming,
     Literature, and the Undoing of Lesbian and Gay History* (Chicago, IL:
     Chicago University Press, 2007).

21   Farson, *The Gilded Gutter*, p. 84; and O'Neill, *London*, p. 113.

22   Amelia Jones, ' "Clothes make the man": The Male Artist as a Performative
     Function', *Oxford Art Journal* 18.2 (1995), pp. 18–32.

23   Patricia Phillippy, *Painting Women: Cosmetics, Canvases, and Early Modern
     Culture* (Baltimore, ML: Johns Hopkins University Press, 2006).

24   Michael Peppiatt, *Francis Bacon in the 1950s* (Norwich: Sainsbury Centre for
     the Visual Arts, 2006), p. 3.

25   Quoted in Houlbrook, *Queer London*, p. 139.

26   'Poof, *n.*', *Oxford English Dictionary*, 3rd edn. (2006). http://www.oed.com
     (accessed 20 May 2014).

27   Rictor Norton, *Mother Clap's Molly House* (London: GMP, 1992).

28   Tanya Cassidy, 'People, Place, and Performance: Theoretically Revisiting
     Mother Clap's Molly House', in Chris Mounsey and Caroline Gonda (eds),
     Queer People: Negotiations and Expressions of Homosexuality, 1700–1800
     (Lewisburg, PA: Bucknell University Press, 2007), pp. 99–113; and Thomas
     A. King, *The Gendering of Men, 1600–1750*, vol. 2: *Queer Articulations*
     (Madison, WI: University of Wisconsin Press, 2008), p. 87.

29   King, *Gendering of Men*, p. 11.

30   Ibid., p. 199.

31   There is an extensive literature on Fanny and Stella: Charles Upchurch,
     'Forgetting the Unthinkable: Cross-Dressers and British Society in the Case
     of the Queen vs. Boulton and Others', *Gender and History* 12.1 (2000),
     pp. 127–57; Maurice B. Kaplan, *Sodom on the Thames: Sex, Love and
     Scandal in Wilde Times* (Ithaca: Cornell University Press, 2005); Michelle Liu
     Carriger, 'The Unnatural History and Petticoat Mystery of Boulton and Park:
     A Victorian Sex Scandal and the Theatre Defense', *TDR* 57.4 (2013),
     pp. 135–56; and Neil McKenna, *Fanny and Stella: The Young Men Who
     Shocked Victorian England* (London: Faber and Faber, 2013).

32   Anon., 'Charge of Personating Women', *Morning Post*, 14 May 1870, p. 6.

33   Anon., 'Young Men Who Are Got Up', *Huddersfield Daily Chronicle*,
     4 April 1893, p. 4 (this article was widely syndicated in the provincial press).

34   Max Beerbohm, 'A Defense of Cosmetics', *Yellow Book* 1 (April 1894),
     pp. 65–82.

35   Quoted in Hugo Vickers, *Cecil Beaton: A Biography* (New York: Primus,
     1985), p. 23.

36 Houlbrook, 'Man with the Powder Puff', p. 154.

37 E. Patrick Johnson, '"Quare studies", or (Almost) Everything I Know about Queer Studies I Learned from My Grandmother', *Callaloo* 23.1 (2000), pp. 1–25, 20.

38 Mark Armstrong, 'A Room in Chelsea: Quentin Crisp at Home', *Visual Culture in Britain* 12.2 (2011), pp. 155–69.

39 Quentin Crisp, *The Naked Civil Servant* (London: Fontana, 1977) (first published 1968), p. 61.

40 Andy Medhurst, 'One Queen and His Screen: Lesbian and Gay Television', in Glyn Davis and Gary Needham (eds), *Queer TV: Theories, Histories, Politics* (London: Routledge, 2009), pp. 79–97, 82. On Crisp in general, see Kelly, *Quentin Crisp*.

41 Crisp, *Naked*, p. 7.

42 Ibid., p. 156.

43 See, for instance, David J. Allen and Terry Oleson, 'Shame and Internalised Homophobia', *Journal of Homosexuality* 37.3 (1999), pp. 33–43; Sally Munt, *Queer Attachments: The Cultural Politics of Shame* (Aldershot: Ashgate, 2008); and David Halperin (ed.), *Gay Shame* (Chicago, IL: Chicago University Press, 2009).

44 Margarita Cappock, *Francis Bacon's Studio* (London: Merrell, 2005), pp. 7–8, explains that Bacon made four references in notes and annotations to pictures in his studio to a 'bed of crime', and p. 188 gives further references to scenes of crime.

45 Statement, Chief Inspector Robert Sygrove, Met. Police D Division, 8 January 1927 (CRIM 1/387, National Archives, London).

46 List of exhibits in *Rex v. Britt and Others* (CRIM 1/387) and Houlbrook (2005), pp. 131–3.

47 Statement, Superintendent George Collings, 17 January 1927 (CRIM 1/387).

48 Statement, Chief Inspector Sygrove, 2 February 1927 (CRIM 1/387).

49 Peppiat, *Francis Bacon in the 1950s*, p. 35.

50 Julie Jones and Stephen Pugh, 'Ageing Gay Men: Lessons from the Sociology of Embodiment', *Men and Masculinities* 7.3 (2005), pp. 248–60, 258.

51 John K. Noyes, *The Mastery of Submission: Inventions of Masochism* (Ithaca, NY: Cornell University Press, 1997), p. 6.

52 Bersani, *Homos*, pp. 48, 87.

53 Ibid., p. 85.

54 Noyes, *Mastery of Submission*, p. 12.

55 Peter Cosgrove, 'Edmund Burke, Gilles Deleuze, and the Subversive Masochism of the Image', *ELH* 66.2 (1999), pp. 405–37, 434. See also Dominic Janes, '"Eternal master": Masochism and the Sublime at the National

Shrine of the Immaculate Conception, Washington, DC', *Theology and Sexuality* 15.2 (2009), pp. 161–75.

56 Chare, *After Francis Bacon*, 96.

57 Darren Patrick Blaney, '1964: The Birth of Gay Theater', *Gay and Lesbian Review* (worldwide edition) (January–February 2014), pp. 17–21, 19.

58 Ariel Nereson, 'Queens "campin'" Onstage: Performing Queerness in Mae West's "gay plays"', *Theatre Journal* 64.4 (2012), pp. 513–32. George Chauncey, *Gay New York: Gender, Urban Culture, and the Makings of the Gay Male World*, 1890–1940 (New York: Basic Books, 1994), indicates that interwar New York was richer in queer culture than its counterpart in the post-war age.

59 Judith Halberstam, *The Queer Art of Failure* (Durham, NC: Duke University Press, 2011), p. 96.

CHAPTER TWELVE

Mingling with the Ungodly: Simeon Solomon in Queer Victorian London

Carolyn Conroy

*Our hitherto dear Servant SS hath most grossly
sinned against our Majesty.*

He hath mingled with the Ungodly.

*He hath done those things which he
ought not to have done*
Simeon Solomon to Herbert Horne, c. 1890

Following his arrest and conviction for attempted sodomy in 1873, the homosexual Anglo-Jewish artist Simeon Solomon spent the remaining thirty-two years of his life living in varying degrees of poverty and hardship in and around the Holborn and Bloomsbury areas of central London. Records indicate that during this time, Solomon's residences alternated between lowly common lodging houses, rooms in cheap private rentals, the workhouse and the workhouse's casual wards for vagrants – a life which was in direct contrast to his former prosperous and comfortable existence among London's artistic elite. This chapter charts the second half of Solomon's life, focusing particularly on the artist's lived experience in queer

Victorian London from the early 1870s until his death in 1905, and from his fascination with the notorious transvestites 'Fanny and Stella' to his relationship with the outrageous Aesthete and friend of Oscar Wilde, Count Eric Stanislaus Stenbock.

In the 1880s and 1890s, Solomon corresponded with one of his most important patrons, art collector and founder of the *Century Guild* publishing company, Herbert Horne, through notes and letters written and sent by way of the City News Room at Ludgate Circus.[1] Among these documents is an intriguing letter composed by Solomon which takes the form of a parody and is addressed to himself from 'the Angel Gabriel, Upper Circle, Heaven'.[2] In the letter the celestial messenger describes in a mocking tone how Solomon 'hath most grossly sinned against our Majesty…hath done those things which he ought not to have done' and 'mingled with the Ungodly'.[3] These lines by Solomon reference his conviction in 1873 and the words echo those found on the artist's arrest documents which state that Solomon had 'wickedly' and 'against the order of nature' committed the 'detestable and abominable crime of buggery against the peace of our Lady the Queen, her Crown and Dignity'.[4] Solomon's allusion to his 'mingling' with the Biblical idea of the ungodly certainly refers to the city's other impious and wicked sodomites whom he had consorted with, and his use of the Angel Gabriel as the deliverer of this condemnation is apt since Gabriel was sent by God to destroy the cities of Sodom and Gomorrah.[5]

However, Solomon's use of the term 'ungodly' could also have been a reference to the destitute, impoverished and outcast peoples that he made his home among in the notorious slum areas of London's St Giles. Writing in 1937, tabloid news journalist Bernard Falk reasoned that Solomon was both 'tainted with perverse inclinations', preferred 'to be a vagabond' and 'consort with the ne'er-do-wells of London'.[6] Likewise, Oscar Wilde's former lover, Robert Ross, had earlier subscribed to the same doctrine as Falk, suggesting that Solomon had chosen a sordid life and that in respectable London he became 'impossible' and had 'no place'.[7] While it is apparent that Solomon was shunned by the city's artistic bourgeoisie after his arrest, it is also reasonable to argue that ultimately he found a place in the city in which he could exist, unconstrained and unhindered by middle-class convention and morality, to pursue his passion for queer 'exotic vice'.[8]

As Matt Cook explains, the definition of 'queer' can be slippery, variable and unfixed, but in the context of this chapter, queer is used to describe both the possibilities of male same-sex desire in the city and Solomon's encounters and engagement with this space not only as a convicted sodomite but also as a working artist pursuing themes of homosexual love and desire.[9] Queer is also used in this chapter to designate what Cook describes as a 'sense of oddity or eccentricity' and the imprecise way that that sense of incongruity might have signalled sexual difference to others.[10] With that in mind, this chapter also studies the early published responses to Solomon's seemingly inexplicable self-exile from middle-class respectability which early commentators such as Falk and Ross found incomprehensible and therefore attributed to the artist's bohemian 'insanity', as evidenced by his arrest, a refusal to conform and an apparent desire to continue to have sex with other men.[11] A comparison was also made by these and other writers between Solomon and other 'failed' decadents and Aesthetes of the *fin de siècle* such as Paul Verlaine whose destructive Bohemianism was blamed as the main contributing factor in their 'downfall'. It is worth noting that contemporary assertions that Solomon's 'persistent lack of self-control' described as 'indistinguishable from madness' was also a notion held and subsequently acted upon by Solomon's family directly after his arrest in 1873, when he was admitted twice to private asylums for 'insane gentlemen'.[12]

Since Falk and Ross's contributions to the myth of the tragic, reckless and hopeless Solomon have been so powerful and influential to successive scholars, this chapter also examines the language used by both men in their writing. In Falk's case, it suggests a possible relationship between the journalist's persistent reference to Solomon as a vagabond and the new late nineteenth-century medicalized theories which linked London's homeless men, tramps and vagrants with same-sex desire.

*

Solomon's early life is fairly well documented. He was born in 1840 and brought up in a prosperous Anglo-Jewish merchant family living on the eastern borders of the old City of London in Sandy's Street, Bishopsgate Without. By the age of eighteen, Solomon was seen as something of an artistic prodigy among his peers and had met and befriended his hero Pre-Raphaelite artist, Dante Gabriel Rossetti. Solomon's early paintings reflected his familiarity with Jewish Old Testament themes which were influenced by Rossetti's Pre-Raphaelite style, but these were gradually replaced by the Classical subjects preferred by his new friend, Algernon Swinburne, and ultimately with the poet's encouragement these would manifest into Solomon's choice of sexually charged homoerotic and sado-masochistic imagery. These ideas were often subtly and implicitly implied and therefore the actual intent was often missed by contemporary newspapers of the time. Early reviews of Solomon's work recorded the real genius and wonderful merit of the paintings: however, amidst all of the accolades, and at the height of his artistic fame, Solomon was arrested in a public urinal with sixty-year-old stableman George Roberts and charged with attempting to commit the 'abominable crime of buggery'.[13] He was thirty-two years old.

The incident took place on the evening of 11 February 1873. Solomon was arrested by police constable William Mitchell around the corner from Marylebone Police Station, in a public urinal situated in Stratford Place Mews off Oxford Street. Solomon and Roberts were held overnight in the police station on Marylebone Lane, intimately examined by a police surgeon for signs of 'sodomitical behaviour' and subsequently tried before a jury at the Middlesex Sessions House in Clerkenwell where both men were found guilty of the charge.[14] Fortunately Solomon was able to avoid a custodial sentence probably because of his social status and close family connections with one of the wealthiest Jewish families in London; however, the unfortunate Roberts was sentenced to a punishing eighteen months hard labour in the House of Detention at Cold Bath Fields.[15]

Despite regaining his liberty, the impact of Solomon's arrest and conviction was sudden and immediate. Former friends and colleagues from London's artistic elite, including members of Rossetti's circle of painters and poets, instantly distanced themselves from him. With his patrons disappearing, commissions drying up and a reliance on alcohol becoming increasingly more evident, Solomon was in desperate straits by the end of the 1870s. By February 1879, during one of the coldest winters on record, the artist's need had become so great that he was forced to approach the City of London Guardians and request admission to the workhouse.[16] He was sent directly to the Homerton Workhouse in Hackney where he spent the next ten days as an inmate.

Workhouse records indicate that by the time of his admission Solomon was resident in the St Giles area, and living in a mean common lodging house at 27 Castle Street (now called Shelton Street), housing 160 mostly single men.[17] The majority of his workhouse admissions over the following twenty-five years were to the St Giles workhouse on Endell Street. The records of the St Giles workhouse chart many of the locations where Solomon lived during this period and list addresses which include Dyott Street, Fullwood's Rents (now called Fulwood Place), Wakefield Street, off Regent's Square, Betterton Street, Newton Street and Macklin Street, which were all located within a mile of the St Giles workhouse.[18] According to his family, Solomon expressed a preference for living in and around the Endell Street workhouse in the St Giles area because it was 'so central'.[19] While this is a typical example among many of the artist's mischievous humour, it is of course also an accurate statement in terms of the city's geography. But there was almost certainly more to Solomon's decision to remain in this area than mere convenience. In order to better understand why, it is important to ask the question, what for Solomon was the area so 'central' for?

According to Harry Cocks, by the mid-nineteenth century, areas around Holborn, Drury Lane, the Strand and the lower end of Regent Street were all said to be habitual haunts of 'Margeries' and 'Pooffs'.[20] As Matt Cook explains, the *Yokel's Preceptor,* or *More Sprees in London*, published in 1855, offered an underworld guidebook to the activities of these men with their 'effeminate air and fashionable dress'.[21] It is possible that Solomon was drawn to the Drury Lane area and to its theatricality, especially in relation to the activity of male cross-dressing. In 1870, the artist had attended the trial of the infamous transvestites 'Fanny and Stella', Ernest Boulton and Frederick Park, who had been arrested one evening at the Strand Theatre for 'personating women'.[22] Writing to his close friend and illicit lover, Cambridge don Oscar Browning in May 1870, Solomon revealed that he had been intrigued by the newspaper coverage of the arrest and, somewhat tongue-in-cheek, supposed that they were probably 'a most disreputable set of young men'.[23]

After both men were acquitted in March 1871, Solomon became friends with Boulton, a budding actor, and attended the Prince's Theatre in Manchester with him later that year, with Boulton cross-dressed as his alter-ego Stella. Solomon wrote that he went to see the pantomime *Bluebeard* with Boulton on his arm, describing him as 'a charming young lady'.[24] Documentation also links Solomon with many other male actors such as Johnston Forbes-Robertson who, as a young man, posed for one of the figures in Solomon's drawing *Until the Day Break and the Shadows Flee Away* (1869). Another actor, active in the Drury Lane Theatres during the 1880s and 1890s, was Cecil Frederick Crofton, an avid collector of Solomon's homoerotic art which he subsequently bequeathed to the Birmingham Museums and Art Gallery in 1908.[25] Crofton – who remained a bachelor all his life, lived with various young men and left much of his outstanding estate to two young male friends – was likely personally acquainted with Solomon during this period, given his large collection of Solomon's work and the artist's affinity with the area.[26]

Whatever Solomon's personal reasons for remaining in this locality, Falk was clear in his opinion that the artist's decision was fuelled by some kind of 'perverse' gratification. The journalist wrote in 1937 that Solomon was 'happy in his degradation...dragging himself from one hovel to another' and similarly Ross commented that Solomon 'rejected fiercely' all attempts at rescue and reform because he 'thoroughly enjoyed, in his own particular way...drifting from the stream of social existence into a Bohemian backwater'.[27] The many obituaries to Solomon published in various national and international newspapers and journals also offered a similar perspective. The *Manchester Guardian* argued that despite the offer of commissions and agreements of work, Solomon always 'went back into the wilds', living the life of 'squalid Bohemianism among the dregs of the town'.[28] The *Daily Mirror* wrote that the artist was 'dead to redemption' and the *Adelaide Advertiser* felt that there was a parallel between the artist's life and that of the late eighteenth-century poverty-stricken painter of animals and rustic scenes, George Morland, who had died in a 'sponging house' not far from 'Solomon's last shelter in the slums of Drury-lane'.[29] Other newspapers placed Solomon firmly in the same company as other artists experiencing what Ross described as 'appalling Bohemianism'.[30] The *Dundee Evening Telegraph* suggested that Solomon was the 'Paul Verlaine of the brush', content in 'his vagabondage', seeking the hospitality of the workhouse when he had 'made an end of his money in drink'.[31]

The comparison between Solomon and Verlaine is clear. The French poet was a contemporary of Solomon's, and the connection made by the newspapers between the two men was predominantly based on their poverty, sexuality and criminal status. In Havelock Ellis and John Addington Symonds's study, *Sexual Inversion* (1897), Verlaine was described as a 'psychosexual hermaphrodite' who oscillated between 'normal and homosexual love'.[32] In the same year that Solomon was convicted for attempted sodomy in London, Verlaine was sentenced to two years in jail in Paris for shooting his lover, the poet Arthur Rimbaud, in the wrist after a violent row.[33] It is also possible that the connection between Solomon and Verlaine is closer still since they are likely to have met through Herbert Horne and Arthur Symons when both men organized Verlaine's visit to London to give a series of lectures in November 1893. In addition, Verlaine's signature appears on the frame of one of Solomon's chalk drawings, *The Winged and Poppied Sleep* (1889), currently in the Aberdeen Art Gallery and Museums collection.[34] The androgynous sleeping figure in this drawing has been seen as an example of the influence that French and Belgian Symbolist artists had on Solomon's work particularly during this period.[35] It seems probable, then, that this drawing, with its closed-eye introspection and identification with French Symbolism, would have appealed to Verlaine, although its reference to the drug-induced sleep of poppies seems incongruous with the poet's noted addictions since Verlaine deemed opium a poison and refrained from using it.[36] Verlaine died prematurely in 1896 at the age of 51. He had become an alcoholic with a particular dependency on absinthe and the last ten years of his life were lived in poverty among Paris's prostitutes and pimps in the notorious Latin Quarter. The poet's obituaries bear a striking resemblance to Solomon's, with writers closely identifying Verlaine with a life of Bohemia and poverty and, as Jerrold Seigel has suggested, 'deeply tangling the two identities of poet/artist and Bohemian'.[37]

The term 'Bohemian' (originally a word meaning 'gypsy' in the eighteenth and early nineteenth centuries) was only associated with the idea of the middle-class artist, poet or writer who chose to reject the established way of life of the Bourgeoisie around 1851 by writer Henri Murger. Murger's hugely successful autobiographical book, *Scènes de la vie de bohème*, describes a reckless hand-to-mouth, living-for-the-moment, artistic existence in Paris's Latin Quarter.[38] This Romantic artistic ideal was intensely powerful but, to the world beyond Paris, artists were perceived to be set on an unthinkable course towards self-destruction. However, in contrast to Solomon, many of Verlaine's peers appear to have demonstrated a more sympathetic view of this life of self-imposed destitution. Verlaine's biographer, Joanna Richardson, proposed that Marguerite Moreno, French actress and wife of writer Marcel Schwob, was fascinated by Verlaine's legend and suggested that Verlaine 'loved poverty' and the 'sin and the fear of hell'.[39] Richardson also advocated that the unorthodox allure that poverty had on Verlaine was part of his growing legend, that he identified himself with the saintly beggar and that he was not unaware of the 'nobility of poverty'.[40] This benevolent attitude to Verlaine's life of hardship was also upheld by those among the Parisian authorities. According to Seigel, Verlaine was sheltered and protected by the Parisian police force and the commissioner of police went as far as to give orders that Verlaine was never to be arrested, no matter what he did.[41] The Parisian toleration of the city's Bohemians was identified by German writer Max Nordau in 1878 as having historical origins.[42] Nordau, who would subsequently attack the idea of 'degenerates' and 'degenerate art', suggested that this acceptance stemmed from the role that it had played in early nineteenth-century French culture and the lessons learned by the Parisian authorities when they had, as Seigel puts it, denied recognition to some of the great talents later hailed as national heroes.[43]

In stark contrast, the British attitude to Solomon's life in poverty in London was one of derision, and a direct link was made with this condition and the evils of decadence and *fin-de-siècle* Aestheticism. As a convicted sodomite, the memory of Solomon's life was also tainted with the memory of Oscar Wilde and Wilde's three very public trials and ultimate conviction for gross indecency in 1895. As an example of this contempt, writing in 1945, British art historian William Gaunt claimed that Solomon was the first casualty of art for art's sake and that his life was 'a warning to others' who might take aestheticism too seriously.[44] Gaunt scorned the Aesthetic movement for its 'gutter-crazy' participants, of whom Solomon was particularly singled out as one of the worst, unable to take part in a middle-class world because of their 'craving for abjection' and 'romanticization of sin'.[45] A link is also inferred by Gaunt between poverty, Bohemianism and homosexuality in London, which he described as being full of flourishing Verlaines all eager to seek out their 'sordid destiny'.[46] It seems clear then that much of this recorded distaste for Solomon's decision not to be redeemed originates from the idea of the later nineteenth-century Aesthetic sensibility and the comparison with the self-exiled Bohemianism of artists such as Verlaine.

There are few surviving documents that might give us clues to Solomon's life and his thinking during this period, but from various contemporary accounts we get the strong impression that Solomon had indeed resisted the consistent efforts of his family and friends to return him to the conventions of Victorian middle-class society. Solomon's nephew, Redcliffe Nathan Salaman, recalled a conversation between his father Myer and mother Sarah around 1890 which appears to reinforce the idea of the Bohemian Solomon. According to Salaman, his father had seen Simeon that day and had given him a couple of shirts. Simeon had accepted one and refused the second, saying, 'You know my dear Myer, I cannot be burdened with property.'[47] In support of this idea, Ross described how the artist 'rejected fiercely' all attempts at rescue or reform and 'thoroughly enjoyed in his own particular way' the 'main sewer'.[48] Indeed, when Ross met with Solomon in 1893, he found the artist 'extremely cheerful' and not 'aggressively alcoholic'.[49] To Ross, Solomon appeared to have no grievances and no bitter stories about former friends, no scandalous tales about contemporaries and no indignant feelings towards those who assisted him. Ross reported that Solomon was full of 'delightful and racy stories' about poets and painters, policemen and prisons and 'enjoyed his drink, his overpowering dirt, and his vicious life' in St Giles.[50]

It is possible, then, that the parish of St Giles and its surrounding areas of poverty provided the kind of 'vicious life' which, according to Ross, Solomon enjoyed. From accounts of St Giles in the eighteenth and nineteenth centuries, the area historically held a fascination which both attracted and repulsed. Both St Giles and its neighbour, the Seven Dials area, were renowned for their overcrowding, poverty and deplorable conditions. In the mid-eighteenth century, Henry Fielding reported the alarming rise in gin consumption at St Giles, which William Hogarth famously illustrated in his engraving from 1751, *Gin Lane*.[51] In 1837, Charles Dickens wrote a vivid description of the Seven Dials area in *Bell's Life in London*.[52] Dickens deliberated over the complicated maze of streets, courts, lanes and alleys which provided a mixture of Englishmen and Irishmen accommodated in dirty, straggling houses.[53] In 1861, he revisited the St Giles area in a short story entitled 'On Duty with Inspector Field', and described 'tumbling houses amidst a compound of sickening smells, and heaps of filth with their vile contents, animate, and inanimate, slimily overflowing into the black road'.[54] The novelist's early fascination with the area is recorded in John Forster's 1872 *Life of Charles Dickens*.[55] Forster noted that, as a young boy, Dickens had a 'profound attraction of repulsion' to St Giles and frequently persuaded a guardian to walk him through the Seven Dials area. Dickens later recalled to Forster 'what wild visions of prodigies of wickedness, want, and beggary arose in my mind out of that place!'[56] Dickens employed his early childhood memories of this area later in his fiction. F.S. Schwarzbach suggests that the attraction of repulsion to the St Giles area that Dickens experienced was a culmination of the suffering he had endured as a child and the suffering of others he witnessed in these areas of poverty, both of which contained elements that were genuinely attractive to the writer.[57]

However, in his work on the late-Victorian middle-class fascination with slumming, Seth Koven suggests that the slums of London were not only seen as sites of physical and social disorder but as 'spaces hospitable to *queer* lives and *queer* sexual desires'.[58] As Koven remarks, in the mid-nineteenth century the term 'queer' was originally associated with the idea of something out of the ordinary but that later, from the 1880s, it was used in specific contexts to imply oddness and the possibility of irregular sexuality.[59] Falk did not use the term 'queer' to define either Solomon or his life in the slums of St Giles in his forceful writing about the artist; instead, the journalist used the word 'vagabond' to describe what Falk called Solomon's 'perverse inclinations'.[60] Falk believed that Solomon preferred to be a vagabond and had been incapable of being reclaimed from a vagabond life.[61] The term literally means itinerant beggar, loafer or tramp, and was used repeatedly by Falk in his writing to describe Solomon's status. To Falk, Solomon was not just another one of the desperate outcast poor; he was different because he was 'happy in his degradation', living among 'the very dregs' of humanity.[62]

It seems conceivable, then, that Falk understood the connection that had been made in the nineteenth century between homosexuality and tramps or homeless men, and perhaps chose to use the term 'vagabond' as a coded alternative with which to subtly imply Solomon's sexuality. As Koven suggests, it is likely that the connection between tramps and male same-sex desire took place as early as the 1860s with the publication of *A Night in a Workhouse*, written by the editor of the *Pall Mall Gazette*, Frederick Greenwood.[63]

A Night in a Workhouse was published as a series of reports by Frederick Greenwood's brother, James, who disguised himself as a homeless tramp in order that he could experience what it was like to spend a night in the casual ward of Lambeth Workhouse. Koven suggests that James, dubbed the 'Amateur Casual', believed that he had witnessed 'an orgiastic scene of sex between men and youths'.[64] As a journalist working for London newspapers, Falk would have undoubtedly been aware of the Greenwood brothers' *A Night*, for as Koven has suggested, it 'routed the literal and imaginative footsteps' of London's journalists after it was published.[65]

Koven also believes that the Greenwoods' publication had a direct influence on Ellis and Symonds's 1897 work on the 'sexual invert' since this study suggests that sexual inversion was prevalent among tramps.[66] The study also included an important contribution to the idea of tramps and male same-sex desire in an essay by Josiah Flint. Flint's essay, entitled 'Homosexuality Amongst Tramps', described how the general impression made on him by the 'sexually perverted men' he had met in vagabondage was that they were 'abnormally masculine'.[67] Indeed, Flint revealed how he had spent eight consecutive months living among tramps and was clear that a number of male tramps in England had no hesitation in declaring their preference for their own sex.[68] Koven remarks that *A Night* had a 'volcanic effect' on Symonds, who wrote in his autobiography that, 'overwhelmed by same-sex urges', he would 'wander through the sordid streets' between his home and Regent's Park looking for 'sensual pleasure'.[69]

In addition to the area's apparent power to seduce homosexual men such as Symonds, the artistic middle-class Bohemian writers and decadents of this era were similarly allured. In 1897, the caricaturist and writer Max Beerbohm chose to site his satirical decadent character, Enoch Soames, at Solomon's former residence at Dyott Street, close to Endell Street and the workhouse.[70] In the late 1890s, the decadent poet and Rhymers' Club member, Ernest Dowson, in the company of author Robert Thurston Hopkins, played a regular game of 'Blind Chivvy' through the by-ways, alleys and courts of central London.[71] Hopkins described this game with Dowson in his essay 'A London Phantom'.[72] The two men sometimes rove forlornly about the foggy London streets, 'initiated bohemians, tasting each other's enthusiasms, sharing money and confessions'.[73] The route that they took from the Bun House at 417 The Strand to Dowson's lodgings at 152 Euston Street would have taken them straight through the St Giles area, passing through Solomon's former residence at Dyott Street.[74] Hopkins described these streets as the 'slinking alleys and byways which then were not well known to the average London man'.[75] There is, perhaps, a sense of excitement and titillation in Hopkins's telling of this tale as the story culminates in the two men being dramatically chased through the streets by a derelict hawker with a Gladstone bag who aroused an 'essence of terror and repulsion' in them.[76]

It is apparent that members of the Rhymers' poetry group, in addition to their noted repulsion of attraction to these areas of poverty and vice, were for similar reasons also seductively drawn towards Solomon. Poets W.B. Yeats, Ernest Rhys and Lionel Johnson appear to have held a certain curiosity and veneration not only for the artist's homoerotic imagery but for the artist himself. Certainly, many of the Rhymers' poets, including Oscar Wilde, had been introduced to Solomon's artwork as undergraduates at Oxford during the late 1870s and 1880s, a period some years after the artist's arrest and during a time when Solomon's name had been somewhat lost to obscurity and myth. Wilde described Solomon as that 'strange genius' and Yeats recalled that Johnson's rooms at Fitzroy Street were walled with 'overpowering pictures' by Solomon, many of them collected during his time at Oxford.[77] Yeats also described how one might meet the 'ragged figure' of Solomon as of some 'fallen dynasty' in the rooms of one of the Rhymers' Club members. To the Rhymers, Solomon was an enigma, a Bohemian artist like Verlaine, who had appeared to cast aside all the trappings of wealth and all attempts at respectability and was willingly living in poverty in the area of St Giles that so attracted other Decadents such as Ernest Dowson.

The Baltic-German aristocrat, Count Eric Stanislaus Stenbock, a close associate of Dowson, Johnson and Wilde, was also fascinated by Solomon and his homoerotic art and would become one of Solomon's most fervent supporters during the 1880s. Despite his wealthy aristocratic background, like the Rhymers, Stenbock was attracted to Solomon's unfettered Bohemianism and was undeterred by the artist's life of poverty in St Giles and reputation as a convicted sodomite. On the contrary, the flamboyant, eccentric, Aesthetic and decadent Count became infatuated with the artist.

Stenbock was a poet and short-story writer who had lived on his family's vast estates in Estonia before going up to Oxford and arriving in London in the mid-1880s. Here he established friendships with Decadent writers and artists Aubrey Beardsley, Wilde's friend More Adey, Arthur Symons, publisher Herbert Horne, Yeats, Johnson and others.[78] Yeats portrayed Stenbock as a 'scholar, connoisseur, drunkard, poet, pervert' and the 'most charming of men', while Symons described him as 'bizarre, fantastic, feverish, eccentric, extravagant, morbid and perverse'.[79] Stenbock's fervour for Solomon is discernible, according to John Adlard, in some of the poet's work during 1881 written when he was only twenty-one. Adlard suggests that in a manuscript book of Stenbock's, discovered in Sweden, the aristocratic poet transcribed a poem that was based on a picture by Solomon, which in turn was very much influenced by Solomon's homoerotic prose poem, *A Vision of Love Revealed in Sleep*.[80] Stenbock's passion for Solomon is also revealed in the poet's first privately published book of poetry, *Myrtle, Rue and Cypress*, in which he dedicates 'the myrtle thereof' to Solomon.[81] The symbolic significance of the myrtle is apt, since in the Renaissance myrtle symbolized everlasting love and conjugal fidelity. By dedicating the myrtle to Solomon, Stenbock appeared to be revealing the intensity of feeling that he had for Solomon and his artwork. In addition, Stenbock's fascination with Solomon is also evident in the similarity between the poet's staff-and-serpent monogram and Solomon's own monogram, which appears on the dedication page of *Myrtle, Rue and Cypress*. Solomon acknowledged this likeness himself in a letter of 1885 when he suggested that he had designed a new monogram for Stenbock after the poet had adopted his old one.[82]

It is probable from the extant evidence that Stenbock met Solomon around the mid-1880s while the artist was resident in the St Giles area. Stenbock had written to Solomon (probably care of the photographer Frederick Hollyer, who had been producing and selling platinotype copies of Solomon's artworks), asking for Solomon to go to him 'as soon as possible'.[83] Solomon described in a letter to Hollyer how he had had a 'delightful day' with Stenbock, whose kindness was 'most singular'.[84] He suggested that Stenbock had met him with a 'low and truly Oriental salute while swinging a silver censer before an altar covered with lilies, myrtles, lighted candles and a sanctuary lamp burning with scented oil'.[85] The artist depicted Stenbock as 'a tall, graceful intellectual looking girl' who was 'not exactly good-looking' but whose eyes and expression were 'very beautiful'.[86] The artist described a truly Aesthetic and decadent scene with Stenbock appearing to Solomon in a 'magnificent blood red silk robe embroidered in gold and silver', engaging with the artist 'about everything' while playing beautiful religious music on the piano and harmonium.[87] Stenbock would subsequently offer Solomon the use of his room to work in and inundate the artist with gifts of money and clothes. Solomon also describes in his letters various trips with the Count to the Grosvenor Gallery, the then unofficial home of the Aesthetic movement, which was cleverly satirized in Gilbert and Sullivan's opera *Patience* as 'the greenery-yallery, Grosvenor Gallery'.[88]

It is unclear from the extant correspondence where Stenbock was lodging in London during this time, although by 1891 he is recorded as living at 11 Sloane Terrace in Knightsbridge. There is a suggestion that Stenbock had wished Solomon to take a room near him; however, the artist declined, which perhaps reinforces the notion that Solomon preferred to remain in the St Giles area rather than take lodgings in a more affluent area of London.[89] Simon Reynolds remarked in his 1985 monograph on Solomon that by 1888 the artist was entertaining hopes of being commissioned to decorate Stenbock's home, but that their initial flurry of friendship was waning with the Count tiring of Solomon's continued importunities.[90] There may be some legitimacy to Reynolds's suggestion, given that Stenbock had recorded in a letter to his family in Estonia that the artist was in the worst condition and 'the bane' of his life.[91] Certainly this was a difficult time for Solomon. Both his mother and beloved sister Rebecca had died within three weeks of each other in November and December 1886. Rebecca had died tragically under the wheels of a hansom cab on the Euston Road with Solomon's mother dying only weeks after. Despite this, Solomon had continued to produce artwork during this year, and there are at least seventeen works in existence, many of which were apparently commissioned by Stenbock who recorded that he had acquired 'lots more Sims'.[92]

In 1895, Stenbock died tragically at his mother's home in Brighton. Adlard describes how the poet, now heavily dependent on alcohol and opium, had toppled into the grate while trying to strike his step-father with a poker – he was thirty-five years old.[93] Despite spending nearly half his life living in poverty, Solomon would outlive Stenbock, Johnson, Dowson, Verlaine and a host of other decadents and aesthetes including Wilde, who would bemoan the loss of his Solomon pictures in his long letter to Lord Alfred Douglas, published as *De Profundis*, in 1897.[94] Instead, Solomon continued to live in the St Giles area for another ten years after Stenbock's death, in continuing conditions of hardship, poverty and illness until, on the morning of 14 August 1905, he died in the dining area of the Endell Street Workhouse. He would leave behind a legacy of some five-hundred-plus paintings and drawings, all executed after his arrest in 1873.

Solomon's withdrawal from respectable society, his alcoholism and his apparent unwillingness to cooperate with any kind of rehabilitation, either physical or psychological, is still seen as a sign of his vulnerability caused by a reaction to the similar situation that was presented to the very different Wilde twenty years later. By examining the period of Solomon's life after his arrest, it is possible to suggest that the way in which Solomon conducted his life after 1873 epitomizes the potential non-repentant homosexual, as identified by more recent scholars including Richard Dellamora.[95] Dellamora believes that homosexual men at this time responded to their situations not simply in panic, self-ignorance or confusion, but in resourceful and creative ways that were at times inevitably circumscribed and painful.[96] Harry Cocks also suggests that Oscar Wilde has too long been seen as the originator of the homosexual identity and that his encounter with Victorian justice has provided historians with the paradigm of the persecuted homosexual.[97] While not seeking to downplay the persecution that Solomon suffered, this chapter has examined the unconventionality of Solomon's response as the convicted sodomite, his decision to remain living among London's 'ungodly' and, by his determination, to pursue his personal iconography of same-sex love within his artwork – a decision which, as shown, has previously been seen by early critics as a sign of mental illness and Bohemian 'insanity'. Indeed, despite Ross and Falk's suggestions that Solomon 'rejected fiercely all attempts at rescue and reform', it is now evident from recently discovered correspondence that Solomon believed that he still had many 'sterling friends' who had come forward when he was in great need.[98] In a letter to Oscar Browning, written around 1884, it is also apparent that Solomon had felt some sense of contrition over his perceived 'bad behaviour' and his decision to remain withdrawn from respectable society. He remarks in the letter that he hoped that Browning would 'pardon what he had done'.[99]

Notes

1   There are fifty or so letters and notes addressed to Horne from Solomon in the collection of the Museo Horne, via dei Benci, Florence, Italy.

2   Simeon Solomon, 'Written on Memorandum Sheets', in *Herbert Horne Letters* (Museo Horne, Florence, Italy, c.1880s).

3   Ibid.

4   'Indictment – Middlesex Sessions Roll', in *London Metropolitan Archive* (London, 1883).

5   Genesis, 18.

6   Bernard Falk, *Five Years Dead: A Postscript to 'He Laughed in Fleet Street'* (London: Hutchinson & Co., 1937), p. 16.

7   Robert Ross, 'Simeon Solomon (a Biography)', *The Bibelot* 17 (1911), pp. 150–51.

8   Redcliffe Nathan Salaman, 'Boyhood and the Family Background: Unpublished Memoirs'. The idea that Solomon enjoyed 'exotic vice' is taken from these family memoirs. My thanks go to Peter Hamburger for providing me with a copy of this text.

9   Matt Cook, *Queer Domesticities: Homosexuality and Home Life in Twentieth-Century London* (Basingstoke: Palgrave Macmillan, 2014), p. 8.

10   Ibid.

11   Solomon was arrested in a public urinal in Paris a year after his original arrest in London and spent three months in a Parisian jail.

12   Falk, *Five Years Dead*, pp. 311–12. Solomon was admitted to Sussex House and Munster House insane asylums in March and April of 1873: 'Lunacy Patients Admission Registers, Series MH 94'. The National Archives, Kew.

13   'Indictment – Middlesex Sessions Roll'.

14   'Calendar of Prisoners', in *London Metropolitan Archive* (London, 1873); 'Middlesex Sessions Roll: Adjourned Sessions', in *London Metropolitan Archive* (London, 1873).

15   'Calendar of Prisoners'. Solomon's first cousin, Myer Salaman, paid a substantial surety to the court which allowed Solomon to be freed.

16   'City of London Union Workhouse: Admissions and Discharge Register 1877–1879' (London Metropolitan Archive, 1879).

17   Ibid.

18   Relieving Officer, 'Parish of St Giles-in-the-Fields & St George, Bloomsbury *Workhouse Examinations*: Folio No. 65320', in *London Metropolitan Archive* (London, 1884).

19   Quoted in G.M. Seymour, *The Life and Work of Simeon Solomon (1840–1905)* (PhD thesis, University of California, Santa Barbara, 1986), p. 222. The source of this quote is ascribed to Raphael Salaman, grandson of Myer Salaman.

20   Harry G. Cocks, *Nameless Offences: Homosexual Desire in the Nineteenth Century* (London and New York: I.B. Tauris, 2003), p. 58.

21   Matt Cook, *London and the Culture of Homosexuality, 1885–1914* (Cambridge: Cambridge University Press, 2003), p. 13.

22   'The Charge of Personating Women', *The Times*, 7 May 1870.

23   Simeon Solomon, 'Letter to Oscar Browning from Simeon Solomon, 1870', *Oscar Browning Collection* (Cambridge: King's College Library and Archive).

24   Simeon Solomon, 'Letter from Simeon Solomon to George Powell, 1871', *George Powell Collection* (Aberystwyth: National Library of Wales, c.1871).

25   Crofton owned, and subsequently bequeathed to Birmingham Museum and Art Gallery, eight of Solomon's works.

26   Information taken from the 1901 England Census, the England and Wales National Probate Calendar 1858–1966, and Crofton's obituary in *The Times*: 'Mr Cecil Crofton', *The Times*, 26 November 1935.

27   Falk, *Five Years Dead*, p. 146.

28   'Miscellany', *The Manchester Guardian*, 29 August 1905.

29   'Tragedy of Blighted Genius', *Daily Mirror*, 19 August 1905; 'A Wasted Genius. A Tragedy of Art', *Advertiser*, 27 September 1905.

30   'A Note on Simeon Solomon', *Westminster Gazette*, 24 August 1905.

31   'End of a Genius', *Dundee Evening Telegraph*, 19 August 1905.

32   Henry Havelock Ellis and John Addington Symonds, *Sexual Inversion*, 6 vols, Vol. 1: Studies in the Psychology of Sex (London: Wilson and Macmillan, 1897; reprinted 1975, 1994), p. 21.

33   Graham Robb, *Strangers: Homosexual Love in the 19th Century* (London: W.W. Norton, 2003).

34   Jennifer Melville, *A Scottish Collection: Treasures from Aberdeen Art Gallery* (The Yomiuri Shimbun/Japan Association of Art Museums, 2000). Ann Steed makes the suggestion that Verlaine may have met Solomon in 1893: see pp. 92–93.

35   Colin Cruise, *Love Revealed: Simeon Solomon and the Pre-Raphaelites* (London: Merrell Publishers, 2005), p. 168, fig. 134.

36   Joanna Richardson, *Verlaine* (London: Wiedenfeld and Nicolson, 1971), p. 246.

37   Jerrold Seigel, *Bohemian Paris: Culture, Politics, and the Boundaries of Bourgeois Life, 1830–1930*, 2nd edn. (Baltimore, MD: John Hopkins University Press, 1999), p. 243.

38 Henri Murger, *Scènes De La Vie De Bohème* (Paris: Michel Levy, 1851).

39 Richardson, *Verlaine*, p. 283.

40 Ibid., p. 282.

41 Seigel, *Bohemian Paris*, pp. 242–43.

42 Max Nordau, *Aus Dem Wahren Milliardenlande: Pariser Studien Und Bilder* (Leipzig: Duncker & Humblot, 1878), pp. 225–36.

43 Seigel, *Bohemian Paris*, p. 242. See also Max Nordau, *Degeneration*, 2nd edn. (Lincoln: University of Nebraska Press, 1993).

44 William Gaunt, *The Aesthetic Adventure* (Oxford: Alden Press, 1945), pp. 48, 128.

45 Ibid., p. 128.

46 Ibid.

47 Salaman, 'Boyhood and the Family Background: Unpublished Memoirs'.

48 Ross, 'Simeon Solomon (a Biography)', p. 146.

49 Ibid.

50 Ibid.

51 Henry Fielding, *An Enquiry into the Causes of the Late Increase of Robbers and Related Writings* (Dublin: G. Faulkner, 1751), p. 140.

52 *Bell's Life in London*, 27 September 1837 ('Scenes and Characters No. 15'). Reprinted in Michael Slater (ed.), *Dickens' Journalism: Sketches by Boz and Other Early Papers, 1833–39* (Columbus, OH: Ohio State University Press, 1994), pp. 70–75.

53 Slater, *Dickens' Journalism*, pp. 70–75.

54 Charles Dickens, *The Works of Charles Dickens in Thirty-Four Volumes*, 34 vols, Vol. 34 (London: Gadshill, 1868), p. 176.

55 John Forster, *The Life of Charles Dickens*, 2 vols, Vol. 1 (London: Chapman and Hall, 1872), p. 19.

56 Ibid.

57 F.S. Schwarzback, *Dickens and the City* (London: The Athlone Press, 1979), p. 25.

58 Seth Koven, *Slumming: Sexual and Social Politics in Victorian London* (Princeton, NJ: Princeton University Press, 2006), p. 183.

59 Ibid., p. 303, n. 15.

60 Falk, *Five Years Dead*, p. 312.

61 Ibid., pp. 16, 311.

62 Ibid., p. 316.

63 Koven, *Slumming*, p. 25.

64 Ibid., p. 47.

65   Ibid., p. 74.

66   Ellis and Symonds, *Sexual Inversion*, Vol. 1, p. 13.

67   Ibid., p. 257.

68   Ibid., p. 256.

69   Koven, *Slumming*, p. 70.

70   Max Beerbohm, *Seven Men* (London: William Heinemann, 1919), p. 14.

71   Desmond Flower and Henry Maas (eds), *The Letters of Ernest Dowson* (London and Melbourne: Cassell, 1967), p. 440.

72   Ibid., pp. 440–3.

73   Ibid., p. 440.

74   'The Bun Shop' was a Yates's Wine Lodge, frequented, according to Thurston, by Dowson.

75   Flower and Maas, *The Letters of Ernest Dowson*, p. 440.

76   Ibid., pp. 442–3.

77   Oscar Wilde, 'The Grosvenor Gallery', *Dublin University Magazine* 90 (1877), pp. 118–26; John Sloan (ed.), *Selected Poems and Prose of John Davidson* (Oxford: Clarendon Press, 1995), p. 175.

78   For more on Stenbock, see John Adlard, *Stenbock, Yeats and the Nineties* (London: Cecil & Amelia Woolf, 1969).

79   W.B. Yeats, *Autobiographies* (London and Basingstoke: Macmillan, 1955).

80   Adlard, *Stenbock, Yeats and the Nineties*, p. 21.

81   Eric Stanilaus Stenbock, *Myrtle, Rue and Cypress* (London: Hermitage Books, 1992).

82   Ibid., Dedication Page.

83   Brian Reade (ed.), *Sexual Heretics: Male Homosexuality in English Literature from 1850–1900* (London: Routledge & K. Paul, 1970), p. 37.

84   Ibid.

85   Ibid.

86   Ibid.

87   Ibid.

88   Also called *Bunthorne's Bride*, the opera premiered on 23 April 1881 at the *Opéra Comique*.

89   Reade, *Sexual Heretics*, p. 37.

90   Simon Reynolds, *The Vision of Simeon Solomon* (Stroud: Catalpa Press, 1985), p. 89.

91   Adlard, *Stenbock, Yeats and the Nineties*, p. 48.

92   Ibid., p. 75.

93 Ibid., p. 85.

94 Oscar Wilde, *De Profundis* (London: Methuen & Co., 1905).

95 Richard Dellamora, *Masculine Desire: The Sexual Politics of Victorian Aestheticism* (Chapel Hill and London: University of North Carolina Press, 1990), p. 22.

96 Ibid., p. 22.

97 Cocks, *Nameless Offences*, p. 159.

98 Ross, 'Simeon Solomon (a Biography)', p. 146.

99 Simeon Solomon, 'Letter to Oscar Browning from Simeon Solomon', in Oscar Browning Collection, King's College Library and Archive, University of Cambridge.

CHAPTER THIRTEEN

Alan Hollinghurst's Fictional Ways of Queering London

Bart Eeckhout

The internationally acclaimed novelist Alan Hollinghurst is usually regarded as a gay rather than a queer writer. This is understandable when we recall the splash he made with his debut, *The Swimming-Pool Library*, in 1988. One of Hollinghurst's main ambitions in writing this novel was to present its principal characters unapologetically as gay men who were not inclined to reflect upon – let alone question – their sexual identities, and who showed little interest in extending their sexual activities into a politically radical, norm-breaking social project.[1] This premise remained at the heart of Hollinghurst's next two novels, *The Folding Star* (1994) and *The Spell* (1998). From the start, this writer's characters were quite simply and resolutely gay. In all three novels, non-normative sexualities and sexual identities were not being presented as social realities whose epistemic conditions needed to be queried along the lines of the then-emerging field of queer theory.

The context in which the present collection of essays is developed, with its emphasis on queer histories of London, offers an excellent opportunity for reconsidering Hollinghurst's reputation and submitting his work to an interpretation which might stimulate interest in it from a more critically queer perspective as well. As I hope to demonstrate, such a reconsideration is also prompted by a number of shifts in emphasis and approach in the writer's more recent novels, *The Line of Beauty* (2004) and *The Stranger's Child* (2011). To be able to make this point, I will start with a reconsideration of *The Swimming-Pool Library*. In my reading of it, Hollinghurst's first novel offers a richly documented, quasi-anthropological exploration of the various ways in which 'gay' spaces were constructed in London during the early

1980s – an exploration also undertaken with a historical eye for such spaces' twentieth-century genealogies. Thus what *The Swimming-Pool Library* presents may be understood as a fictional version of what we have come to call the 'queering' of spaces, though the term is to be used only loosely in this case, without its typical association of a querying or questioning attitude.

While *The Line of Beauty* displays a similar interest in the sexual politics of spatial environments, its later backward glance at the Thatcher era resists the temptation to return also to a documentary mode. The home of the Tory family in Kensington Park Gardens, around which this novel is organized, is quite different from any of the spaces documented in the writer's debut. It serves as a bulwark rather of what in queer theory has come to be labelled 'heteronormativity'. Thus the attention in Hollinghurst's Booker Prize–winning novel comes to lie on the many ways in which the heteronormative core of Thatcher's England is constantly queered by the presence of the book's gay protagonist, Nick, and of other characters observed through his eyes.

Finally, I argue that *The Stranger's Child* is Hollinghurst's first novel to take such constant delight in playing around with the epistemic instabilities associated with queer theory. Simultaneously mimicking and undercutting genre conventions of the family saga and the country house novel, Hollinghurst dramatizes how biographical narratives that seek to include people's sexual lives are inevitably riddled by empirical gaps and irreducible forms of alterity. The ironic historical revisionism of *The Stranger's Child* squares well with queer theory's insistence not just on non-normative sexualities but on the fundamental uncontainability of sexual desires, and on the impossibility of translating such desires into identities that may be fixed and categorized. To demonstrate this, I look more closely at the Sawles' family estate on the outskirts of London in Stanmore. Early on, we observe how the idyllic chronotope which it figures is queered both by what George Sawle describes as 'priapic figures in the trees and bushes' and by the novel's opening episode being situated on the verge of the Great War.[2] The demise of this little bit of Georgian pastoral is completed later in the novel when the would-be biographer Paul Bryant hunts for the house and is unable to evoke it in words when he finds it. Through this later scene, Hollinghurst provides the reader with a felt sense of the material and mental limits encountered by any historiographer wishing to revive the sexual lives of Londoners. More than in any of his previous novels, *The Stranger's Child* shows Hollinghurst actively queering the history of the city in which he lives.

The Swimming-Pool Library: Exploring the city's sex-sharp circuits

In the opening pages of Hollinghurst's first novel, the protagonist and narrator, William Beckwith, describes himself as continuously roaming through 'the sex-sharp little circuits of discos and pubs and cottages' in the London of 1983.[3] He talks of 'the sexed immediacy of London life',[4] whose experience he is bent on recording. Offering an account of gay life in London on the cusp of the AIDS crisis was one of the main purposes of this ambitious novel. To achieve the desired effect, Hollinghurst invented a usefully privileged protagonist: a 25-year-old aristocrat with all the money, leisure time, good looks and sex drive to devote his energies to sexual cruising, and all the class privileges to have access to a wide range of spaces in the city. As a strategy for heightening the reader's attention to such spaces, the writer gave his narrator the additional feature of a strong architectural interest. Will briefly works on the staff of the Cubitt *Dictionary of Architecture* and constantly has an eye out for the aesthetic features and cultural history of built environments. He presents himself as 'a perfect Gemini…tugged between two versions of myself, one of them the hedonist and the other…an almost scholarly figure'.[5] The intelligent, Oxford-educated scholar in Will serves as our architectural and quasi-anthropological guide during the novel's explorations of gay London.

In hindsight, *The Swimming-Pool Library* should clearly be understood in its 1980s context of gay liberation, the dynamics of which it embodies in literary terms. The work was a conscious attempt at opening up the realm of *belles lettres* to subject matter previously evoked only in erotica. The literary reader's attention was deliberately shifted away from the prevalent psychodrama of coming-out narratives, with their habitual focus on family conflicts and the inner turmoil of characters painstakingly and melodramatically coming to terms with their sexual identities. Instead, Hollinghurst sought to queer the great tradition of the urban novel, offering the reader a new set of metropolitan experiences whose social range, complexity and wealth of locations proved just as encompassing as that of any previous urban novel. We may call this project – retroactively and anachronistically – a moderate form of 'queering' because the verb reminds us of the subversive quality of the writer's literary gambit back in the 1980s. Hollinghurst forced his reader to listen to the self-complacent voice of a sexually promiscuous gay narrator who has all the stylistic talent and wit to let his adventures come to life, and who proves eager to tell them not just to a gay niche but to a mainstream audience. This required a certain amount of compromise: under these circumstances, Will Beckwith could not be made simultaneously into a queer character in the later sense of a socially marginal, oppositional figure who questions the limits of a sexual identity politics. Yet one of the unmistakable advantages of Hollinghurst's aesthetic choices was that they invited the reader to reflect on what it might mean to 'queer' London's spaces.

Since material spaces do not have a sexual orientation or identity, there is only what the urban theorist Henri Lefebvre called the social production of space.[6] When we join Will on his guided tour as a sexual *flâneur*,[7] we develop a palpable sense of how this social production works for a wide array of the city's spaces, whose different forms of availability to erotic appropriation are being explored in the course of the novel. Spaces in the book appear to be queered in one of two principal ways: either by being appropriated collectively as gay institutions or by being sexualized through gay individuals who inhabit or pass through them. Most interestingly, the novel introduces us to a variety of spaces situated somewhere along the axis between these two poles. Frequently located in an ambiguous, liminal realm that is semi-public and semi-private, the latter kind of space contributes significantly to the complexity of situations and the drama of encounters which are crucial to the book's plot development.

Hollinghurst's interest in ambiguities and complexities explains why the most obvious examples of collective gay appropriation get relatively short shrift in the narrative.[8] These are the bars and clubs specifically designed to cater to a gay clientele. Will briefly meets up with his only Platonic friend, James, at the Volunteer, which he describes as an uninspiring 'second-division gay pub'.[9] And we find him reminiscing just once about his habitual pattern of visits to the Shaft, an 'airless, electrifying cellar in the West End' to which he used to be 'addict[ed]' and which he 'hardly ever left alone'.[10] By contrast, we spend considerably more time at the other end of the spectrum, in those domestic spaces that gay individuals turn into emblems of their private subjectivities. On several occasions, Will's luxurious flat near Holland Park becomes the locus of sexual dramas and comic scenes which serve as forms of metonymical characterization. We are given a similar opportunity to understand the overworked and sexually unsuccessful James through the description of his flat in Notting Hill: the space is notable for its 'featurelessness', 'fatalistic disdain of possessions' and enormous collection of Shostakovich records expressing their owner's self-indulgent gloom.[11] But it is the house of Charles Nantwich, the octogenarian lord befriended by Will early on in the story, which exerts the greatest fascination and invites the most lavish description. That house – the possession of an aging man through whose biography we are gradually given insight into the gay life of a pre-emancipatory British elite – is tellingly located in the margins of London: it is to be found 'in a street off Huggin Hill, so narrow that it had been closed to traffic and was no longer marked in the London *A-Z*'.[12] Upon first seeing it, Will finds himself 'surprisingly taken back, by its air of secrecy and exclusion, to the invalidish world of Edwardian ghost stories, to a world where people never went out'.[13] This is a house whose interior, in accordance with the camp aesthetic of older generations, combines the accoutrements of old money with blatantly phallic figures, and whose cellar – possibly the site of sometime orgies[14] – contains the remains of a homoerotic Roman mosaic along with a more recently fabricated frieze of 'homosexual parodies'.[15]

Nantwich's house gets such elaborate attention because Will is fascinated by the old man, so much so that through him he begins to excavate the city's invisible gay histories. But it is only one of many spaces in London through which the narrator roams in his capacity as an urban explorer. Outside of

Nantwich's private domain, Will proves notably eager to enjoy the freedom of his sexual autonomy. Following his adventures, we come to understand that this autonomy is dynamically defined and constrained by a variety of heteronomous forces, and that it entails what urban theorists call a spatial politics.[16]

Thus on several occasions we find Will alone in public space. His travels on the Underground build a recurrent motif in this regard. 'I made the best of the Tube', he notes, 'and found it often sexy and strange, like a gigantic game of chance, in which one got jammed up against many queer kinds of person'.[17] Will enjoys 'the drama of the pick-up' whenever he uses public transportation, propelled as he is by 'the erection which even the shortest journey on tube or bus always gives me'.[18] Nantwich's diary, through one of the historically refracted revelations it repeatedly affords, comments indirectly on Will's habits when it talks of 'the daring "chic" of slumming it'.[19] This aspect of daring becomes increasingly clear when Will is made to encounter the limits of his sexual autonomy in the course of the narrative. The first incident occurs when he travels east on the Central Line, gets off at Mile End and finds himself in alien territory. Cruising through a churchyard, he is predictably attracted to a youth seemingly waiting to be picked up. Before he makes his move, Will ponders:

> There is always that question, which can only be answered by instinct, of what to do about strangers. Leading my life the way I did, it was strangers who by their very strangeness quickened my pulse and made me feel I was alive – that and the irrational sense of absolute security that came from the conspiracy of sex with men I had never seen before and might never see again. Yet those daring instincts were by no means infallible: their exhilaration was sharpened by the courted risk of rejection, misunderstanding, abuse.[20]

Even if in the scene that follows the rejection is slight (the boy expects to see money), it rankles the narcissistic and domineering Will: 'I resented his ability to resist me, and that I had no power over someone so young.'[21] Yet a later scene ends less comically: when Will strikes out into impoverished dockland territory and tries to find his way around a cluster of depressing housing blocks, he is mugged by a gang of skinheads who taunt him as a 'poof' and a 'nigger-fucker'.[22]

In the mugging scene, Will faces up to the limits of his urban freedom whenever he goes cruising by himself through public space. Indirectly, the sensational limit-case augments our sense of the more subtle spatial politics dramatized elsewhere in the novel. Most of the scenes present us with situations in which Will makes use of semi-public/semi-private spaces with variously restricted access. Often in these spaces there is a better possibility for gay collectivities to blossom, no matter how ephemerally. The first example is that of the transient meeting-place in which Will and

Nantwich are brought together in the opening pages: the public lavatories (cottages) to which gay men gravitate for a quick sexual fix. This quasi-abject place, fit for representing both the city's underbelly and its dreams of sexual egalitarianism, is set off against a number of conspicuously elitist places which are markers of the protagonists' upper-class privileges. Will is invited into Nantwich's gentlemen's club, where 'some residual public-school thing, quintessential to Clubs, infected the atmosphere'.[23] Despite the club's mustiness, however, this all-male environment proves to be a hotbed for gay sex: some of the clubs' patrons and carefully picked staff appear to be involved, later in the story, in the making of a gay porn film. In addition, the kitchen of Nantwich's exclusive club becomes the scene for a quick fuck in which Will is taken 'with a thrilling leisured vehemence' by the black cook Abdul, who summarily disposes of him afterwards.[24] A sexually sublimated but symbolically no less aggressive scene occurs at another elitist venue. When Will and James attend a performance of Benjamin Britten's opera *Billy Budd* at Covent Garden in the company of Will's grandfather (whose career will turn out to have been founded on his virulent homophobia back in the 1950s), a dramatic configuration unfolds: 'The three of us in our hot little box were trapped with this intensely British problem: the opera that was, but wasn't, gay, the two young gay friends on good behaviour, the mandarin patriarch giving nothing of his feelings away.'[25]

Less exclusive than either Nantwich's club or the Royal Opera House are the two semi-public/semi-private spaces which Will uses most regularly in the course of the novel and which thus come to be his most defining urban habitats: the Corinthian Club (aka the Corry) in Great Russell Street and the nearby Queensberry Hotel at Russell Square, both imaginatively grafted upon real-life venues (today known as the Central YMCA and Hotel Russell, respectively). The Corry's downstairs gym, swimming pool and showers, and the complex circuits for staff and clientele in the hotel, offer the perfect spaces – bustling, transient and cosmopolitan, yet sufficiently secure and available for appropriation as a 'sexual commonwealth'[26] – for a young gay man of privilege such as Will. As a result, he is quite unabashed in declaring his affection for the Corry: 'It was a place I loved, a gloomy and functional underworld full of life, purpose and sexuality.'[27] And the grand Victorian Queensberry, ironically named after the peer who brought about Oscar Wilde's downfall, comes to be filled in due course with Will's desire, all the way up to the attic room to which he retreats with his lover Phil, and even the roof on which the two go sunbathing naked.

Hollinghurst sends his fictive pioneer on London's gay frontier through all these spaces like an ethnographer, returning for the reader with elaborate and vivid description. The novel's near-didactic impetus in this respect is best illustrated by my final example of a semi-public/semi-private space collectively appropriated by gay men as a sexual hunting ground. When Will visits the Brutus Cinema in Frith Street, he explains that '[i]t wasn't so much to see a film as to sit in a dark, anonymous place and do dark, anonymous things'.[28] Starting on his architectural and ethnographic evocation of the Brutus, which runs on for several pages, he tells us how the little cinema

> occupied the basement of one of those Soho houses which, above ground-floor level, maintain their beautiful Caroline fenestration, and seemed a kind of emblem of gay life (the *piano nobile* elegant above the squalid, jolly *sous-sol*) in the far-off spring of 1983. One entered from the street by pushing back the dirty red curtain in the doorway beside an unlettered shop window, painted over white but with a stencil of Michelangelo's David stuck in the middle. This tussle with the curtain – one never knew whether to shoulder it aside to the right or the left, and often tangled with another punter coming out – seemed a symbolic act, done in the sight of passers-by, and always gave me a little jab of pride.[29]

This passage sums up various key strategies used by Hollinghurst to queer London in his sexually liberating first novel: spaces are investigated for how they present 'emblem[s] of gay life', and they are navigated with a modicum of 'pride' by the narrator, who simultaneously betrays his class background in the ostensibly self-mocking way in which he not only uses the impersonal pronoun 'one' to cast himself as the ethnographic observer but also goes on to ironize the unintentionally funny protocol of trying to move in and out of the city's fleeting gay scenes. It is this multi-layered and dynamic quality of spatial evocations in *The Swimming-Pool Library*, with its deft combination of the scholarly and the erotic, that continues to lend complexity and vividness to Hollinghurst's representations of gay men's appropriations of London back in the early 1980s.

The Line of Beauty: Queering heteronormative space from within

When Hollinghurst worked on *The Line of Beauty* almost a decade and a half after writing *The Swimming-Pool Library*, he consciously returned to unfinished business: whereas his first novel ended in the summer of 1983, the backward view he took in the later book started out at the same moment in history but proceeded to take the narrative four more years into the decade. This made possible a focus on two contextual elements which were merely hinted at in his debut: the impact of the Thatcher years and the AIDS crisis on gay life in the city.

In several ways, *The Line of Beauty* follows through on the spatial descriptions in its predecessor, though it clearly resists the temptation to make use again of a conspicuously documentary mode. Its evocations of buildings are integrated more subtly into the larger social canvas which is the novel's main focus. This is not to say that a queer exploration of

London's spatial politics is only of secondary interest to the later novel. On the contrary, it emerges almost automatically as soon as we notice how individual chapters are organized around particular locations rather than around the temporal development more typical of plot-oriented narratives. Drawing its satirical inspiration partly from the eighteenth-century painter William Hogarth's *The Rake's Progress* (1732–33), *The Line of Beauty* is set up as a series of spatially organized tableaux.

The radial centre in this novel is occupied by a self-important house in Kensington Park Gardens. It is inhabited by the aristocratic Tory MP Gerald Fedden and his family as well as, for an unusually long time, the novel's allegorically named middle-class protagonist, Nick Guest, through whom the entire third-person narration is focalized. The reader is being warned from the beginning, through a striking witticism, about Nick's eager assimilation into this lush environment: 'Like his hero Henry James, Nick felt that he could "stand a great deal of gilt".'[30] From the Fedden house the novel's radii extend in various directions: to both straight and gay pubs, the contrasting figure of a black lover's working-class home in Willesden (where the logic of the closet is equally at work, if differently), a Men Only swimming pond on Hampstead Heath, a number of pompous and tacky homes for the newly rich, a handful of fashionable 1980s restaurants, as well as a few places outside London, such as a wealthy banker's late-Victorian country house.

What is most crucial to my argument here is that the home of the Feddens is different in kind from the spaces in the writer's picaresque first novel. It is a figurative cornerstone of Thatcherite England and by the same token resolutely heteronormative – a bulwark for traditional family values. While in the first of the novel's three parts the Fedden house is still able to embody 'Nick's romance of London'[31] and his sense of being on 'the brink of some new promise',[32] a central point of attention becomes how the heteronormative façade that the house projects to the outside world and the gay appropriation it half-allows on the inside become intertwined and set on a collision course. Thus we are able to watch up close how the heteronormative core of Thatcher's England is increasingly queered by Nick's roaming presence and peripheral participation. As a seemingly permanent guest on which the Fedden family has come to depend for their own functioning, Nick turns into a narrative device for analysing not only how political power is constantly performed, negotiated and materialized, but also how it tends to be destabilized from within through the uncontainable forces of same-sex desire. In line with Hollinghurst's previous protagonists, Nick is presented as unambiguously gay, assuming his identity rather than questioning it, but his narrative function in the constellation in which he is inserted is not so simple: in many ways he serves the role of the queer Other that is always already lodged, as a structural necessity, within the heteronormative system or matrix.

Having been taken to task over the limiting aestheticism of his previous novel, *The Spell* (1998), Hollinghurst clearly intended *The Line of Beauty* as a multifaceted interrogation of the ways in which his aesthetic penchant at once sharpens and constrains the social canvases he is so adept at drawing. In Julie Rivkin's words, the 'narrative line' in this ambitious and capacious novel is one that 'links aesthetic experience to all that enables it' and that gradually comes to display the 'subordination of the line of beauty to the laws of property'.[33] Hollinghurst places his protagonist in a series of carefully selected, predominantly heteronormative spaces, allowing the reader to study how each of these environments responds to the presence of a gay assimilationist middle-class aesthete whose observations are simultaneously privileged, astute and blinkered.

Once we begin to understand that the study of different social spaces and their underlying power dynamics is a major compositional strategy in *The Line of Beauty*, we start to see recurrent patterns of subverting and queering the locales in which chapters are placed. Thus in the opening part, set in 1983, we witness Nick's first sexual experience with a black council worker, Leo. The two men meet in a local straight pub (apparently modelled after the Windsor Castle on Campden Hill Road[34]) where they must signal their sexual attraction to each other while hiding it from public view. When they finally get ready to have sex, the limits of their sexual autonomy are brought home to them when – unlike the insouciantly rich Will Beckwith – neither proves to have a private space of their own: as a shy lodger at the Feddens', Nick cannot bring himself to smuggle Leo into his temporary home, while as an unmarried son with a modest income, Leo is still living with his deeply religious mother, who is unaware of her son's sexual orientation. As a result, the couple are forced into outdoor sex. Nick takes Leo into a very particular type of space which bears the imprint of London's history at the centre of England's capitalist class society: the semi-privatized 'communal gardens', accessible to key-holders only, at the back of Kensington Park Gardens. In the dark shrubs behind the Feddens' home, half privileged by its hospitality but also half trespassing upon it, Nick has his first sex ever with another man. Hollinghurst makes sure to underscore the conditionality of the couple's embryonic relationship in this semi-secure space by staging two reactions from passers-by upon Nick and Leo's leaving the gardens, one implicitly racist, the other blatantly homophobic.

What is so intelligent and complex about this scene of would-be sexual intimacy is how Hollinghurst sets up an unstable triangle between the upper-class Fedden house in the background, the white middle-class Nick and the black working-class Leo – one of those configurations that supports Rivkin's reading of the novel in terms of the 'inseparability of business and aesthetic (and sexual) pleasure'.[35] It is a kind of unstable triangle, at once propelling and constraining the flow of sexual desire, that will recur in various guises throughout the novel – for instance, when the opening chapter of Part Two, set three years later, culminates in a threesome between the *nouveau-riche* Lebanese immigrant Wani Ouradi, Nick and an unemployed man (with no small thanks to Thatcher's economic policies) whom Wani and Nick have picked up at a swimming pond. Although this sexual tryst still takes place in the privacy of Wani's postmodern flat in Abingdon Road, with its architectural 'system of minimized stress, of guaranteed flattery',[36] it is mirrored by a similar threesome at the end of the closing chapter of Part Two, this time upstairs in the Feddens' home while the prime minister is paying her only visit to the house. In this chapter, which brings the novel's large central part to a climax, the coke-induced sex takes place between Wani, Nick and the Madeiran waiter Tristão. To enhance its decentring effect, it follows immediately upon Nick's *moment de gloire* in the novel as a result of yet another coke-induced dare: his stepping up to Margaret Thatcher to invite her to dance. While dancing with the prime minister inside a bastion of heteronormative Tory ideology, Nick is fleetingly seen to occupy the centre of power on whose uncomprehending margins he has been living all along like 'an eye-catching unnamed attendant in a history painting'.[37] Thus he might be said, from an allegorical perspective, to have finally infiltrated and even penetrated the Fedden house down to its deepest ideological core, only to mess with it instantly through his secret consumption of illicit drugs and the anti-normative sex he engages in upstairs.

To complicate matters further, the seeds of Nick's ultimate disturbance of the house appear to have been planted in the family's holiday *manoir* in the south of France, far away from London in space and time: Nick and Wani's secret sex there eventually returns at the centre of the mediatized scandal that comes crashing down, in the novel's final part, on the Feddens' home more than a year later. In other words, there appears to be no uncompromised space outside of politics and sexual desire for any of the characters in the story. In *The Line of Beauty*, the very bulwarks and cornerstones of Thatcher's heteronormative England are always already queered from within. The belated attempt by the Feddens, in the final pages of the novel, to expel this queer element and treat it as an alien parasite merely serves to enhance the reader's sense of the hypocritical and violent premises on which the heteronormative matrix historically rests.

The Stranger's Child: Tracing the irretrievability of queer lives

Although I have identified a shift from the quasi-anthropological and documentary depiction of gay-appropriated spaces in *The Swimming-Pool Library* to a more complex narrative in *The Line of Beauty* which allows heteronormative spaces and their political ideology to be destabilized and queered from within, these two novels admittedly still share their reliance on a single protagonist-observer who is unambiguously gay-identified. Hollinghurst's most recent novel, by contrast, presents us with neither a single protagonist nor sexualities that are quite so transparent. Here, for the first time, the epistemic instabilities which we tend to associate with queer theory become relevant to the many secrets and ambiguities characterizing both the life stories and material spaces evoked in the novel. *The Stranger's Child* subverts the drive for closure. As Richard Canning has noted, architectural spaces in this novel 'perpetually act and interact dynamically with individual lives'.[38] The dynamism is such that it proves to be uncontainable, keeping the interaction forever on a temporal axis.

At first sight, the novel may perhaps strike readers as too conventional to be deemed queer. It looks suspiciously like a combination of familiar genres: the socially sweeping 'grand narrative' in the tradition of Victorian and Edwardian realism that joins elements of the family saga and the country house novel. But to stick such labels on the book is to overlook how it undercuts these traditions. While Hollinghurst takes visible delight in exploiting genre conventions, he puts them at the service of a work that is out to achieve a very different effect. If, for instance, he appears to restore the grand narrative of realism, he does so by punching enormous holes in it, rendering it fundamentally elliptical and open-ended. Between the five episodes which he elaborates and which are set respectively in 1913, 1926, 1967, 1979–80 and 2008, there is no traditional narrative continuity: the world in which we find ourselves thrown at any moment is an altogether different one, with new characters and circumstances and greatly changed contexts. Moreover, the secondary continuities that gradually surface need to be decoded painstakingly for an extended portrait to emerge. And this portrait is constrained by time, which invariably takes the upper hand over any attempt at rounding off the narrative. The novel's underlying world view is less nineteenth century than Proustian: it invariably insists on the flow and losses of time.

What Hollinghurst poignantly dramatizes in *The Stranger's Child* are the empirical gaps and irreducible alterities that threaten all biographical narratives seeking to include people's sexual lives. In interviews following the book's appearance, he emphasized the fundamental unknowability and ambiguous evidence about people's private lives. Along the same lines, his idea was 'to write a multi-generational family saga where all the multi-generational family saga was *left out*, or sometimes summed up in a kind of bewildering formula like Daphne saying that her second husband's half-sister was married to her father's elder brother'.[39] There is an aspect of ironic historical revisionism to this approach that squares well with queer theory's insistence not just on non-heteronormative sexualities but on the basic uncertainties which riddle the social and discursive construction of sexualities. It even fits those branches of queer theory which have sought to subvert the cultural norm of the biological family – what Lee Edelman, in a much more polemical manner, has critiqued as the hegemonic logic of 'reproductive futurism'.[40] After all, the disconnections between the novel's episodes were directly inspired, in Hollinghurst's own admission, by the 'question of what the shape of one's life is if one doesn't settle down and have children. Some people do have those clear markers of the passage of time and generations, which a lot of gay people are less bound by'.[41]

The book's alternative organization of a kinship history affects the novel in multiple ways: far from offering a straightforward family saga, the narrative presents us with a series of uncertain biological connections, new alliances through serial marriages and secret love relationships (both gay and straight, in and out of wedlock). By the same token, the usual identifying link between houses and families is ruptured: the two main houses whose partial histories we read display no continuity of possession and inhabitation. The continuity which is supposed to lend an identity and unified history to such spaces is repeatedly questioned by the narrative and shown to be an illusion on the part of those who temporarily inhabit them and try to impose their logic of possession and self-possession upon them. In this sense, the novel's approach towards history accords well with Mark Turner's Benjaminian attempt 'to think about the fragments, rather than the unifying, overarching narratives of urban modernity'.[42]

To anchor this reading of Hollinghurst's queering of space and time in the context of London, I propose to look at the house with which we become acquainted early in the novel, which is to say in the early twentieth century. This is an 'estate' for the upper middle class called Two Acres. Over time, it undergoes a number of changes until, by the beginning of the twenty-first century, we hear it has been demolished. A number of characters whose experiences illustrate the book's concern with the disappearing secrets of (sexual) history are situated in and around Two Acres. The picture which the reader is able to cobble together in the course of the fragmented narrative is that of a house originally built in the 1880s and owned by the Sawle family between 1890 and 1920. It is in Stanmore, then still a little village to the northwest of London. In 1913, this means that it is reachable by train if one gets off at Harrow and Wealdstone; the Harrow station, built in 1880, was one of the early extensions of the Metropolitan Railway corridor established to the northwest of London into Middlesex – a corridor which became synonymous with early twentieth-century suburbanization.[43] We are, in other words, in the pastoral area which, soon after we meet the Sawles in 1913, will come to be known as 'Metroland'.

The Arts and Crafts style of the house is explicitly so named, and one of the Sawle children who grew up in it deplores how it 'had a way of "resolving itself into nooks"'[44] – the ideal receptacle for little privacies and secrecies. Yet Two Acres does not just function as a marker of historical realism but also as a larger cultural synecdoche: it figures a late-Victorian – or by the time we meet it, Georgian – idyllic pastoral on the cusp of the Great War that is about to change the face of the century. The opening scene shows us Daphne Sawle as a young girl lying in a hammock, reading Tennyson and waiting for the arrival of her brother George with his awe-inspiring new friend from Cambridge, the aristocratic young poet Cecil

Valance. Idyllically, but also wittily, 'the sunset sky turned pink above the rockery' while she waits.[45]

The usage of idyllic settings in early twentieth-century fiction stereotypically depended on the staging of a safe inside world that would protect the inhabitants from an unruly world outside. Yet Hollinghurst immediately ruptures this illusion by smuggling fluid desires and hard-to-resolve secrets into the cosy inside of Two Acres. When George's mother and her German friend agree that George is 'blooming',[46] the pastoral metaphor covers up – to themselves more than to the reader – the secret cause of George's recent transformation. Likewise, when Daphne later the same evening ventures out into the dark garden in a romantic pastoral mood – 'There were privet smells and earth smells and rose smells that she took in without naming them in her heady swoop across the lawn'[47] – her openness to sensuality segues into her first sexual *frisson* when she finds Cecil and George in the hammock together.

This part of Hollinghurst's narrative culminates in George's backward glance from the 1920s, when he acknowledges to himself that '[t]he English idyll had its secret paragraphs, priapic figures in the trees and bushes'.[48] From the beginning, in other words, when the suburban Arts and Crafts house and pastoral surroundings still seemed to promise an idyllic immunity from corrupting urban forces, Two Acres was already being queered from within through the uncontainable energies of the libido. At the same time, it was also being queered from without by the forces of history, for the banality of the weekend's anecdotal events relayed in Part One are placed on the verge of one of the twentieth century's worst global carnages. Thus Hollinghurst also ruptures the structure of eternal repetition which constitutes the temporal logic of the idyllic illusion and its supposed protection against the future – which, through the dramatic irony he so deftly exploits, we already know to be calamitous.

Throughout the novel's first episode, Hollinghurst plants the seeds for his Georgian pastoral's demise, which is figured most clearly by the comically queer hunt for the house almost seventy years later by the biographer Paul Bryant. The lower-middle-class Paul, whose identity politics are resolutely gay, lives in a very different social and mental world from that of the Sawles and Valances we encountered earlier on. Yet it is only through his dubious eyes that we can revisit the house in 1980. Stanmore is now part of North London and the final stop on the Jubilee Line. Paul arrives full of misconceptions about his destination. Walking up and around Stanmore Hill, he has trouble finding the remains of Two Acres; he soon 'wished he was more expert at looking at houses, and knowing how old they were'.[49] Eventually he does come upon the house, or rather its shell, hidden behind a chained and padlocked fence, occupying a much smaller plot than it used to do. In the allegory that imposes itself, it critically resists being visited or even looked at. Paul is forced to trespass on the neighbour's property and crawl under a wall of old firs to reach the overgrown garden, emerging scratched.

In line with what I regard as Hollinghurst's queer approach in much of the book, the expected sense of apotheosis fails to follow: 'Somehow he couldn't take the house in; but he would take photographs, so as to see it all later.'[50] Paul finds the Sawles' former home 'empty, and therefore in a way his',[51] yet the way is not that of epistemic control or of a magical flashback to private lives nearly seventy years ago. It is not even the way of literal penetration: English history guards its secrets well in this case as an alarm by the name of Albion Security keeps Paul from breaking in. The only thing Paul detects is evidence suggesting that 'at some stage, before this latest degradation, "Two Acres" had been divided up, three flats, probably – like almost every house in London'.[52] Hollinghurst concludes his evocation in a marvel of stylized ruminations full of rhythmic and acoustical echoes of the days of Edwardian poetry writing:

> He'd had the idea that he would find things more or less as they had been in 1913 – more deeply settled in, of course, discreetly modernized, tastefully adapted, but the rockery still there, the 'glinting spinney' a beautiful wood, and the trees where the hammock had been slung still bearing the ridges of the ropes in their bark. He thought other resourceful people would have come, over the years, to look at it, and that the house would wear its own mild frown of self-regard, a certain half-friendly awareness of being admired…But really there was nothing to see. The upstairs windows seemed to ponder blankly on the reflections of clouds.[53]

This scene, I would like to suggest, offers a telling instance of the short-circuit between present and past when a 'stranger's child' without a rich imagination, who nevertheless wants to be a biographer, faces up to a queer house in London that has been scarred and silenced by history. The encounter with the house forces upon him the irreducibility of material change and the irretrievability of people's subjective (including sexual) lives – those same lives into which, as readers of *The Stranger's Child*, we are given exclusive access through the novelist's more capacious and polyphonic imagination. In this sense, Hollinghurst's scene of disconnection between present and past, which is also a scene of disconnection between generations of same-sex-loving men and women in London, is of a piece with Lee Edelman's resistance to

> the ideological conflation of historical development and genetic narrative, what Paul de Man calls 'the pre-assumed concept of history as a generative process[,]…of history as a temporal hierarchy that resembles a parental structure in which the past is like an ancestor begetting, in a moment of unmediated presence, a future capable of repeating in its turn the same generative process'.[54]

Viewed through this theoretical lens, Paul Bryant's inability to grasp the past experiences of those individuals whose lives he nevertheless believes capable of recording in a published biography is a very queer way of reminding us, on the part of Hollinghurst, of how ephemeral and uncontainable all those queer lives lived in and around London really are – and how much of their sexual histories is bound to remain forever unwritten.

Notes

1   As one recent overview contends,

> [c]haracters in novels by Alan Hollinghurst…enjoy adventurous sex lives but are in most respects conservative rather than radical; cruising and sex in these novels are forms of entertainment, pleasurable diversions rather than acts of resistance. The gay man of Hollinghurst's fiction does not confine his sex life to monogamous couplehood, but in other ways he is an establishment figure, wanting to resist the status quo only when the status quo is hostile to homosexuality.

      Hugh Stevens, 'Normality and Queerness in Gay Fiction', in Hugh Stevens (ed.), *The Cambridge Companion to Gay and Lesbian Writing* (Cambridge: Cambridge University Press, 2011), p. 86.

2   Alan Hollinghurst, *The Stranger's Child* (London: Picador, 2011), p. 159.

3   Alan Hollinghurst, *The Swimming-Pool Library* (London: Penguin, 1988), p. 5.

4   Ibid., p. 5.

5   Ibid., p. 4.

6   Henri Lefebvre, *The Production of Space*, trans. Donald Nicholson-Smith (Oxford: Wiley-Blackwell, 1991).

7   Julie Cleminson develops the connection between Will and the figure of the *flâneur* in her PhD dissertation, 'Walking in London: The Fiction of Neil Bartlett, Sarah Waters and Alan Hollinghurst' (Brunel University, 2009), p. 239. http://bura.brunel.ac.uk/bitstream/2438/4356/1/FulltextThesis.pdf (accessed 14 April 2014). The connection also underlies the generic definition of Hollinghurst's novel as 'loiterature' in Ross Chambers, 'Messing Around: Gayness and Loiterature in Alan Hollinghurst's *The Swimming-Pool Library*', in Judith Still and Michael Worton (eds), *Textuality and Sexuality: Reading Theories and Practices* (Manchester: Manchester University Press, 1993), pp. 207–17.

8   For a reading of the novel in which 'the growth of an urban and largely commercial scene' for gay men is regarded as a form of cultural 'deterioration' by Hollinghurst, see David Alderson, 'Desire as Nostalgia: The Novels of Alan Hollinghurst', in David Alderson and Linda Anderson (eds), *Territories of Desire in Queer Culture: Refiguring Contemporary Boundaries* (Manchester: Manchester University Press, 2000), p. 36.

9   Hollinghurst, *Swimming-Pool Library*, p. 17.

10 Ibid., p. 192.

11 Ibid., pp. 213–14.

12 Ibid., p. 70.

13 Ibid.

14 Ibid., p. 265.

15 Ibid., p. 80.

16 Examples of the use of this terminology are to be found in David Featherstone
    and Joe Painter (eds), *Spatial Politics: Essays for Doreen Massey* (Oxford:
    Wiley-Blackwell, 2013); and Rosalyn Deutsche's *Evictions: Art and Spatial
    Politics* (Cambridge, MA: MIT Press, 1996).

17 Hollinghurst, *Swimming-Pool Library*, p. 47.

18 Ibid., p. 93.

19 Ibid., p. 152.

20 Ibid., p. 132.

21 Ibid., p. 134.

22 Ibid., pp. 172, 173.

23 Ibid., p. 37.

24 Ibid., p. 262.

25 Ibid., p. 120.

26 Alderson, 'Desire as Nostalgia', p. 32.

27 Hollinghurst, *Swimming-Pool Library*, p. 9.

28 Ibid., p. 47.

29 Ibid., p. 48.

30 Alan Hollinghurst, *The Line of Beauty* (London: Picador, 2004), p. 6.

31 Ibid., p. 15.

32 Ibid., p. 19.

33 Julie Rivkin, 'Writing the Gay 80s with Henry James: David Leavitt's *A Place
    I've Never Been* and Alan Hollinghurst's *The Line of Beauty*', *Henry James
    Review* 26.3 (Fall 2005), pp. 289, 290.

34 See 'Locations Manager Patrick Schweitzer on Where The Line of Beauty Was
    Filmed'. http://www.bbc.co.uk/drama/lineofbeauty/backstage.shtml (accessed
    14 June 2006).

35 Rivkin, 'Writing the Gay 80s', p. 290.

36 Hollinghurst, *Line of Beauty*, p. 199.

37 Ibid., p. 375.

38 Richard Canning, 'The Stranger's Child, by Alan Hollinghurst', *The
    Independent*, 17 June 2011. http://www.independent.co.uk/arts-entertainment

/books/reviews/the-strangers-child-by-alan-hollinghurst-2298468.html (accessed 5 April 2014).

39 Alan Hollinghurst, interview with author, 19 November 2011.

40 See Lee Edelman, *No Future: Queer Theory and the Death Drive* (Durham, NC: Duke University Press, 2004).

41 Emily Stokes, 'Lunch with the FT: Alan Hollinghurst', *The Financial Times*, 24 June 2011. http://www.ft.com/cms/s/2/a9229750-9cbe-11e0-bf57-00144feabdc0.html#axzz1mpy0Le2J (accessed 5 April 2014).

42 Mark W. Turner, *Backward Glances: Cruising the Queer Streets of New York and London* (London: Reaktion Books, 2003), p. 36.

43 See the Wikipedia entries for 'Harrow-on-the-Hill Station' and 'Metropolitan Railway'. https://en.wikipedia.org/wiki/Harrow-on-the-Hill_station and https://en.wikipedia.org/wiki/Metroplitan_Railway (accessed 5 April 2014).

44 Hollinghurst, *Stranger's Child*, p. 8.

45 Ibid., p. 3.

46 Ibid., p. 10.

47 Ibid., p. 32.

48 Ibid., p. 159.

49 Ibid., p. 382.

50 Ibid., p. 385.

51 Ibid.

52 Ibid., p. 386.

53 Ibid., p. 387.

54 Lee Edelman, 'Ever After', in Janet Halley and Andrew Parker (eds), *After Sex? On Writing since Queer Theory* (Durham, NC: Duke University Press, 2011), p. 117.

CHAPTER FOURTEEN

Sink Street: The Sapphic World of Pre-Chinatown Soho

Anne Witchard

In her poem 'Caves of Harmony' (c.1925), lesbian writer Sylvia Townsend Warner captures a quintessential moment of queer modernity – a jammed dance-floor after midnight, the plaintive strains of a black saxophonist, the poignant complicity of outsiders: 'Play, dark musician, play –/…/ Music's his paramour;/ And yours, and mine, since we dance here tonight' (ll.1; 15–16). The poem takes its title from Elsa Lanchester's avant-garde nightclub, The Cave of Harmony, the club's name, in fact, coming from Townsend Warner's own suggestion.[1]

It is generally accepted that there was no lesbian nightlife in early twentieth-century London, certainly nothing comparable to what we know of interwar Paris from Brassaï's images of Le Monocle, the celebrated *boîte de nuit* hosted by the flagrantly cross-dressed Lulu de Montparnasse, or the intriguingly discreet accounts of Berlin's '*damenklubs*' – Harmonie, Tatjana's, Violetta or Sappho.[2] Relative to the entertainments of its continental counterparts, London's after-dark lesbian establishments, such as they were, have gone unconsidered. This chapter attempts to discover a lesbian scene, oscillating as it did among the bewildering variety of West End nightclubs and underground bars that mushroomed during the years surrounding the Great War. These places were uncommercialized, unlicensed and generally located in hidden premises in back streets, so by their nature historically evanescent.

Ironically, it was thanks to the narcotics and alcohol restrictions of the wartime Defence of the Realm Act (DORA) that Soho's pre-war promise of a new kind of nightlife heralded by Frida Strindberg's Cave of the

Golden Calf came good in an ever-growing number of shifting speakeasies.[3] A loophole in the law meant that registering as a 'private members club' avoided the requirement for a license to provide alcoholic drinks, dancing or gambling. The questionable legality of such places proved a fertile ground for other illicit practices: 'the cocainer and opium smoker and the dopeist', it was wryly observed, 'have followed swiftly on the restrictions that made it impossible for a man to get a glass of beer or a tot of whisky after ten o' clock at night'.[4] The police files and depositions of their prosecutors, and the memoirs, anecdotes and fictional evocations of their patrons, leave lingering textual traces of these places, where, in an unprecedented egalitarianism, elites mixed with low-life types, dope peddlers with debutantes, while the influx of 'coloured musicians' allowed opportunities for mixed-race as well as same-sex erotic encounters.

This chapter takes its title from one such fiction. 'Sink Street' is Evelyn Waugh's dysphemistic designation of Soho's Gerrard Street in *A Handful of Dust* (1934), a location that he returns to a decade later in *Brideshead Revisited* (1945).[5] These two novels span the period of inter-war modernity and indict the existential emptiness, as Waugh saw it, evidenced by the Bright Young People of his set in their quest for novel sensation. In *A Handful of Dust*, a taxi ride to a certain 'lousy joint' at No. 100 Sink Street, known as 'the Old Hundredth', must make towards Regent Street, turn 'into Golden Square and then down Sink Street'.[6] In the US edition of the novel, textual alterations have the cab heading 'towards Shaftesbury Avenue', turning 'down Wardour Street and then into Sink Street' to 'the old Sixty-four' (at No. 64).[7] *Brideshead Revisited* has 'Ma Mayfield's Old Hundreth' at 'A hundred Sink Street ... [j]ust off Leicester Square'.[8] Waugh's disreputable Sink Street nightclub is unmistakably Mrs Kate Meyrick's legendary '43 Club', named for its address at No. 43 Gerrard Street. The different textual versions describe, between them, the periphery of Soho's 'Black Mile', bounded by Regent Street and Leicester Square, intersected by Shaftesbury Avenue with Wardour Street and Golden Square lying within. Nestled at the centre is the street Waugh chose to designate with a fictional name and which provides my queer orientation for mapping an emergent lesbian nightlife in London.[9]

Gerrard Street: 'The centre of life' (Virginia Woolf, 1918)

In *A Handful of Dust*, Sink Street is 'a dingy little place inhabited for the most part by Asiatics'.[10] In those days, any connection between Gerrard Street and London's Chinese was on account of a widely publicized case in 1922 involving 'Snow King' Billy 'Brilliant' Chang and the unfortunate demise of a cocaine-sniffing dance hostess Freda Kempton.[11] Kempton frequented

Mrs Kate Meyrick's '43' and Chang had interests in the Palm Court Club opposite, both relatively upmarket establishments that flourished among the neighbourhood's many dive bars, 'coloured clubs' and other disreputable places peopled largely, according to police files, by 'sexual perverts, lesbians and sodomites'.[12] Gerrard Street's chief renown back then was as a red light district, the 'rather melancholy haunt of prostitutes', as Leonard Woolf recalled, who patrolled its length 'daily from 2.30pm onwards'.[13] Waugh's reference to 'Asiatics' would have been recognized at the time as designating the types who gathered just across the street from No. 43 at No. 4. This shabby Georgian townhouse was the premises of the 1917 Club founded by Woolf with Oliver Strachey, its name commemorating the Bolshevik revolution of that year in Russia.[14]

In January 1918, shortly after its opening, Virginia Woolf wrote to her sister that '[t]he centre of life I should say is now undoubtedly the 17 club'.[15] Here, according to writer and member Douglas Goldring, were to be found:

> Hindus, Parsees, puritans, free lovers, Quakers, teetotallers, heavy drinkers, Morris Dancers and Folk Song experts…members of the London School of Economics, Trades Union officials, journalists, poets, actors and actresses, Communists, theosophists. In short every colour and creed, every 'ism' and 'ist' was represented.[16]

The general atmosphere was one of benevolent bohemianism: 'darkies, actresses, cranks…that's the sort of creature one meets there', noted Virginia in 1922, adding with uncharacteristic circumspection, 'well I don't boast. I'm only one of them myself'.[17] Afternoons were given over to talks on culture and science, encouraging the frank discussion of controversial sexual subjects. The club established a reputation as – according to one's standpoint – fashionably or 'unfashionably bisexual'.[18] It became a regular venue for 'Bloomsberries', members of the British Society for the Study of Sex Psychology, and attracted students of Freudian analysis from the nearby Tavistock Square Clinic (founded in 1920).[19] The novelist Stella Benson was nervously disparaging in her description of the club's younger patrons. Dining there in 1927 with her girlhood friend, Laura Hutton, she discovered 'Laura's Bolshevik Club' to be 'a dirty little place, pimpled with dusty-haired earnest or olympically sneering young men and women'.[20] Hutton was now a qualified clinician in psychiatry at the Tavistock Square Clinic and Benson the reluctant recipient of her passionate devotion. Unequivocal about her own lesbianism, their relationship would form a case study for Hutton's book *The Single Woman and Her Emotional Problems* (1935).[21]

From the early 1920s, popular interest in Freudianism created 'an apparent boom in lesbianism'.[22] Whether female homosexuality was actually growing more prevalent, its representation and scrutiny were certainly more overt. The hoydenish new freedoms and androgynous appearance of the post-war flapper were linked with an uneasy confusion as to her sexual orientation. Psychologist Phyllis Blanchard's widely read studies of female adolescence warned of the 'increasing role which homosexuality is coming to play in the life of the modern girl'.[23] Foremost among the 1917 Club's eclectically 'queer crowd of *avant-gardists*' memorialized by Goldring, or the 'Asiatics' of Waugh's summative Othering, was that disturbing creature, the 'modern girl'.[24]

This free-spirited new breed offered an unprecedented challenge to clubland's standard demarcations of social class and propriety. Elsa Lanchester, the daughter of defiantly unmarried Marxist-Suffragette parents, prided herself on being, at 16, one of the youngest members of the 1917 Club and something of a mascot there (her bust by Jacob Epstein was installed above the door).[25] Her antics inspired a satirical verse which gives an idea of the diversions the 'modern girl' brought to the 1917 Club in the years following the war:

In nineteen seventeen they founded a club
Partly as brothel and partly as pub,
The members were all of them horrible bores
Except for the Girl in Giotto-pink drawers.[26]

From its earliest days, Virginia Woolf had been drawn to the 'shabby, loose, crop-haired, small faced bright young women' who attended the club.[27] Overhearing one of them declaring that she intended to be England's first woman printer, the Woolfs promptly hired Marjorie Thompson, a student at the nearby London School of Economics, to work at their new Hogarth Press, despite Virginia's misgivings that she wore 'too much powder and scent'.[28] The brassiness of the modern girl, 'putting on too much make-up, drinking too many cocktails', was something much commented upon.[29] While sartorial breaches of gender etiquette – an Eton crop, flattened breasts and boyish garb – intrigued Woolf, certain class sensibilities remained entrenched. She regretted Marjorie Thompson's 'common' accent, in short that she was not 'a lady', while her fascination with Katherine Mansfield's self-styled bohemian ways, her use of scent as much as her sexual recklessness, provoked Woolf's often-quoted observation that she stunk 'like a civet cat that had taken to street walking'.[30] When Leonard Woolf rather proudly referred to the 1917 Club as the 'zenith of disreputability', he was describing its radical socio-sexual hybridity as much as its squalid Soho situation 'opposite Ma Meyrick's "43" in a street infested by tarts'.[31]

In the early 1920s, whenever he could escape from Oxford, Evelyn Waugh would head for Gerrard Street. He might have supper in the 1917 Club's 'dingy basement dining-room' that smelled of cats.[32] Afterwards, along with other of the club's 'less high-minded' members, he would cross the road for illicit drinks and dancing at the '43'.[33] Sometimes they would go on to the 50–50 Club in nearby Wardour Street.[34] The 50–50 was run by gay matinee idol Ivor Novello with his best friend, actress Constance Collier, 'catering exclusively to "Us"', which ostensibly meant 'theatre people', but given their prevalence, clearly indicated the club's preferred homosexual clientele.[35] The perambulations of Waugh and his circle illustrate the overlappings of London's *haute bohème* and artistic intelligentsia with the West End's flamboyant theatre crowd. In 1924, Elsa Lanchester launched a club that catered quite specifically to the intersection of these worlds: The Cave of Harmony.[36]

As a child, Lanchester had been taken to see Maud Allan perform and had 'never been quite the same after that'.[37] Her passion for modern dance led her to train at Isadora Duncan's school in Paris. Duncan's innovative barefoot technique took inspiration from classical Grecian dance and its roots as a sacred art. Her teaching abhorred patriarchal convention and sexual prudery, celebrating women's natural, uncorseted form. This liberating craze for 'Greek' dancing was seen by many as 'wild, disruptive and lesbian'.[38]

When the war forced Duncan's school to disband, Lanchester joined the movement's chief proponent in London, Margaret Morris, who employed her to give lessons in modern movement and eurhythmics at her School of Dance in the Kings Road. Here Morris held a tri-monthly event, the Margaret Morris Club, which became a regular Chelsea outpost for many of those painters, writers and musicians who met at the 1917 Club.[39] Most importantly for Morris, her club answered the pressing need for a place where women might come and go freely and respectably, as women did to bars in Paris.[40]

In wartime London, unaccompanied women were decidedly suspect. Compton Mackenzie's 'Café d'Orange' in the novel *Sinister Street* (1914) is typical of such West End venues where, between the large painted mirrors and advertisements for drinks that decorated the walls:

> at intervals hung notices warning ladies that they must not stay longer than twenty minutes unless accompanied by a gentleman, and with a final stroke of ironic propriety that they must not smoke unless accompanied by a gentleman. The tawdry beer hall with its reek of alcohol and fog of tobacco-smoke, with its harbourage of all the flotsam of the underworld, must preserve a fiction of polite manners.[41]

Morris understood that female liberation entailed the creation of a new physical and social order in the revolt against hierarchy and tradition, and, most importantly for women like Radclyffe Hall, her dance lessons were refreshingly 'far from a system for introducing the rules of the game of flirtation, courtship and marriage'.[42] In a lesser-known novel, *A Saturday Life* (1925), Hall acknowledges Morris's pioneering zeal.[43] Rumour of the naked cavorting in the school cloakroom of unblushing young protagonist, Sidonia, draws masculine condemnation that, in its allusion to Sapphic pollution, was to prove ominously prescient of the kind of attention *The Well of Loneliness* (1928) would receive:

> He pointed out that although England was an island, it was, thank God, a very different island from one that he might mention. (An allusion completely lost on Miss Valery)...He even went so far as to condemn the Valery School, comparing it to a cesspool of ancient iniquity...and that he wished to withdraw his niece immediately from further contamination.[44]

'Tu t'habilles en garçon. Tu le comportes en garçon'[45]

While the post-war craze for dancing of all kinds was so inclusive that 'even the most learned members' of the 1917 Club were 'caught' by it, for some it was inevitably inhibiting.[46] Fox-trots and tangos, just like the outmoded waltzes, were activities that conformed to heterosexual norms and, as Rishona Zimring's attention to Woolf's debutante days shows, 'conformity to these norms' might be 'experienced anxiously' by some women.[47] Morris's work, as Zimring recognizes, 'exemplified the most liberating possibilities for social dance to promote a newly hybrid, cosmopolitan social fabric'.[48] Radclyffe Hall, with her partner Una Troubridge and friend the painter Romaine Brooks, practised the newest steps in congenial company at the Margaret Morris Club.[49] The artist's model Viva King recalled that the club's band:

> was under the direction of a female pianist called Dicky, who, with her short hair, conventional dinner jacket, white shirt and black tie, I naturally took to be a man, if a small one. I was much astonished to see a skirt rather than trousers when she stood up. We had not seen the like until then.[50]

Indeed, it was partly because of what Morris was doing at her Chelsea club nights that Lanchester started The Cave of Harmony. Lanchester's programmes interspersed radical short plays by the likes of Luigi Pirandello, Anton Chekhov and, closer to home, Aldous Huxley, with her own camp repertoire of Cockney coster songs and the suggestive hanky panky of cross-dressed acts inspired by Vesta Tilley.[51] When, after the midnight cabaret, the audience took to the diminutive dance floor, women might dance with other women. The place features in Huxley's novel, *Antic Hay* (1923): it is 'a gala night at the cabaret' and young women are provocatively cross-dressed 'as callipygous Florentine pages, blue-breeched Gondoliers, black-breeched Toreadors'.[52] Jane Marcus has suggested that the title of Hall's novel of lesbian angst, *The Well of Loneliness*, was a deliberate inversion of

The Cave of Harmony, a poignant reference to a place where women felt comfortable expressing their sexuality, both in the way they might dress and by dancing with each other.[53]

The pervasive post-war penchant for male attire is dismissed by the narrator of Compton Mackenzie's *Extraordinary Women* (1928) as 'a purely decorative expression of the instinct that led other young women to drive lorries in France'.[54] This is an acerbic nod to the largely lesbian composition of Barbara 'Toupie' Lowther's all-women ambulance unit which would find its representation in *The Well of Loneliness* as the milieu in which Stephen (modelled on Lowther) finally meets kindred types and finds her great love, Mary. At the same time, it perhaps infers that lesbianism itself, in the aftermath of the war, had become a performative affectation.

Toupie Lowther and Radclyffe Hall were frequent visitors to The Cave of Harmony. Together 'they roared through London' on their motorbikes 'to night-clubs, and bars' and after-hours bottle parties.[55] In the immediate post-war years, their mannish clothing appeared rather less odd than hitherto. Many women had learned to drive – if not through shell fire at the front, then buses and trucks through air raids at home. They had done men's work during the war and wanted clothes that accommodated their new pursuits. To call yourself Billie, Pat or Jo, crop your hair, and wear tailored jackets with Oxford bags were now things that chic heterosexual women did, too. There were 'straight' clubs like Soho's Ham Bone Club where the post-war shortage of men made the sight of women dancing together familiar and unthreatening and therefore attractive to the upper echelons of lesbian bohemia.[56]

Modern girls expressed an open-minded bravura about female homosexuality. Aimee Stuart was co-author with her husband of an all-female play, *Nine Till Six* (1930), about women's work in the fashion industry, and *Love of Women* (1934) which would be banned by the Lord Chamberlain for its lesbian intimations. Stuart was pivotal to a gay salon culture, holding frequent gatherings at her flat in Carlton House Terrace, St James's: 'we talked endlessly about free love and homosexuality', recalled her young protégé, the writer Nerina Shute, who was then diffident about her own preference for women and ongoing affair with 'Josephine', a Roman Catholic who assured her that '[t]here is nothing in the Bible against lesbians'.[57] Shute sported a man's broad-brimmed black hat in an era of tiny cloches and was passionate about sexual politics. In 1927, aged 19, she was hired on the strength of her outspoken opinion as gossip columnist for *Film Weekly* and, in 1931, published *Another Man's Poison*, notorious for its frank depiction of female homosexuality: 'Paula was what we then called ambi-sextrous'.[58] This was a term coined by Aimee Stuart to describe their circle and famously adopted by actress, Tallulah Bankhead, to describe herself. Rebecca West's review of *Another Man's Poison* in the *Daily Telegraph* established Shute, however backhandedly, as the definitive 'modern girl': 'Miss Shute writes, not so much badly as barbarously, as if she had never read anything but a magazine, never seen a picture but a moving one, never heard any music except at restaurants. Yet she is full of talent.'[59] The review secured Shute a contract with the *Sunday Graphic* for a series of articles giving the opinion of 'an ultra-modern girl' under the byline 'The Girl with the Barbarous Touch'.

A favourite rendezvous of that period for Shute, Tallulah Bankhead, Aimee Stuart and others of their theatrical set was The Little Club, another Kate Meyrick venture, located in Soho's Golden Square. Not for nothing is Waugh's Sink Street approached via Golden Square. In 1924, *The People* professed concern in a pruriently titled article, 'The Smear Across London' (23 November). Journalist Frederick Hannen Swaffer discovered 'a "definite cult" of "decadent" people (of both sexes), addicted to "perversion" and "the unnatural" who congregated around the theatre and literary world'.[60] It was followed the Sunday after by 'Another Phase of the Smear: Women Friendships that People Talk About' (30 November). London's lesbian nightlife culture was emerging with increasing visibility as part of this theatrical scene operating on the fringes of the criminal underworld:

> Socially they [homosexual women and men] seem to seek each other … It is, perhaps, because they have in common the fact of their outcast or chosen – according to the way they look at it – state. But it is also because the society of degenerates and semi-degenerates in London exists as a society and claims for its own the vicious of whatever stamp … [T]hey are of all types – drug-takers, uteromaniacs, perverts, alcoholists.[61]

By the time of the trial of *The Well of Loneliness* in 1928, the prevalence of 'decadent' – that is, lesbian – women 'among artists, theatrical and society people' had become an established occasion of moral outrage, provoking James Douglas's editorial tirade against the novel in *The Sunday Express*: 'They flaunt themselves in public places with increasing effrontery and more insolently provocative bravado'.[62]

The Sink of Solitude

> In London streets the groves of Lesbos bloom –
> Man-hatted girls, tweed-coated, light the gloom.
> Women in love now only love themselves
> And men are left (like duller books) on shelves.[63]

Beresford Egan turned to the defunct mode of the illustrated lampoon to excoriate the trial and fuss around *The Well of Loneliness*. The *Yellow Book* graphics and pastiched Victorian melodrama of its telling title *The Sink of Solitude* (1928) were hallmarks of Bright Young People style, of which Egan was an exemplar. No one gets off lightly in maverick publisher

P.R. Stephensen's preface. Putting to one side 'the feebleness of *The Well of Loneliness* either as a work of art or as a moral argument', he berates not just 'the pathetic post-war lesbians with their "mannish" modes and poses' and the 'sentimental scientificality of psychopaths like Havelock Ellis who ponderously "explain" them', but equally the morbid journalists who beset these women. He calls for James Douglas to be repressed as a public nuisance and lambastes the loathly leprosy of newspaper sensationalism for doping England into imbecility.[64]

Meanwhile, Nerina Shute's sharp-tongued media profile earned her a summons from Lord Beaverbrook, curious about 'the modern girl'. She accordingly clued him up, informing him that 'those young women with closely cropped hair who strutted down the Kings Road, Chelsea dressed as men' cited such historical luminaries as 'Sappho and Christina of Sweden' in justification:

> To be a lesbian, I told him, was not illegal, not condemned in the Bible, and since the Great War, as Lord Beaverbrook agreed, there were not enough Englishmen to go round. 'What was wrong', I said, 'with being a lesbian?' Again he nodded. He had read The Well of Loneliness by Radclyffe Hall. So had I. At that time everyone I knew in London was reading it, or discussing it … Well, said Lord Beaverbrook, at last, I suppose you think you're a typical modern girl?[65]

Beaverbrook evidently thought so. In something of a *volte face* given his publication's stance against Hall's novel, he offered her a column in the *Daily Express*. In another account of this interview, Shute credits *The Well of Loneliness* for having made 'the whole proceeding [lesbianism] appear interesting'.[66] For many girls, to be 'ambi-sextrous' was to be ultra-modern, an aspect of the hedonistic license of the post-Armistice world: 'we were giving birth to the permissive age', Shute would later recall with pride.[67] Throughout the 1920s, in popular newspapers and middlebrow fiction, drug-taking, alcoholism and 'unnatural' sexualities had been presented as 'almost exclusively diversions of the well-born'.[68] *The Well of Loneliness* offered lesbian women of all classes of society a new interpretive framework for their experience and, as Shute with some satisfaction observed, 'encouraged everyone concerned'.[69]

Gateways to the underworld

> wealthy women of abnormal tastes do not often seek recreation from chance encounters in the street, or other public places. It is at the gateways to the underworld, fascinating little café bars, dance clubs, feverish centres of excitement and emotional stimuli that you will find them.[70]

Every time Tallulah Bankhead performed in the West End, the theatre was mobbed by 'Gallery Girls'. The young women who thronged the cheap seats whenever Bankhead was on stage were mostly working-class Londoners – shop-girls, tailoresses, typists, domestic servants – who adored her and revelled in her every move.[71] Arnold Bennett described the 'terrific, wild, passionate, hysterical roar and shriek' of the girls' applause.[72] Their hysteria grew such that extra policemen were assigned on opening nights and West End traffic redirected. Her London Gallery Girls, comments biographer Lee Israel, 'if not outright lesbian, were undeniably homoemotional and strongly so in their vociferous reactions to Tallulah. But there was an innocence about these girls in terms of what they didn't know about themselves'.[73]

Dennis Archer in his exhaustive delvings into the capital's underworld in *The Cloven Hoof: A Study of Contemporary London Vices* (1932), without suggesting the reason for it, notes the social shift effected since *The Well of Loneliness*. In a chapter concerning 'manifestations of Lesbianism as they affect the life of London', he makes the observation that 'until quite recently':

> the 'aware' type of lesbian seemed only to exist among two classes, the well-to-do and sophisticated, and the highly educated and philosophical. It is only of recent years that servant girls and shop assistants, fully conscious of the peculiarities of their own natures, have begun openly to discuss it, and to imitate in manner, and even occasionally in dress, the more prosperous. But the cult is certainly beginning to spread among them, and a number of such girls, under the impression, perhaps, that it is *chic* and modern, at any rate to know about it, have grown intensely curious in the matter.[74]

How to identify devotees of 'the cult' as it diffused downwards into the lower classes, in an era when off-the-peg clothing was only just beginning to become available, clearly presented a problem. Archer claims that there were 'only about five modistes in London' that specialized in the type of clothing that 'Lesbians' preferred: 'One sees frequently among them the tailored coat and skirt, high collar, and man's tie ... very often a man's wristlet watch ... and a signet ring.' However, bespoke tailoring was expensive:

> costing as much as twenty-two guineas for a coat and skirt, and three guineas for a shirt. The result is that the few conscious Lesbians among the poorer classes rarely indulge in a specialized form of dress, since such costumes are the one style of clothing most difficult to imitate successfully at a low figure.[75]

The lesbian of the 'well-to-do and sophisticated' class was inevitably presented as predatory.[76] Archer suggests her malign influence operating through networks that included certain 'Beauty Salons existing for the purpose of procuring fresh girls for older women' and the salons of 'certain of the *modistes'* which did business as rendezvous for clients to engage with *mannequins*. Actual networks of lesbian sociability seem to have eluded Archer. He suggests they might be spotted by the company they kept:

> In teashops and cafes Lesbians may be seen with groups of urnings [homosexual men], and also at their parties. There are very few exclusively Lesbian rendezvous in London, only one tea-place being famous for it.[77]

Archer is most likely referring to the first-floor restaurant of the Lyons Corner House in Coventry Street, off Leicester Square. It was known as the Lily Pond, so named, recalls Ellen, a West End chorus girl, because:

> all the 'boys' used to go there for afternoon tea on a Sunday, and the 'girls' started to get in – it was well known. It was a sight to come and see in London, the 'Lily Pond'... The girls were very butch.[78]

Archer evidently never visited the Coffee Ann 'around the backstreets of Tottenham Court Road...a very arty sort of place' where lesbians felt comfortable.[79] Ellen was taken there by a girlfriend in the early 1930s:

> It was most famous and from there I met loads of people. I went to a club in Gerrard St, and it was 42 Gerrard St, and called the 42nd...And all the girls used to gather there night after night. This is where I met Marion – 'Billy' – She lived in Croydon, and was a secretary in quite a well-known furniture company.[80]

Ellen misremembers the number of Kate Meyrick's 43. In *Madness After Midnight*, the memoir of Kate Meyrick's sometime trombonist Jack Glicco, the Coffee Ann is described as:

> without doubt the worst joint in London's West End. If Sandy's Bar was bad, this was ten times worse. Here congregated a cosmopolitan and degraded crowd. Every nationality in the world was represented and every person was either thief, drug-taker, prostitute, pervert or blackmailer.[81]

Despite getting into a brawl with a Spanish pimp, Glicco goes back there, conceding that '[t]here was one curious feature of the Coffee Ann – bad though it was – and that was the amount of genuine artistic talent that congregated there'.[82]

By the mid-1930s, Soho's nightlife was no longer confined to nightclubs. As Glicco explains, a post-night club crowd, including those night owls who could not afford the price of admission to a club, were attracted by the West End's new coffee bars. Sandy's Bar was at No. 25 Oxenden Street, by the Prince of Wales Theatre in the Haymarket. Here in the small hours,

Glicco tells us, 'congregated Lesbians, queers, homosexuals, bi-sexuals'.[83] He details a close call with a convincing transvestite and bears witness to 'two lesbians fighting one minute and kissing and crying on each other's shoulders the next'.[84] Sandy's had seen better days. It was the West End's very first sandwich bar, set up in 1925 by the actor Kenelm Foss, inspired by a trip to New York City where coffee and sandwich bars had become popular during prohibition. Initially Sandy's attracted fashionable bohemia with its fast food and celebrity customers, the actresses and revue girls whose autographed photos were pinned to the walls: 'Gertrude Lawrence, Beatrice Lillie, Sybil Thorndike and Fay Compton'.[85] The *Weekly Dispatch* described the post-theatre crowd as follows: 'Women in gorgeous lamé cloaks sit on high stools and rest their feathered fans upon the bar counter, while their escorts sit holding their silk hats, waiting for the sandwich of their choice.'[86] While some ladies were accompanied by escorts in silk hats, not all were. In a further touch of modernity, a note inside the menu assured female customers that 'Ladies may enter alone with the utmost assurance of courtesy and consideration in every way and from all who may be present'.[87] A cartoon, which was captioned 'Two Ducks, One Honey – and a Large Seasonable – Waiting', shows four unaccompanied women waiting at the bar, their orders being a play on their physical 'types' (see Figure 14.1).[88] There is the familiar blowzy, be-feathered Cockney tart, and three 'modern girls', one of whom, 'the Honey', is clearly Sapphic.

FIGURE 14.1 *Sandy's Bar.*

Sandy's employed bohemian types, among them the future historical novelist Marguerite Steen, then eking a rackety existence between backstage theatre jobs and taking Greek dance classes with Margaret Morris: '"You know such queer people," said my aunt Williama...I could have retorted that all her friends were equally "queer" to me. They were all huntin' and fishin' and shootin'.'[89] Her family's disapproval was couched in the terms that, in the early 1920s clearly spelled out what they disapproved of: '"I don't like my girl being mixed up in unhealthy friendships. With – with –" she groped for the word – "depravity. And you know dam' well what I mean".'[90]

Police accounts corroborate a widening in the location of a lesbian presence from the wealthy nightclub scene to coffee bars and all-night cafés: 'I had not been at West End Central Police Station long', writes WPC Condor, 'before I had pointed out to me certain notorious lesbians who were in the habit of frequenting snack-bars in the hope of finding a "pick-up"'.[91] Maxies Café in Gerrard Street was remembered by Zoe Progl as 'the rendezvous of every type of villain and thug, including ponces, pimps, prostitutes, drug addicts, lesbians and homosexuals'.[92]

It is in Gerrard Street that we find the earliest mention of what seems to have been a predominantly lesbian nightclub. Smokey Joe's was a basement members' club or 'bottle club', 'a very bad place indeed', according to Glicco.[93] It crops up in a number of memoirs of the period. Violet Powell (née Pakenham), one of Waugh's circle, gives us a brief glimpse: 'Descending the spiral of pleasure by the way of the Bag 'O Nails...the bottom might be said to have been reached at a club in Gerrard Street called Smokey Joe's.'[94] At Smokey Joe's there were drag acts, a blues pianist played all night and the lavatories were unspeakable: 'Vice can seldom have worn a dirtier face than it did in this squalid cellar where ladies in check coats and skirts did not hesitate to dance aggressively together'.[95] Pakenham was then a student at the London School of Economics. She may have been acquainted with a young man named Gerwyn Elidor Lewis, also a student at the LSE, who records that 'Smoky Joe' [sic] was his favourite nightspot. Although dubbed the Club King by his fellow students (out on the town two nights a week!), Lewis was in fact a rather naive young man. He particularly liked Smokey Joe's because the place was always full of women though the reason did not dawn on him for quite some months: 'I discovered why it was always full of girls – it was a lesbian club!'[96]

Despite regular police raids, Smokey Joe's survived into the mid-1930s. Jan Gabrial, an American actress newly arrived in London (who would later marry the writer Malcolm Lowry), describes going out one evening with the artist's model, Betty May, and poet Edgell Rickword, to the Fitzroy Tavern in Charlotte Street and finally, 'Betty insisting, to Smokey Joe's, a speakeasy-cum-lesbian pub'.[97] Less fortunate was the Oriental-styled Caravan Club in nearby Endell Street. It advertised itself as 'London's Greatest Bohemian Rendezvous said to be the most unconventional spot in town.' In this 'sink of iniquity', a police raid discovered 'men dancing with men and women with women' and arrested them.[98] The club was shut down.

The moral hypocrisy of the popular press discovering 'sinks of iniquity' at every turn is part of the cultural malaise indicted in *Brideshead Revisited*. But despite Waugh's gloom, some of the indignities encompassed in his albeit ambiguous notion of Sink Street disappeared with the Second World War. Gerrard Street's club scene was enlivened by a boom in new jazz styles, the area's racial mix celebrated in the bebop song 'Gerrard Street' by the Trinidadian saxophonist, Al 'King' Timothy. Among the crazy and comical uproar of the dance club is the sight of 'an old Chinaman upon the floor'.[99] Gerrard Street's cheap rents had encouraged the Chinese to open restaurants serving the area's late-night clientele and a colourful Chinatown had begun to develop. A more forgiving age saw the gradual transition of a serendipitously named club, Gateways, in Chelsea's Kings Road, from a bohemian arts venue into its establishment as a women-only nightclub. Not least of the achievements of the 'modern girl' was that if she wanted to meet other girls she no longer had to seek them out at 'the gateways to the underworld'.

Notes

1   See Jane Marcus, *Virginia Woolf and the Languages of Patriarchy* (Bloomington: Indiana University Press, 1987), p. 169.

2   Florence Tamagne, *History of Homosexuality in Europe, Berlin, London, Paris, 1919–1939*, Vol. I (New York: Algora, 2004), pp. 55, 57, 69.

3   For an account of The Cave of the Golden Calf, see Lisa Tickner, *Modern Life and Modern Subjects: British Art in the Early Twentieth Century* (New Haven, CT: Yale University Press, 2000).

4   Charles Sheridan Jones, *London in War-Time* (London: Grafton, 1917), p. 5.

5   Evelyn Waugh, *A Handful of Dust* (London: Penguin Books, 2000 [1934]), p. 73; *Brideshead Revisited* (London: Penguin, 1983 [1945]), p. 110.

6   Waugh, *A Handful of Dust*, p. 73.

7   Ibid; see appendix, p. 253.

8   Waugh, *Brideshead Revisited*, p. 110.

9   The Black Mile was a name given to Soho by the police and thriller writers.

10 Waugh, *A Handful of Dust*, p. 73.

11 For an account of this, see Kohn, *Dope Girls* (London: Lawrence & Wishart, 1922), chapter 8, and Lucy Bland, *Modern Women on Trial: Sexual Transgression in the Age of the Flapper* (Manchester: Manchester University Press, 2013), chapter 2.

12 Cited in Rebecca Jennings, *Tomboys and Bachelor Girls: A Lesbian History of Post-War Britain, 1945–7* (Manchester: Manchester University Press, 2007), p. 110.

13 Leonard Woolf, *Beginning Again: An Autobiography of the Years 1911 to 1918* (London: The Hogarth Press Ltd, 1964), p. 216.

14 Douglas Goldring, *Odd Man Out: The Autobiography of a 'Propaganda' Novelist* (London: Chapman & Hall Ltd, 1935), p. 267.

15 Cited in Holly Henry, *Virginia Woolf and the Discourse of Science: The Aesthetics of Astronomy* (Cambridge: Cambridge University Press, 2003), p. 81.

16 Douglas Goldring, *The Nineteen-Twenties: A General Survey and Some Personal Memories* (London: Nicholson & Watson, 1945), p. 147.

17 Virginia Woolf, *The Question of Things Happening: The Letters of Virginia Wool*, Vol. II (London: The Hogarth Press, 1976), p. 554.

18 Belinda Humphrey, *Recollections of the Powys Brothers: Llewelyn, Theodore, and John Cowper* (London: Peter Owen Publishers, 1980), p. 81.

19 Lesley Hall, '"Disinterested Enthusiasm for Sexual Misconduct": The British Society for the Study of Sex Psychology, 1913–47', *Journal of Contemporary History* 30.4 (October 1995), pp. 665–86.

20 Cited in Joy Grant, *Stella Benson: A Biography* (London: Macmillan, 1987), p. 238.

21 Laura Hutton, *The Single Woman and Her Emotional Problems* (London: Balliere, Tindell & Cox, 1935).

22 Sherrie A. Innes, *The Lesbian Menace: Ideology, Identity, and the Representation of Lesbian Life* (Amherst: University of Massachusetts Press, 1997), p. 18.

23 Ibid., p. 19.

24 Goldring, *The Nineteen-Twenties*, p. 138.

25 John Houseman, *Front and Center* (New York: Simon & Schuster, 1979), p. 229.

26 Goldring, *The Nineteen-Twenties*, p. 146.

27 Cited in Victoria Glendinning, *Leonard Woolf: A Biography* (New York: Simon & Schuster, 2008), p. 221.

28 Virginia Woolf's concern is discussed in Sean Latham, *'Am I A Snob?': Modernism and the Novel* (Ithaca, NY: Cornell University Press, 2003), p. 65.

29 Alec Waugh, 'The Modern Girl', 1927, cited in John Howard Wilson, *Evelyn Waugh: A Literary Biography, 1924–1966* (Madison, NJ: Fairleigh Dickinson University Press, 2001), p. 40.

30 Jeffrey Meyer, *Katherine Mansfield: A Darker View* (New York: Rowman & Littlefield, 2002), p. 138.

31 Woolf is cited in Winston James, 'A Race Outcast from an Outcast Class: Claude McKay's Experience and Analysis of Britain', in Bill Schwarz (ed.), *West Indian Intellectuals in Britain* (Manchester: Manchester University Press, 2003), p. 79. The description of Gerrard Street is from Goldring, *The Nineteen-Twenties*, p. 151.

32 Goldring, *Odd Man Out*, p. 267.

33 Goldring, *The Nineteen-Twenties*, p. 145.

34 Wilson, *Evelyn Waugh*, p. 22. On one occasion an evening at the 1917 was followed by the 50–50. Another evening he records taking in the '"43" before the "50–50"'.

35 Philip Hoare, *Noel Coward: A Biography* (Chicago: University of Chicago Press, 1998), p. 138.

36 In Charlotte Street, then later in Chenies Mews, Bloomsbury. See Rohan McWilliam, 'Elsa Lanchester and Bohemian London in the Early Twentieth Century', *Women's History Review* 23.2 (2014), pp. 171–87.

37 Elsa Lanchester, *Elsa Lanchester Herself* (New York: St Martins, 1983), p. 19. Maud Allen inspired legions of adoring schoolgirl fans.

38 Grace Ledbetter, Review of Fiona Macintosh, *The Ancient Dancer in the Modern World: Responses to Greek and Roman Dance* (Oxford: Oxford University Press, 2012). http://cj.camws.org/sites/default/files/reviews/2014.12.11%20Ledbetter%20on%20Macintosh.pdf (accessed 12 June 2015). In 1918, Maud Allan had brought libel proceedings against the Independent MP, Noel Pemberton Billing, for his accusation that she was at the centre of a Cult of the Clitoris, 'the filthy words' explained by her counsel in 'less gross language as lesbianism'. See Bland, *Modern Women on Trial*, chapter 1.

39 Margaret Morris, *The Art of J. D. Fergusson: A Biased Biography* (London: Blackie, 1974), p. 97; and Margaret Morris, *Life in Movement* (London: Peter Owen, 1969), p. 25.

40 Morris, *My Life in Movement*, p. 25.

41 Compton Mackenzie, *Sinister Street*, vol. 2 (New York: D. Appleton & Co, 1914), p. 895.

42 Rishona Zimring, *Social Dance and the Modernist Imagination in Interwar Britain* (Farnham: Ashgate, 2013), p. 177.

43 Radclyffe Hall, *A Saturday Life* (London: Virago, 1927), p. 37.

44 Ibid., p. 23.

45 Compton Mackenzie, *Extraordinary Women* (New York: Macy-Masius, 1928), p. 39.

46 Goldring, *The Nineteen-Twenties*, p. 147.

47 Zimring, *Social Dance and the Modernist Imagination in Interwar Britain*, p. 177.

48 Ibid., p. 176.

49 Sally Cline, *Radclyffe Hall: A Woman Called John* (New York: The Overlook Press, 1997), p. 187.

50 Viva King, *The Weeping and the Laughter* (London: Macdonald and Jane's, 1976), p. 75.

51 Huxley's play was called 'Happy Families', inspired by Russian symbolist theatre and published in *Limbo* (1919). See Nicholas Murray, *Aldous Huxley: An English Intellectual* (London: Abacus, 2002), p. 145.

52 Aldous Huxley, *Antic Hay* (London: Random House, 2008), p. 192.

53 Marcus, *Virginia Woolf and the Languages of Patriarchy*, p. 167.

54 Mackenzie, *Extraordinary Women*, p. 41.

55 Cline, *Radclyffe Hall*, p. 153.

56 Virginia Nicholson, *Singled Out: How Two Million Women Survived Without Men After the First World War* (London: Penguin, 2007), p. 204.

57 Nerina Shute, *Passionate Friendships: Memoirs and Confessions of a Rebel* (London: Robert Hale, 1992), pp. 38, 46.

58 Nerina Shute, *Another Man's Poison* (London: Grant Richards, 1931), p. 24.

59 Nerina Shute, *We Mixed Our Drinks: The Story of a Generation* (London: Jarrolds Ltd, 1945), p. 26.

60 Cited in Alison Oram, '"A Sudden Orgy of Decadence": Writing about Sex between Women in the Interwar Popular Press', in L. Doan and J. Garrity (eds), *Sapphic Modernities* (Basingstoke: Palgrave Macmillan, 2006), pp. 165–80, 165.

61 Dennis Archer, *The Cloven Hoof: A Study of Contemporary London Vices* (London: Taylor Croft, 1932), p. 83.

62 'A Book That Must Be Suppressed', *Sunday Express*, 9 August 1928, p. 10.

63 Beresford Egan, *The Sink of Solitude: Being a Series of Satirical Drawings Occasioned By Some Recent Events* (London: Hermes Press, 1928).

64 Ibid., preface.

65 Shute, *Passionate Friendships*, p. 30.

66 Shute, *We Mixed Our Drinks*, p. 23.

67 Shute, *Passionate Friendships*, p. 25.

68 Colin Watson, *Snobbery with Violence* (London: Eyre and Spottiswoode, 1971), p. 105.

69 Shute, *We Mixed Our Drinks*, p. 23.

70 Ada Chesterton, *Women of the London Underworld* (London: Stanley Paul, 1928).

71 Lee Israel, *Miss Tallulah Bankhead* (London and New York: W.H. Allen, 1972), p. 305.

72 Cited in Robert Gottlieb, *Lives and Letters* (London: Macmillan, 2011), p. 6.

73 Israel, *Miss Tallulah Bankhead*, p. 305.

74 Archer, *The Cloven Hoof*, p. 81.

75 Ibid.

76　This had been a commonplace of medical discourses on lesbianism since the nineteenth century.

77　Archer, *The Cloven Hoof*, p. 84.

78　Suzanne Neild and Rosalind Pearson, *Women Like Us* (London: The Women's Press, 1992), p. 47.

79　Ibid., p. 59.

80　Ibid., p. 45.

81　Jack Glicco, *Madness After Midnight* (London: Elek Books, 1956), p. 120.

82　Ibid., p. 122.

83　Ibid., p. 115.

84　Ibid., p. 116.

85　Fanny Burney, *Stage, Screen and Sandwiches: The Remarkable Life of Kenelm Foss* (London: Athena Press, 2007), pp. ix–x.

86　Ibid.

87　Ibid.

88　Unattributed newspaper clipping, 1925. Every possible effort has been made to source the copyright holder and we would be happy to acknowledge them in future editions should they get in touch.

89　Marguerite Steen, *Looking Glass: An Autobiography* (London: Longmans, 1966), pp. 79–80.

90　Ibid., p. 40.

91　Stella Condor, *Woman on the Beat: The True Story of a Policewoman* (London: Robert Hale, 1960), p. 149.

92　Zoe Progl, *Woman of the Underworld* (London: Arthur Baker, 1964), pp. 23–24.

93　Glicco, *Madness After Midnight*, p. 82.

94　Violet Powell, *Within the Family Circle: An Autobiography* (London: Heinemann, 1976), p. 162.

95　Ibid.

96　G.E. Lewis, *Out East: In the Malay Peninsula* (Petaling Jaya: Penerbit Fajar Bakti Sdn. Bhd., 1991), p. 22.

97　Jan Gabrial, *Inside the Volcano: My Life with Malcolm Lowry* (New York: St Martin's Press, 2000), p. 36.

98　Cited in Jennings, *Tomboys and Bachelor Girls*, p. 110.

99　Lyrics to 'Gerrard Street', *London Is the Place for Me*, Vol. 2. http://www.allmusic.com/album/london-is-the-place-for-me-vol-2-mw0000643989 (accessed 12 June 2015).

CHAPTER FIFTEEN

Chasing Community: From Old Compton Street to the Online World of Grindr

Marco Venturi

The word 'community' is one of the most controversial in use today. Academics of various disciplines have proposed several definitions, with differences often arising from within the same branch of knowledge. Over the last few decades, the multiplicity of perspectives seems to have undermined the concept of community itself. Even in everyday life, the term 'community' is used indiscriminately to define such a broad variety of different things, from specific interests to needs and beliefs, that its usefulness as a descriptive term is now being questioned.

A first discussion around the term 'community' arose across the end of the nineteenth and the beginning of the twentieth centuries following the advent of mass society and urbanization. The progression from personal face-to-face interactions of small groups of people in rural areas to those defined by more impersonal relations in urban spaces was seen as a symptom of human alienation and a push towards the end of community. Even though small urban groups, such as neighbourhoods, were initially seen as the only spaces where a sort of communal feeling may have been reproduced within the city, by the 1960s, due to processes of gentrification and urban development, this view started to be challenged, too. With the advent of deindustrialization and globalization in the 1980s, even urban neighbourhoods could not provide a space for community anymore. Space was reorganized, urban communities were displaced, people became mobile and cities became global.

Accordingly, Benedict Anderson has argued that 'all communities larger than primordial villages of face to face contact (and perhaps even these) are imagined'.[1] In fact, thanks to the advent of modern technology, people no longer needed to know each other or to share the same space to form a community. Today, it is possible to imagine a plurality of communities, often interconnected, whose members can enter and leave as they like because boundaries have become more malleable and porous. Moreover, these communities are not based on previous hierarchical structures, such as family, nor do they oblige members to follow strict rules of behaviour. They are composed by the self-identification of different individuals who share a commonality such as similar tastes, lifestyles or needs. Therefore, the sense of belonging to these communities will only be a consequence of processes of identification, not the base on which identity is formed.[2] More specifically, as a result of capitalism, access into community can now be purchased, transforming members into consumers and consumers into members. However, given that identity and community are now often based on consumption, it is clear that they also become exclusive, as not every individual will have the possibilities, or the will, to purchase access into them.

In the last few years, virtual communities have become central to the discussion. They are understood as more fluid and temporary forms of social relations which are redefining space and identity. Virtual communities not only empower people but, as Gerald Delanty has noticed, are also more democratic in the formation of plural identities.[3] People can access these communities regardless of their socio-economic background and can build new identities which they would not be able to create in real life. Interestingly, Manuel Castells has argued that virtual communities could best be defined as *social networks* more than communities since it is the lack of community in the first place that makes them attractive.[4]

As the previous examples show, community is far from being a weak concept. Even though the definition has constantly been challenged, active discussion around it demonstrates that community is still central for our understanding of the world. What is important to notice is that today, more than ever before, the idea of community has gained new multiple meanings and that its understanding will always depend on the context in which the term is used. In this chapter, I reconsider the role that the district of Soho plays in the community-making process for gay men in London and how the area interacts with the new virtual space of Grindr. To do so, I analyse both the history of the district as well as the main characteristics that have turned Grindr into such a major cultural and social phenomenon. If we accept the idea of urban spaces as unable to (re-)create community, what is the contemporary function of Soho? Likewise, if virtual communities are the expression of a lack of community in the first place, what are the consequences for those gay men who use Grindr as a means of interaction with other gay men? Most importantly, should Soho and Grindr really be considered as two different realities or should they be analysed as two sides of the same coin? The understanding of their similarities, differences and interrelations will, I hope, contribute to the discussion of how community is formed and what particular meanings it gains for gay men in London.

Throughout the chapter, I use both the term 'queer' and the term 'gay' to refer to homosexual men. However, these terms are not used as synonyms. The first one is employed in relation to a specific time frame (namely the late 1980s and early 1990s) when a new sexual identity was emerging as a reaction to the inability of both society and gay rights groups to respond to the AIDS crisis. In that context, 'queer' was a politically charged term which differs very much from its current definition as an umbrella term that includes any self-identified non-normative expression of sexual identity (be it gay, lesbian, bi, trans or straight). Consequently, I favour 'gay' as a general term that is currently more widespread and less tied to a specific historical or political period. Although queer men and women initially constituted a key presence and had an active role in the definition of Soho as a gay district, as I will explain, the identity that was promoted in Soho had less to do with politics than it had with consumption. Contemporary Soho may have been born queer, but it definitely developed as gay.

(Un)Changing Soho

As Jonathan Fryer notes, Soho is often identified as 'the tight little grid of streets north and south of Old Compton Street'.[5] This part represents both its heart and its oldest area. Here, on what were once hunting fields of Crown property, the first households were built to accommodate the large movement of people from the City of London towards the surrounding unpopulated fields following the Great Plague of 1665 and the Great Fire of 1666. Notwithstanding, Daniel Farson argues that there is no clear understanding of where its boundaries are situated.[6] Soho could be enclosed within Piccadilly, Oxford, St Giles and Cambridge Circuses and delimited by Oxford Street to the north, Regent Street to the west, Charing Cross Road to the east, and Coventry Street and Leicester Square to the south – although Shaftesbury Avenue is often mistakenly envisioned as its modern south border. These Georgian and Victorian streets were built following a process of modernization that redesigned the map of London in the nineteenth century in order to facilitate the capital's traffic flow. In so doing, Soho assumed, in Judith Summers's phrasing, the form of a 'small island land-locked in London's West End'.[7] This characteristic contributed to preserving its village-like atmosphere throughout the years.[8] Not even the development of a public transport system affected the area. No buses run through Soho, apart from along Shaftesbury Avenue, and the underground stations of Oxford Circus, Tottenham Court Road, Piccadilly Circus and Leicester Square are situated in correspondence with the four *imagined* corners of the district and also serve other important areas such as Marylebone, Fitzrovia, Bloomsbury, Covent Garden, St James and Mayfair.

Even though it was initially conceived for the aristocracy, Soho soon became home to many foreign refugees: from the Greeks escaping the Turks at the end of the 1670s to the French Huguenots who were in turn escaping the religious discrimination of Louis XIV; from the Irish escaping the Potato Famine between 1845 and 1852, to the Italian refugees of the 1860s and the Polish and Russian Jews escaping anti-Semitism in the 1880s and 1890s. All these people had one thing in common: they were escaping from somewhere. As Summers notes, 'persecution comes in many shapes and forms, and in whatever incarnation it appears – political, religious, social or sexual – Soho has always seemed to provide the persecuted with shelter and with the freedom to be themselves'.[9] Nevertheless, the foreign character of the district strengthened the image of Soho as a slum on a more general level. The district soon became synonymous with poverty and its potential consequences such as prostitution, gambling and crime.

The sleazy and indulgent character of the district contributed to the development of a lively nightlife during the interwar years and transformed the area into the place to be. In fact, between the late 1950s and the early 1960s, many different kinds of revolution took place in Soho. The countercultural youth revolution was born in the district's streets, in its shop windows and, most of all, in its new coffee bars and clubs. Jazz and rock 'n' roll went hand in hand with a change in fashion and clothing. The intervention of the newly formed Soho Society, in the 1970s, also forced Westminster Council to restrict the number of sex establishments – more than two hundred – that had appeared at every corner throughout the years. As Frank Mort suggests, film, television and publishing industries, together with local businesses, rapidly started to advertise the foreign nature of Soho as the more attractive and lucrative theme of cosmopolitanism.[10] Soho had gradually been cleaned up and its frontiers had increasingly been opened to a wider crowd.

In this period, between the end of the 1970s and the beginning of the 1980s, the new male-oriented consumeristic culture invaded the area and transformed it into something of an open-air mall where the 'yuppy' (the young successful business man) could purchase style, goods and, to some extent, identity.[11] Thom O'Dwyer pointed out that men's fashion was 'coming out of the closets'.[12] Indeed, the commercialization of masculine identities in Soho represented a huge attraction for many homosexual men who were, at the time, becoming visible both to each other and mainstream society. Still, if style and clothes worked as representational tools, it was in the new clubs and bars that the interaction was taking place. American-style clubs, on the model of Studio One in Los Angeles or Studio 54 in New York, were opened in and around Soho. The most famous were the Sundown Club in the basement of the Astoria Theatre in Charing Cross Road, which opened in 1976 and offered three main nights (*Bang!* on Mondays and Saturdays, and *Propaganda* on Thursdays), and Heaven, which was inaugurated in 1980 under the Arches in Villier Street. Consequently, homosexual men started to be seen as a profitable target by many other types of business in the area. In just a few years, new bars appeared all over Soho and its surroundings, including Bar Code, KuBar, Kudos, Village Soho and The Yard, along with cafés and restaurants such as The Edge, Freedom and Balans, and shops such as Boy Zone, Clone Zone and Paradiso.

Soho therefore functioned as a rendezvous, as a place where gay identities were shaped and displayed outside in the streets as well as inside in its bars. At the same time, the pliability of the district let the performance of these identities shape its own structure and image. Nikki Usher and Eleanor Morrison have suggested that, similar to the areas with a high concentration of immigrants, those with a large presence of gay people were born out of the need to create a safe environment on the basis of a shared identity. These neighbourhoods make gay men visible 'through the claiming of spaces such as storefronts, sidewalks, and public parks as gay, as well as through the performance of gay or queer identity in these places'.[13] Soho represented the first urban district in London where such a high concentration of gay activities arose in the public eye.

Beyond doubt, in contrast to previous gay venues characterized by their anonymity and their underground activity, those that appeared in Soho were defined by a more explicit and 'in your face' attitude. Clean and bright interiors were employed in the design of the new venues as a marketing strategy and as a visual response to the AIDS crisis. Many bars featured large windows at street level which allowed customers to see outside as well as pedestrians to see inside.[14] After decades of forced invisibility, homosexuals were finally becoming visible. In February 1993, during the Queer Valentine Carnival, two thousand gay men and lesbians marched through Soho's streets to reclaim the area as theirs. Soho was now gay; as gay as it would ever be. Most importantly, it seemed that gay men had finally found a home.

Gay men from all over Britain and, more recently, from all over Europe and the rest of the world have found shelter and recognition in this area, building up an intense network of connections. Gradually, even for those who were not regular visitors or who had never visited the area, it did not take long to associate the name of the district with ideas and stereotypes of homosexuality and 'camp'. Be that as it may, the development of gay identities and community based on the consumption of a particular lifestyle might be viewed as 'double-edged': it is true that gay men managed to give new meanings to the city and its spaces, but this process also distanced many people from the initial ideals of political activism and change that had shaped the community itself.[15] Chris Woods sees consumerism as something 'sold as a tool of empowerment' but it could also be seen to represent a way of taking advantage of

> the need of most homosexuals for a sense of community by packaging and then selling to gay men and lesbians real or imagined aspects of their

identity or lifestyle. The commodification of homosexuality has less to do with the politics of liberation or community than with the cynical creation and maintenance of a gullible niche market.[16]

In addition, it is important to keep in mind that trends and fashions change with time and that, most of all, even though gay men are often seen as a uniform group of wealthy consumers, not everyone can, or wants to, afford the same lifestyle. Consequently, as Alan Sinfield emphasized in 1998, even though 'Old Compton Street has given London its gay village … it has only done so for a short eight years'.[17] When, in May 1999, three people were killed and at least 70 were wounded in the bombing of the Admiral Duncan pub on Old Compton Street, it became clear that Soho was not the gay haven that many had initially proclaimed.

In the first decade of the twenty-first century, Soho still attracted a large number of gay visitors and its fame as a gay district became consolidated in many people's imaginations on both a national and an international level, helping to promote the image of London as a cosmopolitan city. However, it could be said that Soho as a gay area has been the victim of its own success. New concepts of gay identity, and community at large, are undermining the very spirit and image of Soho, to the point that its function and future as a magnet for gay men is at risk. Even Clayton Littlewood, one of the most honest observers of contemporary Soho, seems often divided on his position towards the district and its people: 'this place pulls me backwards and forwards. One minute, it's the greatest love of my life, and the next, a love affair that's coated in sadness wherever I turn'.[18] On the one hand, the opening of Soho's services and infrastructures to a more heterosexual clientele, its 'straightening', has changed the composition and the target of its devotees. Many heterosexuals are, in fact, attracted to gay spaces not so much as spaces of sexual experimentation but as spaces of consumption. Here, straight men and women can consume the (safe) exotic 'other' and feel cosmopolitan.[19] Unquestionably, heterosexual tourism, often in the form of hen nights and stag parties, has become a common presence in Soho. On the other hand, the growing visibility and inclusion of homosexuals into mainstream society and politics, the so-called gay sprawl, has reduced, in the last few years, the need for a specifically gay place and, to some extent, the need for a distinctive sexual identity.[20] Consequently, many gay men are now trying to get away from Soho and the stereotypes of camp and gayness which it may represent in British culture, with obvious repercussions on the district, its businesses and its image.

Moving spaces

At the present moment, no district or urban area in London can represent the idea of gay community for gay men the same way Soho used to. In fact, despite the presence of gay bars and clubs in other districts of London, such as Vauxhall, Clapham or Shoreditch, none of these areas has so far played a leading role in the production and re-production of a concept of cohesion for the community itself. Nonetheless, a new place seems to have appeared, only it is not in Soho, or Vauxhall, or Clapham, or Shoreditch, and yet it is present in all these places at once: the Internet. Online media are having a huge impact on our lives. Throughout the day, we spend a large amount of time connected to the Internet, which has clearly radically changed the way we interact. However, this is no news to gay men. Websites like Gaydar or Gayromeo, to name just two, have been active for more than ten years and many gay men will admit to having or having had an active profile online at some point in their lives. Indeed, as Larry Gross emphasizes, homosexuals were among the first to realize the potential of the new medium, becoming both the main consumers and the main producers.[21] Living in a world where no one teaches you how to be gay and where sexual identities always need to be negotiated within a heteronormative 'reality', the Internet has become the place where gay men can not only learn what it means to be gay but also, and most importantly, where they can build their own space, with their own meanings, and connect with people in a similar situation. Coming out videos, chat rooms, virtual communities, porn movies, networking: they are all aspects of a fervent activity that is reshaping the idea of homosexuality itself. The anonymity of the Internet and the protection offered by the mediation of the screen can help people who are struggling with their sexuality to explore and experience gay connections in a less invasive way. Many gay men, for example, find it easier to come out online before doing so in 'real life'. Similarly, gay men who are already aware of their identity can try to negotiate new aspects of their sexuality without feeling the pressure to fit a precise stereotype. In other words, the Internet seems to have freed many gay men from the constrictions of the physical world and to have expanded their possibilities for connection.

In particular, what really changed the situation was the Apple Revolution. Following the globalization of the smartphone industry and its exponential growth in numbers, functions and availability, the way we conceive notions of space and our connections to space have completely changed. The Internet has become something that does not imply a computer and a desk – that is, a specific location in space – but something which can be accessed from a smartphone at any time that a telephone or a wifi connection is detectable, with no limit of mobility. Furthermore, the localization of devices by specific programs (GPS) makes it easy not only to access the virtual space but also to determine one's own position in both this space and the physical world. We move in the city, we walk down the streets, we enter different buildings, we use different modes of transport, and so does the Internet, or at least so does our virtual being. Apps are now giving new meanings to spatiality and how we interact with each other. From the point of view of the gay community, not only do they offer a new means of creating individual sexual identities online but they also offer an alternative space for cruising and community-making.

Consequently, mobile applications such as Grindr have been hugely successful. The Grindr app was launched by Joel Simkhai on 25 March 2009 for the Apple iPhone 3G – which for the first time included GPS programs – but it was soon extended to BlackBerries and Androids. Grindr rapidly became the world's biggest mobile network, with more than five million men in 192 countries.[22] In 2011, London topped the list of the cities of users with almost 400,000 users, and numbers have increased exponentially since then. The simple mention of it by Stephen Fry on BBC's *Top Gear* (Series 13, Episode 2, 2009) caused a massive reaction with about 10,000 downloads on the same night.[23] Over a million people worldwide use Grindr on a daily basis, sending more than seven million messages and two million pictures. They do so for an average of one-and-a-half hours every day and it is estimated that almost 200,000 users are logged on at any given moment.[24]

The success of Grindr may also be due to its simple and appealing design. The app shows small square thumbnail images of hundreds of gay men available in the surrounding areas, often within walking distance, ordered by proximity and without the limit of the physical boundaries that a bar or a club would imply. As Sharif Mowlabocus highlights,

> in what is perhaps the most direct digital interaction of the term 'Gaydar' – the original use of the term as opposed to the website – these applications 'scan' the local area and allow the user to not only see who else nearby is subscribed to the service, but also provide the means for instant communication.[25]

Grindr is not officially described as a space devoted to sexual pursuit and explicit reference to any sexual content (both texts and images) is strictly prohibited in the public area. Its creators describe it as a way to find 'a new date, buddy, or friend' but they also highlight another implicit goal:

> 0 feet away: Our mission for you. Grindr's different because it's uncomplicated and meant to help you meet guys while you're on the go. It's not your average dating site – you know, the ones that make you sit in front of a faraway computer filling out complex, detailed profiles and answering invasive psychological questions. We'd rather you were zero feet away. With Grindr, '0 Feet Away' isn't just a cute slogan we print on our T-shirts. It's a state of mind, a way of life – a new kind of dating experience. Turning Grindr off and being there in-person [*sic*] with that guy you were chatting with is the final goal of using the app. Being 0 feet away is our mission for you.[26]

In other words, breaking with past online experiences that required more effort and time, Grindr markets itself as a quick and easy way to find other gay men. It can be accessed at any time, from any location, even if someone is on the move. In theory, Grindr could represent a new and safer way to cruise the world, a space where only members are allowed, one that is protected from the heterosexual/mainstream judgement and presence, where the whole process of trying to understand if someone is gay or not is eliminated by the fact that, supposedly, everybody using the application is gay or is looking for a connection with another man. Most importantly, it incentivizes physical encounters more than deep and meaningful conversations online. The final goal, as expressed by its creators, is that of finding yourself in front of the person you were chatting with as quickly as possible.

However, the immediacy and facility of this encounter implies that, on one level, the effort put into getting to know each other beforehand will be pretty low and, on the other, it also entails that as quickly and easily as the first date, a second one can be found. The whole communal experience that could be lived in Soho, such as going out for a drink or a meal and socializing with the people around you, no matter what your intentions, is then replaced by the centrality of the cruising and the immediacy of the meeting. Consequently, it does not take long to understand that cruising and sexual encounters are actually the real driving force of this application. Whereas meeting someone demands not only interest but a considerable amount of time (and often money), users of the app can find a possible match by only scrolling down the screen and, in this way, reducing both the effort and the money invested while increasing the possible choice. In this sense, the 'urgency' of Grindr 'works to bring down the investment' while also representing 'the epitome of instant gratification'.[27]

It becomes clear, then, that on Grindr a great stress is placed on the visual, more than the textual. The image not only reflects the idea of one's own opinion of self and the way one wants to represent oneself, but it also allows an authentication from other users. In effect, as Mowlabocus notes, digital images 'appear as a stabilizing force for identity formation and cultural legibility, offering a structuring device for the proliferation of specific ideas as to what it is to be a gay man in contemporary Western culture'.[28] The pictures uploaded on Grindr and similar applications become a currency used in what Mowlabocus defines as 'the Gaydar economy'.[29] Users are required to find the best way to promote their profile and to get the attention of others: 'the profile is as much a mechanism for self-identification as it is one of self-promotion'.[30] This visual emphasis is combined with a brief but very clear textual message. Unlike previous websites, the profile that can be created on the app is very basic: a username, a headline, information such as height and age, and a very short description. In just a few words, users often manage not only to describe themselves but also what, or who, they are looking for on Grindr. The textual, as well as the visual, functions to create new standards and requirements which must be fulfilled in order to promote one's own profile successfully.

However, it is astonishing how many users express their racial, age, body and sexual preferences. Far from being politically correct, Grindr texts often display stipulations such as 'white men only', 'no Asians', 'no fatties', 'not into older guys', 'no twinks', 'only for tops' and 'Brits only'. Moreover, users very often stress and praise a straight-acting identity. Requests like 'straight-acting lads only', 'be masculine', 'only real men', 'no camp' or 'act straight' appear on many profiles. It is interesting to notice how, on an app for gay men, the word 'straight' is used much more frequently than the word 'gay' itself. Camp and 'effeminacy', as well as a strong inclusive pride in being 'queer' and being 'here', have been replaced by a new idea of male homosexuality that differentiates itself from heterosexuality only by the nature of the sexual act. If, on the one hand, this desire of absolute detachment from the gay community and its culture can be seen as an example of integration by the mainstream society of a sexual minority, on the other, it might assume a questioning and a denial of one's own sexual identity in order to be accepted. What the straight-acting homosexual denies, then, both online and offline, is not his own sexuality, as it might have been in the past, but his own sexual identity and the chance of being identified with a gay community that promotes different expressions of homosexuality.

Of great significance, in this sense, is the use that most users make of the 'block' button in order to delete other users' profiles from their view and deny these same users the chance to contact them again. Through this process, they can create their own community based on the exclusion of the other. In Jaime Woo's opinion, 'the beauty of Grindr is that it decoupled hooking up from the specific places, away from the bars, bathhouses, parks, and washrooms'.[31] Yet, whereas no client in a Soho bar can decide who should be allowed in the premises, or what age, ethnic or other specific group he wants to be surrounded by, on Grindr users can block and eliminate other people to their liking. Sexual racism, as a form of sexual discrimination based on racial connotations, is enacted and disguised as personal preferences legitimated by the private nature of the application itself.[32] The same mechanism is then enacted for all other physical features such as age or body type, as well as for the degree of perceived masculinity or the sexual preference of the users. Consequently, the promoted image of the Internet as a new space for sexual freedom and connection becomes in truth a very narrow one. Stereotypes, commonplaces and power relations are recreated in the online world and users not only carry with them their cultural baggage but they also impose it over other users through the celebration of specific images and identities as well as the exclusion of others. The promise of a new-found land seems, once again, to have been breached.

Rethinking community

For most of its existence, Soho has represented many things to many people, being considered, in Mort's view, 'as both a real and an imagined space, where complex economic and social relationships intersected with the equally rich resources of urban fantasy'.[33] Its permeable boundaries have managed to preserve the area almost unchanged for hundreds of years while allowing it to evolve and recreate itself according to the needs of different communities. The understanding of its nature and the way it managed to evolve throughout history is a necessary tool for comprehending the contemporary situation. As previously explained, Soho as we know it is a fairly recent invention. Its streets and bars have functioned as a place where gay identities have been made and, at the same time, a place made by the performance of these identities. In fact, 'like Greenwich Village, Soho was projected as part of the geographies of the imagination and as an intensely compressed but mutable social environment', becoming 'a major site for cultural and sexual experimentation throughout the twentieth century'.[34]

However, because homosexuality is now so widely accepted in British society, it seems that those who still identify Soho as a safe space where it is possible to express their sexual identity freely may also be excluding themselves from a deeper experience available almost everywhere else in the city. Soho, the place where gay men first became visible in London, is now perceived by many as a ghetto. Its boundaries have become too rigid for gay men, showing that gay spaces may be in decline or, at least, may be changing their nature. It is possible today to find gay venues scattered around London, sometimes miles away from one another. Physical concentration of gay activities is not seen as a necessary feature in order to guarantee safety and create community. Many gay men feel safe to express their identity outside of these venues and, similarly, outside of gay communities. Moreover, with the advent of the Internet, gay men seem to have now moved online and to have colonized a whole new space. Yet, even though online technologies may represent a new space for interaction which overcomes the limits imposed by physical areas, Grindr shows that this is not completely true. For instance, Mort talks of membership when referring to the purchase of masculinities/identities in Soho.[35] The same idea can be applied to Grindr as gay men need to create and negotiate their masculinity/identity online in order to play. Following the same line of thought, Gross explains that 'the Internet is not utopia'. In his opinion, the Internet does offer a new world to inhabit but, similar to physical gay spaces, online communities can also be both spaces of freedom and of restraint. Given that most users will bring along the same preconceptions that they have in real life, the Internet will automatically recreate the same hierarchy and the same power relations.[36]

Still, considering online and offline spaces as something separate, or seeing the first as 'an escape from, or a response to' the latter, would be misleading because, as Mowlabocus argues, 'these two concepts are not discrete but pervade one another' in a relationship of 'dialogue'.[37] Grindr cannot be a substitute for the physical space. Even if connections are made online, given the sexual aspect of Grindr, they are likely to take form in the physical space, be it Soho or another place. For this reason, Woo argues that

Grindr will not eliminate physical gay spaces. It only becomes a threat if we take for granted the fact that gay men use Grindr as a substitute for Soho. If, on the contrary, we acknowledge their interrelation and structure the nature and needs of gay venues accordingly, then physical gay spaces will continue to exist.[38] However, as already mentioned, the discourse around the disappearance of Soho as the gay district of London is not limited to the offline/online dichotomy but also involves other factors which characterize contemporary society. The inclusion of gay men into mainstream society, combined with Soho's natural need to reinvent itself, is already producing a visible change in both the composition of the district and the attitudes towards it. This is not to say that every gay bar will disappear from Soho. As Italian and French restaurants can still be found in the district, as well as retail shops and jazz clubs, so will gay spaces. Their function, nonetheless, may become more touristic than communal, a reminder of what it used to be more than an expression of what it actually is.

Conclusion

As the case of Soho and Grindr shows, defining community is a very challenging task. To complicate the picture, the demise of those communities based in specific spaces and their movement to the online world of the Internet have meant that, today, community is ever-present while also being harder to identify given that it is experienced in a more individualistic way. In the specific case of gay men, if we understand the gay 'community' as an exclusive term aimed at the definition of a precise number of members, to which someone either belongs or not, then its use becomes completely arbitrary. Soho has never represented the gay community as a whole, but nor has, or will, Grindr, given that it often preserves the same stereotypes and contradictions. Sure enough, everybody experiences community in a different way and, even though at the beginning of the gay rights movement it seemed possible to achieve a universal gay community into which everybody would fit regardless of ethnicity, class, age, gender, sex, body type or sexual identity, this has never really been achieved.

On the contrary, if we interpret the definition of community as an inclusive, mobile term, we can see how both Soho and Grindr become spaces of representation. One's own idea of community is usually connected to the degree of involvement in the community itself and, although it might not be representative, this idea still represents a useful tool for the expression of a more personal feeling of belonging. When identifying themselves with the gay community, gay men express their need and will to feel part of a group of people who share a particular experience. The duration, the terms, and the degree of involvement in this experience will obviously depend on their personal choices. In fact, it must be kept in mind that, because the gay community is something someone gets to and not something someone comes from (as it may be with a religious or an ethnic community), belonging for gay men is always optional and the result of an often long and difficult path of identification. Today, the term 'gay community' should then be understood in a postmodern sense: it is mobile (can move from one space to the other), imagined (members do not need to know each other), open (members can enter or leave at any time), plural (there is not just one gay community) and placeless (or present in different spaces).

Still, this nature of the gay community, while expanding its potential, also tends to transform it into a very private experience. It is true that nowadays online applications such as Grindr are experiencing a huge success at the expense of gay districts such as Soho, but the problem with online spaces is that, in contrast to their physical counterparts, they are actually invisible to those who are not members and basically impossible to come across unless someone is specifically looking for them. Whereas in the past, being gay, although not a choice, still implied a radical choice to be taken – whether to live in or out of the closet – nowadays we are witnessing an historical period where the inclusion of homosexuality into the current political and social agenda, even reflecting a huge cultural shift, has transformed gay politics into a much less radical movement. Equality implies inclusion, but so far the inclusion has happened on what appears to be heteronormative conditions, reflecting, with the new normal 'straight-like' gay identity being more respectable than the previous self-identified gay identity, a deep confusion of what it means to be gay and what actually makes the gay community. The risk is that the idea of gay community and culture, which took centuries to be developed and which still represents a very fragile concept, might in the near future be erased and that gay men, in order to be accepted into mainstream society, will sacrifice their culture and their visibility in districts such as Soho and will adapt once again to being hidden in the closet – only this time, a virtual one.

Notes

1   Benedict Anderson, *Imagined Communities: Reflections on the Origins and Spread of Nationalism*, 2nd edn. (London: Verso, 1991), p. 6.

2   Zygmunt Bauman, *Does Ethics Have a Chance in a World of Consumers?* (Cambridge, MA: Harvard University Press, 2008), pp. 120–21.

3   Gerard Delanty, *Community* (London: Routledge, 2003), p. 182.

4   Manuel Castells, *The Internet Galaxy: Reflections on the Internet, Business, and Society* (Oxford: Oxford University Press, 2001), p. 128.

5   Jonathan Fryer, *Soho in the Fifties and Sixties* (London: National Portrait Gallery Publications, 1998), p. 5.

6   Daniel Farson, *Soho in the Fifties* (London: Michael Joseph, 1987), p. 4.

7   Judith Summers, *Soho: A History of London's Most Colourful Neighbourhood*
      (London: Bloomsbury, 1989), p. 1.

8   Richard Tames, *Soho Past* (London: Historical Publications Ltd, 1994), p. 9.

9   Summers, *Soho: A History*, p. 38.

10   Frank Mort, *Capital Affairs: London and the Making of the Permissive Society*
      (New Haven, CT: Yale University Press, 2010), p. 241.

11   Frank Mort, *Cultures of Consumption: Masculinities and Social Space in
      Late Twentieth-Century Britain*, 2nd edn. (Abingdon: Routledge, 2009),
      pp. 157–63.

12   Thom O' Dwyer, 'Liberated Man Power Arrives', *Men's Wear*
      (23 August 1984), p. 8; quoted in Mort, *Cultures of Consumption*, p. 16.

13   Nikki Usher and Eleanor Morrison, 'The Demise of the Gay Enclave', in
      Christopher Pullen and Margaret Cooper (eds), *LGBT Identity and Online
      New Media* (New York: Routledge, 2010), p. 274.

14   Johan Andersson, 'East End Localism and Urban Decay: Shoreditch's
      Re-Emerging Gay Scene', *The London Journal* 34.1 (2009), pp. 55–71, 55.

15   Mort, *Cultures of Consumption*, p. 166.

16   Chris Woods, *The State of the Queer Nation: A Critique of Gay and Lesbian
      Politics in 1990s Britain* (London: Cassell, 1995), p. 41.

17   Alan Sinfield, *Gay and After: Gender, Culture and Consumption* (London:
      Serpent's Tail, 1998), p. 196.

18   Clayton Littlewood, *Dirty White Boy: Tales of Soho* (Berkeley, CA: Cleis Press,
      2008), p. 57.

19   See Jon Binnie and Beverley Skeggs, 'Cosmopolitan Knowledge and the
      Production and Consumption of Sexualized Space: Manchester's Gay Village',
      in Jon Binnie *et al.* (eds), *Cosmopolitan Urbanism* (New York: Routledge,
      2006), pp. 220–45.

20   Usher and Morrison, 'The Demise of the Gay Enclave', p. 276.

21   Larry Gross, 'Forward', in Kate O' Riordan and David J. Phillips (eds), *Queer
      Online: Media, Technology, and Sexuality* (New York: Peter Lang Publishing,
      2007), p. ix.

22   See Grindr's official webpage: http://grindr.com/learn-more (accessed
      28 March 2014).

23   Laurence Watts, 'Feature: The Grindr Story', *PinkNews*, 22 February 2012.
      http://www.pinknews.co.uk/2011/02/22/feature-the-grindr-story/ (accessed
      28 March 2014).

24   Amy Ashenden, 'Study: Six Million Users Log onto Grindr an Average of
      Eight Times a Day', *PinkNews*, 27 March 2013. http://www.pinknews
      .co.uk/2013/03/27/study-six-million-users-log-onto-grindr-an-average-of-
      eight-times-a-day/ (accessed 28 March 2014).

25   Sharif Mowlabocus, *Gaydar Culture: Gay Men, Technology and Embodiment
      in the Digital Age* (Farnham: Ashgate Publishing, 2010), p. 195.

26 See Grindr's official webpage: http://grindr.com/learn-more (accessed 28 March 2014).

27 Jamie Woo, *Meet Grindr: How One App Changed the Way We Connect* (Canada: Jamie Woo, 2013), pp. 14, 22, 45.

28 Sharif Mowlabocus, 'Look at Me!: Images, Validation, and Cultural Currency on Gaydar', in C. Pullen and M. Cooper (eds), *LGBT Identity and Online New Media* (New York: Routledge, 2010), pp. 201–14, 201.

29 Mowlabocus, *Gaydar Culture*, pp. 104–5.

30 Ibid., p. 92.

31 Woo, *Meet Grindr*, p. 22.

32 See Nathaniel Adam Tobias Coleman, 'What? What? In the (Black) Butt', *Apa Newsletters: Newsletter on Philosophy and Lesbian, Gay, Bisexual and Transgender Issues* 11.1 (2011), p. 12.

33 Mort, *Capital Affairs*, p. 202.

34 Ibid.

35 Mort, *Cultures of Consumption*, p. 165.

36 Gross, 'Forward', p. x.

37 Mowlabocus, *Gaydar Culture*, pp. 2, 21.

38 Woo, *Meet Grindr*, p. 26.

CHAPTER SIXTEEN

Being 'There': Contemporary London, Facebook and Queer Historical Feeling

Sam McBean

At the Lambeth Women's Project in May 2012, Joan Nestle was in conversation with Christa Holka. In the late 1950s and 1960s, Nestle was a notable figure in the New York City gay and lesbian bar scene and became active in the gay liberation movement following the Stonewall riots. As well as being a Lambda award-winning author, she also, perhaps most notably, co-founded the Lesbian Herstory Archives in 1974, in what was then her apartment. The Lesbian Herstory Archives is now widely considered to be the world's largest archive of materials by and about lesbians and their communities. Nestle's work to build and sustain this monumental institution makes her an integral figure in the archiving of lesbian history. Holka is an American photographer who lives and works primarily in London. Her photographs range from classically styled portraits of her friends, to a series which documents queer club nights, to work which records LGBT cultural events in London. As Holka describes it on her website, she is interested in 'documenting and archiving the communities in which she exists'.[1] Holka's photographs are much more centred around her personal experiences than Nestle's archive – Holka's work is fundamentally linked to a community in which she imagines herself as belonging, whereas Nestle collects and preserves objects, narratives, images and stories from lesbian-identified women around the world. Yet both Holka and Nestle share an investment in the importance of accumulating evidence of queer lives and communities.

This shared investment in the necessity of documenting queer existence seemingly motivated the pairing of Nestle and Holka at the talk at the Lambeth Women's Project. In pairing Nestle and Holka, the event drew attention, or imagined a lineage of commitment, to the documenting of queer communities. As such, the pairing becomes a site for considering what this lineage might be, or what the relationship is between archives of the past and archives of a contemporary queer London. Of particular interest to me here is the way that Holka's photographs might be part of, as well as constitute, an online archive of queer community. While Holka's images have been exhibited at numerous galleries in cities around the world, they also have an active circulation online, where in particular her images of queer club nights are posted, shared and re-posted on Facebook and Tumblr. Given that Nestle's archive is housed within the Lesbian Herstory Archive's Brooklyn brownstone and Holka's photographs circulate online, the dialogue also seemingly invites consideration of what the relationship might be between these two archival sites. Indeed, I take the pairing of Nestle and Holka as an invitation to consider the relationship between 'old' archives and 'new' archives, particularly in relation to queer subjects. In this chapter, I read Holka's photographs and their existence online not as a contemporary version of Nestle's Lesbian Herstory Archive. Instead, I argue that we might draw a less linear relationship between contemporary archives and archives of the past.

Of particular interest to me is Holka's photographic project 'I WAS THERE', a series which documents a number of parties in East London – nights which were either promoted explicitly to, or primarily attended by, lesbian, gay, bisexual or trans people and their allies. If, as a whole, Holka's work displays a commitment to documenting her friends and the queer communities in which she participates, this series is composed of images taken in dark basements and on sweaty dance floors, capturing people who are both unaware of her lens as well as those who are knowingly posing with their friends or fellow partygoers. The series evokes the energies of nights out, performances of being seen and of being in a queer space. While the official series is temporally bound (2009–11) and composed of a select number of images, Holka's snaps of club nights exceed the series itself. A wider range of Holka's photographs of club nights have been featured on Facebook (on various club nights' Facebook pages) as well as on the UK-based lesbian website *The Most Cake*. It is this less 'bound' archive that is most interesting, as the hundreds if not thousands of images taken by Holka circulate freely online. Importantly, these 'scene shots', as they might be described, collectively circulate online as documentation of a particular contemporary queer London.

For queer subjects, the process of 'seeing' oneself in an archive is frequently wrought with difficulties – both in terms of the lack of documentation of forms of non-normative intimacy and sexuality in archives, and in terms of the inevitable problems with 'finding' contemporary identities in the past. I became interested in these photographs because I watched Holka documenting partygoers at club nights. I watched people's desire to be captured by her lens. Moreover, I knew the importance of not only being photographed by Holka, but of having this image then belong to the event's Facebook page. In other words, the desire to be photographed by Holka was also a desire to have the image included in an archive of the night. This inclusion not only offered a professional photo of one's self that could be tagged or passed around via online social networks, but it also acted as evidence of an individual's inclusion in a contemporary queer London scene. I thus became interested in how these contemporary desires and this contemporary archive might be linked to queerness' past invisibility. In other words, might the desire to be in these Facebook archives be more than a performance of self online, and instead be connected to desires to be present in archives? It is with this in mind that I aim to consider what kinds of queer historical affects might circulate online, and particularly in Holka's archives of contemporary London.

Holka's emphatic 'I WAS THERE' is a seemingly straightforward utterance of presence in contemporary queer London. In being photographed by Holka, subjects insist on their presence at a contemporary party and they perform this presence on Facebook. Yet 'I WAS THERE' might also be read as a claiming of past existence – where the 'I' insists on a historical presence. Perhaps the claim stretches beyond the immediate past (the party last night, the event last week), and instead asserts a deeper historical reach (I, as a queer subject, have a history, 'I was there'). Or, finally, 'I WAS THERE', with its all too emphatic caps lock, might also belie anxieties about being present, insecurities about the archivability of contemporary queer London. If queer lives and communities have escaped archival sites, or have proved difficult to document and evidence, the sheer volume of Facebook photographs of queer club nights seems to almost over-evidence contemporary queer existence. Yet, as I suggest, this excess of documentation might reveal the difficulty, or perhaps impossibility, of photographs shared via social media sites being able to evidence the specificity of place (London), as well as queerness more broadly. I consider the entanglement of these three readings of 'I WAS THERE', producing an argument about an archive of contemporary queer London that links it to desires for queer historicity as well as anxieties about contemporary queer London as archivable.

The Facebook archive

Similar to Nestle's work to archive proof of the existence of lesbian lives, Holka's project to document the communities in which she exists provides vital evidence of a queer present. It is frequently from within marginalized communities that the labour to document and archive comes, as queer lives are a challenge to traditional archives and archival documentation.

Traditional and institutional archives have often proven insufficient for, or incapable of, recognizing and protecting forms of life that do not show up in the already sanctioned sites of what is considered collective memory. As Ann Cvetkovich suggests, gay and lesbian archives are '[f]orged around sexuality and intimacy, and hence forms of privacy and invisibility that are both chosen and enforced'. In this way, 'gay and lesbian cultures often leave ephemeral and unusual traces'.[2] Slipping through dominant archival sites, evidence of gay and lesbian existence is often housed as memory, or as 'ephemeral and personal collections of objects' which 'offer alternative modes of knowledge'.[3] Lesbian and gay lives challenge dominant archives as evidence of intimacy, sexuality and desire often falls through the cracks of official documentation, thus both calling into question what counts as archival material and revealing the failure of archival authority.

In some ways, the ease of collaboratively collecting and sharing images online has introduced new possibilities for archives. As these technologies 'expand our capacity to record everything', the process of archiving might be stretched to include our everyday practices of managing, indexing and classifying digital information.[4] As Mike Featherstone explains, 'to be is to record and to record in volume means to classify, index and archive'.[5] Individuals organize an incredible amount of digital data on an almost daily basis – whether it be music files, digitized albums, or hard drive back-ups – so that archiving has become part of our everyday routines. Facebook has emerged as central to personal archival practices, so that in Joanne Garde-Hansen's words, 'Facebook can be seen then as sine qua non of digital memory-making and personal archive building'.[6] Jennifer Pybus refers to an individual's Facebook profile as a 'user profile archive'. For users of Facebook, uploading a photo is 'a highly curated moment' that evidences 'an intentional archival event'.[7] Of course, Facebook does not merely exist as a platform for individuals to 'use', but instead it shapes what narratives can be told through delineating the form in which they must exist. As Jacques Derrida explains, 'the technical structure of the *archiving* archive also determines the structure of the *archivable* content even in its very coming into existence and in its relationship to the future.' The archive inevitably structures what can be saved, so that '[t]he archivization produces as much as it records the event'.[8] In choosing to focus on Facebook as a contemporary archive in this chapter, I do not aim to claim it as a utopian space for documenting queer lives. Rather, I would suggest its archival and affective promises be taken seriously for what they might offer specifically to queer subjects. Indeed, this necessitates seeing Facebook's archival potential as not only personal or individual but also as collaborative in nature. For instance, through Holka's photographs of club nights, she produces on Facebook an archive of not just a personal nature, but of a particular time and place in London. In other words, Holka's drive to personally archive the community of which she is a part extends to producing an archive that is not just personal.

Moreover, Facebook is not only or merely 'new'. Formally, Facebook's use of a 'timeline' structure and its appropriation of photo albums as a primary feature of the site both reference and draw on 'older' techniques of mapping and saving memories. This has been well-explored in new media theory, where concepts such as 'cultural convergence', 'media archaeology' and 'remediation' have emerged to name the way that new media does not exist in a teleological relationship to other media forms.[9] Each term, in its own way, challenges the 'newness' of new media through disrupting linear narratives. I am particularly drawn to Jay David Bolter and Richard Grusin's concept of 'remediation', which names the way media forms that might be described as 'new' are always drawing on so-called older forms.[10] In other words, remediation invites us to consider the ways in which 'new media' might be read for how it reworks forms that are often designated as 'older' – a way to consider how media forms do not work in isolation from each other. This, as Sarah Kember and Joanna Zylinska explain, is a means of rejecting seeing media or 'media time' as a 'series of discrete spacialized objects, or products that succeed one another' where 'we are said to progress *from* photography *to* Flickr, *from* books *to* e-readers'.[11] As they explain, '[o]ld media come around again in this framework, as a result of which history is not seen as linear and progressive but rather as nonlinear and cyclical'.[12] Remediation helps to name the process by which Facebook, in a formal capacity, remediates what might be considered older archival forms.

If contemporary media sites are understood as always already in complex non-linear relationships to media forms with longer genealogies, what remains unexplored is what kinds of affects – affects that might be seen as 'past' – might be bound to new media archival sites. If the past is remediated in relation to media form, the affective structure of this collision between past and present is worth exploring. If contemporary 'new' media sites are always already 'old', how might we read the affective force of this for gay and lesbian subjects in particular? If 'older' archives have had a tendency to fail to capture the 'evidence' of queer existence, what effect does this past absence have on contemporary archives? Might there be something of this past invisibility lingering in the pleasures of a contemporary moment in which hundreds or thousands of images are produced which purport to evidence queerness? Indeed, might there be an affective force attached to contemporary archives – an affective force produced through past invisibility? In this queer take on remediation, what is remediated in and through the digital Facebook archive is not so much the technology of photography itself (the 'old' media), but instead affect. Adi Kuntsman, in her introduction to the edited collection *Digital Cultures and the Politics of Emotion* (2012), argues that we might do well to frame the digital through the following questions: 'How does affect work in online networks and digital assemblages? What are the structures of feeling that operate in our everyday digital life, and what kind of virtual public spheres do they create?'[13] Indeed, online sites such as Facebook, blogs and YouTube are increasingly being read with a focus on affect, feeling and emotion – or in other words, with an insistence that feeling is central to these sites.[14] As Jodi Dean argues, social networks and online platforms 'produce and circulate affect as a binding technique',[15] or, in Kuntsman's words, the digital might be framed through its *affective fabric*.[16] This brings me back to Holka and Nestle, and an insistence on reading Holka's project not as a 'new' archive, where Nestle's would be 'old'. The historical invisibility in dominant institutional archives means that there is an intense affective force in archives such as Nestle's – in their insistence that queer people 'have' a history. The affect attached to 'the queer archive' then becomes, I suggest, remediated in the present, where contemporary subjects' insistence on 'presence' might not be so easily separable from historical invisibility.

Queer historical feelings

Contemporary queer London, and Holka's contemporary archive of queer London on Facebook in particular, might carry with it something of the past. While, as Elizabeth Freeman points out, queer theory has a long history of being interested in temporality, the last decade and a half has seen a number of thinkers turn to engage more explicitly with this theme – many of whom participated in a roundtable published in *GLQ* in 2007, entitled 'Theorizing Queer Temporalities'.[17] The concerns of these various thinkers are diverse, as are their explorations of what it might mean to engage in queering temporality, queering historiography, or in unpacking the ways in which temporality and historiography might already be queer. Part of this recent work in relation to history has, as Heather Love explains it, 'shifted the focus away from epistemological questions in the approach to the queer past' and instead 'traced the identifications, the desires, the longings, and the love that structure the encounter with the queer past'.[18] These explorations of the potential queer experiences of time and history have, however, been primarily focused on literature and experimental art practices.[19] Queer work that does turn to new media sites has tended to explore how contemporary queer identities and communities are being forged on or in relation to interactions with social media or new technologies.[20] A useful exception here is Alex Cho's work on the queer temporalities of Tumblr, in which he argues that interaction on the platform is 'based on a nonlinear, atemporal rhizomal exchange of affect and sensation, a "queer reverb" of repeat and repeat'.[21] In other words, for Cho, the platform provides an opportunity for queer experiences of time – experiences which fall outside of, or re-organize, the linear historical.

Desires to be 'there' in Holka's photographs are, I argue, structured by a longer genealogy of queer feeling. In other words, they might recall the past in queer ways. The promise of being captured in one of her images, and of having that image circulate online as part of a queer event in London, is the promise of inclusion in a queer archive. Being present in a contemporary archive offers queer subjects an opportunity, in Christopher Nealon's words, to *'feel historical'*.[22] As Love puts it, '[t]he longing for community across time is a crucial feature of queer historical experience, one produced by the historical isolation of individual queers as well as by the damaged quality of the historical archive'.[23] In *Foundlings* (2002), Nealon argues that an archive of early twentieth-century queer literary production might be read for how this fiction imagines queerness as an orientation towards the historical. Exploring how authors imagined queerness neither through the dominant, individualizing pathological models associated with sexology nor the emerging late twentieth-century lesbian and gay community model, Nealon argues that 'queer writers and artists were groping their way toward a notion of homosexuality defined by a particular relationship to the idea of history'.[24] Here, queerness signifies or indexes the gap between present impossibility and a desire for future legibility, leading Nealon to insist on a model of the 'historical' that encompasses 'the desire for its conditions'.[25] Queerness, then, might be attached to desires for historicity, as much as it might point us towards the necessity of expanding what it means to feel historical.

Connecting Nealon's work to my analysis of Holka's series is the word 'there'. At the end of Nealon's book, 'there' makes a striking appearance. It becomes central to the historical affect that Nealon aims to tease out through his reading of early twentieth-century literature. In the concluding chapter, Nealon offers a reading of James Baldwin's *Go Tell It on the Mountain* (1953), using this example as indicative of the desire for history that he reads as being characteristic of certain twentieth-century writing. In Baldwin's novel, Nealon reads a possible queer desire in the main character John's admiration for his friend, Elisha, a leader in his church congregation. After John experiences his religious transformation at the end of the novel, Nealon quotes John's words to Elisha: ' "Elisha," he said, "no matter what happens to me, where I go, what folks say about me, no matter what *any*body says, you remember – please remember – I was saved. I was *there*".'[26] Nealon reads John's public display of religiosity not as a commitment to the present of his family and church, but instead as a transcendence that might 'operate as a message in a bottle to his beloved, a sign that will turn out to have been some historical "other" place from which the unspeakability of his love can gain audition'. The 'there', in Nealon's description, thus houses the 'future-anteriority of historical uncertainty'.[27] Concluding Nealon's book on the relationship between queer and feeling historical, this 'there' acts as a linguistic marker of the possibility, the uncertain possibility, of future legibility – a reaching out towards a moment in which one's desire might be read.

While Baldwin italicizes his *'there'*, Holka's series 'I WAS THERE' screams the entire sentence. If, in Nealon's reading, the italicized *there* holds the weight of historical feelings, the caps lock of Holka's series similarly registers an affective force. Here, however, this affective force might be read less as a 'message in a bottle' to an unknown future and instead a claim in the present to historicity. The performance of presence in Holka's series does not necessarily yearn for a future in which one's historicity might be legible, so much as it insists on the present as historical. Repeating Baldwin's *'there'*, Holka's series invests in the importance of queer claims to archival presence through insisting on the importance of the present. Holka's 'THERE' is not just a revision of Baldwin's *'there'* – 'I WAS THERE' is a claim inflected and affectively charged by past queer archival invisibility where the queer past might be understood not as over, but instead as that which has unexpected life in the present.[28] As Love puts it, the past might be experienced 'as something dissonant, beyond our control, and capable of touching us in the present'.[29] Indeed, this resistance to moving progressively 'on' from the past might be seen as the marker of queer historiography, where its practitioners, in Dana Luciano's words, 'ask what it means to think history as something other than a linear chronology, a public record of steady "progress" enabled and stabilized by the domestic-familial reproduction of successive generations'.[30] As an example of this kind of historical inquiry, Luciano produces a reading of the lipstick marks on Oscar Wilde's grave. Luciano argues that the 'pressure of lips on stone suggests a different form of contact with the past', one that resists a generational reproduction. This contact refuses a progressive narrative of linearity that moves on from Wilde, and instead the lips 'bend time through the location of partial affinities' and 'kiss into being an expansively queer *now*'.[31] As Luciano herself notes, this epitomizes Carolyn Dinshaw's concept of 'touches across time', where Dinshaw suggests that 'queerly historical' questioning might explore what it means when the 'past touches the present'.[32] Performances of contemporary queer London on Facebook, in their insistence on the present's historicity, might thus, perhaps paradoxically, be a way of making contact with the past.

Perhaps looking less like lipstick marks on a grave, touches across time are legible in new media sites. A recent post on the website *Autostraddle*, which bills itself as a site for 'kick ass lesbian, bisexual, and otherwise inclined ladies (and their friends)', shares archival event flyers advertising lesbian or queer women events from the 1930s to the 1970s.[33] The post is titled '25 Queer Parties You Should Go To If You Have A Time Machine' and the flyers are introduced as follows:

> If you were reading this website in 2010 but didn't live in New York, you're probably really devastated that you missed our epic Rodeo Disco Pride Party, especially if you enjoy riding mechanical bulls. But actually it's likely that you've missed a lot more parties than just that party. Luckily, we've assembled so many of them here so you can really think about what you're doing with your life.

This post, on the one hand, remediates the event flyers from the past through the website format. Through this remediation, it quite directly links the Rodeo Disco Pride Party to a Gay Liberation dance in the 1970s or a 1930s

Berlin party. One click brings you from the poster from the 1930s onto the website of the Rodeo Disco Pride Party. It also insists that the contemporary party is in a lineage of queer parties. This linking of the present with the past insists on the historical and cultural importance of this present, of being present. Through referencing the contemporary party as an introduction to the parties of the more distant past, it inserts the contemporary New York Pride Party into an historical archive. Moreover, it also suggests that while you may not have a time machine to travel back to Berlin in the 1930s, the parties that are happening in contemporary New York are somehow linked to this history. The best way to be there (in the archive, in the queer past, in contact with this queer past) is, consequently, to be here.

The 'I WAS THERE' of Holka's series emphatically screams of presence. The 'was there' is directed towards a prior event and, combined with images of East London partygoers, references attendance at a particular place in the recent past. Shared online and archived on lesbian websites and the Facebook pages of queer events, Holka's photographs evidence a contemporary queer scene. The compulsive archiving of this scene seemingly attempts to give weight to the importance of this present – both these queer parties and the various incarnations of 'I' that were in attendance. Holka's photographs – designated as they are as contemporary queer evidence – promise a performance of the self in the queer archive of the present. If the archival impulse behind the Lesbian Herstory Archive is in part a motivation to evidence the existence of queer lives, the impulse to document contemporary queers is similarly about evidencing a queer present. However, these Facebook archives of Holka's photographs might promise the contemporary and its subjects a relationship to queer history. Dinshaw and Luciano both describe queer historical affect as a fattening of the present – for Dinshaw, this is an 'extended now' and for Luciano an 'expansively queer *now*'.[34] The desire to perform presence in contemporary archives, similar to the desire to attend contemporary parties as voiced in the *Autostraddle* post, is not disconnected from affect attached to the inability to have been 'there' in archives of the past. Through performing presence in Holka's archives, contemporary queer subjects are not just performing a presence in the 'present', but also in an archive. It is this performance of presence in an archive that seems to me to be inseparable from certain queer historical affects – namely anxieties about past 'unattendance', about one's ability to be historical. Contemporary presence in archives, ghosted as it is by past invisibility, is thus not separate from ongoing desires for queer historicity.

Queer London

In some ways, I have been tracing feelings of precarity or unease with regard to archiving queerness. As much as Holka's series seems to ameliorate contemporary subjects' desires for historicity through its archival promise, it also might yet again fail, finally, to capture 'queer London'. In other words, if thus far I have been exploring how the series might promise queer subjects the possibility of feeling historical, the circulation of these photographs online might fundamentally challenge their ability to act as evidence of a contemporary queer London. If, on the one hand, the series' claim that its subjects were 'there' might be read as an archival or historical claim, it is also a claim to having been at specific parties. Holka explained the 'I WAS THERE' project in a talk in May 2012: 'I was there to document a particular time and place in London, a dance floor, an energy, a moment that lives in these images, online, in various blogs, and in their travels all over the world, online and off.'[35] Referencing the title of the series, Holka insists on her own presence 'there' at a particular time and place in London. It is her presence in this moment that enables her to document the energy of London dance floors. In this statement of presence, Holka describes her photographs as evidencing not only a temporally specific, but also a geographically specific location: London. However, she also references the way in which this documentation has its own kind of movement – online, in its movement around the world, across blogs, Tumblr and Facebook. This movement, while not contained in the original images, is integral to considering how these images might represent contemporary London.

Holka's series, as she narrates it, might be read as offering particular representations of a particular group of individuals who move in and out of spaces in London. Holka's photographs contribute to a certain visual representation of, particularly, East London queer club life. In this, Holka's series might be closely related to a number of photographic projects which aim to document and locate the specificities of queer subjects in relation to place – for example, the work of the South African photographer Zanele Muholi, whose photography includes portraits of lesbians in South Africa, or Molly Landreth's project 'Embodiment: A Portrait of Queer Life in America'. Landreth's project, as she describes it on the project's website, 'is an archive and a journey through a rapidly changing community and the people who offer brave new visions of what it means to be queer in America today'.[36] This is a distinctly place-based project that aims to document queer life as it is lived in America in the present. On the project's website, images of queer subjects across the United States are featured. The photograph of the individual, couple or family is labelled with both the name(s) of the subject(s) and the geographic location of where they live. Emphasizing further the importance of place to the project, a Google map is included which pinpoints the location of the individual(s) featured. Viewers are thus invited to locate the subjects not only in the United States as a country, but also in much more specific geographic locations across the nation. Indeed, widening popular conceptions of where it is that queers are traditionally seen as located (that is, major cities) seems to be one of the project's explicit aims.

Yet these photographs of queer subjects that are in some ways linked quite explicitly to place and time cannot hold this specificity when they are housed online. Online, Holka's photographs can be removed from their context, via online sharing, linking and re-posting. As Featherstone argues, digital archives differ from 'the ledger on the shelf in the archive' in that meaning 'ceases to be contained in a bounded physical textual form, the page or document, but is able to flow through network nodes'.[37] In this movement, it becomes less certain that these photographs can signify a particular time and place. The photographs could document any number of parties in any number of locations and it becomes unclear how they might represent a contemporary London. In the artist's talk from 2012, Holka narrates how she discovered that individuals were taking her images and re-posting them on various sites. Tracking the movement of some of her images, Holka describes how her pictures rapidly travelled across blogs, websites and Tumblr – too many for her to trace.[38] It is this act of movement that Sonja Vivienne and Jean Burgess describe as key to digital photography. They argue that 'the web has changed how and what it means to *share* photographs'.[39] Importantly, the sharing of photographs online means that Holka's archive exists within larger networks and flows – images can be downloaded and appropriated in any number of ways, from being posted on Tumblr to being added to Facebook groups or timelines. As Pybus argues, '[u]nlike the static repositories of information stored in a traditional archive, digital archives are constantly being worked on, their contents always in the middle of being recombined, recontextualized, and re-searched'.[40] On the one hand, this is surely one of the pleasures of Facebook, the ease with which images can be passed around friend circles. It is precisely the sharing, posting and re-posting of images in networks of circulation that produce the affective pleasures of platforms such as Facebook. However, this circulation might also produce a sense of unease as it unhinges photographs from their specific referent. As Cho explores in relation to vintage erotica on Tumblr, the images become 'empty of narrative' even as they might 'hint at a subterranean queer history'.[41] Holka's photographs, then, as they might circulate without captions or credits, as profile photographs for users of Facebook or as images incorporated into individuals' Tumblr pages, are removed from their specific time and place. This movement, this constant reconfiguration of documentation, makes it difficult to see how any of Holka's photographs, out of context, might evidence a contemporary queer London. Downloaded from Facebook, shared without a credit on Tumblr or conjoined to an individual website, the photographs themselves do not easily signify London. Through the sharing, the tagging, the re-posting, and the interaction with this archive of a particular time and place in London, London might disappear – or at least the photographs might no longer index or evidence London.

Moreover, what might also be lost is the photographs' evidencing of queerness. The digital expands the possible meanings of the emphatic

'THERE' in 'I WAS THERE'. In some sense, the 'there' performatively locates its subjects in a particular time and place: London. However, its all too emphatic nature perhaps haunts the insecurity that 'there' in relation to place has in some sense become unhinged. If Holka describes her anxieties about losing track of her images, we might also consider how, as these images travel, they lose their embeddedness in a particular time and place: queer London. So we are returned to the anxieties at the heart of the relationship between queerness and the archive – that the queer communities documented in Holka's photographs might again evade the archive. These contemporary archives are, I suggest, haunted by a past absence. The caps lock 'I WAS THERE', in its over-enthusiastic claiming of past presence, seems to contain within it a reference to fears, anxieties or uncertainties about whether 'I' was indeed 'there'. I am suggesting that, similar to Nealon's argument that Baldwin's *there* houses a future anterior historical uncertainty, the archive of Holka's photographs online might not only claim a historical presence, but might also contain within it an uncertainty about this presence. Through referencing the failure of queerness to be documented in the past, this contemporary evidence of queer London might also be haunted by the potential failure of queerness to be captured in this archival present.

Conclusion

This project started because I wanted to understand why individuals were so captivated by Holka's camera at these queer parties. I watched people watching Holka, waiting for her to turn her lens onto them. I watched Holka often immediately turn the camera around to show them the image she had just captured of them dancing or posing with friends. I witnessed first-hand the desire to be documented at these club nights. Moreover, I saw and experienced the importance of this photograph then making its way onto the online archive of the night. In other words, it was not enough just to be photographed by Holka but it was necessary for this photograph then to be included in the Facebook album of the event night. This move from the photograph to the online archive seemed to promise a certain security of presence in a contemporary queer London. I am hesitant to read this as just another performance of self that online platforms such as Facebook enable – the construction of certain identities through photography and presence at parties. Instead, I suggest that there is a queer specificity to this desire to be in a particular Facebook album. This specificity is an effect of the way in which queer subjects have often been denied access to seeing 'themselves' in the past – either because of a lack of evidence of queerness or because of a knowingness that what we might identify 'as' is a historically contingent configuration of desires, acts and relationalities. As Valerie Rohy describes it, the imperative to resist 'ahistoricism' or 'anachronism' has been central to queer historical critique.[42] Denied this ability to recognize queerness in the past, it seems to me that archival presence is particularly affectively charged for contemporary queer subjects. As such, the desire to be captured by Holka's camera exceeds the promise of the here and now, the present queer London.

Instead, Holka's photographic archive is much more entangled with the queer past. As we think about the sheer number of photographs of this East London scene and its parties – this particular time and place, London – what is seemingly unavoidable for me in these narratives is a sense that past invisibility haunts the contemporary. It haunts the contemporary as a desire to be in the archive and also as a threat that this archive will similarly fail to capture or evidence queerness. The emphatic 'I WAS THERE' points in multiple directions yet it also perhaps fails to evidence the very presence that it emphatically claims. It claims a certainty that is perhaps inevitably a failure to be 'there' – the caps lock insistence reveals a slipperiness around the 'there'. It references a past queer invisibility in the archive, yet the abundance of photographs similarly alludes to the ongoing failure of these photographs to evidence queerness. So if, as Love or Dinshaw suggests, the past has unexpected and unpredictable affective holds on our present, this digital archival space seemingly offers not only a means of exploring contemporary queer life, but of considering the way in which contemporary representations might be bound to queer historical feelings.

Notes

1   Christa Holka, 'About'. http://www.christaholka.com/index.php? /about/bio/ (accessed 9 June 2014).

2   Ann Cvetkovich, *An Archive of Feeling: Trauma, Sexuality and Public Cultures* (Durham, NC and London: Duke University Press, 2003), p. 8.

3   Ibid., p. 8.

4   Mike Featherstone, 'Archive', *Theory, Culture and Society* 23.2–3 (2006), pp. 591–96, 595.

5   Ibid., p. 595.

6   Joanne Garde-Hansen, 'My Memories?: Personal Digital Archive Fever and Facebook', in Joanne Garde-Hansen, Andrew Hoskins and Ann Reading (eds), *Save As… Digital Memories* (Basingstoke and New York: Palgrave Macmillan, 2009), pp. 135–50, 144.

7   Jennifer Pybus, 'Accumulating Affect: Social Networks and Their Archives of Feelings', in Ken Hillis, Susanna Paasonen and Michael Petit (eds), *Networked Affect* (Cambridge, MA and London: MIT Press, 2015), pp. 235–50, 241.

8   Jacques Derrida, 'Archive Fever: A Freudian Impression', trans. E. Prenowitz, *Diacritics* 25.2 (1995), pp. 9–63, 17.

9   See Henry Jenkins, *Convergence Culture: Where Old and New Media Collide* (New York and London: New York University Press, 2006); Erkki Huhtamo and Jussi Parikka, *Media Archaeology: Approaches, Applications, and Implications* (Berkeley, CA and London: University of California Press, 2011); Jay David Bolter and Richard Grusin, *Remediation: Understanding New Media* (Cambridge, MA and London: MIT Press, 1999).

10 Bolter and Grusin, *Remediation*.

11 Sarah Kember and Joanna Zylinska, *Life After New Media: Mediation as a Vital Process* (Cambridge, MA: MIT Press, 2012), p. 3.

12 Ibid., p. 8.

13 Adi Kuntsman, 'Introduction: Affective Fabrics of Digital Cultures', in Athina Karatzogianni and Adi Kuntsman (eds), *Digital Cultures and the Politics of Emotion: Feelings, Affect and Technological Change* (Basingstoke: Palgrave Macmillan, 2012), p. 4.

14 See Ken Hillis, Susanna Paasonen and Michael Petit (eds), *Networked Affect*; Aimée Morrison, ' "Suffused by Feeling and Affect": The Intimate Public of Personal Mommy Blogging', *Biography* 34.1 (2011), pp. 37–55; Nima Naghibi, 'Diasporic Disclosures: Social Networking, Neda, and the 2009 Iranian Presidential Elections', *Biography* 34.1 (2011), pp. 56–69; Anna Poletti, 'Intimate Economies: PostSecret and the Affect of Confession', *Biography* 34.1 (2011), pp. 25–36.

15 Jodi Dean, *Blog Theory: Feedback and Capture in the Circuits of Drive* (Cambridge and Malden, MA: Polity Press, 2010), p. 21.

16 Kuntsman, 'Introduction', p. 3.

17 Elizabeth Freeman, *Time Binds: Queer Temporalities, Queer Histories* (Durham, NC and London: Duke University Press, 2010), p. xii; Carolyn Dinshaw, 'Temporalities', in Paul Strohm (ed.), *Oxford Twenty-First-Century Approaches to Literature: Middle English* (Oxford: Oxford University Press, 2007), pp. 107–23.

18 Heather Love, *Feeling Backward: Loss and the Politics of Queer History* (Cambridge, MA and London: Harvard University Press, 2007), p. 31.

19 See, for example, Freeman, *Time Binds*; Love, *Feeling Backward*; José Esteban Muñoz, *Cruising Utopia: The Then and There of Queer Futurity* (New York and London: New York University Press, 2009); Christopher Nealon, *Foundlings: Lesbian and Gay Historical Emotion Before Stonewall* (Durham, NC and London: Duke University Press, 2002).

20 See, for example, Kate O'Riordan and David J. Phillips (eds), *Queer Online: Media Technology and Sexuality* (New York: Peter Lang, 2007); Christopher Pullen and Margaret Cooper, *LGBT Identity and Online New Media* (London: Routledge, 2010).

21 Alex Cho, 'Queer Reverb: Tumblr, Affect, Time', in Ken Hillis, Susanna Paasonen and Michael Petit (eds), *Networked Affect*, pp. 43–58, 47.

22 Nealon, *Foundlings*, p. 8.

23 Love, *Feeling Backward*, p. 37.

24 Nealon, *Foundlings*, p. 1.

25 Ibid., p. 13.

26 Ibid., p. 182.

27 Ibid.

28 For explorations of this point, see Carolyn Dinshaw, *Getting Medieval: Sexualities and Communities, Pre- and Postmodern* (Durham, NC and London: Duke University Press, 1999); Love, *Feeling Backward*; Freeman, *Time Binds*.

29 Love, *Feeling Backward*, pp. 9–10.

30 Dana Luciano, 'Nostalgia for an Age Yet to Come: *Velvet Goldmine's* Queer Archive', in E. L. McCallum and Mikko Tuhkanen (eds), *Queer Times, Queer Becomings* (Albany, NY: SUNY Press), pp. 121–55, 123.

31 Ibid., p. 123; emphasis in original.

32 Dinshaw, 'Temporalities', p. 112.

33 Autostraddle, 'About'. http://www.autostraddle.com/about/ (accessed 9 June 2014).

34 Dinshaw, 'Temporalities', p. 110; Luciano, 'Nostalgia', p. 123 (emphasis in original).

35 Christa Holka, 'We Belong'. http://vimeo.com/46000354 (accessed 9 June 2014).

36 Molly Landreth, 'About'. http://embodimentusa.com/?page_id=26 (accessed 9 June 2014).

37 Featherstone, 'Archive', p. 595.

38 Holka, 'We Belong'.

39 Sonja Vivienne and Jean Burgess, 'The Remediation of the Personal Photograph and the Politics of Self-Representation in Digital Storytelling', *Journal of Material Culture* 18.3 (2013), pp. 279–98, 281; emphasis in original.

40 Pybus, 'Accumulating Affect', p. 239.

41 Cho, 'Queer Reverb', p. 50.

42 Valerie Rohy, 'Ahistorical', *GLQ: Journal of Lesbian and Gay Studies* 12.1 (2006), pp. 61–83, 65–6.

BIBLIOGRAPHY

Adlard, J., *Stenbock, Yeats and the Nineties*, London: Cecil & Amelia Woolf, 1969.

Ahmed, S., *The Cultural Politics of Emotion*, New York and London: Routledge, 2004.

Ahmed, S., *Queer Phenomenology: Orientations, Objects, Others*, Durham, NC: Duke University Press, 2006.

Ainley, R., 'Watching the Detectors: Control and the Panopticon', in R. Ainley (ed.), *New Frontiers of Space, Bodies and Gender*, London: Routledge, 1998.

Alderson, D., 'Desire as Nostalgia: The Novels of Alan Hollinghurst', in D. Alderson and L. Anderson (eds), *Territories of Desire in Queer Culture: Refiguring Contemporary Boundaries*, Manchester: Manchester University Press, 2000.

Aldrich, R., *Colonialism and Homosexuality*, London and New York: Routledge, 2003.

Allen, D.J. and T. Oleson, 'Shame and Internalised Homophobia', *Journal of Homosexuality* 37.3 (1999), pp. 33–43.

Alley, R., *Francis Bacon*, London: Thames and Hudson, 1964.

Altman, D., 'Globalisation, Political Economy and HIV/AIDS', *Theory and Society* 28.4 (1999), pp. 559–584.

Altman, D., 'Legitimisation through Disaster', in E. Fee and D.M. Fox (eds), *AIDS: The Burdens of History*, Berkeley: University of California Press, 1988.

Anderson, B., *Imagined Communities: Reflections on the Origin and Spread of Nationalism*, London: Verso, 1983; revised 1991, 2006.

Andersson, J., 'East End Localism and Urban Decay: Shoreditch's Re-Emerging Gay Scene', *The London Journal* 34.1 (2009), pp. 55–71.

André, A. and S. Chang, 'And Then You Cut Your Hair: Genderfucking on the Femme Side of the Spectrum', in M.B. Sycamore (ed.), *Nobody Passes: Rejecting the Rules of Gender and Conformity*, Berkeley, CA: Seal Press, 2006.

Anon, *Anthropologia: In Which Are Included the Proceedings of the London Anthropological Society, 1873–1875*, vol. 1, London: Ballière, Tindall and Cox, 1875.

Anon, 'Bar Wotever', http://www.vauxhalltavern.com/events/event/bar-wotever /(accessed 30 October 2015).

Anon, 'A Book That Must Be Suppressed', *Sunday Express*, 9 August 1928.

Anon, 'The Chairman [Lord Stanley] at Farewell Dinner for Captain [R.F.] Burton', *Anthropological Review* 3.9 (1865), p. 169.

Anon, 'Charge of Personating Women', *Morning Post*, 14 May 1870.

Anon, 'The Charge of Personating Women', *The Times*, 7 May 1870.

Anon, 'Duckie: About', http://www.duckie.co.uk/about (accessed 30 October 2015).

Anon, 'End of a Genius', *Dundee Evening Telegraph*, 19 August 1905.

Anon, 'Location Manager Patrick Schweitzer on Where the Line of Beauty Was Filmed', http://www.bbc.co.uk/drama/lineofbeauty/backstage.shtml (accessed 14 June 2006).

Anon, 'Miscellany', *The Manchester Guardian*, 29 August 1905.

Anon, 'A Note on Simeon Solomon', *Westminster Gazette*, 24 August 1905.

Anon, *Sins of the Cities of the Plain, or the Recollections of a Mary-Ann with Short Essays on Sodomy and Tribadism*, Paris and London: Olympia Press, 2006 [1881].

Anon, 'Tragedy of Blighted Genius', *Daily Mirror*, 19 August 1905.

Anon, 'A Wasted Genius. A Tragedy of Art', *Advertiser*, 27 September 1905.

Anon, 'Young Men Who Are Got Up', *Huddersfield Daily Chronicle*, 4 April 1893.

Antosa, S., *Richard Francis Burton: Victorian Explorer and Translator*, Bern, Oxford and New York: Peter Lang, 2012.

Archer, D., *The Cloven Hoof: A Study of Contemporary London Vices*, London: Taylor Croft, 1932.

Armstrong, M., 'A Room in Chelsea: Quentin Crisp at Home', *Visual Culture in Britain* 12.2 (2011), pp. 155–169.

Arya, R., 'Constructions of Homosexuality in the Art of Francis Bacon', *Journal for Cultural Research* 16.1 (2012), pp. 43–61.

Ashbee, H.S., *Catena Librorum Tacendorum*, London: Privately Printed, 1885.

Ashbee, H.S., *Centuria Librorum Absconditorum*, London: Privately Printed, 1879.

Ashbee, H.S., *Fashionable Lectures: Composed and Delivered with Birch Discipline*, London: J.C. Hotten, 1872.

Ashbee, H.S., *Index Librorum Prohibitorum: Being Notes Bio-Biblio Icono-Graphical and Critical in Curious and Uncommon Books*, London: Privately Printed, 1877.

Ashbee, H.S., *The Library Illustrative of Social Progress*, 8 vols, London: James Hotten, 1860–73.

Ashenden, A., 'Study: Six Million Users Log onto Grindr an Average of Eight Times a Day', *PinkNews*, 27 March 2013, http://www.pinknews.co.uk/2013/03/27/study-six-milion-users-log-onto-grindr-an-average-of-eight-times-a-day/ (accessed 28 March 2014).

Autostraddle, 'About', http://www.autostraddle.com/about/ (accessed 9 June 2014).

Bailey, P., *Music Hall: The Business of Pleasure*, Milton Keynes: Open University Press, 1986.

Bakhtin, M., *Rabelais and His World*, trans. Helene Iswolsky, Bloomington: Indiana University Press, 1984.

Bartley, P., *Prostitution: Prevention and Reform in England, 1860–1914*, London: Routledge, 2000.

Bauer, H. and M. Cook, 'Introduction', in H. Bauer and M. Cook (eds), *Queer 1950s: Rethinking Sexuality in the Postwar Years*, Basingstoke: Palgrave Macmillan, 2012.

Bauman, Z., *Does Ethics Have a Chance in a World of Consumers?*, Cambridge, MA: Harvard University Press, 2008.

Beddoe, J., 'Discussion (of "The Manchester Anthropological Society")', *Anthropological Review* 5 (1867), p. 20.

Beerbohm, M., 'A Defence of Cosmetics', *Yellow Book* 1 (April 1894), pp. 65–82.

Beerbohm, M., *Seven Men*, London: William Heinemann, 1919.

Bell, D. and G. Valentine (eds), *Mapping Desire: Geographies of Sexualities*, London and New York: Routledge, 1995.

Bengry, J., 'Courting the Pink Pound: *Men Only* and the Queer Consumer, 1935–39', *History Workshop Journal* 68.1 (2009), pp. 122–148.

Berridge, V., *AIDS in the UK: The Making of a Policy, 1981–1994*, Oxford: Oxford University Press, 1996.

Bersani, L., *Homos*, Cambridge, MA: Harvard University Press, 1995.

Binnie, J., 'Coming Out of Geography: Towards a Queer Epistemology?', *Environment and Planning D Society and Space* 15 (1997), pp. 223–237.

Binnie, J., 'Trading Places: Consumption, Sexuality and the Production of Queer Space', in D. Bell and G. Valentine (eds), *Mapping Desire: Geographies of Sexualities*, London and New York: Routledge, 1995.

Binnie, J. and B. Skeggs, 'Cosmopolitan Knowledge and the Production and Consumption of Sexualized Space: Manchester's Gay Village', in J. Binnie *et al.* (eds), *Cosmopolitan Urbanism*, New York, NY: Routledge, 2006.

Bland, L., *Banishing the Beast: Feminism, Sex, and Morality*, London: Penguin, 1995.

Bland, L., *Modern Women on Trial: Sexual Transgression in the Age of the Flapper*, Manchester: Manchester University Press, 2013.

Blaney, D.P., '1964: The Birth of Gay Theater', *Gay and Lesbian Review* (worldwide edition) 21.1 (January–February 2014), pp. 17–21.

Bolter, J.D. and R. Grusin, *Remediation: Understanding New Media*, Cambridge, MA and London: MIT Press, 1999.

Boone, J.A., 'Vacation Cruises; Or, the Homoerotics of Orientalism', *PMLA* (Special Topic: Colonialism and the Postcolonial Condition) 110.1 (January 1995), pp. 89–107.

Booth, H.J., 'Claude McKay in Britain: Race, Sexuality and Poetry', in L. Platt (ed.), *Modernism and Race*, Cambridge: Cambridge University Press, 2011.

Bourcier, M.-H., 'F*** the Politics of Disempowerment in the Second Butler', *Paragraph* 35.2 (2012), 235–240.

Bourcier, M.-H., *Queer Zones: Politique des identités sexuelles et des savoirs*, Paris: Editions Amsterdam, 2006.

Bowen, E., *Collected Stories*, London: Vintage, 1999.

Brady, S., *Masculinity and Male Homosexuality, 1861–1913*, Basingstoke: Palgrave, 2005.

Bratton, J.S., 'Irrational Dress', in V. Gardner and S. Rutherford (eds), *The New Woman and Her Sisters*, Hemel Hempstead: Harvester Wheatsheaf, 1992.

Bratton, J.S., 'Jenny Hill: Sex and Sexism in the Victorian Music Hall', in J.S. Bratton (ed.), *Music Hall: Performance and Style*, New York: Taylor and Francis, 1997.

Brintnall, K., *Ecce Homo: The Male-Body-in-Pain as Redemptive Figure*, Chicago, IL: University of Chicago Press, 2011.

Brown, G., K. Browne and J. Lim, 'Introduction', in K. Browne, J. Lim and G. Brown (eds), *Geographies of Sexualities: Theory, Practices and Politics*, Aldershot: Ashgate, 2007.

Brown, M. and L. Knopp, 'Queer Diffusions', *Environment and Planning D: Society and Space* 21 (2003), pp. 409–424.

Browne, F.W.S., 'A New Psychological Society', *International Journal of Ethics* 28 (1917–18), pp. 266–269.

Browne, K., J. Lim and G. Brown (eds), *Geographies of Sexualities: Theory, Practices and Politics*, Aldershot: Ashgate, 2007.

Burney, F., *Stage, Screen and Sandwiches: The Remarkable Life of Kenelm Foss*, London: Athena Press, 2007.

Burrow, J.W., 'Evolution and Anthropology in the 1860s: The Anthropological Society of London, 1863–71', *Victorian Studies* 7.2 (December 1963), pp. 137–154.

Burton, R., 'Notes on Certain Matters Connected with the Dahoman', *Memoirs Read Before the Anthropological Society of London* 1 (1864), pp. 308–321.

Burton, R. (trans.), *Ananga Ranga (Stage of the Bodiless One); or, The Hindu Art of Love*, London: For the Kama Shastra Society of London and Benares, and for private circulation only, 1885.

Burton, R. (trans.), *The Book of a Thousand Nights and a Night: A Plain and Literal Translation of the Arabian Nights' Entertainments*, London and Benares: Kama Shastra Society, 1885.

Burton, R. (trans.), *The Carmina of Caius Valerius Catullus*, London: Printed for the Translators, 1894.

Burton, R. (trans.), *Il Pentamerone*, London: Henry & Co., 1893.

Burton, R. (trans.), *The Kama Sutra of Vatsyayana*, Benares: Printed for the Hindoo Kama Shastra Society, 1883.

Burton, R. (trans.), *The Perfumed Garden of the Cheikh Nefzaoui*, London: For the Kama Shastra Society of London and Benares, and for private circulation only, 1884.

Butler, J., *Gender Trouble: Feminism and the Subversion of Identity*, London: Routledge, 1990.

Butler, J., 'Sexual Politics, Torture, and Secular Time', *The British Journal of Sociology* 59 (2008), pp. 1–23.

Canning, R., 'The Stranger's Child, By Alan Hollinghurst', *The Independent*, 17 June 2011, http://www.independent.co.uk/arts-entertainment/books/reviews/the-strangers-child-by-alan-hollinghurst-2298468.html (accessed 5 April 2014).

Cappock, M., *Francis Bacon's Studio*, London: Merrell, 2005.

Carriger, M.L., 'The Unnatural History and Petticoat Mystery of Boulton and Park: A Victorian Sex Scandal and the Theatre Defense', *TDR* 57.4 (2013), pp. 135–156.

Cassidy, T., 'People, Place, and Performance: Theoretically Revisiting Mother Clap's Molly House', in C. Mounsey and C. Gonda (eds), *Queer People: Negotiations and Expressions of Homosexuality, 1700–1800*, Lewisburg, PA: Bucknell University Press, 2007.

Castells, M., *The City and the Grassroots: A Cross-Cultural Theory of Urban Social Movements*, Berkeley: University of California Press, 1983.

Castells, M., *The Internet Galaxy: Reflections on the Internet, Business, and Society*, Oxford: Oxford University Press, 2001.

Castle, T., *The Apparitional Lesbian: Female Homosexuality and Modern Culture*, New York: Columbia University Press, 1993.

Chambers, R., 'Messing Around: Gayness and Loiterature in Alan Hollinghurst's *The Swimming-Pool Library*', in J. Still and M. Worton (eds), *Textuality and Sexuality: Reading Theories and Practices*, Manchester: Manchester University Press, 1993.

Chanan, M., *From Handel to Hendrix: The Composer in the Public Sphere*, London: Verso, 1999.

Chare, N., *After Francis Bacon: Synaesthesia and Sex in Paint*, Farnham: Ashgate, 2012.

Chauncey, G., *Gay New York: Gender, Urban Culture, and the Makings of the Gay Male World, 1890–1940*, New York: Basic Books, 1994.

Chesterton, A., *Women of the London Underworld*, London: Stanley Paul, 1928.

Cho, A., 'Queer Reverb: Tumblr, Affect, Time', in K. Hillis, S. Paasonen and M. Petit (eds), *Networked Affect*, Cambridge, MA and London: MIT Press, 2015.

Christie, A., *The Mystery of the Blue Train*, London: Harper Collins, 2001.

Clayton, A., *Decadent London*, London: Historical Publications, 2005.

Cleminson, J., 'Walking in London: The Fiction of Neil Bartlett, Sarah Waters and Alan Hollinghurst', PhD thesis, Brunel University, 2009.

Cline, S., *Radclyffe Hall: A Woman Called John*, New York: The Overlook Press, 1997.

Cockin, K., 'Housman, Laurence (1865–1959)', *Oxford Dictionary of National Biography*, Oxford: Oxford University Press, 2004, http://0-www.oxforddnb .com.catalogue.wellcomelibrary.org/view/article/34014 (accessed 19 March 2014).

Cocks, H.G., *Nameless Offences: Homosexual Desire in the Nineteenth Century*, London and New York: I.B. Tauris, 2003.

Cohen, E., *Talk on the Wilde Side: Toward a Genealogy of a Discourse on Male Sexualities*, New York and London: Routledge, 1993.

Coman, N.A.T., 'What? What? In the (Black) Butt', *Apa Newsletters: Newsletter on Philosophy and Lesbian, Gay, Bisexual and Transgender Issues* 11.1 (2011), p. 12.

Condor, S., *Woman on the Beat: The True Story of a Policewoman*, London: Robert Hale, 1960.

Conservatives for the Family Campaign, *HIV Infected Citizens: Charter of Responsibility*, 27 September 1990.

Cook, M., 'AIDS, Mass Observation and the Permissive Turn', *Journal of the History of Sexuality* (forthcoming).

Cook, M., '"Gay Times": Identity, Locality, Memory, and the Brixton Squats in 1970s London', *Twentieth Century British History* 24.1 (2013), pp. 84–109.

Cook, M., 'Ives, George Cecil (1867–1950)', *Oxford Dictionary of National Biography*, Oxford: Oxford University Press, May 2006; online edn, October 2007, http://0-www.oxforddnb.com.catalogue.wellcomelibrary.org/ view/article/57683 (accessed 19 March 2014).

Cook, M., 'Law', in H.G. Cocks and M. Houlbrook (eds), *The Modern History of Sexuality*, Basingstoke: Palgrave Macmillan, 2005.

Cook, M., *London and the Culture of Homosexuality, 1885–1914*, Cambridge: Cambridge University Press, 2003.

Cook, M., *Queer Domesticities: Homosexuality and Home Life in Twentieth-Century London*, Basingstoke: Palgrave Macmillan, 2014.

Cook, M. and J.V. Evans (eds), *Queer Cities, Queer Cultures: Europe Since 1945*, London: Bloomsbury, 2014.

Cooper, E., 'Queer Spectacles', in P. Horne and R. Lewis (eds), *Outlooks: Lesbian and Gay Sexualities and Visual Cultures*. London: Routledge, 1996.

Cooper, W.F., *Claude McKay: Rebel Sojourner in the Harlem Renaissance: A Biography*, Baton Rouge: Louisiana State University Press, 1987; paperback 1996.

Corfield, P.J., *Vauxhall and the Invention of the Urban Pleasure Gardens*, London: History & Social Action Publication, 2008.

Corfield, P.J., *Vauxhall: Sex and Entertainment*, London: History & Social Action Publication, 2012.

Cosgrove, P., 'Edmund Burke, Gilles Deleuze, and the Subversive Masochism of the Image', *ELH* 66.2 (1999), pp. 405–437.

Crisp, Q., *The Naked Civil Servant*, London: Fontana, 1977 [1968].

Crozier, I., 'Nineteenth-Century British Psychiatric Writing About Homosexuality Before Havelock Ellis: The Missing Story', *Journal of the History of Medicine and Allied Sciences* 63 (2008), pp. 65–102.

Cruise, C., *Love Revealed: Simeon Solomon and the Pre-Raphaelites*, London: Merrell Publishers, 2005.

Cvetkovich, A., *An Archive of Feeling: Trauma, Sexuality and Public Cultures*, Durham, NC and London: Duke University Press, 2003.

Davenport, J., *Aphrodisiacs and Anti-aphrodisiacs*, London: Privately Printed, 1869.

Davenport, J., *Curiositates Eroticae Physiologie*, London: Privately Printed, 1875.

Davenport, J., *Esoteric Physiology Sexagyma*, London: Privately Printed, 1888.

David, H., *On Queer Street: A Social History of British Homosexuality 1895–1995*, London: Harper Collins Publishers, 1997.

Davis, T.C., 'Actresses and Prostitutes in Victorian London', *Theatre Research International* 13.3 (1988), http://dx.doi.org/10.1017/S0307883300005794 (accessed 20 May 2015).

Day, P. and R. Klein, 'Interpreting the Unexpected: The Case of AIDS Policy Making in Britain', *Journal of Public Policy* 9.3 (1989), pp. 337–353.

de Certeau, M., *The Practice of Everyday Life*, Oakland: University of California Press, 1984.

de Frece, M., *Recollections of Vesta Tilley*, London: Hutchinson and Co., 1934.

de Lauretis, T., *Alice Doesn't: Feminism, Semiotics, Cinema*, Bloomington: Indiana University Press, 1984.

Dean, J., *Blog Theory: Feedback and Capture in the Circuits of Drive*, Cambridge and Malden, MA: Polity Press, 2010.

Delanty, G., *Community*, London: Routledge, 2003.

Dellamora, R., *Masculine Desire: The Sexual Politics of Victorian Aestheticism*, Chapel Hill and London: University of North Carolina Press, 1990.

Dentith, S., *Bakhtinian Thought*, London: Routledge, 1995.

Derrida, J., 'Archive Fever: A Freudian Impression', trans. E. Prenowitz, *Diacritics* 25.2 (1995), pp. 9–63.

Deutsche, R., *Evictions: Art and Spatial Politics*, Cambridge, MA: MIT Press, 1996.

Dickens, C., *Sketches by Boz*, ed. Dennis Walder, London: Penguin, 1995.

Dickens, C., *The Works of Charles Dickens in Thirty-Four Volumes*, London: Gadshill, 1868.

Dinshaw, C., *Getting Medieval: Sexualities and Communities, Pre- and Postmodern*, Durham, NC and London: Duke University Press, 1999.

Dinshaw, C., 'Got Medieval?' *Journal of the History of Sexuality* 10.2 (2001), pp. 202–212.

Dinshaw, C., 'Temporalities', in P. Strohm (ed.), *Oxford Twenty-First-Century Approaches to Literature: Middle English*, Oxford: Oxford University Press, 2007.

Dinshaw, C., L. Edelman, R.A. Ferguson, C. Freccero, E. Freeman, J. Halberstam, A. Jagose, C. Nealon and N. Tan Hoang, 'Theorizing Queer Temporalities: A Roundtable Discussion', *GLQ* 13.2–3 (2007), pp. 177–196.

Doan, L., *Disturbing Practices: History, Sexuality and Women's Experience of Modern War*, Chicago and London: University of Chicago Press, 2013.

Downing, S.J., *The English Pleasure Garden, 1680–1860*, Oxford: Shire, 2013.

Drorbaugh, E., 'Stormé DeLarverié and The Jewel Box Revue', in L. Ferris (ed.), *Crossing the Stage: Controversies on Cross-Dressing*, London: Routledge, 1993.

Duffy, J.H., *Reading Between the Lines: Claude Simon and the Visual Arts*, Liverpool: Liverpool University Press, 1998.

Duggan, L., *The Twilight of Equality? Neoliberalism, Cultural Politics, and the Attack on Democracy*, Boston: Beacon, 2003.

Dyer, G., *The Colour of Memory*, Edinburgh and London: Canongate, 1989.

Edelman, L., 'Ever After', in J. Halley and A. Parker (eds), *After Sex? On Writing Since Queer Theory*, Durham, NC: Duke University Press, 2011.

Edelman, L., *No Future: Queer Theory and the Death Drive*, Durham, NC: Duke University Press, 2004.

Egan, B., *The Sink of Solitude: Being a Series of Satirical Drawings Occasioned by Some Recent Events*, London: Hermes Press, 1928.

Elder, G., 'Of Moffies, Kaffirs and Perverts: Male Homosexuality and the Discourse of Moral Order in the Apartheid State', in D. Bell and G. Valentine (eds), *Mapping Desire: Geographies of Sexualities*, London: Routledge, 1995.

Ellis, H.H., *My Life*, London: Heinemann, 1940.

Ellis, H.H., *Studies in the Psychology of Sex. Vol. 2: Sexual Inversion*, New York: Random House, 1936.

Ellis, H.H., and J.A. Symonds, *Sexual Inversion*, 6 vols, London: Wilson and Macmillan, 1897.

Ellis, N., 'Black Migrants, White Queers and the Archive of Inclusion in Postwar London', *Interventions: International Journal of Postcolonial Studies* 17.6 (2015), pp. 893–915.

Ellis, N., 'The Eclectic Generation: Caribbean Literary Criticism at the Turn of the Twenty-First Century', in M. Bucknor and A. Donnell (eds), *The Routledge Companion to Anglophone Caribbean Literature*, Abingdon, Oxon: Routledge, 2011.

Epstein Nord, D., 'Night and Day: Illusion and Carnivalesque at Vauxhall', in J. Conlin (ed.), *The Pleasure Garden, from Vauxhall to Coney Island*, Philadelphia: University of Pennsylvania Press, 2013.

Falk, B., *Five Years Dead: A Postscript to 'He Laughed in Fleet Street'*, London: Hutchinson & Co., 1937.

Fanon, F., *Black Skin, White Masks*, London: Pluto Press, 2008.

Farson, D., *The Gilded Gutter Life of Francis Bacon*, London: Century, 1993.

Farson, D., *Soho in the Fifties*, London: Michael Joseph, 1987.

Featherstone, M., 'Archive', *Theory, Culture and Society* 23.2–3 (2006), pp. 591–596.

Featherstone, D. and J. Painter (eds), *Spatial Politics: Essays for Doreen Massey*, Oxford: Wiley-Blackwell, 2013.

Fielding, H., *An Enquiry into the Causes of the Late Increase of Robbers and Related Writings*, Dublin: G. Faulkner, 1751.

Fitzsimons, D., V. Hardy and K. Tolley (eds), *The Economic and Social Impact of AIDS in Europe*, London: Cassell, 1995.

Florida, R., *The Rise of the Creative Class: And How It's Transforming Work, Leisure, Community and Everyday Life*, New York: Basic Books, 2002.

Florida, R., *The Rise of the Creative Class: Revisited*, New York: Basic Books, 2012.

Flower D. and H. Maas (eds), *The Letters of Ernest Dowson*, London and Melbourne: Cassell, 1967.

Forrester, J., 'The English Freud: W.H.R. Rivers, Dreaming, and the Making of the Early Twentieth-Century Human Sciences', in S. Alexander and B. Taylor (eds), *History and Psyche: Culture, Psychoanalysis, and the Past*, New York: Palgrave Macmillan, 2012.

Forster, J., *The Life of Charles Dickens*, 2 vols, London: Chapman and Hall, 1872.

Foucault, M., *The History of Sexuality Volume 1: The Will to Knowledge*, trans. Robert Hurley, London: Penguin, 1990.

Freeman, E., 'Packing History, Count(er)ing Generations', *New Literary History* 31.4 (Autumn, 2000), pp. 727–744.

Freeman, E., *Time Binds: Queer Temporalities, Queer Histories*, Durham, NC and London: Duke University Press, 2010.

Fryer, J., *Soho in the Fifties and Sixties*, London: National Portrait Gallery Publications, 1998.

Gabrial, J., *Inside the Volcano: My Life with Malcolm Lowry*, New York: St Martin's Press, 2000.

Gallop, J., *Feminism and Psychoanalysis: The Daughter's Seduction*, London: Macmillan, 1982.

Garde-Hansen, J., A. Hoskins and A. Reading (eds), *Save As… Digital Memories*, Basingstoke and New York: Palgrave Macmillan, 2009.

Garfield, S., *The End of Innocence: Britain in the Time of AIDS*, London: Faber, 1994.

Gaunt, W., *The Aesthetic Adventure*, Oxford: Alden Press, 1945.

Gay Men's Oral History Group, *Walking After Midnight: Gay Men's Life Stories*, London: Routledge, 1989.

Giffney, N., 'Denormatizing Queer Theory: More Than (Simply) Lesbian and Gay Studies', *Feminist Theory* 5 (2004), pp. 73–78.

Glendinning, V., *Leonard Woolf: A Biography*, New York: Simon & Schuster, 2008.

Glicco, J., *Madness After Midnight*, London: Elek Books, 1952.

Glover, E., *The Diagnosis and Treatment of Telinquency: Being a Clinical Report on the Work of the Institute During the Five Years 1937 to 1941*, London: Institute for the Scientific Treatment of Delinquency, 1944.

Goldring, D., *The Nineteen-Twenties: A General Survey and Some Personal Memories*, London: Nicholson & Watson, 1945.

Goldring, D., *Odd Man Out: The Autobiography of a 'Propaganda' Novelist*, London: Chapman & Hall, 1935.

Gosciak, J., *The Shadowed Country: Claude McKay and the Romance of the Victorians*, New Brunswick, NJ: Rutgers University Press, 2006.

Gottleib, R., *Lives and Letters*, London: Macmillan, 2011.

Gowing, L., 'History', in A. Medhurst and S.R. Munt (eds), *Lesbian and Gay Studies: A Critical Introduction*, London: Cassell, 1997.

Grant, J., *Stella Benson: A Biography*, London: Macmillan, 1987.

Greenblatt, S., *Marvelous Possessions: The Wonder of the New World*, Chicago, IL: University of Chicago Press, 1991.

Groes, S., *The Making of London: London in Contemporary Literature*, Basingstoke: Palgrave Macmillan, 2011.

Gross, L., 'Forward', in K. O' Riordan and D.J. Phillips (eds), *Queer Online: Media, Technology, and Sexuality*, New York: Peter Lang Publishing, 2007.

Halberstam, J., *Female Masculinity*, Durham, NC and London: Duke University, 1999.

Halberstam, J., *In a Queer Time and Place*, New York: New York University Press, 2005.

Halberstam, J., *The Queer Art of Failure*, Durham, NC: Duke University Press, 2011.

Hall, L., '"Disinterested Enthusiasm for Sexual Misconduct": The British Society for the Study of Sex Psychology, 1913–47', *Journal of Contemporary History* 30.4 (October 1995), pp. 665–686.

Hall, L.A., '"The English have hot-water bottles": The Morganatic Marriage Between the British Medical Profession and Sexology Since William Acton', in R. Porter and M. Teich (eds), *Sexual Knowledge, Sexual Science: The History of Attitudes to Sexuality*, Cambridge: Cambridge University Press, 1994.

Hall, R., *A Saturday Life*, London: Virago, 1927.

Halperin, D., *One Hundred Years of Homosexuality: And Other Essays on Greek Love*, New York: Routledge, 1990.

Halperin, D., *Saint Foucault*, Oxford: Oxford University Press, 1995.

Halperin, D. and V. Traub (eds), *Gay Shame*, Chicago, IL: Chicago University Press, 2009.

Hammer M. and C. Stephens, '"Seeing the story of one's time": Appropriations from Nazi Photography in the Work of Francis Bacon', *Visual Culture in Britain* 10.3 (2009), pp. 315–351.

Harper, C.G., *The City of London Guide*, London: Charles G. Harper, 1927.

Harper, C.G., *A Literary Man's London*, London: Cecil Palmer, 1926.

Harper, C.G., *A Londoner's Own London*, London: Cecil Palmer, 1927.

Harper, C.G., *More Queer Things About London*, London: Cecil Palmer, 1924.

Harper, C.G., *Queer Things About London*, London: Cecil Palmer, 1923.

Harris, B., *Politics and the Nation: Britain in the Mid-Eighteenth Century*, Oxford: Oxford University Press, 2002.

Hassan, T. (dir.), *Brixton Fairies: Made Possible by Squatting* (2014).

Hatch, J.H., 'Seeing and Seen: Acts of the Voyeur in the Works of Francis Bacon', in R. Arya (ed.), *Francis Bacon: Critical and Theoretical Perspectives*, Bern: Peter Lang, 2012.

Henry, H., *Virginia Woolf and the Discourse of Science: The Aesthetics of Astronomy*, Cambridge: Cambridge University Press, 2003.

Herman, R.D.K., 'Playing with Restraints: Space, Citizenship and BDSM', in K. Browne, J. Lim and G. Brown (eds), *Geographies of Sexualities: Theory, Practices and Politics*, Aldershot: Ashgate, 2007.

Herring, S., *Queering the Underworld: Slumming, Literature, and the Undoing of Lesbian and Gay History*, Chicago, IL: Chicago University Press, 2007.

Hoad, N., 'Arrested Development or the Queerness of Savages: Resisting Evolutionary Narratives of Difference', *Postcolonial Studies* 3.2 (2000), pp. 133–158.

Hoare, P., *Noel Coward: A Biography*, Chicago: University of Chicago Press, 1998.

Holka, C., 'About', http://www.christaholka.com/index.php?/about/bio
    /(accessed 9 June 2014).
Holka, C., 'We Belong', http://vimeo.com/46000354 (accessed
    9 June 2014).
Hollinghurst, A., *The Line of Beauty*, London: Picador, 2004.
Hollinghurst, A., *The Stranger's Child*, London: Picador, 2011.
Hollinghurst, A., *The Swimming-Pool Library*, London: Penguin, 1988.
Holloway, M. et al., '"Funerals Aren't Nice but It Couldn't Have Been Nicer": The
    Makings of a Good Funeral', *Mortality* 18.1 (2013), pp. 30–53.
hooks, b., *Black Looks: Race and Representation*, London: Turnaround, 1992.
hooks, b., *Reel to Real: Race, Class, and Sex at the Movies*, New York:
    Routledge, 1996.
Hornsey, R., 'Francis Bacon at the Photobooth: Facing the Homosexual in Post-
    War Britain', *Visual Culture in Britain* 8.2 (2007), pp. 83–103.
Hornsey, R., *The Spiv and the Architect: Unruly Life in Postwar London*,
    Minneapolis: University of Minnesota Press, 2010.
Houlbrook, M., 'Cities', in H.G. Cocks and M. Houlbrook (eds), *Palgrave Advances
    in the Modern History of Sexuality*, Basingstoke: Palgrave Macmillan, 2006.
Houlbrook, M., '"Lady Austin's Camp Boys": Constituting the Queer Subject in
    1930s London', *Gender and History* 14.1 (2002), pp. 31–61.
Houlbrook, M., 'The Man with the Powder Puff in Interwar London', *Historical
    Journal* 50.1 (2007), pp. 145–171.
Houlbrook, M., *Queer London: Perils and Pleasures in the Sexual Metropolis,
    1918–1957*, Chicago, IL: Chicago University Press, 2005.
Houseman, J., *Front and Center*, New York: Simon & Schuster, 1979.
Hudson, D., *Munby: Man of Two Worlds. The Life and Diaries of Arthur J. Munby,
    1828–1910*, London: John Murray, 1972.
Huhtamo, E. and J. Parikka (eds), *Media Archaeology: Approaches, Applications,
    and Implications*, Berkeley and London: University of California Press, 2011.
Humphrey, B., *Recollections of the Powys Brothers: Llewelyn, Theodore, and John
    Cowper*, London: Peter Owen Publishers, 1980.
Hunt, J., 'Anniversary Address to the Anthropological Society of London', *Journal
    of the Anthropological Society of London* 5 (1867), pp. lxi–lxii.
Hutton, L., *The Single Woman and Her Emotional Problems*, London: Balliere,
    Tindell & Cox, 1935.
Huxley, A., *Antic Hay*, London: Random House, 2008.
Innes, S.A., *The Lesbian Menace: Ideology, Identity, and the Representation of
    Lesbian Life*, Amherst: University of Massachusetts Press, 1997.
Israel, L., *Miss Tallulah Bankhead*, London and New York: W.H. Allen, 1972.
Jagose, A., *Queer Theory: An Introduction*, New York: New York University
    Press, 1996.
James, W., *A Fierce Hatred of Injustice: Claude McKay's Jamaica and His Poetry of
    Rebellion*, London: Verso, 2000.
James, W., 'A Race Outcast from an Outcast Class: Claude McKay's Experience
    and Analysis of Britain', in B. Schwarz (ed.), *West Indian Intellectuals in Britain*,
    Manchester: Manchester University Press, 2003.
Janes, D., '"Eternal Master": Masochism and the Sublime at the National Shrine
    of the Immaculate Conception, Washington, DC', *Theology and Sexuality* 15.2
    (2009), pp. 161–175.

Janes, D., *Picturing the Closet: Male Secrecy and Homosexual Visibility in Britain*, Oxford: Oxford University Press, 2015.

JanMohamed, A.R., 'Sexuality on/of the Racial Border: Foucault, Wright, and the Articulation of "Racialised Sexuality"', in D.C. Stanton (ed.), *Discourses of Sexuality: From Aristotle to AIDS*, Ann Arbor: University of Michigan, 1992.

Jardine, L., 'Sarah Waters: Sex and the Victorian City'. Interview with Sarah Waters, BBC2, 4 May 2005.

Jarman, D. (dir.), *Blue* (1993).

Jarman, D., *Modern Nature: The Journals of Derek Jarman*, London: Century, 1991.

Jeffreys, S., *The Spinster and Her Enemies: Feminism and Sexuality, 1880–1930*, London: Pandora Press, 1985.

Jeffries, S., 'Scarlet Kisses of Death for Oscar's Tomb', *Guardian*, 29 October 2000, http://www.theguardian.com/world/2000/oct/29/books.booksnews (accessed 11 August 2015).

Jekyll, W. (ed.), *Jamaican Song and Story: Annancy Stories, Digging Sings, Ring Tunes and Dancing Tunes*, London: Pub. for the Folk-lore Society by D. Nutt, 1907.

Jenkins, H., *Convergence Culture: Where Old and New Media Collide*, New York and London: New York University Press, 2006.

Jenkinson, J., *Black 1919: Riots, Racism and Resistance in Imperial Britain*, Liverpool: Liverpool University Press, 2009.

Jennings, R., *Tomboys and Bachelor Girls: A Lesbian History of Post-War Britain, 1945–7*, Manchester: Manchester University Press, 2007.

Jivani, A., *It's Not Unusual: A History of Lesbian and Gay Britain in the Twentieth Century*, London: Michael O'Mara, 1997.

Joannou, M., 'Nancy Cunard's English Journey', *Feminist Review* 78 (2004), pp. 141–163.

Johnson, E.P., '"Quare studies", or (Almost) Everything I Know About Queer Studies I Learned from My Grandmother', *Callaloo* 23.1 (2000), pp. 1–25.

Jones, A.M., '"Clothes Make the Man": The Male Artist as a Performative Function', *Oxford Art Journal* 18.2 (1995), pp. 18–32.

Jones, A.M., *Monopolies of Loss*, London: Faber, 1992.

Jones, C.S., *London in War-Time*, London: Grafton, 1917.

Jones, J. and S. Pugh, 'Ageing Gay Men: Lessons from the Sociology of Embodiment', *Men and Masculinities* 7.3 (2005), pp. 248–260.

Jordan, M.D., 'Touching and Acting, *or* The Closet of Abjection', *Journal of the History of Sexuality* 10.2 (2001), pp. 180–184.

Kaines, J., 'The Ultimate Object of Anthropological Study', *Anthropologia* 1 (1873), pp. 30–37.

Kaines, J., 'Western Anthropologists and Extra Western Communities', *Anthropologia* 1 (1873), pp. 225–235.

Kaplan, M.B., *Sodom on the Thames: Sex, Love and Scandal in Wilde Times*, Ithaca, NY: Cornell University Press, 2005.

Kaplan, M.B., 'Who's Afraid of Jack Saul? Urban Culture and the Politics of Desire in Late Victorian London', *GLQ: A Journal of Lesbian and Gay Studies* 5.3 (1999), pp. 267–314.

Kelly, N., *Quentin Crisp: The Profession of Being*, Jefferson, NC: McFarland, 2011.

Kember, S., and J. Zylinska, *Life After New Media: Mediation as a Vital Process*, Cambridge, MA: MIT Press, 2012.

Kemp, J., *London Triptych*, Brighton: Myriad Editions, 2010.

King, M.B., 'Psychological and Social Problems in HIV Infection: Interviews with General Practitioners in London', *British Medical Journal* 299 (16 September 1989), pp. 713–716.

King, T.A., *The Gendering of Men, 1600–1750. Vol. 2: Queer Articulations*, Madison: University of Wisconsin Press, 2008.

King, V., *The Weeping and the Laughter*, London: Macdonald and Jane's, 1976.

Knopp, L., 'From Lesbian and Gay to Queer Geographies: Pasts, Prospects and Possibilities', in K. Browne, J. Lim and G. Brown (eds), *Geographies of Sexualities: Theory, Practices and Politics*, Aldershot: Ashgate, 2007.

Knopp, L., 'On the Relationship Between Queer and Feminist Geographies', *The Professional Geographer* 59.1 (2007), pp. 47–55.

Knopp, L., 'Sexuality and Urban Space: A Framework for Analysis', in D. Bell and G. Valentine (eds), *Mapping Desire: Geographies of Sexualities*, London and New York: Routledge, 1995.

Knopp, L., 'Some Theoretical Implications of Gay Involvement in an Urban Land Market', *Political Geography Quarterly* 9.4 (1990), pp. 337–352.

Kontou, T., *Spiritualism and Women's Writing: From the Fin-de-Siècle to the Neo-Victorian*, London: Palgrave, 2009.

Koven, S., *Slumming: Sexual and Social Politics in Victorian London*, Princeton, NJ: Princeton University Press, 2004.

Kramer, J.K., 'Bachelor Farmers and Spinsters: Gay and Lesbian Identities and Communities in Rural North Dakota', in D. Bell and G. Valentine (eds), *Mapping Desire: Geographies of Sexualities*, London: Routledge, 1995.

Kuntsman, A., 'Introduction: Affective Fabrics of Digital Cultures', in A. Karatzogianni and A. Kuntsman (eds), *Digital Cultures and the Politics of Emotion: Feelings, Affect and Technological Change*, Basingstoke: Palgrave Macmillan, 2012.

Lanchester, E., *Elsa Lanchester Herself*, New York: St Martins, 1983.

Landreth, M., 'About', http://embodimentusa.com/?page_id=26 (accessed 9 June 2014).

Lang, C.Y. (ed.), *The Swinburne Letters*, New Haven, CT: Yale University Press, 1959–62.

Latham, S., *'Am I A Snob?': Modernism and the Novel*, Ithaca, NY: Cornell University Press, 2003.

Ledbetter, G., 'Review of Fiona Macintosh, *The Ancient Dancer in the Modern World: Responses to Greek and Roman Dance*', http://cj.camws.org/sites/default/files/reviews/2014.12.11%20Ledbetter%20on%20Macintosh.pdf (accessed 12 June 2015).

Lee, R., 'The Extinction of Races', *Journal of the Anthropological Society of London* 2 (1964), p. xcviii.

Lefebvre, H., *The Production of Space*, trans. Donald Nicholson-Smith, Oxford: Wiley-Blackwell, 1991.

Lewis, B. (ed.), *British Queer History: New Approaches and Perspectives*, Manchester: Manchester University Press, 2013.

Lewis, G.E., *Out East: In the Malay Peninsula*, Petaling Jaya: Penerbit Fajar Bakti Sdn. Bhd., 1991.

Littlewood, C., *Dirty White Boy: Tales of Soho*, Berkeley, CA: Cleis Press, 2008.

Louis Crompton, L., *Byron and Greek Love: Homophobia in Nineteenth-Century England*, Berkeley: University of California Press, 1985.

Love, H., *Feeling Backward: Loss and the Politics of Queer History*, Cambridge, MA and London: Harvard University Press, 2007.

Luciano, D., 'Nostalgia for an Age Yet to Come: *Velvet Goldmine*'s Queer Archive', in E.L. McCallum and M. Tuhkanen (eds), *Queer Times, Queer Becomings*, Albany: State University of New York Press, 2011.

Lutz, D., *Pleasure Bound: Victorian Sex Rebels and the New Eroticism*, New York and London: W.W. Norton, 2011.

Mackenzie, C., *Extraordinary Women*, New York: Macy-Masius, 1928.

Mackenzie, C., *Sinister Street*, 2 vols, New York: D. Appleton, 1914.

Maitland, S., *Vesta Tilley*, London: Virago, 1986.

Malchow, H.L., *Gothic Images of Race in Nineteenth-Century Britain*, Stanford, CA: Stanford University Press, 1996.

Manalansan, M., *Global Divas: Filipino Gay Men in the Diaspora*, Durham, NC: Duke University Press, 2003.

Mannheum, K., 'The Problem of Generations', *Psychoanalytic Review* 57.3 (1963), pp. 4–38.

Marcus, J., *Hearts of Darkness: White Women Write Race*, New Brunswick, NJ: Rutgers University Press, 2004.

Marcus, J., *Virginia Woolf and the Languages of Patriarchy*, Bloomington: Indiana University Press, 1987.

Mavrommatis, G., 'A Racial Archaeology of Space: A Journey Through the Political Imaginings of Brixton and Brick Lane, London', *Journal of Ethnic and Migration Studies* 36.4 (2010), pp. 561–579.

Mavrommatis, G., 'Stories from Brixton: Gentrification and Different Differences', *Sociological Research Online* 16.2 (2011), pp. 1–10.

Maxwell, W.J., 'Banjo Meets the Dark Princess: Claude McKay, W.E.B. Du Bois, and the Transnational Novel of the Harlem Renaissance', in G. Hutchinson (ed.), *The Cambridge Companion to the Harlem Renaissance*, Cambridge: Cambridge University Press, 2007.

Mayes, S. and L. Stein (eds), *Positive Lives: Responses to HIV: A Photodocumentary*, London: Cassell, 1993.

McKay, C., 'Boyhood in Jamaica', *Phylon* 14.2 (1953), pp. 134–145.

McKay, C., *A Long Way from Home*, London: Pluto Press, 1985.

McKay, C., *Spring in New Hampshire and Other Poems*, London: Grant Richards, 1920.

McKay, C. and W.J. Maxwell, *Complete Poems*, Urbana: University of Illinois Press, 2004; paperback 2008.

McKenna, N., *Fanny and Stella: The Young Men Who Shocked Victorian England*, London: Faber and Faber, 2013.

McLaren, A., 'Smoke and Mirrors: Willy Clarkson and the Role of Disguises in Inter-war England', *Journal of Social History* 40.3 (2007), pp. 597–618.

McWilliam, R., 'Elsa Lanchester and Bohemian London in the Early Twentieth Century', *Women's History Review* 23.2 (2014), pp. 171–187.

Medhurst, A., 'One Queen and His Screen: Lesbian and Gay Television', in G. Davis and G. Needham (eds), *Queer TV: Theories, Histories, Politics*, London: Routledge, 2009.

Mellor, L., *Reading the Ruins: Modernism, Bombsites and British Culture*, Cambridge: Cambridge University Press, 2011.

Melville, J., *A Scottish Collection: Treasures from Aberdeen Art Gallery*, The Yomiuri Shimbun/Japan Association of Art Galleries, 2000.

Meyer, J., *Katherine Mansfield: A Darker View*, New York: Rowman & Littlefield, 2002.

Mill, J.S., 'The Westminster Election of 1865', in J.M. Robson and B.L. Kinzer (eds), *The Collected Works of John Stuart Mill, Volume XXVIII: Public and Parliamentary Speeches Part I November 1850-November 1868*, Toronto: University of Toronto Press, 1988.

Mills, J., 'The Writer, the Prince and the Scholar: Virginia Woolf, D.S. Mirsky, and Jane Harrison's Translation from Russian of *The Life of the Archpriest Avvakum, by Himself* – A Revaluation of the Radical Politics of the Hogarth Press', in H. Southworth (ed.), *Leonard and Virginia Woolf, the Hogarth Press and the Networks of Modernism*, Edinburgh: Edinburgh University Press, 2010.

Minca, C., 'Postmodernism/Postmodern Geography', in R. Kitchin and N. Thrift (eds), *International Encyclopaedia of Human Geography*, Oxford: Elsevier, 2009.

Moore, O., *PWA: Looking AIDS in the Face*, London: Picador, 1996.

Moran, J., *Interdisciplinarity*, 2nd edn, London: Routledge, 2010.

Moran, L.J. and D. McGhee, 'Perverting London: the Cartographic Practices of Law', in C.F. Stychin and D. Herman (eds), *Sexuality in the Legal Arena*, London: Athlone Press, 2000.

Morris, M., *The Art of J.D. Fergusson: A Biased Biography*, London: Blackie, 1974.

Morris, M., *Life in Movement*, London: Peter Owen, 1969.

Morrison, A., '"Suffused by Feeling and Affect": The Intimate Public of Personal Mommy Blogging', *Biography* 34.1 (2011), pp. 37–55.

Mort, F., *Capital Affairs: London and the Making of the Permissive Society*, New Haven, CT: Yale University Press, 2010.

Mort, F., *Cultures of Consumption: Masculinities and Social Space in Late Twentieth-Century Britain*, 2nd edn, Abingdon: Routledge, 2009.

Moss, S., 'The Importance of Being Merlin', *Guardian*, 24 November 2000, http://www.theguardian.com/books/2000/nov/24/classics.oscarwilde (accessed 11 August 2015).

Mowlabocus, S., *Gaydar Culture: Gay Men, Technology and Embodiment in the Digital Age*, Farnham: Ashgate Publishing, 2010.

Mowlabocus, S., 'Look at Me!: Images, Validation, and Cultural Currency on Gaydar', in C. Pullen and M. Cooper (eds), *LGBT Identity and Online New Media*, London: Routledge, 2010.

Muñoz, J.E., *Cruising Utopia: The Then and There of Queer Futurity*, New York and London: New York University Press, 2009.

Munt, A., *Queer Attachments: The Cultural Politics of Shame*, Aldershot: Ashgate, 2008.

Munt, S., 'The Lesbian *Flâneur*', in D. Bell and G. Valentine (eds), *Mapping Desire: Geographies of Sexualities*, London and New York: Routledge, 1995.

Murger, H., *Scènes De La Vie Bohème*, Paris: Michel Levy, 1851.

Murray, A.J., 'Let Them Take Ecstasy: Class and Jakarta Lesbians', *Journal of Homosexuality* 40 (2001), pp. 165–184.

Murray, D.A.B., 'The (Not So) Straight Story: Queering Migration Narratives of Sexual Orientation and Gendered Identity Refugee Claimants', *Sexualities* 17.4 (2014), pp. 451–471.

Murray, N., *Aldous Huxley: An English Intellectual*, London: Abacus, 2002.

Naghibi, N., 'Diasporic Disclosures: Social Networking, Neda, and the 2009 Iranian Presidential Elections', *Biography* 34.1 (2011), pp. 56–69.

National Lesbian and Gay Survey, *Proust, Cole Porter, Michelangelo, Marc Almond and Me: Writings by Gay Men on Their Lives and Lifestyles from the Archives of the National Lesbian and Gay Survey*, London: Routledge, 1993.

Nealon, C., *Foundlings: Lesbian and Gay Historical Emotion Before Stonewall*, Durham, NC and London: Duke University Press, 2002.

Neild, S. and R. Pearson, *Women Like Us*, London: The Women's Press, 1992.

Nereson, A., 'Queens "Campin'" Onstage: Performing Queerness in Mae West's "Gay Plays"', *Theatre Journal* 64.4 (2012), pp. 513–532.

Newton, E., *Mother Camp: Female Impersonators in America*, Chicago: University of Chicago Press, 1979.

Nicholson, V., *Singled Out: How Two Million Women Survived Without Men After the First World War*, London: Penguin, 2007.

Nordau, M., *Aus Dem Wahren Milliardenlande: Pariser Studien Und Bilder*, Leipzig: Duncker & Humblot, 1878.

Nordau, M., *Degeneration*, Lincoln: University of Nebraska Press, 1993.

Norton, R., *Mother Clap's Molly House*, London: GMP, 1992.

Norton, R., 'Princess Seraphina', http://rictornorton.co.uk/eighteen /seraphin.htm (accessed 25 July 2015).

Noyes, J.K., *The Mastery of Submission: Inventions of Masochism*, Ithaca, NY: Cornell University Press, 1997.

O'Dwyer, T., 'Liberated Man Power Arrives', *Men's Wear*, 23 August 1984.

O'Neill, A., *London: After a Fashion*, London: Reaktion, 2007.

O'Riordan K. and D.J. Phillips (eds), *Queer Online: Media Technology and Sexuality*, New York: Peter Lang, 2007.

Ofield, S., 'Cruising the Archive', *Journal of Visual Culture* 4.3 (2005), pp. 351–364.

Ofield, S., 'Wrestling with Francis Bacon', *Oxford Art Journal* 24.1 (2001), pp. 115–130.

Ogden, M., 'Locating the Macaroni; Luxury, Sexuality and Vision in Vauxhall Gardens', *Textual Practice* 11.3 (1997), pp. 445–461.

Oram, A., 'Cross-Dressing and Transgender', in H.G. Cocks and M. Houlbrook (eds), *Palgrave Advances in the Modern History of Sexuality*, Basingstoke: Palgrave Macmillan, 2006.

Oram, A., '"A Sudden Orgy of Decadence": Writing About Sex Between Women in the Interwar Popular Press', in L. Doan and J. Garrity (eds), *Sapphic Modernities*, Basingstoke: Palgrave Macmillan, 2006.

Oswin, N., 'Critical Geographies and the Uses of Sexuality: Deconstructing Queer Space', *Progress in Human Geography* 32.1 (2008), pp. 89–103.

Owen, A., *The Darkened Room: Women, Power and Spiritualism in Late Nineteenth Century England*, London: Virago, 1989.

Palmer, P., '"She Began to Show Me the Words She Had Written One by One": Lesbian Reading and Writing Practices in the Fiction of Sarah Waters', *Women: A Cultural Review* 19.1 (2008), pp. 69–86.

Peck, J., 'Struggling with Creative Class', *International Journal of Urban and Regional Research* 29.4 (2005), pp. 740–770.

Pellegrini, A., 'Touching the Past; or, Hanging Chad', *Journal of the History of Sexuality* 10.2 (2001), pp. 185–194.

Peppiatt, M., *Francis Bacon in the 1950s*, Norwich: Sainsbury Centre for the Visual Arts, 2006.

Peppiatt, M., *Francis Bacon: Anatomy of an Enigma*, London: Constable and Robinson, 2008.

Phillippy, P., *Painting Women: Cosmetics, Canvases, and Early Modern Culture*, Baltimore, MD: Johns Hopkins University Press, 2006.

Plummer, K., *Telling Sexual Stories: Power, Change and Social Worlds*, London: Routledge, 1995.

Podmore, J.A., 'Lesbians in the Crowd', *Gender, Place and Culture* 8.4 (2001), pp. 333–355.

Pohl, R., 'Sexing the Labyrinth', in K. Mitchell (ed.), *Sarah Waters: Contemporary Critical Perspectives*, London: Bloomsbury, 2013.

Poletti, A., 'Intimate Economies: PostSecret and the Affect of Confession', *Biography* 34.1 (2011), pp. 25–36.

Pope-Hennessey, J., *Monckton Milnes: The Flight of Youth 1851–1885*, London: Constable, 1951.

Powell, V., *Within the Family Circle: An Autobiography*, London: Heinemann, 1976.

Power, L., *No Bath but Plenty of Bubbles: An Oral History of the Gay Liberation Front, 1970–1973*, London: Cassell, 1995.

Prichard, J.C., *Researches into the Physical History of Mankind*, 3rd edn, 5 vols, London: Sherwood, Gilbert and Piper, 1836–47.

Progl, Z., *Woman of the Underworld*, London: Arthur Baker, 1964.

Puar, J.K., 'Queer Times, Queer Assemblages,' *Social Text* 23 (2005), pp. 121–139.

Puar, J.K., 'Rethinking Homonationalism', *International Journal of Middle Eastern Studies* 45 (2013), pp. 336–339.

Puar, J.K., *Terrorist Assemblages: Homonationalism in Queer Times*, Durham, NC: Duke University Press, 2007.

Puar, J.K. and A. Rai, 'Monster, Terrorist, Fag: The War on Terrorism and the Production of Docile Patriots', *Social Text* 20 (2002), pp. 117–148.

Pullen, C. and M. Cooper (eds), *LGBT Identity and Online New Media*, New York: Routledge, 2010.

Pybus, J., 'Accumulating Affect: Social Networks and Their Archives of Feelings', in K. Hillis, S. Paasonen and M. Petit (eds), *Networked Affect*, Cambridge, MA and London: MIT Press, 2015.

Rainger, R., 'Race, Politics and Science: The Anthropological Society of London in the 1860s', *Victorian Studies* 22.1 (Autumn 1978), pp. 51–70.

Ramlow, T.R., 'Queering, Cripping', in *The Ashgate Research Companion to Queer Theory*, Farnham: Ashgate Publishing, 2012.

Rawson, C.J., 'Cannibalism and Fiction II: The Sexual Metaphor', *Genre* 11.2 (1978), pp. 227–234.

Raynsford, N., *Housing Is an AIDS Issue*, London: National AIDS Trust, 1989.

Reade, B. (ed.), *Sexual Heretics: Male Homosexuality in English Literature, 1850–1900*, London: Routledge & K. Paul, 1970.

Rendell, J., '"Serpentine Allurements": Disorderly Bodies/Disorderly Spaces', in I. Borden and J. Rendell (eds), *Intersections: Architectural Histories and Critical Theories*, London: Routledge, 2000.

Reynolds, S., *The Vision of Simeon Solomon*, Stroud: Catalpa Press, 1985.

Rhodes, T., *Hard to Reach or Out of Reach? An Evaluation of an Innovative Model of HIV Outreach Health Education*, London: Tufnell, 1991.

Richardson, J., *Verlaine*, London: Wiedenfeld and Nicolson, 1971.

Rivkin, J., 'Writing the Gay'80s with Henry James: David Leavitt's *A Place I've Never Been* and Alan Hollinghurst's *The Line of Beauty*', *Henry James Review* 26.3 (Fall 2005), pp. 282–292.

Robb, G., *Strangers: Homosexual Love in the 19th Century*, London: W.W. Norton, 2003.

Robertson, M., *Worshipping Whitman: The Whitman Disciples*, Princeton, NJ: Princeton University Press, 2010.

Rocheron, Y. and O. Linne, 'Aids, Moral Panic and Opinion Polls', *European Journal of Communication* 4 (1989), pp. 409–434.

Rodger, G., '"He Isn't a Marrying Man": Gender and Sexuality in the Repertoire of Male Impersonators, 1870–1930', in S. Fuller and L. Whitesell (eds), *Queer Episodes in Music and Modern Identity*, Chicago: University of Illinois Press, 2002.

Rohy, V., 'Ahistorical', *GLQ* 12.1 (2006), pp. 61–83.

Ross, R., 'Simeon Solomon (a Biography)', *The Bibelot* 17 (1911), pp. 150–151.

Rothenberg, T., '"And She Told Two Friends": Lesbians Creating Urban Social Space', in D. Bell and G. Valentine (eds), *Mapping Desire: Geographies of Sexualities*, London and New York: Routledge, 1995.

Said, E., *Orientalism*, Harmondsworth: Penguin, 1978.

Schwarz, A.B.C., *Gay Voices of the Harlem Renaissance*, Bloomington: Indiana University Press, 2003.

Schwarzback, F.S., *Dickens and the City*, London: The Athlone Press, 1979.

Sedgwick, E.K., *Between Men: English Literature and Male Homosocial Desire*, New York: Columbia University Press, 1985.

Sedgwick, E.K., *Epistemology of the Closet*, Berkeley: University of California Press, 1990.

Sedgwick, E.K., *Tendencies*, London: Routledge, 1994.

Seigel, J., *Bohemian Paris: Culture, Politics, and the Boundaries of Bourgeois Life, 1830–1930*, 2nd edn, Baltimore, MD: John Hopkins University Press, 1999.

Sellon, E., *Memoirs Read Before the Anthropological Society of London*, London: Trübner, 1865.

Sellon, E., *The New Epicurean*, London: Thomas Longtool, 1875 [1865].

Sellon, E., *New Ladies Tickler; or, the Adventures of Lady Lovesport and the Audacious Harry*, London: Printed for the Booksellers, 1866.

Sellon, E., *The Ups and Downs of Life*, London: William Dugdale, 1867.

Seymour, G.M., *The Life and Work of Simeon Solomon (1840–1905)*, PhD thesis, University of California, Santa Barbara, 1986.

Shaw, S.J., 'Marketing Ethnoscapes as Places of Consumption: "Banglatown – London's Curry Capital"', *Journal of Town and City Management* 1.4 (2011), pp. 381–195.

Showalter, E., *Sexual Anarchy: Gender and Culture at the Fin de Siècle*, New York: Viking, 1990.

Shute, N., *Another Man's Poison*, London: Grant Richards, 1931.

Shute, N., *Passionate Friendships: Memoirs and Confessions of a Rebel*, London: Robert Hale, 1992.

Shute, N., *We Mixed Our Drinks: The Story of a Generation*, London: Jarrolds Ltd., 1945.

Sigel, L.Z., *Governing Pleasures: Pornography and Social Change in England, 1815–1914*, New Brunswick, NJ: Rutgers University Press, 2002.

Silverstone, S., 'Duckie's *Gay Shame*: Critiquing Pride and Selling Shame in Club Performance', *Contemporary Theatre Review* 22.1 (2012), pp. 62–78.

Sinfield, A., *Gay and After: Gender, Culture and Consumption*, London: Serpent's Tail, 1998.

Slater, M. (ed.), *Dickens' Journalism: Sketches by Boz and Other Early Papers, 1833–39*, Columbus: Ohio State University Press, 1994.

Slater, T., 'The Eviction of Critical Perspectives from Gentrification Research', *International Journal of Urban and Regional Research* 30.4 (2006), pp. 737–757.

Sloan, J. (ed.), *Selected Poems and Prose of John Davidson*, Oxford: Clarendon Press, 1995.

Somerville, S.B., 'Scientific Racism and the Invention of the Homosexual Body', in L. Doan and L. Bland (eds), *Sexology in Culture: Labelling Bodies and Desires*, Cambridge: Polity Press, 1998.

Stacey, J., 'The Families of Man: Gay Male Intimacy and Kinship in a Global Metropolis', *Signs: Journal of Women in Culture and Society* 30.3 (2005), pp. 1911–1935.

Steen, M., *Looking Glass: An Autobiography*, London: Longmans, 1966.

Stenbock, E.S., *Myrtle, Rue and Cypress*, London: Hermitage Books, 1992.

Stephens, M.A., *Black Empire: The Masculine Global Imaginary of Caribbean Intellectuals in the United States, 1914–1962*, Durham, NC: Duke University Press, 2005.

Stevens, H., 'Normality and Queerness in Gay Fiction', in H. Stevens (ed.), *The Cambridge Companion to Gay and Lesbian Writing*, Cambridge: Cambridge University Press, 2011.

Stocking, G.W., *Victorian Anthropology*, New York: Macmillan, 1987.

Stokes, E., 'Lunch with the FT: Alan Hollinghurst', *The Financial Times*, 24 June 2011.

Straub, K., 'The Guilty Pleasures of Female Theatrical Cross-Dressing and the Autobiography of Charlotte Clarke', in J. Epstein and K. Straub (eds), *Body Guards: Cultural Politics and Gender Ambiguity*, London: Routledge, 1991.

Sullivan, N., *A Critical Introduction to Queer Theory*, Edinburgh: Edinburgh University Press, 2003.

Summers, J., *Soho: A History of London's Most Colourful Neighbourhood*, London: Bloomsbury, 1989.

Summerskill, C., *Gateway to Heaven: Fifty Years of Lesbian and Gay Oral History*, London: Tollington, 2013.

Sussman, H., *Victorian Masculinities: Manhood and Masculine Poetics in Early Victorian Literature and Art*, Cambridge: Cambridge University Press, 1995.

Swinburne, A., 'William Blake', reprinted in E. Gosse and T.J. Wise (eds), *The Complete Works of Swinburne*, vol. VI, London: William Heinemann, 1926.

Symonds, J.A., *A Problem in Modern Ethics*, London: Charles R. Dawes Ex Libris, 1896.

Tamagne, F., *History of Homosexuality in Europe, Berlin, London, Paris, 1919–1939*, 2 vols, New York: Algora, 2004.

Tames, R., *Soho Past*, London: Historical Publications, 1994.

Taylor, A., 'A Queer Geography', in A. Medhurst and S.R. Munt (eds), *Lesbian and Gay Studies: A Critical Introduction*, London and Washington: Cassell, 1997.

Terry, J., 'Anxious Slippages Between "Us" and "Them": A Brief History of the Scientific Search for Homosexual Bodies', in J. Terry and J. Urla (eds), *Deviant Bodies: Critical Perspectives on Difference in Science and Popular Culture*, Bloomington: Indiana University Press, 1995.

Thomas, M.W., *Transatlantic Connections: Whitman U.S., Whitman U.K.*, Iowa City: Iowa University Press, 2005.

Tickner, L., *Modern Life and Modern Subjects: British Art in the Early Twentieth Century*, New Haven, CT: Yale University Press, 2000.

Timothy, A., 'Gerrard Street', *London Is The Place for Me*. Vol. 2, http://www.allmusic.com/album/london-is-the-place-for-me-vol-2-mw0000643989 (accessed 12 June 2015).

Titterton, W.R., *From Theatre to Music Hall*, London: Stephen Swift & Co., 1912.

Turner, M.W., *Backward Glances: Cruising the Queer Streets of New York and London*, London: Reaktion Books, 2003.

Upchurch, C., 'Forgetting the Unthinkable: Cross-Dressers and British Society in the Case of the Queen vs. Boulton and Others', *Gender and History* 12.1 (2000), pp. 127–157.

Usher, N. and E. Morrison, 'The Demise of the Gay Enclave', in C. Pullen and M. Cooper (eds), *LGBT Identity and Online New Media*, New York: Routledge, 2010.

Valentine, G., '(Re)negotiating the "Heterosexual Street": Lesbian Productions of Space', in N. Duncan (ed.), *Body Space*, London: Routledge, 1996.

Valocchi, S., 'The Class-Inflected Nature of Gay Identity', *Social Problems* 46.2 (1999), pp. 207–224.

Vickers, H., *Cecil Beaton: A Biography*, New York: Primus, 1985.

Villarejo, A., *Ethereal Queer: Television, Historicity, Desire*, Durham, NC: Duke University Press, 2014.

Villin, E., 'Discussion (of "On Phallic Worship")', *Anthropological Review* 8 (1870), pp. xli–lxii.

Vivienne S. and J. Burgess, 'The Remediation of the Personal Photograph and the Politics of Self-Representation in Digital Storytelling', *Journal of Material Culture* 18.3 (2013), pp. 279–298.

von Krafft-Ebing, R., *Psychopathia Sexualis*, trans. C.G. Chaddock, Philadelphia, PA and London: F.A. Davis Co. Publishers, 1892.

Wahab, A., 'Homophobia as the State of Reason: The Case of Postcolonial Trinidad and Tobago', *GLQ: A Journal of Lesbian and Gay Studies* 18.4 (2012), pp. 481–505.

Walkowitz, J.R., *City of Dreadful Delight: Narratives of Sexual Danger in Late-Victorian London*, Chicago, IL: University of Chicago Press, 1992.

Walkowitz, J.R., *Nights Out: Life in Cosmopolitan London*, New Haven, CT: Yale University Press, 2012.

Waters, C., 'Sexology', in H.G. Cocks and M. Houlbrook (eds), *The Modern History of Sexuality*, Basingstoke: Palgrave Macmillan, 2005.

Waters, S., *Affinity*, London: Virago, 1999.

Waters, S., *Fingersmith*, London: Virago, 2002.

Waters, S., *The Night Watch*, London: Virago, 2006.

Waters, S., *Tipping the Velvet*, London: Virago, 2012 [1998].

Watney, S., *Imagine Hope: AIDS and Gay Identity*, New York: Routledge, 2000.

Watney, S., *Policing Desire: Pornography, AIDS and the Media*, London: Comedia, 1986.

Watson, C., *Snobbery with Violence*, London: Eyre and Spottiswoode, 1971.

Watts, L., 'Feature: The Grindr Story', *PinkNews*, 22 February 2012, http://www.pinknews.co.uk/2011/02/22/feature-the-grindr-story/ (accessed 28 March 2014).

Waugh, E., *Brideshead Revisited*, London: Penguin, 1983 [1945].

Waugh, E., *A Handful of Dust*, London: Penguin Books, 2000 [1934].

Weeks, J., *Coming Out: Homosexual Politics in Britain from the Nineteenth Century to the Present*, London: Quartet Books, 1990 [1977].

Weeks, J., 'Inverts, Perverts and Mary-Annes: Male Prostitution and the Regulation of Homosexuality in England in the Nineteenth and Early Twentieth Centuries', *Journal of Homosexuality* 6.1–2 (1980–81), pp. 113–134.

Weeks, J., *Making Sexual History*, London: Polity Press, 2000.

Weeks, J., *The World We Have Won: The Remaking of Erotic and Intimate Life*, London: Routledge, 2007.

Weigman, R. and E.A. Wilson (eds), 'Queer Theory Without Antinormativity', *Differences: A Journal of Feminist Cultural Studies* 26.1 (2015).

West, R., 'The Freewoman', first published in *Time and Tide*, 16 July 1926, reprinted in D. Spender (ed.), *Time and Tide Wait for No Man*, London: Pandora, 1984.

Whitman, W., *Leaves of Grass and Other Writings*, New York: Norton, 2002.

Wilde, O., *De Profundis*, London: Methuen, 1905.

Wilde, O., 'The Grosvenor Gallery', *Dublin University Magazine* 90 (1877), pp. 118–126.

Wills, W.D., *Homer Lane: A Biography*, London: Allen and Unwin, 1964.

Wilson, E., *Hidden Agendas: Theory, Politics and Experience in the Women's Movement*, London: Tavistock, 1986.

Wilson, E., *The Sphinx in the City: Urban Life, the Control of Disorder, and Women*, London: Virago, 1991.

Wilson, J.H., *Evelyn Waugh: A Literary Biography, 1924–1966*, Madison, NJ: Fairleigh Dickinson University Press, 2001.

Winslow, B., *Sylvia Pankhurst: Sexual Politics and Political Activism*, London: Routledge, 2004 [1996].

Woo, J., *Meet Grindr: How One App Changed the Way We Connect*, Canada: Jamie Woo, 2013.

Woods, C., *The State of the Queer Nation: A Critique of Gay and Lesbian Politics in 1990s Britain*, London: Cassell, 1995.

Woolf, L., *Beginning Again: An Autobiography of the Years 1911 to 1918*, London: The Hogarth Press, 1964.

Woolf, V., *The Diary of Virginia Woolf Volume 1: 1915–19*, London: Penguin, 1979.

Woolf, V., *The Letters of Virginia Woolf, Vol II; The Question of Things Happening*, ed. Nigel Nicolson, London: The Hogarth Press, 1976.

Yates, C., *Building for Immunity: Housing People with HIV Disease and AIDS*, London: National Federation of Housing Associations, 1991.

Yeats, W.B., *Autobiographies*, London and Basingstoke: Macmillan, 1955.

Zimring, R., *Social Dance and the Modernist Imagination in Interwar Britain*, Farnham: Ashgate, 2013.

INDEX

1917 Club (Soho) 117, 121, 123, 137, 223–6
'25 Queer Parties You Should Go To If You Have A Time Machine' 262

Adlard, J. 194, 196
Adventures of a Schoolboy or the Freaks of Youthful Passion (Reddie, 1866) 154
Affinity (Waters, 1999) 42, 81, 83, 86–8
ahistoricism 266
Ahmed, S. 4, 29, 71
AIDS/HIV 241, 243
    awareness of 58
    backlash 56
    cases in London 52–4
    charities 49, 57
    crisis in London 61
    death rates of 51
    de-gaying of 56
    disease of globalization 51
    experience of 54
    fear and insecurity arising from 57–8
    gay men in relation to 50–1
    GLF activism in early 1970s 55–6
    growth of awareness of 58
    homeless people with 52
    identification of 52
    and London 49–64
    national conference on 53
    normalization of 60
    related deaths in UK 50
    reporting of 57
    support, care and treatment 53–5
    treatments for 50
    wards and clinics 54
Ainley, R. 95

Aldrich, R. 151, 160
Allen, D. J. 182
Altman, D. 58
anachronism 266
Anderson, B. 9
androgyny
    elements of 98
    mobilization of 99
    performance of 98
Another Man's Poison (Shute, 1931) 227
Anthropological Society 43, 135, 150, 151–3, 154, 158, 159, 160
anthropometry 152
Antic Hay (Huxley, 1923) 226
anti-gay legislation, Uganda 66
Antosa, S. 31, 42–3, 149
Aphrodisiacs and Anti-Aphrodisiacs: Three Essays on the Power of Reproduction (Davenport, 1869) 157
apparitional lesbian 14
Archer, D. 230, 231
Ashbee, H. S. 90, 137, 154–5
Astoria Theatre 242
Autostraddle 262–3
Avery, S. 24, 29

Backward Glances: Cruising the Queer Streets of New York and London (Turner, 2003) 12, 25
Bacon, Francis 167–84
    bodily performances 172
    career in London 167
    face paintings 172, 178
    make-up, use of 172, 178
    queer sexuality 176
    sadomasochism 167–8
    selection of paintings 169

self-fashioning of 168, 169
sexual tastes 176
violence and transgression 170
visual culture of 176–9
Bakhtin, M. 4, 18 n.5, 82, 83
Bankhead, Tallulah 227–8, 230
Bar Wotever's Female Masculinity
    Appreciation Society 105
Bauer, H. 4, 18 n.1
Beerbohm, M. 175, 181 n.34, 193
Bell, D. 8, 10, 36 n.5
Bennett, A. 230
Bersani, L. 177, 179 n.1
BHC. *See* Brixton Housing Co-op (BHC)
bigot geography 41–2, 65–80
bisexuality 49
Blanchard, P. 224
Blaney, D. P. 178
Bohemianism 44, 117, 187, 189, 191,
    194, 223
'Boi Box' Drag King cabaret night
    103, 105
Bolshevik revolution 223
Bolter, J. D. 259
Book Club Negro Art, exhibition of
    1920, 121
Boone, J. A 151
Booth, H. C. 139
Booth, H. J. 124
Bottomley, H. 102
Boulton, E. 174, 188–9
Bourcier, M.-H./S. 42, 98, 101–4
    concept of Drag King
        performance 98
    pratiques transgenres 42, 98, 101,
        102, 103, 104, 108, 112 n.50
    and queer theory 101
Bowen, E. 83, 91, 92
Brideshead Revisited (Waugh, 1945)
    222, 234
British political discourse, global gay
    rights in 67
British Psycho-Analytical Society 142
British Society for the Study of Sex
    Psychology (BSSSP) 43, 133–48,
    223
    activism 140
    attitudes towards homosexuality
        134

context of metropolis with 137
overlooked precursor for 136–7
role of 134
terms of reform of laws 143
Brixton 65–80
    1981 riots in 70
    racist divisions 71
    sexual history of 73
    sexual possibilities in 74
    spatial relationship to central
        London 69, 71
    'straight' and 'queer' histories of
        75
Brixton Housing Co-op (BHC) 55
brothels 169, 224
Brown, G. 8, 18
Bryant, P. 204, 215–16
BSSSP. *See* British Society for the Study
    of Sex Psychology (BSSSP)
Burgess, J. 265
Burton, R. 43, 135, 150–7, 159–61
    climatic theory 159
    contradictory hypotheses 159
    inequality between races 152
    pederasty 159
    theory of Sotadic Zone 159
Butler, J. 9, 65, 85, 101
    theorizations of gender
        performativity 101

Cannibal Club 31, 43, 135, 150, 151,
    153–60
    informal gatherings of 150
    male social and symbolic spaces of
        154
    sexology 158–60
    symbol of 155
cannibalism 153, 155, 156, 160
Canning, R. 213
capitalism 122, 125, 240
Caribbean migrants 69
carnivalesque, concept of 4, 18 n.5, 42,
    82–3, 87, 93
Carpenter, E. 120, 133, 136, 137, 138,
    158, 159
Castells, M. 240
Castle, T. 14, 92
'Caves of Harmony' (Townsend,
    c.1925) 221

Central London Action on Street
    Health (CLASH) 57
Chanan, M. 5
Chapman, C. 138
charlatanism 86
Chauncey, G. 25
Cho, A. 260, 265
CLASH. *See* Central London Action on
    Street Health (CLASH)
Clayton, A. 13, 214
*The Cloven Hoof: A Study of
    Contemporary London Vices*
    (Archer, 1932) 230
Cocks, H. G. 25, 188, 196
Collins, W. 83, 88
colonialism 69, 76, 119, 121, 152,
    160
The Colour of Memory (Dyer, 1989)
    70
community/communities
    alternative space 246
    collectivism and 56
    concept of 9–10
    definition 239, 250
    feminist 91
    gay identities and 243–4, 248,
        250–1
    heterosexuals and 244
    homosexual sense of 243–5, 248–9,
        251
    modern concept of 239
    notion of 10
    queer performance and 106
    rethinking of 248–50
    sense of 106
    urban 239
    virtual 239–51, 255–67
comparative anatomy 152, 160
    scientific methods of 152
Condor, S. 233
Conroy, C. 42, 44
Constab Ballads (McKay, 1912) 119,
    120, 124
consumers 240, 243–5
conventional masculinity 177–8
Cook, M. 4, 11–13, 25, 26, 31, 41, 45,
    186, 188
Cooper, E. 15, 117, 119, 120
Corfield, P. J. 5

Criminal Law Amendment Act (1885)
    11
Crisp, Q. 171–3, 175, 177, 178
cross-dressing 5, 11, 82, 84, 85, 168,
    176, 188, 189,
    examples of 93
    lesbians and 85
Crozier, I. 135
culture
    England folk 119
    essentialization of 68
    of Francis Bacon 176–9
    Jamaica folk 119
    lesbian identity and 82
    male homosocial 135
    Molly House 11, 173, 174
    and politics of Queer London 12
    queer urban 13
    queer visual 167
    visual 176–9
Cvetkovich, A. 27, 29, 258

Daily Telegraph 227
The Darkened Room (Owen, 1989) 86
Darwin, C. 7
Davenport, J. 157
David, H. 25, 32
Day, P. 5
Deakin, J. 168
Dean, J. 260
de Certeau, M. 60
Defence of the Realm Act (DORA) 221
de Frece, W. 100
Delanty, G. 240
de Lauretis, T. 77 n.2, 101
Dellamora, R. 44, 196
Derrida, J. 258
Dickens, C. 5, 6, 83, 88, 89, 118, 192
digital archives 255–67
*Digital Cultures and the Politics of
    Emotion* (Kuntsman, 2012) 259
Dinshaw, C. 24, 27–33, 262–3, 267
*A Discourse on the Worship of the
    Priapus* (Knight, 1786) 157
Disorderly Houses Act (1751) 169–70
DORA. *See* Defence of the Realm Act
    (DORA)
Douglas, A. 32, 196, 228, 229
Downing, S. J. 7

Dowson, E. 193, 194, 196
Drag King performance 97–108
    Drag Queens and 102–7
    events and performance 97
    lack of understanding of 103
    performance techniques 101,
        104–5
    performers 105
    popularity of 102
    strategies 101
    styles of 102–4
    vocal techniques 100
Drag Queens 102–7
Drag Queens of London (TV show)
    106
Dreadnought (McKay, 1920) 117,
    122–3, 125
Drury Lane Club 117, 125
Dyer, G. 70, 73, 178

Edelman, L. 213, 216
Edwards, E., 121
Eeckhout, B. 13, 41, 44
Egan, B. 228
Ellis, H. H. 43, 74, 133, 136, 140, 143,
    158–60, 190, 193, 229
Ellis, N. 118
'Embodiment: A Portrait of Queer Life
    in America,' (Landreth) 264
Epstein Nord, D. 5
European-style gay bars 49
Evans, J. V. 26
Extraordinary Women (Mackenzie,
    1928) 227

Facebook 256–60, 262–6
Falk, B. 186, 187, 189, 192, 193, 196
Farson, D. 179, 241
Featherstone, M. 258, 265
female cross-dressing, sexual politics
    of 84–5
female masculinity 100, 104, 105
female same-sex desire 15
female sex workers 57
femininity 14, 99–100, 103, 108, 174,
    178
    and androgyny 98
Fielding, H. 192
Film Weekly (magazine) 227

Fingersmith (Waters, 2002) 42, 81, 83,
    88–91, 93
flâneur 12, 14, 42, 44, 83, 85–8, 90
Florida, R. 67, 78 n.11
The Folding Star (Hollinghurst, 1994)
    203
Forster, J. 192
Foucault, M. 88, 149
Foundlings (Nealon, 2002) 261
Fraxi, P. 155
Freeman, E. 27, 29, 260
Freudianism 223
Fryer, J. 241
fundraising 17, 53
    collectivism and community in 56

Gabrial, J. 233
Gallery Girls 230
Gallop, J. 87
Garde-Hansen, J. 258
Gaunt, W. 191
gay bars 49, 245, 250
gay community
    online media, impact on 244–51
        (*see also* Grindr)
    racism 75
gay equality 67
gay friendliness
    in Brixton 71–2
    and homophobia in London 68–9
gay identity
    community concepts 244, 251
    inequality and 65
    Jagose on 108 n.2
    law and 32
    North American context 78 n.8
    race and 80 n.35
    sexual liberation 78 n.13
    spatial concentration 67
Gay Liberation Front (GLF) 53, 55, 74
gay liberation movement 175, 255
Gay Monitoring and Archive
        Project 56
gay progress narratives 65
    in London 65, 68
    stigmatizing and exclusionary
        effects of 66
    and urban change 67–8
    vulnerability of 68

gay rights 241, 250
  in British political discourse 67
  progress for 65–6
gender 26–7, 83, 85, 101, 103, 150,
  168, 171, 173, 174
gentrification
  in Brixton 72, 74, 76
  definition 78 n.8
  effects of 17
  rental costs and rapid processes of
    15–16
  spatial dynamics 15–17, 66–8
  theories of 14
  urban communities 239
Gerrard Street 123, 137, 222–4, 233–4
Getting Medieval (Dinshaw, 1999) 29,
  30
GLF. *See* Gay Liberation Front (GLF)
Glicco, J. 231–3
globalization 51, 239, 245
Glover, E. 142
Goldring, D. 223, 224
Gosciak, J. 115, 116, 119, 121, 124,
  126
Go Tell It on the Mountain (Baldwin,
  1953) 261
Gowing, L. 14
Graham, K. M. 3, 18
Gray, D. 173
Great Exhibition (1851) 7
Great War 204, 214, 221, 229
Grindr 16, 45, 240, 246–51
Groddeck, G. 143
Groes, S. 13
Gross, L. 245, 249
Grusin, R. 259

Haire, N. 134
Halberstam, J. 27, 104, 178
Hall, L. A. 31, 43
Hall, R. 225–7, 229
Halperin, D. 27
A Handful of Dust (Waugh, 1934) 222
Harper, C. G. (*Queer Things About
  London*, 1924) 28–9
The Haunted Host (Patrick, 1964) 178
hauntings, kinds of 59, 60
health education 52
Herford, M. 142

Herman, RDK 7
heteronormativity 9, 204
heterosexual/heterosexuality 154
  behaviours 9
  performance of 9
Hindle, A. 98, 99, 103
Hirschfeld, M. 133, 139
HIV/AIDS. *See* AIDS/HIV
Holcomb, G. E. 117, 118
Holka, C. 24, 45, 255–8, 260–7
  photographs 45, 255–6, 258, 260,
    263–6
Holland, M. 32
Hollinghurst, A. 13, 14, 44. *See also
  specific novels*
  characters in novels 203–16
  on gay spaces 203–14
  heteronormative space 204, 209–13
  on London's history 204–5, 209,
    211–12, 214–16
  on queer lives 212–17
  on queer London 205, 209
  on sexual identities 203, 205
  on sexual intimacy 211
  on time 205–6, 212–16
homoeroticism 151, 153–4
homogeneity, representations of 73
homonormativity 3, 65, 66
  politics of 10
homosexual/homosexuality 26, 28, 29,
  151, 156, 191, 193
  discussions of 135
  emerging models of 159
  vs. homosociality 149
  identification with 139
  laws on 140
  overlapping issues of 153–4
  'problem' of 171
  re-emergence of 34
  societal toleration of 135
  unprogressive views on 68
  urban subcultures 168
homosexual rights 138
homosociality 135, 149, 151, 153–4
Hopkins, R. T. 193–4
Horne, H., 194
Houlbrook, M. 10, 12–15, 18, 24, 25,
  27, 29, 30–2, 34, 43, 117, 171
Housman, L. 140, 141

Humphrey, B. 173
Humphreys, T. 173
Hunt, J. 43, 150–2
Hutton, L. 223
Huxley, A. 226
Hytner, N. 173

Industrial Revolution 82
interdisciplinarity 17
International Socialist Club (ISC) 117,
    125
Internet 24, 50, 60, 245, 248–50
ISC. *See* International Socialist Club
    (ISC)
Israel, L. 230
Ives, G. 136, 140
'I WAS THERE' project (Holka) 45,
    256–7, 261–4, 266–7

Jamaica
    colonial education in 119–20
    folk cultures of 119
Janes, D. 43–4
Jarman, D. 54, 55, 57, 59, 60
jazz clubs 115, 250
Jekyll, W. 119–20, 124
Jennings, R. 138, 142
Jim Crow Laws 120
Joannou, M. 115
Johnson, E. P. 31, 175, 194, 196
Johnson, L. 31–2, 194
Jordan, M. D. 29

Kaplan, M. B. 13
Kember, S. 259
Kemp, J. 13, 14, 32, 33, 35, 222–3
    London Triptych 13, 32–5
Kertbeny, K. M. 159
King, V. 226
Knopp, L. 8, 66
Kontou, T. 87
Koven, S. 25, 192, 193
Kuntsman, A. 259, 260

Lambeth Women's Project (2012)
    255–6
Lanchester, E. 221, 224–6
Landreth, M. 264
Lefebvre, H. 205

Lesbian and Gay Film Festival 56
Lesbian Herstory Archives 255–6, 263
lesbians 31
    cross-dressed 85
    culture 82
    description 82
    feminist community 91
    flâneur 82, 87–8
    gay men *vs.* 56
    identity 14, 82
    'invisibility,' 14
    relationship with metropolis 82
    role in the sexual politics 82
    sociocultural effacement of 92
    and theories of gentrification 14
Lewis, B. 25, 153
Lewis, G. E. 233
LGBT asylum seekers 66
Lilly, C. 93
Lim, J. 8
The Line of Beauty (Hollinghurst,
    2003) 44, 203–4, 209–12, 218
Littlewood, C. 244
*London and the Culture of
    Homosexuality, 1885–1914*
    (Cook, 2003) 11, 20 n.38, 25
London Triptych (Kemp, 2010) 13,
    32–5
Love, H. 27, 29, 37 n.20, 261, 262
Love of Women (Stuart, 1934) 227
Luciano, D. 31, 32, 262, 263
Lutz, D. 156, 159

Mackenzie, C. 225, 227
Madness After Midnight
    (Glicco, 1952) 231
Malchow, H. L. 155
male cross-dressing 188
male homosociality
    bonds 150, 152
    culture 135
    Sedgwick's definition of 151
male impersonation 83, 84, 98, 100,
    103, 107
male impersonators 74, 98–103
*Mapping Desire: Geographies of
    Sexualities* (Bell and Valentine,
    1995) 8, 9, 10
Marcus, J. 123, 226

Margaret Morris Club 225–6
masochism 154, 155, 177–8
Maxwell, W. J. 120
McBean, S. 16, 24, 31, 45
McKay, C. 25, 43, 115–26
  early life of 119
  experiences in London 114–17
  life in British colony 119
  poetry 122–5
  politics and 117–27
  use of creole 118
McKenna, N. 11
Medhurst, A. 175
Mellor, L. 92
Mill, J. S. 134
modern girls 44, 224, 227–9,
  232, 234
Molly House culture 11, 173, 174
Moore, O. 54
morality, public standards of 169
Moran, J. 17, 18
Morland, G. 189
Morris, M. 225, 226, 233
Morrison, E. 243
Mort, F. 242, 248, 249
The Most Cake (UK-based lesbian
  website) 256
Mowlabocus, S. 246, 247, 249
Muñoz, J. E. 27
Munt, S. 14, 82, 85
Murger, H. 190
Murray, G. 134
Music Hall stage 97–8, 102
  male impersonation on 98

National Lesbian and Gay Survey
  (NLGS) 52, 54
Nazi photography 169
Nealon, C. 261, 266
Nestle, J. 255–7, 260
New Spring Gardens. *See* Vauxhall
  Pleasure Gardens
New York Pride Party 263
Night in a Workhouse (Greenwood,
  1860) 193
Nights Out (Walkowitz, 2012)
  116–17
The Night Watch (Waters, 2006) 42,
  81, 83, 91–3

Nine Till Six (Stuart, 1930) 227
NLGS. *See* National Lesbian and Gay
  Survey (NLGS)
Nordau, M. 191
normative sexuality 168, 204, 213
normativity 99–100
Norton, R. 5, 173
Noyes, J. K. 178

O'Dwyer, T. 242
Ofield, S. 11, 12
Old Compton Street 10, 15, 239–51
Operation Cottage (documentary) 57
Oram, A. 5
orientalism 151, 158
Owen, A. 86
*Oxford Dictionary of National
  Biography* 134

Palmer, P. 15, 41–2
Pankhurst, S. 116, 117, 122
Park, F. W. 174
Patrick, R. 178
pederasty 159
Pellegrini, A. 30
Peppiatt, M. 171, 173, 176
Phillippy, P. 172
Podmore, J. A. 14
Pohl, R. 88
polygenesis theory 152
pornography 12, 13, 149–60
Powell, V. 98, 102, 233
pratiques transgenres. *See* Bourcier,
  M.-H./S.
pre-Chinatown Soho 44, 221–34.
  See also Sink Street
Prichard, J. C. 152
primitivism 122
Progl, Z. 233
prostitutes 4, 12, 57, 90, 171, 190,
  233. *See also* sex workers
prostitution 14, 82, 153, 176
Pybus, J. 258, 265

queer
  clubs 169, 255–7, 264
  definition of 27, 29, 186
  historical affect and 257, 260–1,
  263, 267

historicity 45, 257, 263
history 12, 29–30, 75, 203
queer London
    black histories of 65–80, 115-32
    communities 24
    contemporary 256–7, 260, 262–7
    disappearing 16–18
    recovering 11–15
    spatial understanding of 3–22
    theorizing 8–11
*Queer London: Perils and Pleasures in
    the Sexual Metropolis, 1918–
    1957* (Houlbrook, 2005) 117
queer theatre, interwar heritage of 178
queer theory 26, 27, 82, 101, 108 n.2,
    167, 203, 204, 213, 260
Queer Valentine Carnival 243

race
    categories of 152
    philological view of 152
    and sexuality 151
racism 69, 71, 75, 115, 120, 121, 122,
    124–7, 248
Rawson, C. J. 155
rent boys 12, 33
Reynolds, S. 196
Rhys, E. 194
Richardson, J. 190
Rivkin, J. 211
Rodeo Disco Pride Party 262–3
Rodger, G. 98–100
Rohy, V. 27, 266
Romain, G. 9, 15, 25, 42–3, 226
Roman Catholics 169, 227
Ross, R. 31, 186, 187, 189, 192
Rothenberg, T. 14
Royal Vauxhall Tavern (RVT) 7,
    15–17, 106, 112 n.53

sadism 177
Said, E. 151
A Saturday Life (Hall, 1925) 225
Schwarz, A. B. C. 124, 192
Second World War 134, 170, 234
Sedgwick, E. K. 27, 29, 33, 150–2
Seigel, J. 190, 191
Sellon, E. 153, 154, 157
sex workers 57, 85

sexually transmitted infection (STI)
    clinics 54
Sexual Offences Act (1967) 13, 176
sexual psychology 133–48
sex workers 57, 85
Shaw, S. J. 115
Shute, N. 227–9
Sigel, L. Z. 135, 152, 153, 155
Sinfield, A. 244
*The Single Woman and Her Emotional
    Problems* (Hutton, 1935) 223
Sinister Street (Mackenzie, 1914) 225
The Sink of Solitude (Egan, 1928)
    228–9
Sink Street 221–34
    Waugh on 222–8
slavery 152
social networks 240, 257, 260
Soho. *See also* pre-Chinatown Soho
    cafés and restaurants 242–3
    gay venues 242–8
    Grindr and 249–51
    homosexuality 243–5, 248–9, 251,
        261
    masculinities/identities 249
    nightlife 44, 221–2, 228, 231, 242
    Old Compton Street 10, 15, 239,
        241, 244
    online and offline spaces 248–50
    sexual experimentation 244, 249
Solomon, S.
    conviction in 1873 186–8
    early life of 187
    life in poverty in London 191
    'ragged figure' of 194
    residence of 185
    sexuality 185–202
    workhouse records of 188
Somerville, S. B. 159
Songs of Jamaica (McKay, 1912)
    118–20
The Spell (Hollinghurst, 1998) 203,
    210
Spencer, H. 7
spiritualism 86–8
Spruce, E. 16, 31, 41–3
Stacey, J. 55
Steen, M. 233
Stenbock, E. S. 186, 194–7

Stephens, M. 121
Stevenson, J. 141
STI clinics. *See* sexually transmitted infection (STI) clinics
Stokoe, K. 15–16, 42
Stonewall riots 255
The Stranger's Child (Hollinghurst, 2011) 44, 203–4, 212–17
Studies in the Psychology of Sex: Sexual Inversion (Ellis, 1936) 158
Studio 54 242
Studio One 242
Sullivan, N. 4, 195
Summers, J. 241, 242
Sussman, H. 154
The Swimming-Pool Library (Hollinghurst, 1988) 203–5, 209, 212
Swinburne, A. 155, 157, 158, 187
Symonds, J. A. 158–60, 190, 193

Taylor, A. 9–10
telephone advice service 53
Terrence Higgins Trust (THT) 49, 56
Tilley, V. 42, 97–103, 107
Timothy, A. 234
Tipping the Velvet (Waters, 1998) 42, 74, 81, 82, 83–6, 87, 93
Titterton, W. R. 98
Townsend, S. 221
Tumblr 256, 260, 264–5
Turner, M. W. 12, 25, 214

Uganda, anti-gay legislation 66
UK, gay progress narratives in 66
underworld 188, 208, 225, 228–34
urban change, gay progress and 67–8
urban renewal, progress narratives of 70
Usher, N. 243
utopias of belonging 9–10

Valentine, G. 8–10, 82, 243
Vauxhall Pleasure Gardens 4–8, 15
Venturi, M. 9, 16, 31, 45

Verlaine, P. 187, 189, 190–1, 194, 196
Villarejo, A. 25
Villin, E. 158
virtual communities 240, 245
Vivienne, S. 265

Walkowitz, J. R. 116
Waters, C. 10
Waters, S. 10, 42, 74
   Affinity 42, 81, 83, 86–8
   carnivalesque dimension of metropolitan life 82
   Fingersmith 42, 81, 83, 88–91, 93
   narrative strategies 83
   The Night Watch 42, 81, 83, 91–3
   Tipping the Velvet 42, 74, 81, 82, 83–6, 87, 93
Watney, S. 55, 59
Waugh, E. 222–5, 228, 233
The Weekly Dispatch 232
Weeks, J. 153, 158
The Well of Loneliness (Hall, 1928) 226–30
Wesner, E. 98
West, R. 137
Whitman, W. 12, 120, 156–9
Wilde, O. 13, 31–5, 120, 136, 172, 174–6, 186, 191, 194, 196, 208, 262
Wilson, E. A. 82
Witchard, A. 9, 15, 31, 43–4
The Woman in White (Collins, 1860) 83, 88
Woods, C. 243
Woo, J. 248
Woolf, L. 15, 23, 134, 143
The Workers' Dreadnought 117, 122, 123, 125

Yeats, W. B. 194
YouTube 259–60

Zimring, R. 226
Zylinska, J. 259